IN SERVICE
TO THE CITY

IN SERVICE
TO THE CITY

A HISTORY OF THE
UNIVERSITY OF CINCINNATI

David Stradling

University of
CINCINNATI | PRESS

About the University of Cincinnati Press
The University of Cincinnati Press is committed to publishing rigorous, peer reviewed, leading scholarship accessibly to stimulate dialog between the academy, public intellectuals and lay practitioners. The Press endeavors to erase disciplinary boundaries in order to cast fresh light on common problems in our global community. Building on the university's long-standing tradition of social responsibility to the citizens of Cincinnati, state of Ohio, and the world, the press publishes books on topics which expose and resolve disparities at every level of society and have local, national and global impact.

The University of Cincinnati Press, Cincinnati 45221
Copyright © 2018

Published with generous support from Patty and Buck Niehoff and Betsy and Peter Niehoff for the University of Cincinnati Bicentennial.

ucincinnatipress.uc.edu
Published in 2018

ISBN 978-1-947602-07-6 (hardback)
ISBN 978-1-947602-08-3 (e-book, PDF)
ISBN 978-1-947602-09-0 (e-book, EPUB)

Library of Congress Cataloging-in-Publication Data

Names: Stradling, David, author.
Title: In service to the city : a history of the University of Cincinnati /
   David Stradling.
Description: First edition. | Cincinnati : University of Cincinnati Press,
   [2018] | Includes bibliographical references and index.
Identifiers: LCCN 2018008573| ISBN 9781947602076 (hardback) | ISBN
   9781947602083 (pdf) | ISBN 9781947602090 (epub)
Subjects: LCSH: University of Cincinnati--History. | Education,
   Higher--Ohio--Cincinnati--History. | Cincinnati (Ohio)--Intellectual life.
Classification: LCC LD983 .S87 2018 | DDC 378.771/78--dc23 LC record available at
https://lccn.loc.gov/2018008573

Designed and produced for UC Press by Orange Frazer Press, Wilmington, Ohio
Typeset in: Wilmington, Ohio
Printed in the United States of America

First Printing

Dedicated to the memory of
Zane L. Miller
Cincinnati's Historian

Contents

ILLUSTRATIONS

PREFACE

My long history with the University of Cincinnati began in 1972, when my mother started taking classes at the College-Conservatory of Music, commuting down from our Kenwood home nearly every quarter for much of my childhood. On occasion, my brother and I sat in the hallway awaiting the end of her voice lessons or opera history classes. For our patience we were rewarded with hamburgers and fries at McDonald's in the student union. When I got to high school, I frequently came down to campus to conduct research for history and English classes. I remember fondly the long row of cabinets holding the card catalog on the fourth floor of Langsam—and the vending machines on the floor above. These early experiences established in my mind a fundamental conception of UC: it was a campus that welcomed people at any stage of life, anyone who wanted to take advantage of the resources it provided.

After I attended college in New York, I came back to Cincinnati, and to UC, to take several undergraduate classes in education and history to help me prepare for a master's in teaching degree. I took a class with Barbara Ramusack, who, as it turned out, was the department head when I was hired at UC eleven years later. After I finished my MAT, also in New York, I took the National Teachers' Exam in Zimmer Hall, sitting with hundreds of prospective teachers, most of whom, no doubt, had earned their degrees at UC. I decided to continue my education, earning a master's in history at the University of Wisconsin, after which I came back to UC once again, this time to study urban history with Zane L. Miller. I stayed for one year, returning to Wisconsin to complete my doctoral degree there in environmental history.

After teaching at two other institutions, I once again returned to UC to become the urban historian, replacing Zane in the year 2000. I earned tenure and was promoted to full professor and then, recently, I entered administration, becoming the associate dean for humanities in the College of Arts and Sciences. My taking an administrative position was, in part, a somewhat misguided attempt to become a participant observer, to learn about this institution from yet another perspective. It worked—I have learned much about how institutions of higher education function, although it has come at some cost to this book project, given the demands of the position.

In sum, I cannot pretend that I have any semblance of objectivity when it comes to my subject. I have known this place in nearly every possible way. I cannot suggest that my experience hasn't shaped what follows. I will claim that my professional development has been more influential than my personal experience, however. I have picked themes for this book that fit my interests and expertise, as is clear in my focus on the relationship between the university and the city, and in my attention to the physicality of the institution. My interests as an urban environmental historian permeate the book.

All historians run up against the limits of their abilities, and I clearly did so frequently here, in studying the work of scholars and teachers in fields with which I have no familiarity. I also ran up against space limitations. From the outset I determined to write an accessible book, one that could be read cover to cover. This meant I could not take an encyclopedic approach and that some topics would gain attention as part of my narrative thread, while others would play little or no role. Institutional structure and governance appear here only as they relate to the themes of the book, and I have said little about the American Association of University Professors (AAUP) and faculty labor issues. Student life also falls in and out of view. I say essentially nothing about fraternities and sororities. Their absence does not reflect my determination that Greek life has not been important to UC's history, just that it didn't fit into my particular telling of the story.

I have attempted to capture the full complexity of the university, but some colleges clearly receive more attention than others. My own college may play an outsized role here, in part because of my biases and in part because of my chosen themes. In sum, while I have written a comprehensive history of UC, this is not an exhaustive work. I cannot claim that this is *the* story to be told about UC.

I *can* claim to have had considerable help along the way, however. This book owes its existence to Buck Niehoff, who led the charge on the creation of scholarly publications as part of UC's bicentennial celebration. In the spring of 2012, Buck invited me to join him for lunch with Greg Hand, a long-time UC employee who knows more about the institution than anyone. Buck laid out his vision of an independent, scholarly history. Even before he got to the point of asking me to take it on, I had decided this was something I should do, in partial compensation for the opportunities this institution has provided for me. Since that meeting, Greg has been a constant supporter. He read and commented on the entire manuscript, chapter by chapter as I completed them. And Buck's insistence that this be a work of scholarship has ensured that the contents and conclusions of this book are mine alone. Although Greg and other readers have helped me avoid making many mistakes, any residual errors are my responsibility alone.

This book was also made possible by the research support of many graduate students, generously funded by the provost's office. Most important, Nate McGee probably could have written his own book on UC after the amount of research he did for me as he completed his dissertation on bluegrass music in Cincinnati and other cities. I also received essential help from Alyssa McClanahan, Angela Stiefbold, Anne Delano Steinert, Kristen Fleming, and Katherine Ranum, all of them doctoral students in the Department of History. Sarah Muncy helped prepare the book for publication by writing the accessibility captions for the images. Sarah Stradling expertly translated several letters sent to Carl Blegen, because her father does not know German.

The support of UC libraries was also essential, especially at Archives & Rare Books, where Kevin Grace, Suzanne Maggard Reller, and Eira Tansey provided indispensable service. Thanks too to Veronica Buchanan, who guided my research at the Henry R. Winkler Center for the History of the Health Professions, and Gino Pasi, who arranged for the Daniel Drake image. I have relied on librarians at other institutions as well, including Anne Shepherd and others at the Cincinnati Museum Center, home to the Cincinnati History Library and Archives. The Public Library of Cincinnati and Hamilton County contains great collections and employs a helpful staff, including Victoria L. Norman, Whitney Smith, Jessica Hicks, Chelsea Swinford, Shalini N. Teagarden, and Keith Good. Cedric Rose provided help at the Mercantile Library, as did Devhra BennettJones and others at the Lloyd Library. Vicki Newell helped me navigate the Cincinnati Parks Archives at the Bettman Natural Resource Center, and Bob Vitz, a historian and member of the Literary Club, gave me access to archives there. Mark Wetherington and others provided assistance at the Filson Historical Society in Louisville, which is a wonderful place to work. Jennifer Hardin provided assistance at the relatively new and lovely library space at the Cincinnati Art Museum. In addition, Katharine Milar, a professor of psychology at Earlham College, provided documents from her research on Ada Arlitt, and LaDale Winling kindly sent me an advance copy of his book *Building the Ivory Tower*.

Several current and former UC employees gave support and encouragement, including M. B. Reilly and Kristi Nelson, who provided moral support and access to documents. Jodi Shann, director of Environmental Studies, provided me with funds to hire a student to assist one summer, Coleman Williams, who worked with me in the Kehoe collection. Jeff Kramer gave me a tour of the Department of Classics Archive and helped me find the most relevant material, including the images of Carl Blegen. Lisa Ventre, director of photography at UC, gathered and helped me select several of the images. Special thanks to Conrad Kickert, assistant professor of planning, for creating the map of Cincinnati in chapter 7.

In addition to Greg Hand, several other colleagues have read and commented on at least part of the book. Michael Griffith read the entire manuscript, correcting many errors and offering good advice throughout. His keen eye and remarkably broad range of knowledge greatly improved this book. Arnie Miller read the last chapter, offering helpful suggestions to improve clarity and amplify themes. Jack Davis read and commented upon the section about Carl Blegen, and through his correspondence greatly improved my understanding of Greek archeology. Frank Russell read and commented upon the section concerning the Niehoff Urban Studio. Larry Jost shared his thoughts on the section concerning TUC workers. At one of the Department of History's regular research seminars many of my colleagues, including Willard Sunderland and Barbara Ramusack, offered helpful comments on early drafts of chapters 2 and 3. Elissa Yancy read and commented upon the section on E. Lucy Braun. Special thanks to Yonatan Eyal, director of the Graduate School, who read and commented on the entire draft. Many of his thoughts are woven into this final product.

I am grateful to Ken Petren, dean of Arts and Sciences, who afforded me the time to complete this project even though it detracted from my work as his associate, and to my colleagues in the dean's office, Arnie Miller, Margaret Hanson, Jennifer Malat, Lisa Holstrom, Marcia Miladinov, and Cammie Hulett, for their patience and good will. Watching all of them over the last two years has reminded me that institutions are built only through the hard work and dedication of individuals. I hope that theme is apparent in the chapters that follow.

Finally, a special acknowledgment of the patience of my family: Jodie, Sarah, and Nina. For the last two years this book has been an all-consuming endeavor. When I wasn't lost in my reading and writing, I was often lost in thought. I was completely reliant upon their support and understanding.

This book is dedicated to my mentor and colleague Zane L. Miller, who offered me encouragement, opinions, and anecdotes in the research phase of this project. I can only guess at the numerous ways this book would be better had he lived to offer his thoughts on the prose that follows.

IN SERVICE
TO THE CITY

INTRODUCTION

The University *in* Cincinnati

In 2019 the University of Cincinnati celebrates its bicentennial, providing an opportunity to tell stories and take stock. As chancellor of the University of Chicago Robert Hutchins wrote years ago, "It is imperative to force the periodic reconsideration of the purpose of an institution."[1] That seems a fair statement of this book's goal. As with any celebration of longevity, this one brings good reason for the university community to express pride and reflect on the institution's remarkable growth. University boosters should emphasize UC's uniqueness and accomplishments. Publicity surrounding the bicentennial should feature Oscar Robertson, Lucy Braun, Benadryl, cooperative education, and many other distinctive UC personalities and contributions. The university should also look forward and imagine a bright future, imagine how higher education will be different in another fifty years. But there is, I think, greater benefit to telling the story fully and honestly, a greater value to recognizing the struggles that have been at the heart of this institution's past. Dramatic changes to the university and its surroundings in the early twenty-first century might suggest that even the year 2000 is ancient history for a fast-moving institution, but there is special value in taking the longer view, seeing past the last two decades of growth. That longer story imparts entirely different themes: resilience and adaptation. After all, through its history this institution has evolved to accommodate extraordinary economic and social change, from the industrial revolution to the rights revolution. UC has weathered the disruptions of world wars and economic depressions. It grew rapidly when it had to, and more recently it survived cuts to public funding and shifting expectations for what college degrees should mean.

What follows is the story of people—students, faculty, administrators, staff, and neighbors—in continuous struggle to shape an institution so that it might better serve the community. The details matter here, of course, but so too do the broad strokes. UC's long history spans all the major changes in higher education in the United States. Its story begins with a classical education for Cincinnati's elite, designed to elevate the character of the city's future business and political leaders. That original institution, Cincinnati College, occupied a single Neoclassical building near the center of the city. In fits and starts, with a confusion of closures and mergers, it evolved into one of the nation's largest research universities, designed to train a great diversity of students in an incredible array of fields. It now occupies an expansive campus complex perched above the urban core, a center of economic activity second only to downtown Cincinnati in the region. Recounting this evolution, pausing at each significant step, provides a window onto the evolution of UC, the city of Cincinnati, and higher education in the United States altogether. This longer narrative allows us to contemplate the shifting role of higher education in the nation's democracy and economy.

This book does more than tell stories, of course. It asks questions. Most fundamentally, it asks throughout, from founding to failure to rebirth to revision: What are universities for? UC's long evolution has been accompanied by a shifting mission, sometimes unarticulated, sometimes incoherent. What is most remarkable, though, is that the debate was never settled. We ask today the very same questions Daniel Drake asked as he worked to create Cincinnati College. Whom should the college serve? How can it serve them best? What should students learn and how should they learn it? How should this institution relate to the city of Cincinnati and to the broader region? And, perhaps most important, how can we pay for it? That these essential questions are still as alive today as they were two hundred years ago may be the best evidence of higher education's mutability. On the other hand, given the multiple purposes and myriad constituencies of universities, perhaps the debate about mission and priorities could never be settled. Perhaps it need not be, for even though consensus is desirable, it isn't required, even in a democratic institution.

In 1930, the well-known education reformer Abraham Flexner asked a variation of this book's central question: What is "the idea of a *modern* university?" In reflecting on the rapidly growing and diversifying early twentieth-century university—fast on its way to becoming the research university we know today—Flexner took a conservative view, fearful that the traditional mission of higher education would be lost. He applauded institutions for evolving, keeping pace with the changing needs of society. "But," he warned, "a university should not be a weather vane, responsive to every variation of popular whim. Universities must at times give society, not what society wants, but what it needs."[2] Further, he explained, "universities exist, partly at least, in order that they may influence the direction in which thinking and living move."[3] In other words, universities should not merely follow the market, but shape it. This question constitutes one of the central tensions in the history of higher education in the United States: Given the demands that society places upon higher education, to what degree can a university set its own mission?

Despite its never settled nature, UC's mission has had two constants. Both speak to the purpose of all institutions of higher education. First, the university has been a center of disinterested inquiry and open discourse. Each generation of faculty and students has sought truth, whether new or ancient, comforting or disruptive. The topics of inquiry, the techniques of research, and the methods of communication have shifted greatly, but the goals of truth-seeking and truth-speaking have persisted. Second, UC has been consistently dedicated to the public good. Of course the definition of "the public" has changed significantly, and Cincinnatians, like all Americans, have never agreed on who counts as part of the public. So too conceptions of "good" have changed over time. In 1819, a college could most clearly serve the public good by instilling character in its students, and in the citizenry more broadly. Higher education elevated the human spirit through exposure to the best of what has been thought and said, to use Matthew Arnold's nineteenth-century phrase.[4] As Stanford University president David Star Jordan put it just after the turn of the twentieth century, "The highest function of the university is the formation of character, the training of men and women, in purity and strength, in sweetness and light."[5] This is what Flexner feared would be lost. Two hundred years later, conceptions of serving the public good have shifted. Now many people describe the university's purpose as increasing students' earning potential, instilling an entrepreneurial spirit, and, altogether, making contributions to the nation's economic growth.

Here is another tension that runs through the history of higher education. How can universities best serve the public good: educate the elite in culture and aesthetics, creating a leadership class—the nineteenth-century model; or, serve a broader segment of the population, educate as many students as possible, even to the point of providing remediation to facilitate entry into undergraduate programs, in order to improve individual lives, mostly in economic terms? The changing definition of the term notwithstanding, serving the "public good" has remained central to the university's mission, and it is useful to contemplate precisely how this goal shifted in meaning over time—and why.

In addition to the broad goals of seeking truth and serving the public good, UC has maintained a more focused mission, one that relates directly to the argument of this book. Although it has fallen in and out of favor, serving the community, serving the city, has been at the core the university's mission. That service has taken on various, shifting forms, but the recurrence of this theme is difficult to ignore. Faculty and administrators of every generation have sought out larger and larger audiences, educating students, of course, but also nonmatriculated citizens, both directly through lectures, workshops, radio programs, and the like; and indirectly in collaboration with other government entities and not-for-profit organizations. This service mission has woven the university into the community in so many ways that to begin making a list is to recognize the impossibility of making it complete. For citizens of Cincinnati and the region around, the university has operated health clinics, cared for preschool children, broadcast classical music and jazz, tested air quality, created public history displays, counseled victims of sexual assault, advised the Cincinnati City Council and other local governments on public policy, performed plays and musicals, designed buildings, freed innocent prisoners, organized volunteers in response to emergencies, provided entertainment with Division I sports, etcetera.

Since the late 1800s, critics of higher education have spoken of the university as a world apart, an ivory tower filled with scholars with their noses in books, thinking arcane thoughts, poring over obscure data. The university is not the "real world," detractors have long said, for even a modestly traditional education cannot prepare young men and women for the rapidly changing world in which they live. I make the opposite argument here. A university, and the University of Cincinnati in particular, is every bit a part of this "real world." Far from some isolated retreat, UC's campus has been an integral part of the economy and culture of the city in which it has developed. This is not to say that the ivory tower mythos has no basis in fact. Some academics have sought detachment, claiming that only distance from the vagaries of society can protect the objectivity of their research, the purity of their thought. But as the chapters that follow show, this has been a minority position at UC. Connections to the community and service to the city have extended and amplified the teaching and research missions of the university. This book puts the university *in* Cincinnati, so that we can assess its real meaning.

🌿 Themes of the Book

The chapters that follow trace the 200-year history of UC and its predecessors, but some eras get more attention than others. Four of the nine chapters concern the last fifty years, the decades not covered by the previous comprehensive history of UC, Reginald McGrane's *The University of Cincinnati: A Success Story in Urban Higher Education*, published in 1963 at the encouragement of President Walter Langsam, who was himself a historian. McGrane transmitted UC's published record faithfully, including much of what was newsworthy in the past, taking an encyclopedic approach to his institutional history. He announced his only real theme in the title: UC was a success. I have taken a different approach, pressing one central argument concerning service to the city along with several additional themes.

The first of these themes is simple enough: location matters. UC has been in Cincinnati its entire history, of course, but over the course of 200 years it has occupied three different regions in the United States. It was founded as Cincinnati College on the frontier in 1819; founded anew in 1870 as the municipally owned University of Cincinnati in what was then the center of the nation, the thriving industrial heartland;[6] and, by the time it became a state university in 1977, UC was once again on the nation's periphery, part of the declining Rust Belt, far from the thriving coasts. Each of these three regional locations had consequences for UC. The frontier, with its boosterish enthusiasm, contained a remarkable mixing of people and ideas, creating a lively, democratic culture—seemingly an ideal location for the founding of a distinctive college that could serve its distinctive region. In the late 1800s and early 1900s, Ohio's economic glory days, when the state played a critical role in national politics, UC benefited from the patronage of established families and connections to thriving businesses. It became a center of pedagogical innovation as part of a diverse, progressive city. In the second half of the twentieth century, UC found itself imbedded in the nation's flyover territory, a region of lowered expectations, constrained budgets, and managed decline. The reality of stagnation and the prospect of descent inspired the university to initiate yet another era of innovation, one that amplified national and international connections.

Just as regional location has mattered to the university's evolution, so too has its location within the city. The institutions that comprise UC have occupied four dif-

5

ferent locations in Cincinnati: downtown, the hillside overlooking the basin, Burnet Woods and neighboring Corryville, and the distant suburbs. Each location offered its own mix of advantages, such as convenience for students and proximity to other cultural and social resources; and disadvantages, such as noise, pollution, crime, and traffic. In each location the institution attempted to find a balance between centrality and remove. By the turn of the twentieth century, remaining downtown or even on the hillside had become untenable, especially given high rents and urban disamenities. Once settled in Burnet Woods and Avondale, UC adjusted to the changing metropolis by adding new facilities in the suburbs and by intervening in a variety of ways in the neighborhoods surrounding its main campus. These interventions play a significant role in the story that follows.

A second, related theme runs through the book: the fate of the university has been linked to the fate of the city, even though Cincinnati's growth maps imperfectly onto the growth of the university. During the city's era of most rapid growth, the 1840s and 1850s, Cincinnati College consisted of only a law school. The city also had a medical college, but a university had not yet been founded to unite these separate institutions with a liberal arts college. After Charles McMicken's bequest allowed the city to create what became a comprehensive, municipal university, the institution thrived only to the degree that the community could support it, especially through property taxes and the issuance of municipal bonds. In the second half of the twentieth century, as the city began to falter economically and demographically, the university looked beyond Cincinnati for support, and UC transitioned into a state institution. In this later period, the city turned to the university to rekindle its growth, especially through the creation of high-paying research jobs.

The third theme derives from the fact that from the moment of its founding the university has been engaged in a constant struggle to finance its endeavors. To succeed the university has needed the patronage of the city's wealthy families. UC has been a public institution since 1870, which has imbued it with a democratic mission to serve the people, but government—the city and the state—has never provided it with the resources necessary to do so comfortably. Raising funds from benefactors to build buildings and endowments has been essential to the university's growth. Cincinnati's wealthy families—the Longworths, Tafts, Sintons, Gambles, Lindners, and many others—have given money to the institution out of a sense of the university's importance to the city. In more recent decades a broader alumni base has spread the task of building the institution—the number of donors has expanded, but the importance of the endowment itself has never faded, nor has the reliance on the wealthiest Cincinnatians. From its inception, then, the home of independent inquiry, of academic freedom, has been absolutely dependent upon the support of the city's economic elite.

The fourth major theme of the book, and perhaps the only surprising one, is that despite the politically and socially progressive reputation of the university's faculty and their forward-looking, cutting-edge research, the university itself has been a very conservative, often reactionary institution. This does not make UC unique, for institutions of higher education tend not to drive social change. Individuals within higher education may lean toward the left, but the institutions that employ them are as conservative as any large institution is, prone to inertia and long, actionless debate. Budgetary limitations and political considerations can also slow institutional change. These have certainly been factors at UC, which has lagged in any variety of reforms, from providing affordable daycare for employees, to creating a smoke-free work environment, to providing gender-neutral restrooms, to adopting carbon-neutral energy generation. College students and faculty have often been on the front lines of social activism—from the civil rights and women's rights movements to public health and environmental protection—but they are just as likely to be demanding change within their institutions as without.

✿ The Most Democratic of Our Institutions

Not surprisingly the literature on United States higher education is extensive. A wide variety of scholars—sociologists, philosophers, historians—have taken up the task of describing the institutions that employ them. Many great historians, including Allan Nevins, Richard Hofstadter, Merle Curti, and Vernon Carstensen, have contributed to this literature, mostly writing intellectual histories, describing the ideas that have shaped and transformed academia. Many of these books, like this one, describe the history of just one institution, but others take up higher education more broadly, attending to curricular developments, the role of universities in the national economy, and other themes. A good many of these books manage to tell the story of higher education in America without mentioning the University of Cincinnati.[7] The literature tends toward the elite—Harvard, Yale, the University of Chicago, Johns Hopkins, and the like. Perhaps there is good reason for this elite bias, if your goal is to write a history of ideas about higher education. Many important innovations did come out of these large, influential institutions.

But the elite bias in the historical literature has many drawbacks, including that it is also reflects an anti-urban bias. As the historian Steven J. Diner has described, the use of "urban" as a descriptor of universities has served as a handicap in achieving national recognition, partly because urban universities have generally focused on serving local constituencies. This bias has also impeded scholarly assessment of these institutions.[8] This is a mistake for two reasons. First, urban institutions have made significant contributions to the development of higher education. Most pertinently, UC was the first university to create a cooperative education system, first in engineering and then business and architecture. The cooperative program developed directly out of the university's urban location. Second, and I would argue more importantly, UC and other large, democratic, urban universities deserve attention because they have achieved something that no other institutions in the world have: they provide access to a high-quality, competitive education for average citizens, those without great wealth or outstanding academic records. In other words, most people who have studied higher education's history haven't studied the institutions that educate most people. As Diner argues, by the end of the 1910s, the University of Cincinnati was among those institutions that led "the nation in democratizing higher education" by educating "working-class and immigrant day students and adult night students." That accomplishment is worthy of further exploration.[9]

This brings me to one last point before I begin the story in earnest. In the late 1800s, as the number of institutions of higher education grew rapidly in the United States, Western Reserve University president Charles Franklin Thwing declared, "The college is, along with the public school, the most democratic of our institutions. It exists for the people."[10] Thwing praised the accessibility of higher education in the United States, its availability to students of different classes and backgrounds. But the democratic theme runs through the governance of universities, too. University culture has been highly democratic, particularly through the twentieth century, with diffuse power structures and an assumption that all institutional policies should be subject to scrutiny and open debate. They are often, as we shall see, democratic to the point of chaos; they are open, sometimes, to the point of conflict. In this way, and in many others, the modern university may be the most distinctively American institution we have.

1

A FRONTIER INSTITUTION

The College Edifice in the Commercial City

In the fall of 1814, Daniel Drake stood before a small group of men who, somewhat hopefully, called themselves the "School of Literature and the Arts." Engaged in the "introductory labors" of bringing high culture to frontier Cincinnati, theirs was one of many short-lived efforts to connect this western outpost to the traditions of western civilization. Just four years earlier Drake had described Cincinnati as a village with no paved streets, and in many ways it was still what Drake called a "Back-woods" community. But on this night Drake praised the work of the school's members, who over their first year had presented essays on topics as various as the geology of Cincinnati and the internal commerce of the nation. Drake acknowledged that the West was at a disadvantage so far as intellect and learning were concerned; comparisons with Europe's great centers of education—Edinburgh, Paris, or London—would be absurd. "Our lot, gentlemen, is cast in a region abundant in but few things, except the products of a rich and unexhausted soil. Learning, philosophy, and taste, are yet in early infancy, and the standard of excellence in literature and science is proportionally low."[1]

But Drake assured the assembled that the Miami Country, so called because of the two Miami rivers that drained the good farmland north of the city, held more than natural advantages. The young American empire's hold on the West was tenuous, but so too was the influence of "the empire of prejudice." Drake thought these men were in a position to innovate, to improve upon the societies of the East and of Europe. Perhaps most important, "In no country of the same age and numbers, do the immigrants exhibit more diversity."[2] People had come to Cincinnati from every state in the young nation, from England, Ireland, and "the empires of Europe." Drake thought this diverse population gave residents the opportunity to

9

traverse the world and learn the customs of many places without ever leaving the city. According to Drake, "the operations of intellect in an old country are like the waters of a deep canal, which, flowing between artificial banks, pursue an equable and uniform course." But in this "new country" the waters of intellectual life "resemble the stream which cuts its own channel in the wilderness; rolls successively in every direction; has a current, alternately swift and slow; is frequently shallow; but always free, diversified, and natural. The former is eminently useful for a *single* purpose—the latter can be made subservient to *many*." Drake, a brilliant, controversial young man, Cincinnati's most prominent intellectual figure, had found the perfect metaphor to capture the raw potential of the Ohio Valley. The wild waters of the West—metaphorical and real—would reshape the nation. And Cincinnati, Drake hoped, would be at the center of it all.

Born in New Jersey in 1785, Drake had moved with his family at an early age to May's Lick, Kentucky. He came to Cincinnati at fifteen to study medicine as an apprentice to William Goforth, a well-regarded physician. Like Goforth, Drake had varied intellectual interests, and in addition to studying medicine he became a student of the young city and the Ohio Valley region. Among the important early publications of his long and remarkable career were *Notices Concerning Cincinnati*, a pamphlet published in 1810, and the more substantial *A Natural and Statistical View, or Picture of Cincinnati*, published in 1815. Together these pieces not only established Drake as an expert on Cincinnati, but also as one of its most vocal boosters, eager to convey the unique prospect of his adopted city. The Ohio Valley, Drake emphasized, was ruled by its own climate and possessed distinctive flora and fauna; its rocks contained a distinctive fossil record, which was of special interest in the early 1800s because of the Big Bones found across the river in Kentucky. Like all good boosters, Drake was compelled by his desire to know this place, boast of its character, and predict its grand future.

And now, just a month before the Treaty of Ghent brought the War of 1812 to its official close, Drake could affirm an American future in the West. With the removal of British interests and the defeat of confederated Native Americans, migration to the Ohio Valley was sure to surge, and boosters like Drake would direct the flow. Many fledgling cities—including Lexington in the heart of the rich soil of the Kentucky bluegrass region, and Louisville, located downriver at the only substantial falls on the Ohio—competed to attract migrants seeking economic opportunities. Boosters knew that many of the nascent towns would not thrive, that just a few would become substantial places, and only one would become the region's metropolis. Most boosters were primarily concerned about improving commercial traffic and increasing property values—making money— but for some, like Drake, the concern was more than economic. He wanted Cincinnati to become the intellectual and cultural center of the region—the Athens of the West.[3]

Drake was hardly the only booster in Cincinnati. In a historical sketch of the city that accompanied his 1819 directory, Oliver Farnsworth reflected on the changes witnessed by a fictive settler who had arrived in Cincinnati just two decades earlier. "In the course of a few years, he has seen a little village of cabins transformed, as if by magic, into a populous, active, and

Daniel Drake, 1855. This engraving appeared in Edward Mansfield's *Memoirs of the Life and Services of Daniel Drake, M.D.* (Cincinnati: Applegate & Co., 1855). *Courtesy of the Henry R. Winkler Center for the History of the Health Professions, University of Cincinnati Libraries.*

commercial city. He has seen the canoe give way to the barge, and the barge to the steam boat. In short, he has seen hills torn down, marshes filled up, streets laid out, graduated and paved, public buildings erected, manufactories established, and every part of the country around him improved and beautified by the active spirit of enterprise and civilization."[4] In the thirty years since its founding, Cincinnati had grown into an important commercial center, with a bustling public landing that served as a linchpin in the burgeoning river trade. Still, with fewer than 10,000 residents and a credit crunch caused by a banking panic that year, Cincinnati's continued rise was far from guaranteed.

Observer after observer—from resident boosters to touring foreigners—commented on the distinctive feel of the frontier. Even in cities, they felt a certain freedom from custom, a distance from cultural norms and ancient institutions—a liberty to remake oneself and perhaps society. Expressing their faith in democracy, some observers anticipated great experimentation and innovation, not just in economic terms, but in social arrangements as well. Importantly, however, the impulse of settlers everywhere was to fill the structural void with new institutions, usually modeled directly on those they had left behind. Growth created wealth, especially among property owners, and the established elite invested a portion of their gains in ways designed to enrich their lives but also to perpetuate the development of their city.[5] Titian Peale took note of these investments when he stopped in Cincinnati while traveling on the steamboat *Western Engineer* in May 1819. Peale, son of the famed artist Charles Willson Peale, noted that Cincinnati had "risen like a mushroom from the wilderness." The city's growth and diversity had been created by immigrants "every day arriving from all parts of the world." Although much of the growth was quite recent, Peale remarked, "The inhabitants have already founded a college and subscribed eight or ten thousand dollars for a museum."[6] They had done so because only through such investments could Cincinnati hope to become the metropolis of the West.

🌿 A Very Eligible Situation for a Seat of Learning

Cincinnati's effort to create an institution of higher education began in earnest in 1814, with a group of Methodists trying to establish a Lancastrian School under their control. Some residents, however, not wanting the school under the auspices of any single religious body, decided to create their own—the Cincinnati Lancaster Seminary, chartered by the state in 1815. The new school admitted students at a wide range of ages and operated under the educational principles of Joseph Lancaster, an English Quaker who advocated a system in which the older children taught the younger under the supervision of one master. To accommodate the new school, the First Presbyterian Church leased land at the corner of Walnut and Fourth Streets, upon which a two-story building was erected. The Methodists, at first snubbed, joined in the effort, and in the spring of 1815, 420 students enrolled in the school, their families paying a tuition of $8 per term. A few needy youngsters attended on scholarship, a condition set by the Presbyterian Church in exchange for the land.[7]

The Lancaster School competed with several other private schools, but the city itself did not yet provide public education. In 1818, a number of prominent Cincinnatians, including General William Lytle, Judge Jacob Burnet, and John H. Piatt, raised funds to add a college to the Lancastrian School. The $50,000 pledged would have provided a tidy endowment, except for the onset

Cincinnati College, circa 1819. Constructed at the corner of Walnut and Fourth Streets, the Cincinnati College edifice, with its bell tower and gardens, provided a structure worthy of a growing city. Unfortunately, it also created a debt that could not be overcome by the generosity of its patrons. *Photograph files, Archives & Rare Books Library, University of Cincinnati.*

of the Panic of 1819, a financial crisis that triggered two years of economic stagnation. Lytle, son of one of the founders of the city, a famed military man, experienced surveyor, and heir to a considerable fortune, mostly in land, suffered acutely during the crisis. Still, prospects seemed bright on January 22, 1819, when the state of Ohio incorporated the Cincinnati College with a short piece of legislation. (Interestingly, Cincinnati became a city two weeks later, when the General Assembly approved a municipal charter.)

Daniel Drake, who had personally traveled to Columbus to help ensure the passage of the college charter, was ecstatic with the outcome. "There is now a fair prospect of making this city the emporium of the sciences from the Western Country," he wrote in his typically confident tone. The faculty would be led by Elijah Slack, who had moved to Cincinnati to lead the Lancastrian Seminary after a rocky stint at Princeton University. Slack ran the college and taught mathematics, physical sciences, and chemistry. He did so using a laboratory outfitted with his personal apparatus, which he had brought with him from Princeton. The importance of the appearance of this sophisticated equipment on the frontier should not be underestimated. "A very handsome Laboratory has been fitted up," Drake bragged to Dr.

Samuel Brown, "which will receive a hundred pupils and Mr. Slack has furnished it amply and in the best style with apparatus."[8]

The state charter named the first board of trustees and established the rules by which it would operate. The board consisted of twenty prominent men of the city, including Burnet, Lytle, Drake, and Martin Baum, who undertook the building of a grand Palladian home on Pike Street at the same time he helped to build the college.[9] The state authorized the college board to "grant and confer on any candidate, in such form as they may direct, all or any of the degrees that are usually conferred in any college or university in the United States." The college also gained control of the Lancastrian Seminary and its two-story brick building. The school had a central entranceway and staircase, topped with an impressive dome that contained a set of bells.[10] Still, the building was not yet substantial enough to house a college, and the board set out to expand it with a new wing.

In October, Cincinnati newspapers announced that the college would open on November 9 with "the classical course of studies." This would be the winter session, with a summer session to begin in May and end in a September commencement. Admission cost $5, and courses cost $20 per term. To gain admission, students needed some command of Latin and Greek, which they would demonstrate via examination. As was standard, the curriculum was entirely set by the faculty, with no electives. Freshmen took courses in Virgil, Horace, Xenophon, Latin prosody, and the Greek New Testament, among other classical topics. In subsequent years students took geometry, algebra, natural philosophy, chemistry, and astronomy, even while continuing to study Greek and Latin classics. In addition to the demanding coursework, the college established a rigid code of conduct. All students were to attend morning and evening prayers in the college hall and attend "public worship on the Sabbath." Among the many other rules: students could not "go to a tavern or tippling house, for the purpose of entertainment or amusement, without permission from some member of the Faculty"; and, challenging someone to a duel, or merely serving as a second in a duel, would be grounds for expulsion.[11]

The opening of the college brought a great deal of optimism, despite the economic downturn. As Oliver Farnsworth wrote, "It must be obvious to everyone acquainted with the Western Country, that Cincinnati is a very eligible situation for a seat of learning." And now it would have an educational institution befitting its rank as the largest city in the Ohio Valley. The political, cultural, and economic elite of the West could send their sons—and only their sons—to a college in their region's urban center, in the hopes that they would be prepared to lead the next generation. Farnsworth was certain that the institution would succeed, for the commercial connections created by the Ohio River had placed Cincinnati at the center of the region's economic network. Further, Farnsworth noted, "It is a healthy, populous city, and can afford the wealth and talents necessary to endow and foster an institution of the kind."[12] Boosters hoped Cincinnati College would quickly surpass Lexington's Transylvania University, which became the first college west of the Appalachians when founded in 1799. The nationally known Lexington institution provided the best evidence that Cincinnati could not yet claim to be the Athens of the West.[13]

Drake thought Cincinnati College could outcompete Transylvania by taking advantage of its location. In the previous decade, Cincinnati had dramatically

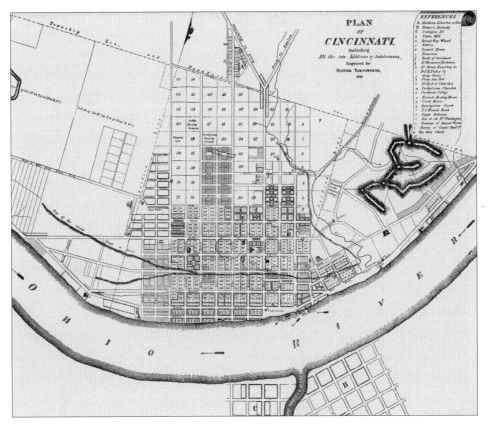

Cincinnati, 1819. This map appeared in Oliver Farnsworth's city directory. It lists the recently created Cincinnati College among the city's prominent sites, at the location of the former Lancaster Seminary. *Photograph files, Archives & Rare Books Library, University of Cincinnati.*

outpaced Lexington in growth, and with the ever-expanding fleet of steamboats on the river, there was no reason to think Cincinnati's economic superiority over its landlocked southern neighbor would diminish. The trick would be translating individual profits into community resources. Residents had begun a subscription library nearly twenty years earlier, and Drake hoped its collection would move to the college to facilitate student use. Drake also thought the Western Museum Society, just organized, would "place its collections in the same building and thus contribute to the promotion of this young and promising institution."[14] Of course, the commercial bustle of the city brought its disadvantages for scholars, too. After two years of study in Cincinnati, John Hough James reflected in his diary after walking into town during a hot and dusty late summer day, "I have often wished for the country where I might pursue my studies undisturbed."[15] For better and worse, Cincinnati College would be an *urban* institution.

The college faculty, numbering just three at the start—Slack, Thomas Osborn, who taught languages, and David Taylor, who tutored students—assessed the abilities of the first set of applicants and placed them in the curriculum based on their proficiencies in Latin and Greek. Three young men entered as juniors and so were prepared for graduation after the summer session in 1821. On September 26, a Wednesday evening, in a ceremony held in the north wing of the college building, President Slack opened the graduation with a prayer. One of Cincinnati's weekly newspapers, the *Western Spy*, reported on the events of the day. "The audience was numerous and respectable, and left the Institution, we trust, equally impressed with its importance and the novelty of the scene which they had just witnessed." This was, according to the paper, "no ordinary moment," one that would be of interest to every class in the city, one "of so much consequence to the republic of science, letters, and refinement." The lengthy report looked forward to the day when the college would "be justly esteemed the first and greatest of the Western Country."[16]

Among the three graduates was William Henry Harrison Jr., son of a general who had gained fame fighting Native Americans and the British before and during the War of 1812. The older Harrison had recently served in the US House of Representatives—and eventually he would be elected president of the United States. Unfortunately, his son, who lived in North Bend with his parents, died before his father's inauguration in 1841. At graduation, the younger Harrison spoke on "Eloquence," a speech the *Western Spy* called "an impassioned, glowing harangue, one delivered with his characteristic impetuosity." The second graduate was Frederick A. Kemper of Walnut Hills, who gave the salutatory address in Latin, precluding comment from the *Spy*'s reporter, who didn't know the language. The third was John Hough James, who graduated at the top of his small class. James delivered "a chaste, appropriate, and highly affecting Valedictory," according to the *Spy*. James himself admitted that he was "flattered with having drawn tears from some of the ladies and some of my fellow students." After the day's events he reflected in his diary, "I have the honour of being the first graduate of Cincinnati College and tho I leave it with the highest honours it can bestow, I leave it with regret."[17]

In 1822, a young, wealthy Scot named William N. Blane passed through Cincinnati as part of a tour of the continent, arriving on the steamboat *United States* from the thriving city of Louisville. He was most impressed with Cincinnati, which he called "the western capital of the Federal Republic." Blane toured the college while in town, even sitting in on a class. "The college is tolerably built," he noted in a published account of his journey, "but is not likely to be well attended until better regulations are established." In an indication that Cincinnati retained its outpost flavor, Blane reported, "I was present at a lecture, and was much shocked at the want of decorum exhibited by the students, who sat down in their plaids and cloaks, and were constantly spitting tobacco juice about the room."[18] Apparently demanding church attendance and prohibiting duels was not enough. The journey from "Back-woods" community to Athens of the West would take some time.

❦ Neatly and Scientifically Arranged

On June 10, 1820, Daniel Drake stood behind the rostrum of the Cincinnati College chapel. Just thirty-five years old, Drake was an established figure in the city, well known to its learned elite. So it wasn't surprising that he should rise before the crowd in celebration of the opening of the Western Museum. Drake had been involved with the museum from the outset, encouraged by William Steele, who had recruited Drake to serve as the Museum Society secretary in 1818. Meetings began the next year. Members contributed $50, a very high sum. The museum opened a year later, occupying prominent space in the college edifice, in close proximity of the students and faculty who might make frequent use of the collections.

The Western Museum contained such a great variety of items that it might have been called a museum of everything. Cabinets displayed "neatly and scientifically arranged" objects, including minerals, fossils, and cultural artifacts, many of them collected from the region. In this way more than just the museum's location was "western."[19] Its finest objects were, too. The most important of these were samples of Big Bones from the famed lick across the river. These included Drake's own collection of fossil bones. Some cabinets held Native American artifacts, which Drake referred to as "curiosities"—"utensils, weapons, and trinkets of our Indian tribes," some of which were taken from the many mounds in the region.[20] Indeed, Drake hoped the museum would "be made an efficient means of inquiry into the aboriginal history of this country" and ultimately explain what happened to the mound-building societies that had disappeared long before white settlers arrived.[21] The room also held preserved animals—taxidermy—"quadrupeds," reptiles, and birds, which captured the rich natural history of the Ohio Valley. The museum even included paintings, mostly produced in the region. Drake noted that in older cities, museums of different specialties would hold these collections separately—art here, native artifacts there, and fossils in still another place.[22] In the new country, these objects would be displayed, appreciated, and understood in relationship to one another.

The museum was curated by Robert Best, who also performed taxidermy and positioned the animals, earning great praise in the local press. Another museum employee also gained notoriety. Four months before the museum opened, young Robert Todd Lytle, who later became one of the early graduates of Cincinnati College, wrote from Louisville, inquiring of his father William, then a trustee of the college, if he could find a place for a man with extraordinary talent. This man, born in Saint-Domingue and raised in France, could serve as professor of French, or perhaps of drawing, for John James Audubon had made a reputation for himself with his art, especially his paintings of birds. "You have no doubt seen some of his paintings in this place," Robert wrote, "and of course will be able to judge that subject for yourself." Audubon had been collecting birds for years as he moved about Kentucky, Missouri, and Louisiana, making just enough money to raise a family on the edge of poverty. All the while he painted birds in realistic settings in the hopes of publishing a complete ornithology of the United States—a work that Lytle thought was nearly finished just as the Western Museum was opening. "The opportunity of employing Mr. Audubon ought not to be neglected," Lytle implored, "as he would be a great acquisition to your institution and to your society."[23]

Audubon's work for the museum gained immediate acclaim in the press. The weekly newspaper, *Liberty Hall*, praised Audubon's "collection of splendid, and we may safely say unrivalled, paintings of birds, animals, &c. from real life." His work constituted just a fraction of the fine art in the new museum. Drake noted that some observers might say that the city is "too poor to encourage the fine arts," that this enterprise is premature for a small city on the western edge of the nation. "I will admit that but few of our citizens have sufficient wealth to become their individual patrons," Drake said, "but this very circumstance constitutes a strong argument for confiding to a collective body, the means and the duty of promoting their introduction to this country." This is what the museum was for, to encourage the introduction and production of fine arts in Cincinnati as well as to promote an understanding of the natural history of the region. Science and art were intimately connected in Drake's mind, just as they were united in Audubon's paintings.[24]

Drake thought of the museum as a perfect supplement to the college, and so their physical connection was important. Drake arranged an agreement with the college trustees that assured the collection a rent-free home in the college building, while students and professors would have unfettered access, including the use of artifacts to illustrate lectures. In this way, the museum provided objects for study to complement the literature provided by the college, although Drake thought that the museum, too, needed an expansive library. "One of the most painful deprivations experienced by the student of nature in these new and remote settlements," Drake wrote, "is the want of books to direct his researches." The library would have to expand, because, "Thousands of years have elapsed since the students of Nature began to unfold her mysteries. Books are the great repository of their discoveries, and he who neglects them, begins, like the first observer, unaided and alone." In an effort to raise money to purchase books, Drake and Slack organized lectures at the museum—Drake on "Mineralogy and Geology" and Slack on "Elements of Natural Philosophy." The lectures, free to members of the museum, were 25 cents for the general public.[25]

The college and the museum were physically united, but each had a specific purpose. "The College is principally a school of literature, the Museum of science, and the arts," said Drake. "The knowledge imparted by one is elementary, by the other practical. Without the former, our sons would be illiterate; without the latter, they would be scholars merely—by the help of both, they may become scholars and philosophers." In other words, complete students must combine scholarly understanding of the world in which all of humanity has existed, with a practical knowledge of the world in which they actually live. Drake also regarded learning at first hand, through travel and field study, to be essential to developing understanding. He argued that Cincinnati's young men and women should know their home before heading off to explore Europe or the eastern cities. "Until we are acquainted with the state of our own country," he wrote, "we must be wretchedly prepared to appreciate that of others."[26] In this way, the mission of the college to connect western residents to classical traditions was balanced by the mission of the museum to familiarize them with the particularities of their own Ohio Valley.

The Western Museum became a necessary stop for travelers passing through the city. W. N. Blane, who had been unimpressed with the college, had a more positive reaction to the museum. "The Museum at Cincinnati, though small, is very interesting to a lover of natural history," he reported. "All the specimens are very neatly arranged." He was especially struck by one of the "remains of the mammoth"—a great tusk eight and a half feet long.[27] Unfortunately, shortly after Blane's visit the poor finances of the museum, unsurprising given the depressed economy, precipitated a crisis that nearly led to the sale of the objects. With no ready buyers, the entire collection was gifted to Joseph Dorfeuille, who had become director in 1823, with the simple stipulation that members continue to have free access. Dorfeuille moved the museum out of the college edifice to the corner of Main and Second Streets, closer to the public landing, where it could more easily attract travelers passing through Cincinnati on the river. Under Dorfeuille's leadership the mission of the museum quickly slid from education to entertainment, and the collection's scientific value waned.[28]

✺ The Philadelphia of the West

Drake had played a significant role in founding of the college and the museum, but his primary professional goal was to create a medical college in Cincinnati. Indeed, Drake secured the incorporation for the Medical College of Ohio just days before that of Cincinnati College in January 1819. His own medical training had begun with an apprenticeship, but he had also received formal training in Philadelphia, where he studied under Benjamin Rush at the University of Pennsylvania's excellent medical school, from which he received a degree in 1816. He then accepted a faculty position at Transylvania University, which started its medical school in 1817. But Drake spent less than a year in Lexington, because he much preferred living in his beloved Cincinnati. Upon returning in early 1818, Drake began to build support for a medical school that would replicate the success of Pennsylvania and eclipse the success of Transylvania. Writing to Dr. Samuel Brown, Drake concluded, in typical booster fashion, "Upon the whole I am convinced that Cincinnati is to be the *Philadelphia* of the West as to medical instruction."[29]

To found a successful school, Drake needed to attract renowned faculty. To this end, he carried on an extensive correspondence with Brown, one of the nation's most highly regarded physicians, who was then at work in Philadelphia. In a lengthy letter, Drake assured Brown that, "we shall not hesitate to encourage the emigration hither of such eminent men as may be necessary to fill the professorships" of this new college. Brown too had trained with Benjamin Rush, and he had attended the University of Edinburgh and the University of Aberdeen, giving him one of the finest pedigrees in the country. Seeing Brown as the linchpin of his school's success, Drake offered him the professorship of anatomy even before the college had been established.[30]

"Of the state of the medical profession in Cincinnati I cannot say much," Drake reported to Brown, displaying the condescension his fellow physicians found so annoying, "but the population of the town (already much greater than that of Lexington) is rapidly increasing." Drake knew that his college would enter into direct competition with the one he had recently left, and so he assured Brown that Cincinnati was "better situated physically, morally and politically, for a medical college, than Lexington." To increase public enthusiasm for a medical school in Cincinnati, Drake gathered together talented physicians—Coleman Rogers and Elijah Slack—and arranged a lecture series. This allowed Drake to report to Brown on "the pulse of the public."[31] The lectures also helped draw the attention of prospective students, including "four respectable young men from the interior of Kentucky and three from other towns in this state," he wrote to Brown, eager to emphasize the ability of Cincinnati to draw talented students away from Lexington.[32]

Drake expected to double the attendance at lectures the next winter, and based on this support he "concluded to make a personal application to the legislature for a law of incorporation." He solicited Brown's thoughts on the language that should be contained in the charter, which Drake himself drafted, and he asked permission to include Brown's name as professor of anatomy. "To this I hope you will consent; and if you have not given us your decision upon the receipt of this letter please to write me immediately at Columbus." Drake expected the school to grow quickly, and he assured Brown, "We do not therefore solicit your cooperation in a transient or insignificant undertaking."[33]

Coleman Rogers also recruited Brown to join the as-yet-unfounded college. He too understood that the real competition was with Transylvania, where Brown had taught for several years after returning from Scotland. Transylvania had been damaged by Drake's departure, which precipitated other departures and a temporary closure of the medical program, and Rogers assured Brown, "[I]t will be impossible to fill the professorships in the school at Lexington for many years; no person will accept who is qualified."[34] Two months after Rogers made his case, Drake returned from Columbus, having secured a charter for the college and the medical school. Brown, however, did not join in Drake's celebration.[35]

Despite the wooing, Brown decided to head to Lexington instead of Cincinnati. Upon hearing the news, Rogers wrote, "I admit you have all the talent that could be asked for to form a school, but you must have more, you must have population so that you may have patients to give your practice; you must have *subjects* for anatomy; to conclude you want *stuff* to work on." Further, Rogers warned, "This you have not—nor can any human effort procure it."[36] Brown's decision to bolster Transylvania's faculty was a heavy blow to Cincinnati, because leaders of both institutions thought the region could support only one excellent medical college. Drake, frustrated by Rogers's ultimate support of Brown's decision, had him dismissed from the college. When classes began in the fall of 1820, four professors—Drake, Slack, and two other local physicians, Jesse Smith and Benjamin Bohrer—constituted the faculty.[37]

In addition to completing the faculty, Drake was intent on assembling a library of medical works. He had asked Brown to gather books in Philadelphia—all the most recent publications in the field. Drake was especially keen on acquiring books from France. "If we conclude to import any books from Europe we should make out an order soon," Drake noted in February, just six months from what he hoped would be the opening of the school. By the time the school did commence in 1820, a year later than he had hoped, the library consisted of over five hundred volumes, a number sufficiently large so as to appear in a marketing circular announcing the commencement of classes.[38] An up-to-date library was a strong selling point with prospective students.

Although he had not assembled the faculty he wanted, Drake continued to work toward the success of the Medical College, including securing the use of a house with room enough to instruct 100 students, although the first class had only 30. He also made arrangements to assure a stream of patients for the students. He made an agreement with the secretary of war to attend to the soldiers at the garrison in Newport, and with the city to attend to the poor. Most important, he went back up to Columbus to secure the creation of the Commercial Hospital and Lunatic Asylum in 1821, for which he also secured state funds and tax support.[39] Students and faculty at the college would have attending rights at the new hospital, constructed on Twelfth Street, a mile north of the riverfront on inexpensive land.

Unfortunately for the Medical College and for Drake, jealousies and animosities developed into a fractured medical community, and after just two years Drake was forced out of the college he had created. Slack, who participated in Drake's ouster, continued on at the college, which managed to erect its own building on Sixth Street in 1826. Drake, meanwhile, returned to Transylvania to teach. When he left town, nearly all of the institutions he had established rested on weak foundations.

❦ Drake's Battle for the Marines and a Place in the City

Charles Fenno Hoffman arrived in Cincinnati via steamboat in the spring of 1834. The young, soon-to-be-famous author was struck by the city's beauty, its "well-washed streets and tasteful private residences." Despite the depression of the early 1820s, Cincinnati's population had more than doubled in a decade. At well over 25,000 residents, Cincinnati was larger than Lexington, Louisville, and St. Louis combined. Construction of the Miami Canal, begun in 1825, had helped fuel the growth by connecting Cincinnati to Dayton and the rich farmland of western Ohio. The city became home to hundreds of new residents every year, and since nearly everyone in Cincinnati came from somewhere else, it was, Hoffman wrote, "in the highest degree absurd to speak of the Cincinnatians as a provincial people in their manners, when the most agreeable persons that figure here hail originally from New-York or Philadelphia, Boston and Baltimore, and are very tenacious of the style of living in which they have been educated." In other words, it wasn't just the fine hotels and the "elegantly furnished drawing-rooms" that revealed Cincinnati's progress. It was the manners of the people, tied as they were to older, eastern places. The frontier had pushed west, the forests had been pushed back, and the city had flourished. Hoffman raved of the "twenty gilded spires gleaming among gardens and shrubbery," and several "principal buildings" drew his attention, among them the Cincinnati College edifice. Unfortunately, in 1834 the college no longer offered classes, and, in fact, the building had been underutilized for nearly a decade. Still a prominent building, the college edifice had begun to show signs of dilapidation.[40]

In the years immediately following its founding, the college gathered considerable moral support but too little financial support. At the time of the first graduation, the *Western Spy* asserted that universities are "mines of wealth to the cities in which they are located." In reality, the flow of wealth would have to move the other direction if the school were to build a firm foundation. Since finances did not improve, the first graduation was one of just four held before the college ceased operations.[41] In 1826, the college suspended operations and began leasing its rooms to help pay down the debt. Students still used the building, to visit private tutors, and several organizations rented rooms for meetings and lectures. The edifice even served as an emergency hospital during the cholera epidemic of 1832. But the college itself existed as a merely legal entity.

Cincinnati College had been part of a wave of new institutions in the West—including Ohio University, founded in 1804, and Miami University, founded five years later.[42] Although both of those rural schools persisted, the failure rate of booster colleges like Cincinnati's was high. Benjamin Drake and E. D. Mansfield wrote hopefully about the college's revival shortly after its closure, but they added, "Until that period shall arrive it is gratifying that our citizens, who have sons to educate, can avail themselves of the advantages of the Miami University, which is located in the vicinity of our city, and is now rising into respectability." Cincinnati's elite would have to send their sons away for college, but not too far away.[43]

In the spring of 1835, the trustees began discussing the possibility of reviving the college through the creation of new medical and law departments. Two years earlier Timothy Walker, a Harvard Law School graduate and recent migrant to Cincinnati, had joined with Edward King and John C. Wright to create the Cincinnati Law School, the first of its kind in the West. At the start lectures were given in Walker and King's law offices on Third Street, but in 1835 the school became a department of the Cincinnati College so that it could confer degrees. The untimely death of King in 1836 left the fledgling school shorthanded, with just two professors. Soon there would be only one—Walker, who, very ably, gave all the lectures.[44]

The college edifice could easily accommodate the small law school, but the building needed considerable work and an enlarged north wing to make it more useful to a new medical department. As the board's building committee summarized, "The object of this wing is to afford, first a laboratory and apparatus room for the professor of chemistry; second, an apartment for the preparations of the professors of special and morbid anatomy, and of surgery and obstetrics; third, a room for practical anatomy." The committee thought that when completed, the revived college would have room for 300 students in the north wing and an equal number in the south. To pay for the work, the board sought donations from wealthy residents, but the faculty also contributed a significant sum. In 1836, with the edifice "reclaimed from decay," as Drake put it, the board agreed to enclose the college grounds with a stone wall and iron fence so that faculty could create a botanical garden to the south of the building, at the corner of Fourth and Walnut. The board also approved planting and protecting a row of shade trees around the whole property and improving the pavement in front of the building. In this way, the revival inside the building would be matched by renewal outside.[45]

While the college refurbished the building, Drake established a faculty. He served as professor of the theory and practice of medicine and as dean. Joining him were Samuel Gross, who taught anatomy and physiology, Joseph McDowell, professor of surgical anatomy, and professor of obstetrics Landon Rives, who had arrived in Cincinnati in 1830 after having studied medicine in Philadelphia. In all, nine physicians took faculty positions, and they instantly made the school a strong rival to the Medical College of Ohio, Drake's earlier creation. Indeed, on the strength of the faculty, the new medical department attracted sixty-six students to its first cohort in 1836. Students came from thirteen states to study with Drake and his colleagues. In just its second year, the Cincinnati College medical department admitted more students than its older rival.[46]

The faculty could attract students, to be sure, but they needed access to patients for clinical training if the college were to succeed. The rival Medical College of Ohio had exclusive access to the only hospital in the city, the Commercial Hospital, and so Drake decided to create another facility, which he called Cincinnati Hospital, directly across the street from Cincinnati College. The new hospital would receive patients from Drake's Eye Infirmary, which he had opened in 1827, but students—and the hospital—would require a larger, more diverse stream of paying customers. For that, Drake turned to merchant marines.[47]

In the mid-1830s, the public landing was the heart of the city. Hundreds of merchants, cartmen, and day laborers mingled with passengers, captains, and boatmen. The landing, which sloped gradually into the rising and falling river, could be cluttered with piles of products that were coming and going. Men rolled barrels on and off the steamboats and flatboats that came and went. About 250 steamboats plied the waters of the west in the mid-1830s, most of them traveling up and down the Mississippi and Ohio Rivers. With an average crew of twenty-two men, inland steamboats employed more than 5,500 men altogether. In addition, every year as many as 6,000 flatboats—each with a crew of four or five men—stopped at Cincinnati as they floated down river.[48]

In January 1836, Drake attended the Medical Convention of Ohio in Columbus, hoping to gather support for the creation of a system of marine hospitals. Such a system already existed along the coast, for which merchant marines contributed 20 cents a month to a federal fund, a tax that Drake thought could be replicated for men working inland waters. In arguing for a new system, Drake specifically linked the Ohio Valley environment with a propensity for disease, noting that great numbers of boatmen traveled through "unhealthy climates" where they were subject to the "insalubrious exhalations" of marshy banks. Many passengers got sick while traveling up the Mississippi, but, according to Drake, even more people died on "the long and sickly descending voyages of the flat bottomed boats, which often depart from the upper waters in summer and early autumn, when they are low, and their shores unhealthy." The arrival of sick boatmen put ports like Cincinnati at risk of contagious diseases and burdened them with the duty and expense of caring for the infirm. What's more, Drake argued, sick boatmen put the entire commercial enterprise at risk. "Nothing is more common than for two out of the five hands, who generally managed one of these boats, to die; and it has even happened, that the whole have perished, and the boat with its cargo been left deserted, to be lost."[49]

Drake was concerned about these men and about the health of his city, but he was more interested in the opportunity the marines represented for his fledgling medical school. Sick and injured marines could provide a variety of clinical experiences, and, equally important, could pay for the services rendered. In the spring of 1836, Drake petitioned Congress to create these inland marine hospitals and then corresponded with Secretary of the Treasury Levi Woodbury to have the boatmen sent to his Cincinnati Hospital. Using the language of the federal law, Drake informed Woodbury that his hospital would furnish "boarding, nursing, lodging, washing, medical treatments, medicine and funeral expenses" to all entitled seamen. Perhaps impressed with Drake's persistence and reputation, Woodbury notified Cincinnati's port surveyor, Robert Punshon, that the taxes he collected from boat captains should go to Drake's hospital.[50]

With this assured stream of paying patients, Drake formally proposed that Cincinnati College create an infirmary as a "school of practical medicine, surgery, and Obstetrics," which the faculty promptly approved. Immediately thereafter, Drake presented a five-year lease for a townhouse owned by William Disney just across the street from the college, the signing of which the faculty also promptly approved. Drake and his colleagues quickly prepared the building to accommodate sick and injured marines, furnishing it as a hospital with their own funds.[51]

This arrangement lasted a year, the length of the original contract, after which Punshon decided to send the marines up to the Commercial Hospital at Twelfth Street and Central Avenue, more than a mile from the public landing, where it had been located in the hope of removing the sick from the unhealthy air and unsettling atmosphere at the heart of the bustling city. The Commercial Hospital had attended to the needs of the marines before Drake's arrangement with Woodbury, and Punshon decided that he would revert to this previous practice. This decision was devastating to Cincinnati Hospital and Cincinnati College. "The loss of this class of patients is quite a calamity to the medical department," Rives noted in a plea to the Board of Trustees, in which he encouraged them to exert their influence over the port supervisor or with officials in Washington.[52]

For Drake, Punshon's decision was a personal affront. He assumed, and with good reason, that Punshon had made the change at the pleading of the Medical College of Ohio faculty, not because they needed the patients, but because they wanted to deprive Drake's new school of the clinical experience. So here was the faculty of the old medical school, which Drake had created, taking steps to destroy his new medical school. Although Drake saw this action as yet another personal attack by jealous physicians, he also understood the ramifications for his new hospital. Drake flatly concluded "without the marines the establishment will not support itself."[53]

Drake complained bitterly to James Whitcomb, commissioner of the General Land Office and his personal liaison to Woodbury. Drake argued that since the Commercial Hospital had city support, it did not need the marines. Drake also claimed that no one had done as much as he had to ensure that Congress created inland marine hospitals, which might have been true.[54] Drake's correspondence with Whitcomb and directly to Secretary Woodbury had the desired effect. Woodbury asked Punshon to explain his actions. In late 1837, Punshon reported a series of complaints against the Cincinnati Hospital, including the "contracted size of the apartments." Most of the complaints concerned the relative settings of the two hospitals, however, one being in the center of the city, and the other on the periphery. Punshon claimed that seamen complain about "the heat and dust in the hot weather together with the noise which exists in the most populous and crowded

Commercial Hospital, 1886. Pictured here several decades after Drake's efforts to secure marine patients for his own hospital, Commercial Hospital won out on arguments concerning its better location at the edge of the city, along the Miami and Erie Canal north of downtown. *Photograph files, Archives & Rare Books Library, University of Cincinnati.*

part of the city." In contrast, the Commercial Hospital was "commodious" and "out of the throng of the city."[55]

When made aware of these complaints, Drake produced an affidavit from Dr. Edward Kimball, resident physician of the Marine Hospital. Kimball claimed he had never heard a complaint from a boatman. He also defended the location of his facility, which became the focus of the battle, claiming "the hospital is situated not on one of the business streets of the city" and that it was near "a garden and grass plot"—the college yard—where "the invalids take exercise."[56] Punshon also created an affidavit signed by several owners and officers of steamboats and Joseph Pierce, the port warden, who swore that the Commercial Hospital had provided their men "good clean and comfortable rooms" in "an airy and healthy situation near the confine of the city of Cincinnati." These men had been surprised that the marines "had been removed to a new institution called the Cincinnati Hospital located in the *heart* of the city." They complained that the new hospital was "subject to the noise and constant tumult of a business street and in the summer season to that of dust." They appealed to Punshon to return the sick and injured sailors to Commercial Hospital.[57]

Drake responded to Punshon's affidavit with yet more affidavits. One, dated April 24, 1838, was signed by several boatmen—pilots, stewards, engineers, captains—stating that Drake's hospital is "well finished, well warmed and properly ventilated." They agreed that the hospital was appropriate for a marine hospital. For good measure, Drake had a long list of doctors add their names to the testimonial, along with the medical students at Cincinnati College, some from Alabama, Tennessee, and Mississippi.[58]

Drake also made clear that Punshon's decision had been motivated by the interests of the older Medical College. Drake even conveyed that "the Surveyor of the Port is a clerk in the Office of one of the Trustees of the Medical College of Ohio, and dependent on him for his daily bread, and all the Trustees of that establishment are enemies of the Cincinnati College." Further, Drake noted that those who signed a petition supporting the change to Commercial Hospital were connected in some way to the rival medical school, including one who admitted to thinking the Medical Department of Cincinnati College ought to be abolished. Drake also defended his hospital's location. "The Hospital stands on the west side of the street, and consequently the dirt in summer is blown from it, and it is on one of the most elegant blocks of the city with low offices and shops on each side of it, and the Cincinnati College with its grounds, for 200 feet on the opposite side of the street," where, now fully revived, 200 students were "taught by lectures and recitations." In addition to the college, there was a female academy and a school for the instruction on the piano, Drake noted, making the case that if this part of the city were quiet enough for educational purposes, it must be quiet enough for a hospital. Drake even attacked Commercial Hospital, which served as the city's poorhouse, claiming "two thirds of its inmates are paupers," clearly an inappropriate arrangement for pilots and engineers who were "respectable men." Drake noted that the college hospital was for sick people only and "at this very moment has four patients in it, who are paying for their accommodations, three of whom have come to it from places in Ohio, Kentucky, and Virginia, more than 300 miles distant."[59]

Cincinnati College trustees put together a committee to investigate and found that Punshon himself had never visited Drake's hospital. And the committee determined that complaints about noise were unfounded because of the presence of the college and because the watermen are "a class of patients whose daily business is prosecuted in the midst of noise and bustle." The committee visited the hospital, found it well furnished and comfortable. The doctors reported that patients had never complained of its location. The committee also believed that since the hospital was a mile closer to the river than the Commercial Hospital, it was of greater advantage to the watermen, especially for "the victims of those severe accidents to which watermen are particularly liable."[60]

By the fall of 1838, Woodbury had washed his hands of the issue and left the decision to Punshon. Drake's only recourse would be to claim Punshon was incompetent or corrupt, a strategy he apparently left untested.[61] Just months later, however, the Medical Department of Cincinnati College was struck with crisis, as Dr. Willard Parker, chair of surgery, left the faculty in mid-summer. With little time to find a replacement before the next session, Drake sent letters to other physicians seeking advice, including to Joshua Martin in Xenia. Martin was certain that no current faculty member could succeed in that most important job. Clearly the success of the college was still predicated on finding talented faculty with strong reputations, and preferably from outside the city.[62]

Drake decided to support Samuel Gross for the chair of surgery, but the board refused to elevate him. The snub caused Gross to retire, leaving the Medical Department in disarray. On August 24, 1839, the Board of Trustees "vacated" the professorships at the Medical Department, although by then several of the remaining faculty had "withdrawn." Rogers and McDowell had already left the city. Although the board was open to a reorganization of the school, Drake could not put the pieces back together.[63] Drake, Gross, and Rives agreed to inventory the property of the department and the Cincinnati Hospital, including furniture, chemical apparatus, and books, and find buyers for everything. Proceeds would pay debts, with any residuals going to the faculty, who had purchased much of the equipment in the first place.[64] With that, the Medical Department of Cincinnati College ceased to be.

❀ Well Lighted, Comfortably Warm

The Medical Department wasn't Cincinnati College's only failed endeavor in the 1830s. In 1836, the trustees gathered to consider creating an Academic Department to offer a classical education. Trustee Robert T. Lytle asked the board to create "a flourishing City University," which would require more than just medical and law departments.[65] Daniel Drake, even while teaching and administering the Medical Department, was fully engaged in the effort to re-create the Academic Department. Drake contacted William Holmes McGuffey, then a professor at Miami University and the author of a recently published children's reader that would make him a household name for more than a century. In addition to wooing McGuffey, just as he had wooed Samuel Brown nearly twenty years earlier, Drake was engaged in fundraising, attempting to secure $1,500 to pay McGuffey's salary, raising much of it by selling $50 subscriptions that entitled holders the right to send a student for a year. Ultimately Drake secured thirty subscriptions, although not all of the donors intended to send students. Nicholas Longworth, one of Cincinnati's wealthiest men, gave $400, and Drake himself gave $200.[66] With the money raised, the trustees elected McGuffey president and professor of intellectual and moral philosophy and the evidences of Christianity. "For the last two days I have been conversing with respectable citizens on the subject of your election," Drake wrote to McGuffey to encourage his acceptance, "and find but one position and feeling. Your acceptance would be followed by a sort of general rejoicing." McGuffey accepted the job the next week.[67]

The Academic Department opened late that fall, enrolling ninety students, most of whom were "sons of citizens of Cincinnati." The board took the strong enrollments as a sign of public support for revival of the college. Still, the institution was on the financial edge, carrying debt taken on in 1835 and 1836 to expand and repair the building, and now it was "indispensable for the Board to acquire the means of putting a new roof on the edifice" and "of repairing and furnishing several of the rooms appropriated to the Academical Department." The board also wanted to furnish the great hall "so as to fit it for the purposes of the College, and for public meetings of the city." And so fundraising continued. In May 1837, with "the aid of the ladies of the city," the college put on an exhibition of fine arts—"chiefly of the paintings and statuary of the numerous ingenious young artists of our city." The Ladies' Fair, as it was called, raised $828 through art sales. Altogether, the board hoped to raise $5,000 to put the college on good footing, relieving it of debt and establishing an endowment. Despite the fundraising efforts, tuition from the 103 students who had enrolled by the end of the spring constituted the largest part of the 1837 budget.[68]

The Academic Department attracted several strong faculty, including Ormsby MacKnight Mitchel, a West Point graduate who taught math and astronomy, and Asa Drury, professor of Latin, Greek, and ancient history. Just three years after its revival, however, the college suffered a blow, when McGuffey accepted the presidency at Ohio University. McGuffey even took a significant pay cut in exchange for the stability afforded by the landed endowment of the rural college. McGuffey, who had quickly tired of living on the edge of insolvency, hoped Ohio University's endowment would ensure a more prosperous and predictable future.

Once again Cincinnati College suffered from bad timing. The financial panic of 1837, sparked by President Andrew Jackson's banking policies, had precipitated an unprecedented depression and undoubtedly had impeded college fundraising. In early 1840, law professor Edward Mansfield updated McGuffey, by then living in Athens, Ohio, on the conditions in Cincinnati. He lamented the "almost universal stagnation of business" that had "crept over the country." He noted that the problems at Cincinnati College were "only a specimen of the general state of things here." The college still had about 125 paying pupils, but the professors were forced to accept a salary cut to allow it to stay open.[69] Two months later Mansfield could report no improvement. "As to literature, there is none in Cincinnati, at this time," he complained to McGuffey. "Everybody is absorbed in the pecuniary distress of the times and whatever light emerges from it,—is the light of fashion."[70] Mansfield later reported that after "lingering a few years," the Academic Department disbanded, "the professors separated; and the college name attached to its walls alone attest that such an institution once existed."[71]

Mansfield exaggerated the demise of the college, for the Law Department persisted, but even that was jeopardized by a catastrophic fire on a Sunday morning, January 18, 1845. The building was fully destroyed, along with the possessions of several occupants, among them the Young Men's Mercantile Library, which had moved into the building in 1840. As it turned out, the presence of the Mercantile Library may have saved the college. With the building destroyed and no significant endowment in hand, the college faced the very real possibility of disappearing. The Mercantile Library, founded in 1835 to cultivate learning among the city's merchants, signed a perpetual lease for space in a new college building, however, providing the capital to start afresh. The Mercantile's annual report noted that, "it was a prudent and safe investment, and that while we aided in the erection of an Edifice, which should give character and credit to the public buildings of the city, the occupancy in it of its finest and most spacious apartments would reflect back, and reciprocate the like benefits to our Association."[72]

When the new college edifice opened in 1846, the trustees decided not to reestablish the Academic Department. The trustees recognized that it could not afford to assemble a complete faculty, but since the college was "central to the city, and its hall well fitted for courses of public lectures," they determined that "lectures on various branches of human knowledge, might be instituted and maintained, with equal credit to the college and advantage not only to the families of those who are stockholders in the institution but to the community at large." In this way, the educational mission of the college would be maintained—which was legally necessary if the building were to remain tax exempt.[73]

The seemingly arcane tax issue became quite real in part because of the new edifice. As was typical of academic buildings, the new college building was Greek in style, with a Dayton marble façade and a cupola modeled on the Tower of the Winds in Athens, but the building had a multipurpose design. The first floor contained eight storefronts facing Walnut, spaces that could earn rent to help pay down the debt and, eventually, create a permanent endowment. It made perfect sense, after all, for a building at the heart of the city to use its location to advantage, and that advantage was retail. The city rented the rear of the ground floor for public offices. The Mercantile Library occupied the front rooms of the second floor, while the grand College Hall, with thirty-one-foot ceilings and three chandeliers, occupied the back half of the building. The hall could accommodate up to 3,000 people. Above, the third floor was reserved for Cincinnati College offices, lecture rooms and private rooms for students, while the Law School occupied the fourth floor.[74]

Joining the Mercantile Library on the second floor was the Chamber of Commerce, which not surprisingly shared a significant membership with the library association. The north room became the Merchants' Exchange. Here members kept careful records of "the imports and exports to and from the city, by the river, canals and railroad; of arrival and departure of steam-boats; of the markets, for demand and supply; of arrivals at the principal hotels, etc.; all of which has been constantly accessible to the examination of subscribers, and furnished in abstract from the Exchange books to each of the daily papers." In addition, the Mercantile subscribed to local, regional, and national periodicals. By 1847, members could come to the reading room to peruse forty-five newspapers, including twenty-seven dailies and twelve weeklies.[75] In this way, together the Mercantile and the Chamber educated their members about business both immediate and far-flung.

The second floor of the college building became a place where a variety of men could mingle and discuss the news of the day. Chamber members met with strangers with business to conduct; masters and first clerks of steamboats and agents of any railroad or company were given free admission to the rooms. Bulletin boards contained notices of "the latest news of general interest, recent reports of important mercantile transactions in this and other markets, copies of steamboats' manifests, with transcripts of their logs, and other commercial intelligence." Members also posted on the bulletin boards, advertising and describing their businesses.[76] Altogether the college had become largely a place of business, without having entirely abandoned its educational mission. Still, the casual observer would have found little in common between the college hall of 1849 and the one that had opened thirty years earlier. Gone were the objects of natural history and the cultural artifacts of lost civilizations. In their stead were the schedules and tables of commerce and all variety of news about current conditions.

The college itself may have been nearly moribund, focused purely on the work of the law school, but the Mercantile Library made certain that the college building remained home to lively intellectual debate and learning. As it still does, the library sponsored a series of lectures each year, and in the late 1840s some of the most learned men of the city took the rostrum. Judge Timothy Walker, the former dean of the law school—and for many years its only professor—discussed "The Morals of Commerce." Others associated with Cincinnati College also spoke, including E. D. Mansfield, on the "Life, Genius and Discoveries of Sir Isaac Newton," and Alexander McGuffey, William's brother, who addressed "The Personal and Poetical Character of Shakespeare." The Mercantile also brought in leading intellectuals from outside Cincinnati, such as Robert Dale Owen, the well-known social reformer and outspoken US representative from New Harmony, Indiana, who discussed "The History of Labor." Perhaps most impressive, Louis Agassiz, the famed Harvard geologist, came to Cincinnati for the American Scientific Association meeting in 1851 and gave a series of lectures at the Mercantile. His topics included "The Relation of Man to the Animal Creation."[77]

Cincinnati College had not become what Drake and the other early boosters had hoped it would be. Its Greek façade alone could not convince the nation that Cincinnati had become the Athens of the West. Undoubtedly a confluence of factors led to its failure to thrive. There was the bad timing, given the coincidence of the founding (and refounding) of the college and severe economic downturns. And the presence of the controversial Drake at the center of these efforts undoubtedly limited interest in some circles. And perhaps the secular nature of the college, unusual in this era, was enough to raise concerns about the moral training it could provide to the city's future leaders. Or perhaps the elite, even in Cincinnati, thought an education in the West could not compare to what the East had to offer.[78]

When Drake died in 1852, having lived a most energetic and engaged life, he could take some comfort in the fact that the city itself had thrived, having grown to over 115,000 residents. Its economy had diversified, with commerce sparking growth in meatpacking and steamboat manufacturing. The clothing, furniture, and carriage industries flourished, too. Cincinnati had also become the West's publishing center, producing books and periodicals consumed around the nation. And it had taken on a nickname, Queen City of the West, befitting its regional stature. The college edifice offered hope that higher learning might someday find a home in the city, and in the meantime, at least the Mercantile Library provided a reading room, "well lighted, comfortably warm, and plainly though neatly furnished," where men of business and boosters of all types could come and talk about the prospect of a bridge spanning the Ohio or perhaps the necessity of building a railroad to the south. Unfortunately, they apparently did too little talking about the need to support higher education, and the creation of a stable university in Cincinnati would await the death of another benefactor, Charles McMicken, who passed away six years after Drake.[79]

2

SHALL IT ALL BE IN ONE PLACE?
Building a University of Cincinnati

Judge John Stallo stood behind the lectern at Pike's Opera House before what the *Enquirer* called a "small but elegant" crowd. Joining Stallo on the stage were seven men and three women, the 1880 graduating class of the University of Cincinnati. Their commencement took place at one of Cincinnati's finest venues, in the heart of the city, the stage decorated with "exotic and indigenous plants." The Cincinnati Orchestra, which called Pike's home, performed the musical interludes that "relieved the literary portion of the program of monotony." As was customary, several of the graduating class read their senior theses. This was the university's third commencement.[1]

A prominent Cincinnati lawyer, Stallo was eight years removed from his famed victory in the defense of the Cincinnati Public School ban on reading the Bible in class. This night he was on stage to deliver the baccalaureate address. After thanking those who had come to celebrate the graduation of ten students from the five-year-old university, Stallo, a former member of the university's Board of Directors, could not help but express his disappointment. "To be candid, I had expected a larger attendance. I had hoped that our citizens, by their participation in the exercises of this evening, would refute the charge, so commonly proffered against the people of the West, that they are wholly absorbed in the pursuit of wealth, and indifferent to everything but its display." As a young man, Stallo had heard Professor Ormsby MacKnight Mitchel give a commencement address at the old Cincinnati College, in which Mitchel had praised the rise of intellectual life in the Ohio Valley. "In a very few years after the delivery of that discourse the faculty of the Cincinnati College was disbanded," Stallo relayed, "the old college building was destroyed, and the main part of the new edifice which has been erected in its stead, is now devoted to the sale of stocks, cheap jewelry and leather trunks; the only things carried on in it which are in some sort suggestive of the original purpose for which the college was founded being the mercantile library and a law school in which preparatory collegiate training is not one of the requisites of admission."[2]

Stallo described the similarly poor trajectories at the city's other institutions of higher learning, among them the Ohio Mechanics Institute, founded in 1828, and the observatory, created in 1843 and led by Ormsby Mitchel. He then stepped back to recognize the impropriety of his topic at this occasion. "It is a disagreeable truth, perhaps, and one which it may not be polite to utter in this presence, but it is a truth nevertheless, that up to the present time Cincinnati has not been distinguished as a seat of learning, and has been a very uncongenial abode for persons of scientific or literary attainments." He had heard the excuses residents made, saying the Queen City was a young place, and Cincinnatians are busy, too busy to learn Greek and calculus. "They have had their hands and heads full in felling the primeval forest," he went on, "in building houses, churches, common schools, factories and machine shops, in grading and digging roads and canals, in constructing steamboats and locomotives, in fighting the Indians first, and slavery afterwards, in founding the city, and helping to organize the body politic."

This was quite a list of distractions, indeed, which had kept Cincinnatians from founding a great university. Stallo went on to exalt the city's accomplishments, sounding very much like Daniel Drake and the other early boosters by declaring, "Cincinnati is the center of one of the most fertile, and prospectively one of the most populous, regions of the globe." But, he was forced to admit, Cincinnati had not become the Athens of the West. Stallo finished his talk, to great applause according to the *Enquirer*, with a plea to the city's generosity. The people of Cincinnati, he hoped, "will insist upon it that the best thought and learning of the century shall have a home and hearth right here in our midst, and that the institution founded by Charles McMicken shall not perish from indifference and neglect as our other colleges have perished before."

Stallo's address highlighted a central tension in the history of higher education, between the pursuit of wealth and the pursuit of knowledge. Older, private universities in the East served the elite, providing a classical foundation in Greek, Latin, and theology. Supporters argued that classical education created complete men and women—contemplative, moral, and civilized. The goal of this type of higher education was not the creation of employers and certainly not employees, but the entire enterprise was predicated on the bequests, donations, and subscriptions of wealthy families, to augment tuition payments from wealthy students. Only the elite expected this type of education; only the elite paid for it.

The University of Cincinnati would have to be different. Founded with a bequest to the city by Charles McMicken in 1858, and later granted tax support from city residents, the University of Cincinnati would have to be responsive to the public, not just the elite. The men who were appointed to the Board of Directors, those who debated the shape of the institution they were charged to create, were some of the city's most prominent figures, Stallo among them, but they imagined a new university that could serve the broader community; they imagined a more democratic institution.

🌹 Charles McMicken's Will

In 1803, a young Charles McMicken moved from his Pennsylvania home to frontier Cincinnati. He lived much of his adult life elsewhere, but he remained attached to the Queen City and the family he had there, especially his nephew Andrew with whom he shared a home for nearly twenty years. McMicken made a living—and a fortune—in river trade and real estate. He moved wheat and cotton by water and converted his profits into land. McMicken followed his trade routes, living the winter months of his adult life in Louisiana and, after 1840, summering in Cincinnati. His real estate portfolio included extensive holdings in Louisiana, especially around Baton Rouge and New Orleans, as well as scattered buildings and lots in Cincinnati. At his death, he owned land in Kentucky and Texas, as well. McMicken also owned slaves who served him at his southern homes, and later in life he became a financial backer of the plan to "colonize" Liberia with Americans of African descent, which provides a hint as to his thinking about the place of African Americans in the United States.[3] He had also supported the Farmers' College, the agricultural school and experimental farm founded in 1846 in a suburb that subsequently took the name College Hill. McMicken's support of this institution, through the endowment of a professorship in agricultural chemistry, gave perhaps the best indication during his life that McMicken would support higher education upon his death. He died of pneumonia in 1858, after having contracted an illness on a steamboat returning to Cincinnati from New Orleans.[4]

McMicken was a very wealthy man, but he wasn't especially well known—at least not until his will was read. Much of the document concerned McMicken's extensive bequests to various relatives, mostly the sons and daughters of his siblings, as McMicken never married and had no children who appeared in his will.[5] But then the document turned to his most lasting legacy: the founding of "an institution, where white boys and girls might be taught, not only a knowledge of their duties to their Creator and their fellow-men, but also receive the benefit of a sound, thorough and practical English education, and such as might fit them for the active duties of life." Even in these opening phrases, McMicken made clear his particular vision. He expected both men and women to have access to higher education, although later in the will McMicken specifies that the city create "two colleges" in separate buildings—one male, one female. When it finally began admitting students in the 1870s, McMicken's university was coeducational, but it did not have two single-sex colleges. This wasn't the only stipulation that wasn't followed by the Board of Directors as they shaped the university. McMicken's phrasing "where white boys and girls might be taught" gives a clear indication that he intended this university to be white only, but since the will did not specifically exclude African Americans, the phrase about whites did not guide the institution. While organizing the university, the Board of Directors, all of them white men, did not discuss the issue of race.[6]

Cincinnati had always been a racially divided city, and in the late 1850s its segregation occurred mostly through the power of cultural exclusion rather than written regulation—except in the realm of education. Cincinnati's public schools were strictly segregated at the time McMicken wrote his will and passed away, and although the separate "Colored Public Schools" provided an invaluable service to the community, McMicken apparently saw no reason to support higher education for African Americans, a position no doubt widely shared in the city before the Civil War. Segregation at the lower levels, which afforded limited opportunities for African Americans to acquire the kind of high school education that would adequately prepare them for a college entrance exam, ensured that regardless of admissions policies African Americans would find it difficult to pursue higher education. That said, the university McMicken founded did admit African American students, including Henry Malachi Griffin, who in 1886 became the first African American to graduate from the University of Cincinnati, having written a thesis entitled "Aeschylus as a Poet and Religious Teacher." Griffin went on to become a teacher and physician, although not in Cincinnati.[7]

Beyond the description of who the university should serve, McMicken's will also included some specific ideas about the education the students should receive. It should be practical and, because McMicken was a religious man (though perhaps no more so than most men of his era), the university should emphasize duty to God and community. The university was to give "instruction in the higher branches of knowledge, except Denominational Theology" as then taught "or may hereafter be taught, in any of the secular College or Universities of the highest grade in the Country."[8] Despite McMicken's exclusion of denominational theology, a reflection of a life lived with openness to several denominations, the will did require that "The Holy Bible of the Protestant version and contained in the Old and New Testament shall be used as a Book of Instruction in the said Colleges."[9] Here too the university failed to honor the wishes of its benefactor, as the board made no stipulations for teaching the Bible as it organized courses for instruction in 1874.[10]

The will also made demands on where the school should operate. "The College Building shall be erected out of the rents and income of my real and personal estate," McMicken wrote, "and on the premises on which I now reside, in the City of Cincinnati." In other words, the new university would have to be built on the hill that ran north from Over-the-Rhine, a hill so steep as to have helped constrain the physical growth of the city. In addition, the will stipulated that university buildings "shall be plain, but neat and substantial in their character." Clearly the Board of Directors took liberties with McMicken's instructions, building one school instead of two, for instance, but that school did rise on the McMicken estate, just above the old McMicken homestead. Honest people might disagree about how long the instructions for "plain, but neat" buildings were followed.[11]

In sum, the will provided the means for creating a new university, but it laid out some constraints, as well. And we shouldn't overlook the most remarkable fact of the bequest. Rather than establish a private trust to run the school, as was usual, McMicken left his property and instructions to the city of Cincinnati. In no other instance in United States history had anyone left a significant portion of their estate to a municipal government to create an institution of higher learning. At the time of the bequest, no city in Ohio operated a university, and very few cities in the nation financially supported higher education. McMicken had only the examples of the College of Charleston, which began to receive financial support from that city in 1837, and the Free Academy in New York City, which opened in 1849 and eventually evolved into the City College of New York. The latter university had an especially democratic mission, to provide a practical education to both rich and poor boys and girls.[12] In other words, McMicken's will, unique in its own right, set

The home of Charles McMicken, circa 1875. McMicken's property ran from the stone wall in the foreground, along the street that later took his name, all the way to the top of the hill to a small bit of land that is now part of Belleview Park. This image appeared in the 1896 *Cincinnatian*, but comes from an earlier time. *C.U. Collection, Archives & Rare Books Library, University of Cincinnati.*

the University of Cincinnati on an unusual path, one that bound an institution of higher education to the city where it would grow.

To create and support its new university, the city of Cincinnati was to receive McMicken's real estate in the city of New Orleans, a substantial tract south of Baton Rouge, property in Delhi Township, just outside Cincinnati, and "all my real estate in the City of Cincinnati." The will gave explicit authority to the city to demolish antiquated buildings and to build new buildings, using proceeds from the estate for the benefit of "securing the largest income," but, importantly, the will specified that none of the property in the city "shall at any time be sold."

Unfortunately for the city, some of McMicken's relatives challenged the will's generosity to higher education. Most significantly, family members in the state of Louisiana claimed that the city of Cincinnati had no legal means of taking ownership of property in that state, demanding instead that the valuable holdings in New Orleans be distributed to relatives. After the Louisiana State Supreme Court ruled against the city of Cincinnati in 1860, removing the Louisiana property from the university bequest, the city struggled to replace the lost endowment. The Board of Directors, elected in 1859 by city council, was now forced to articulate and construct a university while trying to gather the resources necessary to build anything approaching an institution of higher education. For years the board essentially functioned as the directors of a real estate corporation. They managed a portfolio of downtown and riverfront properties, collecting rents, distributing annuities to McMicken relatives as stipulated in the will, and making repairs to aging buildings. (They sold the Delhi Township property.) In the process, the McMicken endowment accumulated essentially no cash over the first ten years of its existence. The value of the real estate increased significantly in value, however, especially during the Civil War years, with rent income rising from about $10,000 per year to over $30,000 during the 1860s. Still, a decade after McMicken's passing, the institution McMicken had imagined didn't seem any closer to being an actual university than it did when lawyers read the will in 1858.[13]

❦ The Completion of Our Present System of Education

With the contested McMicken will settled, the Civil War concluded, and the city properties generating a more substantial income, the Board of Directors was in a better position to actually found a university. By this time the nation was in the process of creating a new kind of institution, one more practically minded, focused on instruction and research in agriculture and the mechanical arts. The Morrill Act of 1862 granted considerable federal resources so that each state could create this new type of school. These land-grant colleges, including Ohio State University, founded in 1870, altered the landscape of higher education by providing greater access for middle-class Americans and ensuring that curricula would tend toward subjects designed to support the nation's economy as much as to encourage intellectual inquiry.[14]

But this was just part of the nation's higher education revolution. Few Americans sought a college degree in the first half of the 1800s, and when they did they attended elite institutions, such as Harvard and Yale. Now, in the last three decades of the 1800s, the United States was witnessing an explosion in new universities, not all of them land-grant colleges. These institutions developed as the classical curriculum fractured, in part due to a growing emphasis on teaching the sciences, but also because new disciplines demanded space in university catalogs.

Offerings in Latin and Greek eroded in favor of instruction in modern languages, especially German and French. Classical philosophy splintered into history and political economy. New social sciences developed, too, most importantly sociology and anthropology.[15] At the same time, following the example of Charles Eliot's Harvard, many universities began liberalizing their curricula, moving away from traditional requirements and toward an elective system that empowered students to select their own coursework. In sum, Cincinnati's leaders were charged with the creation of a new university at a propitious moment, just when a variety of democratic developments in higher education were emerging.[16]

As one would expect, no consensus developed as to the precise shape McMicken's university should take, but among the elite there was agreement that in important ways it should follow the German model. Among those advocating this approach was Charles Phelps Taft, son of Alphonso Taft, one of the city's leading figures, a lawyer, superior court judge, and a member of the university's Board of Directors. In early 1871, just as the University of Cincinnati was being organized in earnest, the younger Taft delivered a paper at the Literary Club of Cincinnati[17] entitled "The German University and the American College." Taft had been educated at Yale and Columbia, earning a law degree at the latter, but he had also spent a year at the University of Heidelberg. It was quite common for upper-class Americans to take some part of their education in Europe, especially in Britain or Germany. Taft admired the entire German education system, which split students into two tracks at an early age. One set of schools, *Gymnasien*, prepared students for university study and the professions. The other type of school, *Realschulen*, prepared students for trade work. Taft argued that the rigor of German universities required this division, by raising the educational expectations for students bound for higher education. "In founding our university," Taft said, "it should be our object to secure the completion of our present system of education. In Germany, the university crowns the educational edifice, of which they are so justly proud. In this the Germans are worthy of our emulation."[18]

Taft most admired the intense competition the German system inspired after graduation from *Gymnasium*: the constant pressure on students, instructors, and professors to work hard and be productive. German universities were state supported, but they paid their professors only a small stipend. Most of their income came from the tuition of the students in their classes. Under this model, the best professors attracted the most students, not just because they gave brilliant lectures, but because of their scholarly reputation. As a result of the "severe race" for the limited number of prized professorships and the "unceasing and unrelenting" competition, Taft clamed, "[t]he twenty-three universities of Germany have placed that country at the head of the nations in respect to literary and scientific knowledge and research."[19] In the United States, Taft saw no such competition, no similar productivity, even though he had attended two of the nation's elite colleges. Taft thought the American professor could "lead a quiet, easy life, retailing the products of the brains of others."[20]

Taft did allow that in one area Americans had the opportunity to improve upon the German system: "the doors of our university may be open not only to the graduates of a Yale or a Harvard, but also to those of a Vassar or a McMicken College for young women."[21] Coeducational institutions were just then becoming more common, as several states organized their land-grant colleges to serve young men and women. This was especially the case in the West and Midwest. (Ohio was home to the nation's first coeducational college, Oberlin, which had opened its doors to women just twenty years before McMicken's will was read.) Cincinnati's university would indeed train men and women, although not without the impingements of gender norms. As Taft noted, university directors had "a rare opportunity before them." Since they were creating an institution out of whole cloth, "They have no deep-rooted prejudices of proud old colleges to overcome. The field is open and clear to establish a first-class university."[22]

Those working to create the fledgling University of Cincinnati, or Cincinnati University or McMicken University, as it was variously known during its first decade, might look to Germany for inspiration, but they could not expect the kind of government support those institutions received. Cincinnati's university would receive no federal or state funding, at least not at the outset. What's more, after the adverse decision regarding the McMicken will, it didn't have nearly the endowment that its benefactor imagined it would. In other words, from its very founding the institution fought to finance its operations adequately; meeting the educational needs of the community and keeping pace with changing expectations of what higher education delivered would be a constant struggle.[23]

Given his will's instructions, McMicken also might have been surprised to see how and where the city began to use his endowment to begin educating students. In the late 1860s, Joseph Longworth, the son of the extraordinarily wealthy Nicholas Longworth, endowed the creation of a school of design through the ground rents generated by a parcel of land near the riverfront. The city combined this endowment with revenue generated by the McMicken properties to create what became known as the McMicken School of Design. McMicken had been a supporter of the arts, having purchased some statuary for the Cincinnati Academy of Fine Arts, which had begun gathering copies of classical statues, Renaissance paintings, and other masterworks in the second half of the 1850s. Those works eventually became the property of the university, where they served as models for art students and, apparently, as inspiration for other patrons of the arts, who eventually formed the Cincinnati Museum Association, which in turn created the Cincinnati Museum of Art.[24]

The university's board of directors hired Thomas Satterwhite Noble to lead the School of Design, which began operating in January of 1869 in the Third and Main Street building that was the crown jewel of the McMicken properties. The stated purpose of the school was "the application of Drawing and Design to the Industrial Arts." Male and female students were to be admitted, and the instruction would be free to all city residents (over the age of twelve). Initially limited to sixty students, all of them to be instructed by Noble, the school's curriculum was supposed to affect "the improvement of the Industrial Arts, by spreading among the operative classes of this city a more thorough technical and scientific education in Art and Design, as applied to manufactures, so as to aid them in obtaining that taste and skill in the fashion and finish of their work."[25]

At first blush, Noble seems an odd choice to provide instruction in industrial arts. A native of Kentucky, Noble was a student of painting, not of "the Industrial Arts." He was hired away from an art studio in New York City, where he had made a name for himself as a romantic painter. (His best-known work, *Margaret Garner* [1867], depicted the horrific scene in which Garner has murdered one of her children rather than see her returned to slavery.) But Noble's work was admired in Cincinnati, and his selection to run the school affirmed elite society's only partial acceptance of the new industrial reality.[26] The creation of the School of Design revealed an understanding that the city's future lay in manufacturing, but it also reflected the hope that the arts might in some way tame and beautify the products of industry, that the rapidly evolving industrial city might remain familiar and civilized. Still, the practical aspect of the education was front and center. Schools of design had been created by governments in Europe, most famously in France, where they "have given great superiority to their fabrics in many most valuable and important branches of industry," according to an advertisement for the McMicken school. "This is proved not only by the results of the great competitive Expositions," the circular continued, but more so "by the contents of our own stores and shops." As much as the board may have desired the School of Design to create a class of industrial artists, Noble, not surprisingly, ran an art school, with the curriculum well focused on the drawing and painting of the human body. Three years after it opened, the School of Design moved into the Cincinnati College building on Fourth and Walnut, occupying the space at no cost except for those of repairs, an arrangement facilitated by Alexander McGuffey, who served both institutions at the time.[27]

Even as the board opened the McMicken School of Design, a new plan emerged to create the institution McMicken had envisioned. The city's Board of Education proposed the consolidation of McMicken, Hughes, Woodward, and Cincinnati College into one university. Actually, the Board of Education proposed the consolidation of the endowments for these institutions, each of them based in city real estate. Hughes and Woodward were the city's finest high schools, the two schools capable of preparing students for college. They had been created by benefactors, Thomas Hughes and William Woodward, for the education of poor children. Both were supported by rents paid on land in Over-the-Rhine, Pendleton, and Mount Auburn, areas where real estate values had increased significantly since the funds had been established in the 1820s and 1830s. In 1851, Hughes and Woodward became part of the city's public system, and their trusts continued to support the schools. Cincinnati College, as we have seen, operated largely through rent paid by tenants in its own building on Walnut. Brought together, the Board of Education believed, income from these properties might support a substantial university.[28]

It is worth pausing to reflect on how much wealth cities created merely through their growth. Many a family fortune was built through the rising value of urban land, and many of those fortunes in turn supported urban institutions, especially museums, public auditoriums, and schools. In Cincinnati this was most evident in the wealth and philanthropy of the Longworth family, but other families too turned modest profits into lasting fortunes by investing in urban real estate. The cultural and educational institutions that became markers of urbanity were also symbols of growth. Importantly, as the Cincinnati struggled to create an impressive university, its wealthy citizens were also gathering funds to build Cincinnati Music Hall, completed in 1878, and support the Cincinnati Art Museum, which opened in Mount Adams in 1886. Although these institutions had their own specific goals, together they were part of a project to secure the city's reputation as a center of high culture by connecting Cincinnati to western traditions in art, music, and education—becoming the "Athens of the West" would require the inspiration of classical statuary as much as the provision of classical education.

Each of these institutions held symbolic value for Cincinnati, but each also held great potential in securing more growth, even if only through the improved reputation of the city. The principal author of the Board of Education plan, J. B. Powell, emphasized this aspect of higher education. "Some of the Fruits of such a University would be to draw together a group of literati whose influence would permeate our whole community," he wrote. "It would open the door of higher education to hundreds in our own midst who are now hopelessly excluded from the same." The report claimed the larger school "would reach the pulpit, the press, the bar, the home of the rich and poor, alike. It would grow up in our midst an aristocracy of intellect and cultivation."[29] This didn't quite sound like a city-run, democratic institution of higher education, of course.

The Board of Education's interest in creating a successful university came out of more than mere civic-mindedness. It reflected a common understanding of a successful educational system, in which a strong university would exert pressure to improve down through the high schools. Schools superintendent John Hancock called the proposed unified institution "the crowning glory of our Public School system." Part of the benefit was physical—parents would not have to send their children away to college. Rather, they could expect to send their children for a college education "under their own eye, as all children should be educated, where it is practicable." Hancock also argued that alongside the classical course of education the university should offer a "polytechnic course," in which students would focus on natural sciences, mathematics, and modern languages—a curriculum designed to "prepare its students for the active affairs of life," a paraphrase of McMicken's will. Further, in his annual report to the school board, Hancock touted the "reflex influence of such an institution on the schools below." The benefits of a strong university would flow down through the system as parents and students strived for achievement.[30]

The Board of Education's enthusiasm for the bringing together of the various educational endowments went unmatched by the other institutions, however, and the plan to create one great Cincinnati university gathered no momentum. The McMicken board didn't take up the topic of consolidation until 1871, again with no immediate effect.[31]

🌿 Alphonso Taft's Questions

In the spring of 1872, three years after McMicken opened its School of Design and the Board of Education proposed its unrealized plan, Alphonso Taft delivered an address before the Young Men's Mercantile Library Association. It was his first time speaking before this group since the old college edifice had burned and the new building had replaced it. In his previous talk, Taft had encouraged residents to support the construction of railroads, claiming Cincinnati had fallen behind other cities that were investing heavily in new lines. "Since then," Taft was pleased to say, "the city

has put forth her iron tracks to all the cardinal points. She has reached the confines of the nation in all directions, except the South." This last direction, of course, was the most important, the direction in which Cincinnati might have had some competitive advantage over Chicago, which had catapulted over Cincinnati in size and was clearly destined to become the region's metropolis. South was also the direction in which the city was in the process of building its own line—the Southern Railway—through a reluctant Kentucky, which had delayed the project, and on to Chattanooga, Tennessee.[32]

Alphonso Taft, circa 1872. This portrait of Taft appeared in James Landy's *Cincinnati Past and Present* (Cincinnati: Elm Street Publishing Co., 1872). The lengthy biography that appeared with the photo praised Taft's wisdom as a judge, lawyer, and city council member, as well as his special role in protecting Charles McMicken's bequest to the city of Cincinnati to establish a university. *Rare Books Collection, Archives & Rare Books Library, University of Cincinnati.*

It was this spirit of perseverance and municipal activism that Taft hoped to access as he spoke on a new theme, "Cincinnati and her University." Taft had joined the Board of Directors in December 1870, after the state of Ohio passed a law allowing cities of the first

48

class, such as Cincinnati, to create and support universities. This enabling legislation was designed to remove all doubt about the city's authority to operate an institution of higher learning. Under the law, Cincinnati created a new board for the University of Cincinnati. Along with Taft, the city council appointed several other prominent men, including George Hoadly, a superior court judge (and future Ohio governor), and Alex McGuffey, a member of the Cincinnati College Board.[33]

So Taft was before the members of the Mercantile Library to speak practically about the creation of the university, a process in which he had a significant voice. He opened with a quotation from Pliny the Younger, who wrote to his friend Tacitus about the benefit of young men taking their education close to home: "Your sons should receive their education here…For where can they be placed more agreeably than in their own country, or instructed with more safety and less expense than at home, and under the eye of their parents." After presenting this ideal, Taft raised several questions. "The first practical difficulty is to determine what this University, as it is called by the law and by the public, shall actually be; what departments or schools it shall have, and how they shall be supported," he said. "The second question, which has its practical difficulties, is where the University shall be located. Shall it be upon the hill top, or below? Shall it all be in one place?"[34]

The board had been struggling with these very questions. Most fundamentally, whom should they hire and what shall they teach? In the spring of 1871, Hoadly proposed that the board resolve to establish a "college of science and the useful arts," which would include "the building and equipment of an observatory, and instruction in Mathematics, Astronomy, Natural Philosophy, Chemistry, Mineralogy, and Metallurgy, Mechanics, Civil and Mining Engineering, Geology and Natural History, Architecture and the Arts of Design, the Modern Languages, Veterinary Surgery, also in the Bible as required by the Will of Charles McMicken." This is quite an inclusive list of sciences, but with few exceptions a list of *only* sciences. Significantly, Hoadly, a graduate of Western Reserve College and Harvard Law, did not include classical subjects: Latin, Greek, and philosophy. Here, of course, was the crux of the debate. Should the University of Cincinnati emulate the finest colleges in America—the institutions that most of the board members had attended themselves? Or, as Hoadly proposed, should the board chart a bolder course and establish a fully modern institution?[35]

Hoadly's proposed "college of science and the useful arts" moved further from traditional education than many his fellow board members were willing to go, and so when a final vote came a few months later, the board created five new departments (anticipating just one faculty member per department), which would join the extant School of Design: Ancient Literature and Languages; Modern Languages; Mathematics, Natural Philosophy (physics), and Astronomy; Mechanical, Mining, and Civil Engineering; Chemistry and Mineralogy. In sum, the University of Cincinnati would retain classical elements but prepare students for an economy increasingly driven by science.[36] The board remained divided even after months of discussion. In the end Taft sided with the majority, while Hoadly remained opposed to classical instruction. As Taft told the Mercantile members a year after the split vote, "Our ideal, like that of Mr. [Ezra] Cornell, is 'an institution where any person can find instruction in any study'—an ideal, however, which cannot be realized without time and means." In other words, like Cornell, who had combined his considerable wealth with support from the Morrill Act to create a land-grant institution in Ithaca, New York, Taft imagined the creation of a large and practical-minded university. "The scientific part of it is not likely to be attacked, and needs no defense," Taft told his audience. "But the value of classical study has often been denied, and is constantly challenged." As he had before the board, Taft defended classical studies, claiming that they would remain critical to educated people for "a thousand years to come." He allowed that the university would change, though not so radically as to give up Greek and Latin. "We shall expect to make room, from time to time, for such of the industrial sciences as may be most needed and first provided for by endowments, but without prejudice to classical literature and the natural sciences, in both of which we must have instruction not inferior to the best." According to Taft, the University of Cincinnati must be both innovative and traditional.[37]

Taft's second question proved as difficult to answer as the first, and the board debated the location of the school for months. McMicken's will required that the university be constructed on his homestead, but the property ran from the base of the hill all the way to the top, with the lot split nearly in half by Clifton Avenue, which sliced diagonally up the steep grade. The board debated whether the school should sit at the top or somewhere near the bottom. After examinations of the rock, much of which was well exposed by the grading that made Clifton Avenue possible, the board was advised to build in the lower half. In theory this location would better accommodate growth, because the McMicken property included little space at the very top. For his part, Taft was not so terribly concerned about space. He thought perhaps the third floor of the college edifice, the building where he spoke before the Mercantile, would suffice, especially if the college and university combined, as he thought they should. Taft assumed the university would need little space. What it needed most was "brains." In this conclusion, and in others, Taft echoed public school superintendent Hancock, who hoped that university directors would set aside "the too common practice" of "investing largely in costly buildings," and instead "attract to their service some of the foremost men of the world as their professors." According to both Taft and Hancock, the university needed "brains instead of bricks."[38]

Of course, without any university building at all, this was not strictly true. And the absence of a building helped ensure that Taft's last question—Shall it all be in one place?—would be all the more vexing. The city had several institutions of higher learning, none of them especially financially viable: the observatory, the School of Design, the Ohio Mechanics Institute, and, of course, the Cincinnati College, which had been thrown into debt and its future put in doubt by the fire that had destroyed its building. The Board of Education's consolidation plan hadn't moved forward, but the idea of gathering together the city's institutions of higher education persisted through the decades. In 1884, Isaac M. Wise, founder and president of Hebrew Union College, created a fictive Cincinnati University while delivering the commencement address at the actual University of Cincinnati. According to Wise, this large and complete university included the "Law College over yonder," and the College of Music, and the Art School, and, of course, the two medical schools. "Unite them in one building and under one management and you have already one of the greatest Universities in the country." Ironically, just as Wise spoke of uniting the various schools, the university let go its School of Design, which, at the request (and with the financial support) of Nicholas Longworth II, became the property of the Cincinnati Museum Association in 1884 and became known as the Cincinnati Art Academy. It then joined the Cincinnati Art Museum in Eden Park three years later, occupying a building paid for by David Sinton, one of Cincinnati's wealthiest men, who had made his money largely in industry.[39]

The year Wise described the fictive Cincinnati University, the actual university president Jacob D. Cox asked the board of directors to pursue a "cooperative union" among all the degree-granting institutions, including the law school, the medical colleges, dental college, pharmaceutical college, College of Music, Art School, even St. Xavier College, a small Jesuit college that had opened downtown in 1840. According to Cox, the creation of this single "University organization" would not require "any surrender of property or income, or name, or share in government." Efficiency of

operation was not the goal. "The belief is that in this way our city can exhibit an array of well-organized schools that legitimately constitute departments of a university,
and that a union of them would, in an imposing manner command the attention
of the nation, and justify our claim of widely performing university work." In other
words, the primary goal was to increase the city's national reputation for higher education—to change the way the nation saw Cincinnati, to rectify the problem that
Stallo had identified at the 1880 commencement.[40]

The call for union brought some positive replies. The first came from the Cincinnati Hospital, which operated a Clinical and Pathological School. Upon affiliation
with the university in 1887, it became the basis of the medical department. Among
its staff was Dr. Cornelius Comegys, who had served on the university board since
day one. The College of Pharmacy was also among the first institutions to take up
the offer of union. Open since 1871, its faculty included John Uri Lloyd, one of the
nation's leading pharmacists. The 1886 affiliation allowed the institutions to function
independently, however, and Pharmacy did not become an actual college in the university until 1954. The Ohio College of Dental Surgery,[41] which dated to 1845, also
affiliated in 1887, and seven years later the Cincinnati College of Medicine, created
in 1851, affiliated too. Among its faculty was Charles A. L. Reed, a prominent physician who had also joined the university's Board of Directors.

In sum, through coordination and combination with existing institutions the
University of Cincinnati gradually began to look more like an actual university,
along the lines of the definition laid out by Charles Phelps Taft back in 1871:
"a universal school, in which are taught all the branches of learning."[42] But the
university remained scattered about the city—the College of Medicine on Vine
Street, Pharmacy on Court Street, and Pathology on Central. The administration
was hardly more centralized, as each school retained its own board and separate
faculty, as Cox had proposed. In subsequent decades, especially as many of these
institutions eventually sought more tangible benefits of union, "Shall it all be in one
place?" became a guiding question for the university.

❧ The Best Opportunities Consistent with Available Funds

With a modest financial foundation, the University of Cincinnati began humbly,
offering classes at Woodward High School in 1873 while its own building took
form a mile away. Seven courses welcomed a total of fifty-eight students, of whom
forty were women. Five of the classes were in languages—two each in French and

German, one in Latin and Greek. The other courses were in mathematics and chemistry. In October 1875, the Academic Department moved to the new university building, perched halfway up the hill north of Over-the-Rhine, on the old McMicken estate. Tall and stately, with four full floors below its mansard roof, pocked with chimneys and gables, the university building loomed over the city's basin neighborhoods. The city's university now had a physical dimension and a prominent visual presence. Still, the opening of the building should in no way suggest that discussions about the shape of the institution were closed. Debate about the university's mission and future never ceased.[43]

Within four years the university was admitting students to pursue seven different degrees—doctor of philosophy, master of arts, master of science, bachelor of arts, bachelor of letters, bachelor of science, and a normal (teaching) diploma. This was a remarkable range of degrees given the small faculty, which in 1876 was composed of just eleven men, four of whom taught languages—two ancient and two modern. In addition to admitting students to pursue each of these degrees, the

The University Building, circa 1875. This image captures the problem created by the placement of the original building in the middle of the hill. Although it was accessible via Clifton Avenue, on the other side of the building, most students had to climb many flights of stairs to reach classes from the streets below. *Photograph files, Archives & Rare Books Library, University of Cincinnati.*

university also made room for "special students," those who wished to take courses but not enroll in a particular degree program. By 1880, 91 nonmatriculated students were taking courses, largely in languages and literature—this out of a total student body of 128 in the Academic Department. (More students were taking classes in the School of Design downtown.) Thus, from the very beginning the University of Cincinnati endeavored to serve a variety of students and their interests, even those who were uncertain if they could or should pursue a degree.[44]

Not surprisingly, in the early years roughly two-thirds of the students came from the city of Cincinnati. A few came from Covington and Newport, across the river, and several others came from nearby suburbs, such as Clifton and Madisonville, both of which would eventually become part of the city. After granting one degree in 1877, UC held its first commencement ceremony at Pike's Opera House a year later. The university celebrated the graduation of eight students. Among the seven men earning diplomas, one was from Brazil. Indeed, three more Brazilians graduated the next year—all of them earning degrees in engineering. That particular international connection did not persist, however, and for decades the university served an overwhelmingly local population.[45] A more lasting connection developed between UC and nearby Hebrew Union College, which began admitting students in 1875. A small rabbinical college, Hebrew Union relied on UC to offer the range of courses necessary for its students to earn a bachelor of arts, including Israel Aaron, who graduated from UC in 1880, on his way to earning his rabbinical degree three years later. Through this relationship, UC helped Hebrew Union succeed as the first Jewish institution of higher education in the United States. All of the early rabbinical candidates were men, but perhaps more important to UC's early identity were the female students. Among them, joining the first graduating class in 1878, was Winona Lee Hawthorne, of Newport, Kentucky, who became the first woman to earn a University of Cincinnati degree.[46]

As the first decade of UC came to a close, the chair of the Board of Directors Samuel Hunt summarized the progress made and the promise held out by "the university idea." Hunt, who had formerly served as an Ohio state senator and had introduced the bill that allowed the creation of the university in 1870, understood that resources would limit what UC could accomplish, particularly if the various schools in the city failed to unite in one great university. Still, Hunt promised that UC would pursue "the best opportunities consistent with available funds," perhaps a fitting motto for a striving but perpetually underfunded institution.[47]

3

TO THE WOODS

An Urban University Moves Away from Urban Problems

For a time the old McMicken homestead seemed poised to be the one place where higher education might take root and expand in the city. Halfway up the hill, just below Clifton Avenue, the college sat at a location that screamed compromise: not on the top, where it would have had the advantages of view and distance from the bustle of the city; not at the bottom, where students would have had easy access on foot or via streetcar. In front of the building, a little to the east, sat the old McMicken homestead, a surprisingly modest clapboard home with four windows facing down the hill, over the city and the gardens that were once the real attraction of the place. A stone wall marked the southern end of the property on Hamilton Road, which took the name McMicken Avenue after the college opened. Despite the fact that the university overlooked the city and was clearly visible from town, many people associated with it—students, faculty, board members—complained that during its first decade of existence the university was largely overlooked by the city. And everyone knew that the mere completion of the building did not guarantee that the institution would persist. In fact, years of modest growth in reputation and student numbers suggested the opposite.[1]

The university's failure to thrive was at the heart of an internal battle in 1882, when several members of the Board of Directors accused the university's rector, Thomas Vickers, of incompetence. In leveling his complaints, Cornelius Comegys considered the city as a whole, noting that its two fine high schools—Woodward and Hughes—prepared many young men and women for college. What's more, Cincinnati's growth and position in the nation essentially demanded the complementary growth of the university. "Our city is now a great railroad center, and is about the center, too, of the national population," Comegys wrote, "and on account of its vast manufacturing and mercantile interests, our great public works in engineering science, such as bridges, hydraulic apparatus, mills of all sorts, railroad shops, and other innumerable establishments in various industries and arts, is one of the richest fields in the nation for the practical observation of all the elements of industrial and political economy." Comegys was describing how, in the second half of the nineteenth century, the thriving commercial river city had evolved into a modern industrial metropolis with a remarkably diverse economy. Cincinnati manufactured clothing, shoes and boots, furniture, and carriages. It shaped iron and steel into hardware and machines. It brewed beer and packed meat. Comegys argued that because the city had developed a diverse and prosperous economy, it should also be able to support a "great school of science and arts." He concluded that the university's failure to grow could be traced to the fact that Vickers, a former Unitarian minister and librarian, was not a trained academic (he was a political appointee), or perhaps because he spent too much time in saloons. Either way, Comegys's attack echoed that of students writing in the school newspaper, *Academica*, who also wondered why the school had progressed so slowly.[2]

Tangled in the Vickers controversy was the continued conflict over the role of the Bible in education. UC had formed its curriculum in the shadow of the Bible War, during which the city fought to keep the reading of the King James Bible out of public schools, a policy passed by the school board in 1869. Several of Cincinnati's Protestant preachers and religious conservatives sued the public schools to force a reversal of the policy. A well-known lawyer, and a member of the UC board, Rufus King, made a defense of the Bible before the superior court, on which sat Alphonso Taft. Taft, a liberal Unitarian, had been a member of Thomas Vickers's congregation at a time when Vickers was among the most prominent voices demanding the removal of the Bible from public schools. Taft issued an impassioned defense of religious liberty in 1870 when the superior court decided the case, but his was the only dissenting voice. The case went to the Ohio Supreme Court, which ruled in favor of the public schools in 1873. But the issue was still raw at the university, which, per McMicken's bequest, was supposed to teach the Bible. Comegys had consistently encouraged the Board of Directors to take up the issue, determined to keep Bible instruction on campus. (He was a Bible instructor himself.) And so, as the board entertained reports on the leadership of Vickers, a central force in the removal of the Bible for schools, its membership included several key participants in the case, notably the conservative King, the Unitarian Taft, the freethinking John Stallo, and the Unitarian George Hoadly, who had aided Stallo in the defense of the public school's right to discontinue Bible instruction. Indeed, it is entirely possible that the liberal religious reputations among so many of the university's leaders may have encouraged some devout Protestants to send their sons and daughters elsewhere for college.[3]

As Cincinnati struggled to build a strong university, it succeeded in building a spectacular Music Hall in Over-the-Rhine, less than a mile down Elm Street from McMicken. Completed in 1878, the massive Gothic Revival hall, designed by Cincinnati's Samuel Hannaford, became the city's most prominent symbol of cultural attainment. As Music Hall rose aside Washington Park, the university tried to get comfortable on its sloping campus, clinging to one of the steep hills that had concentrated the city in the basin. Cincinnati was composed of uncommonly dense neighborhoods, with the majority of the city's 250,000 residents living in the West End, Over-the-Rhine, and downtown. This density brought with it a number of environmental disamenities, including noise and smoke, both of which consistently drew the attention of university leaders.[4]

But in the decades after the Civil War the city was in the process of bursting out of its confined core. By 1880, streetcars carried passengers over seventy-six miles of track, and a series of inclined planes transported streetcars, wagons, and pedestrians up the steep grades to the hilltop districts of Mount Adams, Clifton, and Price Hill. Soon electrification made the streetcars even more efficient, and their lines reached farther into the suburbs. By 1912, 222 miles of track laced the city, allowing more and more people to seek homes on the hilltops—and beyond. The city responded to this expansion by annexing surrounding areas, growing rapidly from its six-square-mile core to a fifty-square-mile metropolis. Together the streetcars and inclines helped satisfy the city's need to be on the move. They would do the same for the university.[5]

❧ Ruined Almost Entirely by the Smoke

Ironically, a fire may have provided the catalyst required to ensure permanence. In the early morning hours of Saturday, November 7, 1885, a passerby noticed flames coming from the university building. The fire seems to have started in the chemistry laboratory in the cellar, which was completely destroyed. Several other rooms were badly damaged, mostly in the southwest corner of the building, above the lab. City officials examined the damage the next morning, declaring some of the rooms a "total loss," but noting that several rooms were still in good condition, including the natural history room on the third floor. Despite the heroic work of the firemen, which saved the building from total destruction, *Academica* declared the fire a "terrible calamity."[6]

Less than twelve hours after the fire had been spotted, the Board of Directors held an emergency meeting in one of the dry rooms of the building. Board members knew that classes would have to be moved during repairs. The first order of business at the meeting was the reading of a note from Isaac M. Wise. "The University building being burned down," Wise wrote, "I take pleasure in informing you and the Board that the Hebrew Union College building and each room thereof, is at your service to be used as temporary quarters by the University of Cincinnati." Hebrew Union College had just moved into a former mansion on West Sixth Street five years earlier. Since the college's modest number of students took classes at the University of Cincinnati, the collaboration made good sense. Wise noted that his three-floor building had sufficient room for university classes, concluding, "The Hebrew Union College building is at your service daily up to two P.M. as long as you may deem proper to use it." The Board of Directors accepted the offer immediately.[7]

Almost as soon as the smoke had cleared, the press began to speculate about rebuilding. Even in its coverage of the fire itself, the *Enquirer* noted that the scene had been visited by thousands of curious residents, "and some regrets were heard that, since the fire had started, it was somewhat of a pity the work had not been complete, so that a new structure might have been erected nearer the level of Mc-Micken Avenue than to have it where it is, on an almost inaccessible bluff, reachable without fatigue by nothing except Rocky Mountain goats."[8] Even though the destruction had been incomplete, the *Times-Star* asked if "now is the time to suggest that a change of location would be advantageous." The paper claimed the current location "would be very valuable for manufacturing purposes, while the University buildings might be put up on some of the hills where they would not only show to better advantage, but would be improved in every way." Because streetcar lines had expanded through the city, a university on top of the hill would not be out of reach. As the *Times-Star* put it, "rapid transit between the town proper and the suburbs is every year annihilating distance." And, the paper noted, the university was "situated in the midst of the smoke and dirt of a manufacturing part of the city," and concluded that the current location "has been a drawback to the University's progress, and now the time has come when a change can conveniently be made."[9]

At its first regular meeting after the fire, while sorting through the insurance policies that would pay for the damage, the Board of Directors also considered the legal impediment regarding a move: the McMicken will. The board generally agreed, as Comegys reported, "the interests of the University imperatively demand either a change in the location of the University Building or the acquisition of additional property and the erection of other buildings for University purposes or both." The board directed its law committee to inquire as to the possibility of moving off the McMicken property.[10]

The smoke from the fire may have cleared as the city debated moving the university, but the smoke of the city persisted, eventually becoming one of the central complaints about the current location. Indeed, even as the board had debated the building's placement in 1872, some members supported making a "chemical test of the air," in an effort to show that air quality was better at the top of the hill than down by the old homestead. (That resolution failed and the tests didn't take place.)[11] Complaints about industrial pollution peaked as the push to move up the hill gathered momentum. "There is immense smoke that pours out of the chimneys from the breweries," Comegys observed, while shifting blame for the university's slow growth from Vickers to the school's location. Several professors said that constant smoke damaged books and instruments. Clarence L. Herriot, a professor of natural history, described the difficulty of teaching biology in the university building. "In the first place, the collections suitable to such a department, illustrating the different branches of the animal kingdom, are very soon ruined by the smoke," he said. Herriot had even turned down an offer "of a collection of European insects which would have been of very material use to us, but I was unable to accept them from the fact that in a year or two, at most, they would have been destroyed by the smoke and dust. That is true, also," he continued, "of a collection of birds which we have—a very valuable collection—which is ruined almost entirely by the smoke and dust and soot which passes through our department." What's more, Herriot noted, "Labels on all our collections are very soon rendered illegible by the smoke."[12] Professor Edward W. Hyde, who had been at the university since the building opened, noted that teaching math wasn't badly compromised by conditions, but engineering and drafting were. "At present," he said in 1891, "the main difficulty is in the dirt injuring the books rapidly, and the darkness, which makes it frequently necessary to light the gas in the morning to carry on our work because of the city atmosphere." Clearly this wasn't an ideal educational environment.[13]

But it wasn't just the smoke. Comegys complained that "the movement of trains on the incline plane agitates the building and makes noise, and is a disturbing agent in the university."[14] The Elm Street Incline, also called the Bellevue Incline, connected the end of Elm Street to the Bellevue House, a restaurant, saloon, and entertainment venue perched at the top of the hill. The incline had opened in September 1876, just a year after the university, and it passed within forty feet of the building. The incline lifted streetcars and pedestrians up the hill, many of them on their way to and from expanding residential neighborhoods, others on their way to a respite from the city in Burnet Woods, the city's largest park. Unfortunately, the incline provided no advantage to the university, since it simply rolled past the building mid-trip to the top or the bottom of the hill without stopping. In addition to the noise and vibrations caused by the passing cars, which many of the professors complained of as well, the incline itself served as the reminder of the many disadvantages of standing on the middle of the hill.

Both student and city newspapers kept the pressure on the university to move. "Everyone is of the opinion that at the present time there could be no worse place for a college than the present situation," *Academica* editorialized in 1885, a couple of months after the fire. "We have a large campus, to be sure, but its slope is so peculiar that even a goat would find himself beset with difficulties if he undertook to gambol upon the delightful green sward." Worse than the campus itself, however, was the neighborhood. According to *Academica*, "The place is a great manufacturing center, and we get all the benefit of the peculiar odors that arise from soap factories, glue factories, breweries, etc. These are pretty well mixed by the time they reach the hill-top, and form a compound that makes the chemical student's old friend, sulphuretted hydrogen [rotten egg smell], hang its head in shame."[15]

The *Enquirer* asked in 1886, "Shall a more appropriate and fitting site be selected?" The paper suggested that the university move to College Hill and join with the former Farmers' College, now known as Belmont.[16] Moving to College Hill would be difficult, however, in part because of the distance from the center of town, but also because that neighborhood was not yet part of the city, to which McMicken had made his bequest. Indeed, Isaac Wise, who had been a member of the Board of Directors since 1882 and had become a more vocal member after the fire, asked his colleagues to resolve *not* to move out of the city. The board tabled the resolution in an effort to keep all options open. Of course, there were several locations inside the city under consideration, including Over-the-Rhine, perhaps around Washington Park, although that neighborhood also suffered from smoke, noise, and expensive land. Others proposed Mount Lookout, largely because it had recently become home to the observatory, which had joined the university in 1871. The observatory had relocated from Mount Adams in 1873 to property donated to the city by John Kilgour, who had just that year created the Consolidated Street Railway Company. Mount Lookout might have been a good location for an observatory, as it was well away from city smoke, but, as *Academica* noted, it was not so good for commuting students, even if they could afford to take Kilgour's streetcars. For its part, the student newspaper seemed to prefer simply moving up the hill, either to Bellevue, to a couple of acres already owned by the university at the end of Ohio Avenue, next to the incline landing, or to "Ten to twenty acres of the southwest corner of Burnet Woods," which "could probably be gotten free, and it has every advantage of light, pure air, cleanliness, convenience to the city and is most certainly a desirable location."[17] By 1890 changes in the city had reshaped student demographics. Fifteen years earlier the vast majority of the students came from the densely packed neighborhoods of the West End, Over-the-Rhine, and downtown. Now, just over 40 percent of the student body came from the heart of the city. More students—48 percent—came from the "upper level," including 20 percent from Walnut Hills, and 4 percent from Clifton and Avondale. Cumminsville (now called Northside) was home to 3 percent of the students, while 6 percent came from areas in the county north of the city. Thomas H. Norton, professor of chemistry since 1883 and simultaneously the university's registrar, used residential figures to make the case for moving the school to Burnet Woods. The walking city had grown into a riding city, Norton noted, claiming "at the present time we have no student who is not within easy reach by rail or street car of the university."[18]

With accessibility for students becoming less of an issue, factors such as the attractiveness of the immediate surroundings began to take precedence. Regardless of location, though, there was a growing consensus that the university would have to move to thrive.

There Must Be Some Sentiment Connected with It

Even after the repaired building reopened, the university continued to debate moving off the McMicken homestead. The building had been improved in many ways during the repairs, but the flaws of its surroundings could not be fixed. While professors grumbled about noise and smoke, students were much more likely to complain about the sloping campus and the lack of space for athletics. Students had use of the McMicken gardens, but sports were essentially impossible around the school, since flat land was at a premium anywhere near the building. Student athletes had to seek open fields at a distance, including at the top of the hill. As athletics became more important to university life around the country, especially as organized football thrust universities into competition with one another, students called for better facilities. Athletes needed space to practice, and even non-athletes began to call for better space so they could exercise. The university building didn't even have a gymnasium, much to the dismay of students, who as early as October 1875, just as the building opened, had petitioned the Board of Directors to equip a room for athletics—the first of many such petitions.[19]

Pleas for improvements in athletic opportunities persisted through the early 1880s, including a brief treatise on the value of "Physical Culture" by William Stecher, a gymnastics instructor, which noted that several schools in the East and West "have inserted gymnastics in the regular course of their institutions." If schools were to develop complete men and women, Stecher argued, the body must be instructed as well as the mind.[20] In 1887, students were still trying to get a gymnasium, now asking simply for use of the storage space in the basement of the repaired university building. The *McMicken Review*, the latest version of the student paper, noted that faculty need not worry about noise from the gym interrupting classes, claiming, "If the students had some place where they could pleasantly pass vacant hours they would perhaps avoid places much more objectionable."[21] A month later, the *Review* was more assertive, making an argument that sounded decades ahead of its time: "We need a gymnasium and we need it badly. Excellence in athletic sports does as much in attracting students to a college as does a well-arranged curriculum and a fine corps of professors."[22] The paper argued that the annual Field Day, in which students participated in a range of competitions at a nearby park, provided an opportunity not just to exhibit athletic abilities, but also to create community and to gather momentum toward the creation of more organized sports.

The student papers could be merciless in their criticisms of the university. In 1880, a tongue-in-cheek editorial in the student newspaper *Belatrasco* addressed the many "advantages" of the McMicken campus. The "the non-existence of dormitories" forced students "to reside in their own homes, subjecting them to home influences and forcing them to take some exercise, at least, in reaching the school"— clearly a dig at the hillside campus. "This plan avoids many of the evils of college life," the editorial continued, "the disgraceful conduct and riots, the distraction and diversion of many from their studies by boating, balling, etc."[23] In the years after the fire, more critics would take up the absence of a true campus, arguing that this greatly impeded student involvement in activities, since students generally returned home after classes, which stunted school spirit.

In 1890, the *Review* published a remarkably complete critique of the university's situation. The unattributed "Student Complaint" tried to answer the question, "Why is it that the University hasn't a larger attendance?" There must be something the matter with the school, the author proposed, but it wasn't the faculty or the coursework. Instead, the campus—and the absence of a gym—was at the heart of the complaint. "We have a campus that makes us heave many a deep sigh in the mornings when we climb it. Oh, why did anybody ever think of building a university on the side of a hill that rises about thirty feet in a hundred! Let us hurry and move to Burnet Woods, where we can have a campus." The complaint also mentioned the lack of a library on campus. (Students had access to the impressive public library, although it was more than a mile from the university, on Vine Street south of Seventh.) Perhaps worse, according to the author, the university had no athletic standing to use in recruiting more students. The author concluded, "You know the students are the University, and without students there is no University; and if there is nothing to attract students except merely what they can learn from the professors, it will be a very small university."[24]

A little over a year later, after the university lost an early season football game to the YMCA of Dayton, the hand-wringing about the team turned inevitably to the lack of practice time, which was directly related to the absence of practice space. "We have no campus," a *McMicken Review* editorial pointed out. "We have been looking forward to Burnet Woods as the fulfilment of our want in this respect." With the move up the hill seemingly still uncertain and at least a year off, the student paper proposed that the school at least rent a field to allow regular practices by the various sports teams.[25] Fortunately, the 1891 season turned around, and in the end the *Review* called it great advertising for the university. "The many press notices have given much free advertising and if there is a man in Cincinnati who does not know that we have here a splendid University, he is either a dolt or cannot read."[26] (In either case, he might not have been an appropriate candidate for admission.)

Back in 1888, the board had again asked its law committee to investigate whether the university could move and sell or lease the current property for manufacturing, which seemed its highest and best use. The committee determined that such action would be unwise, noting that it would probably "bring about litigation and might possibly endanger the city's title to the McMicken bequest."[27] Despite the warning, the board soon voted to pursue city council approval of a move to Burnet Woods. The board's committee on location even claimed that moving the university to Burnet Woods would be a win-win. A pamphlet circulated to drum up public support declared, "[T]he proposed location in Burnet Woods Park is peculiarly suitable for the site of a great university; and the picturesque grouping of handsome buildings in this now unimproved section of the Park, the establishment of a magnificent botanical garden, and the laying out of drives, walks, and lawns, will, instead of detracting from the attractions of this part of the Park, add tenfold to its beauties and popularity."[28]

Council was convinced. In the fall of 1889, it passed, unanimously, an ordinance "Relating to the occupancy of part of Burnet Woods Park by the University

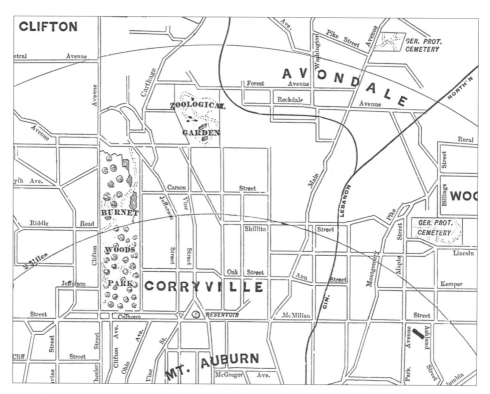

Map of Burnet Woods and surroundings, 1890. When UC moved up the hill to Burnet Woods it was still less than two miles from Fountain Square in the center of the city, but the steep hill made it seem much farther removed. This map was published by Rand McNally in 1890, five years before the university moved into the park. *Photograph files, Archives & Rare Books Library, University of Cincinnati.*

of Cincinnati," which granted forever just over forty-three acres to the university "for all proper university purposes." Since both the park and the university were city-owned, the cost was just $1. The ordinance allowed the university to erect "its main building at whatever point that it may select" within the southeast corner of the park, and stipulated that "it shall have exclusive control in and over so much of said lot as lies within a radius of one hundred (100) feet" of the building, at least within the acres marked off for university use. Importantly, the ordinance also required that land not used for buildings, or within 100 feet of a building, was "to remain open to the public as a part of Burnet Woods Park forever." The ordinance also required that within five years the university would have expended at least $100,000 for the construction of buildings and other improvements.[29]

Despite the unanimous council vote, not everyone agreed that the move would be in the best interest of the park, or of the city generally. The fiercest opposition came from the McMicken family, and, as expected, the issue moved to court when Andrew McMicken sued to keep the university where it was. Hiram Peck, a former member of the Board of Directors, respected lawyer, former judge, and current member of the law school's faculty, offered his services to defend the move. Peck's legal theory was that conditions in the neighborhood of the McMicken homestead had changed so dramatically that the location was no longer suitable for a university. To document these changes, Peck deposed a number of prominent Cincinnatians with deep memories and, mostly, long connections to the university. Witnesses described the nearly rural character of the old homestead in the 1850s, when Charles McMicken wrote his will, noting that the northern part of Over-the-Rhine had yet to industrialize. (The family's lawyer pointed out that many of the university's witnesses had forgotten how old some of the breweries actually were.) Witnesses also spoke in unison about the current conditions, emphasizing the smoke and noise. The goal was to suggest that if Charles McMicken were alive, he too would want the university moved. In arguing that university surroundings must be "pleasant to the scholars and students," Charles Taft went further in his reasoning than most. Claiming that attending college should be about more than just learning, Taft asserted, "In addition to acquiring the knowledge of any of the sciences or of languages, in order to gain the fullest benefit of a college education there must be some sentiment connected with it. There must be esprit de corps." In other words, students needed to feel connected to their school, to the campus. "In my view it is very difficult, almost impossible, to have that from a school situation where this university building now is."[30]

Lawyers for the McMicken family countered that the Burnet Woods site had flaws too, emphasizing that the neighborhood on the southern boundary of the park had become dense with saloons, with perhaps twenty drinking establishments along Calhoun Street. But Professor Hyde, who had taken his engineering students to survey Burnet Woods, testified that because of the topography the "most eligible location" for building would be in the northwest corner of the forty acres to be given, and therefore far from the rough part of Corryville.[31] Altogether Hyde found Burnet Woods a much superior location, partly because at least a quarter mile "would lie between the university buildings and any objectionable surroundings, such as beer-saloons, and so on," but also because, "[t]here are no manufacturing establishments in the immediate neighborhood," meaning the site was not subject to shrouds of smoke. Hyde added that because of the ample space, "there would be abundance of room for athletic grounds, and for laying out the grounds in an attractive and desirable manner, which would make it attractive to students."[32]

Peck's witnesses argued that the Burnet Woods location would be quiet enough for contemplation, clean enough for scientific experimentation, and spacious enough for physical exercise—three qualities that the old homestead never or no longer possessed. The case made its way up to the Ohio Supreme Court, which in the spring of 1893 determined that the university did have a right to move. It affirmed the circuit court ruling that, "the desire and intention of [Charles McMicken] was to found a *College of the highest character*, but not to restrict the location of the buildings perpetually to *one* spot." The university was heading up the hill and to the woods.[33]

At 163 acres when granted to the city by Robert W. Burnet and William S. Groesbeck "for park and other purposes" in 1872, Burnet Woods contained large stands of old trees separated by winding carriage paths.[34] Its hilly ground sloped to the north, down toward Clifton, an in-city suburb of mansions and, increasingly, fashionable apartment buildings along the streetcar lines. By the time the university proposed moving into the park, Burnet Woods contained several popular picnic areas and a small artificial lake, used for boating. The southwest corner of the park, the acreage granted by the city, would most assuredly "remain in its present rough, neglected condition indefinitely," university officials argued, and the construction of the campus would thus improve the site, even for recreation. Unsurprisingly, not everyone agreed with this assessment. The parks had been poorly managed for more than a decade, but the city created a new advocate for them in 1891: the Board of Park Commissioners. In its first annual report, Jeptha Garrard, president of the board, lamented the transfer of land to the university. "The topography of that part of Burnet Woods given to the University is such that if the ceded tract is used by the University it will cease to be of value to the people as a park."[35]

Despite Garrard's conclusion, the initial grant to the university was approved without public opposition, perhaps because the park was lightly used or, more likely, because most residents recognized the limitations the hillside location had placed on the university. At the same time, most residents would not have guessed how much of the park the university would eventually take, and just how completely the campus would transform Burnet Woods. At first even the university's board conceived of the park as a home for a few buildings and an athletic field. And, as required by the 1889 ordinance, "The public would not be excluded at any time from any part of the grounds." Thus, the discussion surrounding the move to Burnet Woods made clear that at least some people thought the university and park could coexist, even on the same acreage. Befitting the commingling of these uses, the site became known as the "Burnet Woods Campus."

On Tuesday, October 4, 1892, several members of the university board, including Cornelius Comegys, Charles Reed, and James Brown, chair of the building committee, made an on-site visit to Burnet Woods. The primary object of the trip was to show Park Commissioner Garrard where the university would build first. The men gathered at the university and then proceeded up the hill, where they found Ward Baldwin, professor of civil engineering, standing among stakes he'd driven into the ground, marking the spot for the new McMicken Hall. The building committee agreed to the location, praising its view over Clifton Avenue and the Mill Creek Valley beyond, and, despite the protests of Garrard who thought the spot too obtrusive, work on the foundation began almost immediately.[36]

So the university would be in the park. With that question settled, another came to the fore: What other institutions would join the Academic Department in Burnet Woods?

🌿 A Building Appropriate to the Location

On the morning of March 9, 1894, Alexander McGuffey, the long-serving secretary and treasurer of the Cincinnati College and a former member of the university's

Board of Directors, arrived at the Hamilton County Courthouse carrying nearly all of the extant documents relating to Cincinnati College. McGuffey had served as Daniel Drake's executor, which is how he came to possess "the package labeled 'All real estate papers,'" many of which were written in Drake's hand. Now, forty years after Drake's death, McGuffey had been called to court to explain college governance. Who were the shareholders in the college and how did they come to their decisions? The questions, and there were many of them, came from Gustavus Wald, a prominent Cincinnati lawyer who represented the University of Cincinnati. Sitting with Wald at the plaintiff's table was Joseph Foraker, former governor of Ohio, who served as co-counsel. In essence, these men, and many other powerful citizens, were in court to answer Alphonso Taft's question: Shall it all be in one place?

The case began, oddly enough, when the Mercantile Library attempted to get electricity put into its reading room on the second floor of the college building. The Mercantile's frustrations with its location had grown in recent years, and some members felt their long lease with its poorer sibling, the college, was holding back their association. Not surprisingly, the initial response was to create a committee, which might have led to nothing except for the leadership of Edmund K. Stallo, son of Judge John Stallo and a well-regarded lawyer in his own right. At the time, the younger Stallo sat on the boards of both the Mercantile and the university, and he saw a way forward that united the interests of each. First the committee laid out a case for action: "The present quarters of The Young Men's Mercantile Library Association are not only dingy, uninviting, poorly lighted and poorly ventilated, but owing to the library's association with an institution that seems in every way disinclined to improve the building in which the library is situated, there seems to be no remedy of this state of affairs." As the premises were neither "adequate" nor "profitable"—language used in the lease— the Mercantile was justified in seeking some significant alteration.[37]

That alteration turned out to be the proposed destruction of the college as a legal entity and its combination with the University of Cincinnati. The committee determined that since the college had given up on teaching everything but law, it had violated its own lease for the property and its charter from the state. The college had ceased to be a true college, the argument ran, so the state could alter its charter. What's more, the committee argued: "The Cincinnati University is an institution of learning that not only merits the support of every public spirited citizen of the city of Cincinnati, but it is an institution that fully embraces the functions contemplated by the charter of The Cincinnati College." The committee went so far as to claim that the Cincinnati College trustees must be accumulating money, because the law school was small and the rent for the building, mostly coming from the shops on the first floor, must be large. "If this surplus does exist," the committee determined, "it should be devoted to the erection of a building appropriate to the location of the lot on which the Cincinnati College building at present stands."[38]

The phrase "appropriate to the location" is especially revealing, as it indicates just how much rent pressure influenced the conversation about the college. The committee's solution was to get legal counsel—Stallo contacted Foraker first—and seek a legislative solution. With well-connected counsel, it didn't take long for a law satisfying both the Mercantile and the university to make its way through the State House. In March of 1892 the legislature declared that since "the endowment of The Cincinnati College, as at present invested and managed, is not sufficient to enable it to carry out the purposes of its charter," and because "it would be advantageous to The Cincinnati College and to The University of Cincinnati, and to the public generally, that the government of the two institutions should be joined and consolidated," the state placed the college under the control of the university's Board of Directors, removing the Cincinnati College board altogether.[39]

This is how McGuffey wound up in court with Daniel Drake's papers. He was defending the right of the college to exist. The college's board had simply refused to relinquish its position, had held on to its documents, continued to occupy the building and operate the law school, and now denied the right of the state to alter its charter. The shareholders, McGuffey claimed, had voted unanimously in favor of challenging the law. The case, it turns out, was mostly about these shareholders. With a long series of questions, Wald hoped to make clear that the college really had no original documents indicating who owned stock, no actual stock certificates from 1819, the year of its creation, or even 1835, the year of its re-creation. Instead, the college had created a new list of shareholders and issued new stock in 1872 because, in the words of McGuffey, there was "danger in this uncertainty that the stock may be lost, or its ownership disputed." In reality, the danger came from the new university, just then preparing to offer classes at Woodward High School, and the talk swirling around town that the college should be absorbed by the university. In excruciating detail, Wald forced McGuffey to admit that many shares had been issued to people who were dead at the time and that through a rather opaque process these shares came back to McGuffey in the form of proxies. (He cast more than half of the votes at shareholder meetings.)

Despite the college's obvious recordkeeping problems, even to the point of failing to keep track of who had the right to vote at shareholder meetings, the Ohio Supreme Court ruled in its favor: the legislature did not have the right to alter the charter in 1892. The ruling left the Mercantile Library with few good options. The university, on the other hand, took dramatic action, when, in 1896, after further negotiations with the college failed to lead to union, it created its own law department, appointing William Howard Taft as dean and Wald as one of the faculty. Not surprisingly, given the quality of the faculty and the weight of the university behind it, the Law Department was an instant success. An initial class of forty students met in a university-owned building on Fourth Street, half a block from Cincinnati College. By the spring of 1897, the college was feeling considerable pressure. In addition to the competitor right around the corner, new law schools had recently opened in Cleveland, Columbus, and Indianapolis, all of which drew students away from the Cincinnati Law School. The college trustees finally consented to consolidation, even though it meant several faculty members were forced to retire. Taft became dean of the con-solidated school; the new Law School opened in the college building the next spring, where the students had access to the fine law library the college had built over the previous fifty years.[40]

🌿 University Purposes

In the fall of 1895 McMicken Hall opened in Burnet Woods. Led by Alfred K. Nippert and Frank Sanford Brown, the Alumni Association organized donations to ensure that the new building was equipped with a gymnasium, seventy feet by fifty feet, complemented by showers and lockers. As the *Enquirer* reported, the fa-cility filled "a long-felt want."[41] The president of the Alumni Association, Henry Bettmann, helped open the gymnasium with a speech that described the training of mind and body in Greek and Roman societies, which also connected this new facility with traditional classical education. After Bettmann's speech, and others from the dean and the president of the board, Bettmann announced that the uni-versity had received a $500 gift from the American Book Company, solicited by Professor William Sproull for the purpose of further equipping the gym. After the cheering and the singing of school songs, students danced to music played by harp and violin. Meanwhile, the football team geared up and headed out to practice on a rough field just south of the building.[42]

McMicken Hall, circa 1910. The move to Burnet Woods allowed UC to create a real campus atmosphere. McMicken's prominent location on the ridge above Clifton Avenue allowed the university to maintain a parklike front yard while retaining easy access via streetcar. *Photograph files, Archives & Rare Books Library, University of Cincinnati.*

Altogether the scene made clear that the Burnet Woods Campus would transform university life. The 1896 yearbook, *The Cincinnatian*, affirmed that from McMicken Hall and its surroundings in the park, "the students have imbibed college spirit. Instead of the smoky, dusty factories, we have always before our eyes the charming Mill Creek Valley, and we live in a world entirely different from the city. Now we can begin to realize college life; now we have a fixed home around which we can gradually create a mist of tradition."[43]

The campus would not be complete, however, until the university had a real athletic field. At first the university proposed using the high ground south of Mc-Micken, where the team was practicing, and where knolls could be leveled to create a full field. City officials preferred giving the university access to the hollow southeast of the building.[44] In 1896, Professor Baldwin, who had laid out the spot for McMicken Hall and had continued his surveying of the park, declared the low spot quite suitable for an athletic field. "The hills here form a perfect amphitheater," he said, "and seats could be placed on the hillside with but slight expense."[45]

But conflict arose between the university and other city administrators, especially Reuben Warder, superintendent of parks, over the use of park lands. Warder thought the hollow would be a fine location for a botanical garden. The student newspaper, now called the *Burnet Woods Echo*, reported in detail the saga of the university's search for a suitable field. "To those unacquainted with the real facts in the case it may seem strange that after the City of Cincinnati had granted to the University forty acres to be used for 'University purposes,' it should deny to it the right to devote a small portion of the tract to college athletics, which are as indissolubly connected with the University as any of the courses laid down in the catalogue." The *Echo* determined that Warder was hostile toward the university because he never accepted its move to the park. As the university and the park board wrangled over the hollow, university sports continued to be played off campus, including at League Park, the West End home of the Cincinnati Reds.

The city ultimately sided with the university, but construction awaited sufficient funds to move earth and prepare the field, which would eventually accommodate home football and baseball games and include a quarter-mile track. The fundraising was capped in 1901 by a $2,000 donation from Mayor Julius Fleischmann.[46] As the university graded the hollow for an athletic field in the summer of 1902, it petitioned the parks board to allow the construction of a fence, mostly so that it could charge admission to its games. The university spent $5,000 on the field, which had been "redeemed from a state of impenetrable bramble and briar break," according to the student paper.[47] The fence would allow the university to charge for the use of grandstands and defray the cost of maintaining what became Carson Field, named in honor of the UC coach Arch Carson. Several members of the city's Board of Public Service objected, noting that the legislation allowing the university's move to the park clearly stated that the public would not be excluded from any part of the grounds.[48] Supporters tried to allay fears by noting that spectators would still be able to see games for free, because the hillside would allow them to overlook the fence and the field.[49]

By the fall of 1902, the field was finished, but the university had yet to add seats and the city had yet to permit a fence. The matter became so urgent that President Howard Ayers spoke to the Board of Directors, claiming that it "is absolutely necessary that the grounds be enclosed," and asking that board members lobby city officials.[50] A month later, a split Board of Public Service allowed the fence. The *Enquirer* thought the vote was justified, "as athletics is one of the chief features of university life." In other words, the field would be as integral to the university as an academic building, which had been specified in the original grant of park use. Somewhat less positively, the *Enquirer* also noted that the fence would "protect the students from being interfered with in their games by crowds of hoodlums."[51]

The fence controversy continued when the university erected a fence made of seven-foot boards in November.[52] Protests within the neighborhood and divided interests inside city government led to an awkward lawsuit. The city, represented by Hunt, who personally supported the fence, sued the university to force the field to remain open to the public. In the spring of 1903, the superior court of Cincinnati ruled in favor of the university's right to enclose the field, noting, "an athletic field is a well-recognized part of every modern college or university."[53]

Clearly the fence took on great symbolic value. Opponents expressed concerns about exclusivity in a public park, and no doubt fear that university incursions in the park would continue. Supporters, on the other hand, simply demanded that the city meet at least the basic needs of a quality university. "Let us have a first-class university or none at all," Hunt declared, as if he were discussing something much more important than a fence, or even an athletic field. But the debate and the court case also reflected the enduring problem of public institutions in a democratic society. The university found itself unable to serve a divided public, for the decision to enclose the field impinged on the rights of residents to use public land—a complaint also made by the Turners of North Cincinnati,[54] who had hoped to use the field for exercises. Obviously this would not be the last time that the university would run afoul of varied interests in the city, nor the last time neighbors would resent the expanding institution.[55]

❦ Subversive of the Interests of the Law School

As the University of Cincinnati moved to Burnet Woods, the nation suffered through a terrible depression. A financial panic in 1893 sparked a prolonged downturn, with high unemployment lingering until the end of the century. When the economy finally stirred, Cincinnati's skyline exploded upward. New skyscrapers crowded downtown, especially along Fourth Street. In late 1901, the nineteen-story Union Savings Bank and Trust building opened on the corner of Fourth and Walnut, casting a new late afternoon shadow over the college edifice across the street.

73

Designed by famed Chicago architect Daniel Burnham, Union Trust was the tallest building in Cincinnati, and it was the leading edge of a wave of construction that would transform downtown over the next dozen years. That wave included the First National Bank building, also designed by Burnham and completed in 1904. It also rose at the corner of Fourth and Walnut.

Even before the construction boom was in full swing, Cincinnati College, which retained a separate board even after the union of the law schools, created a committee to investigate the potential sale of its low-rise edifice. In early 1900, the committee reported to President Edmund W. Kittredge that an insurance company would offer something around $300,000 for a perpetual lease, demolish the college building, and "erect a large and modern office structure upon all of the College property." Negotiations were complicated by the Mercantile Library's own long-term lease, but the association was as eager for a new building as the college was for the opportunity to wring equity from its property.[56] In the end, the board accepted an offer from T. J. and J. J. Emery—Thomas Emery's Sons, a real estate development firm—and with the agreement of the Mercantile Library in 1901 the parties signed a perpetual lease for the old college edifice for $325,000.[57]

With a good deal of cash and no building, the Law School now had to make a choice. Where should it relocate? The faculty, led by Gustavus Wald, then dean of the Law School, preferred to stay downtown, and just a month after the sale was completed, the college trustees voted to build a new building a half mile north, on Ninth Street. The college agreed to purchase property between Vine and Race Streets, on which sat an old school building owned, but unused, by the Ninth Street Baptist Church. The building, which would be demolished, occupied a 50-by-120-foot lot between the church and the Phoenix Club, an impressive structure built to serve the city's Jewish businessmen. The trustees were forgoing the advantages of the free land in Burnet Woods and, perhaps just as important, the advantages of being in the same place as the university: access to the libraries and the gymnasium and other amenities on campus. The argument for downtown rested on convenience, the small matter of carfare to commute up to the woods, and the larger matter of students having access to law offices, where many of them worked while in school. Of course, downtown was more convenient for faculty members, too, many of whom also maintained practices in the city.[58]

Even after the school had purchased the property, at a reasonable price, trustees felt pressure to move the school up the hill. President Ayers, who had

The Cincinnati Law School, circa 1915. Upon selling its lot at Fourth and Walnut, the Cincinnati Law School moved to this handsome Samuel Hannaford building on Ninth Street—despite concerted efforts to move it to Burnet Woods to join the university. *Photograph files, Archives & Rare Books Library, University of Cincinnati.*

some control over the law faculty but none over the college trustees, lobbied Kittredge in the hope that "a new home for the Law School" could be part of a group of buildings envisioned by McKim, Mead & White, the famed New York architecture firm he had recently hired to draw up plans for university expansion. "I felt and I still feel that the erection of the new building on ninth street [sic] is a mistake and subversive of the interests of the Law School, both immediate and in the future," Ayers wrote. "It is not too late to reconsider the question and I would look upon such rediscussion of the question as a great favor, since I am confident that some of the gentlemen, whose votes decide the matter, are not fully informed of all the facts in the case, particularly those from the University standpoint." Kittredge and the rest of the college board considered themselves fully informed, however, and they were well aware of the "extra expense of building the school downtown."[59]

In March, another prominent voice expressed concern about construction of a new building downtown. Former Law School dean William Howard Taft was visiting the city for the first time since becoming the governor of the Philippines. At a Queen City Club event in his honor, Taft expressed strong support for moving the Law School to Burnet Woods. Taft was not in favor of students working while in school, and he thought the removal of the school to the park would force students to concentrate more fully on their studies. Taft met privately with Kittredge and several faculty members, but to no avail. Dean Wald, who strongly opposed the move up the hill, was able to maintain support for the downtown location, and soon the building, designed by Samuel Hannaford and Sons, was under construction. The handsome three-story building opened in October 1903.[60]

❧ The University Belongs to Them

In 1895, twenty-four years after Charles Taft's lecture before the Literary Club extolling the German education system, William O. Sproull, professor of Latin and Arabic at the university, delivered a paper to the same organization entitled simply "The University of Cincinnati." The new McMicken Hall had just opened in Burnet Woods, but clearly the institution was still trying to find its place in the city, still struggling to define its mission. Sproull was a well-regarded professor who had recently served as dean of the Academic Department. He had earned his doctorate in Leipzig in 1877, and like Charles Taft he considered Germany's system of higher education the envy of the world. It trained many of America's academics as well as its own. And like Taft, Sproull thought that German universities, with their focus on graduate instruction and research, could still serve as a model for the United States. "The university is properly for investigation and research, not primarily teaching," Sproull claimed. "Its success is to be measured by its contributions of knowledge and by the number of persons it has trained who also have become contributors thereto." After Sproull recounted his own university's history, he said pointedly: "The question which must be faced is: *Shall the University become a university in reality? or, Shall it remain a college, a local institution? Shall it enter into honorable rivalry with institutions of a national reputation?*"[61]

It was clear how Sproull would answer those questions. He had been at the university for fifteen years, arriving the year Judge Stallo gave his Baccalaureate address. Like Stallo, Sproull called upon Cincinnatians to support their university. "Professors, apparatus, libraries make an institution, and money can procure all these," he said. He asked the city's wealthy citizens, many of whom were in the room listening to his paper, to support an institution that could rival the nation's finest universities and could keep the city's most talented students home.[62]

Just a couple of months before Sproull gave his paper at the Literary Club, on June 26, 1895, chairman of the Board of Directors Cornelius Comegys, who had done more than anyone to see that McMicken's bequest became the foundation of a viable university, spoke at length before the board. Comegys, who was also a prominent physician in the city, noted that the university faced special pressure to be excellent because of the public support it received. He knew the school would need more, however, and he favored putting a small tax levy before the people so that the university could purchase better scientific apparatus. "It is a painful fact that we are losing students in our advanced grades because of the insufficiency of apparatus," he told the board. Comegys also argued that the city should lobby for the return of money sent to Columbus to support state institutions of higher learning. Since there were no state schools in Hamilton County, Comegys wondered why its residents should send their dollars to Columbus. Perhaps, he argued, undoubtedly with tongue in cheek, the University of Cincinnati should open its own school of agriculture and veterinary medicine, replicating programs that existed at Ohio State University.

What Comegys was most interested in, however, was making the university more useful to the residents of Cincinnati. Noting his approval for extension work—reaching out to the people of the city—Comegys hoped that more courses could be offered, especially in modern languages. "It is of great importance that a knowledge of the Spanish language can be obtained by our young merchants and manufacturers," he said, making an argument that was well ahead of its time. "We are so contiguous to millions of Spanish speaking people that a great effort should be made, in the interests of commerce at least, to give suitable culture in that language." He also thought the university "should encourage evening studies in drawing and scientific lectures by our younger mechanics and among the labor unions of our working mechanics." This last suggestion was especially important, because "by our co-operation with the working classes," Comegys argued, the university could "prove to the people" that it "is not intended alone for the favored classes of citizens but for all the people to open the way for scientific knowledge to all inquiries of whatever position in life." He concluded his talk with an even fuller call for democratizing the institution. "Finally in some way, in all ways, the people shall come to understand the University belongs to them, and they will cherish and sustain it, that it is to be kept open to all in some form all the year round."[63]

The press paid some attention to Comegys's report, but the board meeting contained more immediate and important news: a local businessman, Henry Hanna, had given the university $45,000 to complete the north wing of the new university building. Comegys, nearly overcome with emotion, asked that the gathered "return our thanks to Almighty God for the magnificent generosity of Henry Hanna." The board was silent for a moment and then rose and bowed their heads as Rabbi Isaac M. Wise, still a member of the board, offered a prayer of thanks. Hanna Hall opened to a great celebration in the spring of 1897. Some of the advanced students led tours through the new chemical laboratory and civil engineering department. Former congressman John Follett delivered the major speech of the day. He praised those who had given so much to institutions of higher learning, calling out the generosity of Hughes, Woodward, and McMicken, and, of course, Henry Hanna, who was in attendance. He closed, however, by praising the generosity of Cornelius Comegys, who had passed away the previous year at the age of eighty.[64]

4

A PROGRESSIVE INSTITUTION

The University in the Age of Reform

In the second half of the 1800s, Cincinnatians had translated the city's prosperity into a set of admirable civic institutions—a new art museum, an impressive library, an even more impressive music hall, and a fledgling university. But in the early 1900s, these symbols of cultural attainment alone could no longer secure the city's stature. Increasingly, wealthier Americans looked to improve their communities through broader reforms designed to create more livable cities. Industrial Cincinnati had grown rapidly, if somewhat chaotically. Its people had grown wealthy, although unevenly so. As the nineteenth century moved toward its close, residents were wondering if all that growth and wealth might be put to better use. Might Cincinnati become a more pleasant, healthful place to live? Might experts in all fields—from engineering to medicine to political science—help create more efficient cities, where all citizens could more fully enjoy the fruits of prosperity? These broad questions drove much of the reform fervor of the Progressive Era. They also helped transform UC into a model municipal university.

Cincinnatians tend to think of their city as a conservative place. At the heart of this myth of conservatism is the image of the frumpy Queen City bested by broad-shouldered Chicago, an outcome that was all but ensured by the former's inability to adapt to a shifting national economy. Cincinnatians tell the story of how Chicago embraced railroads while their own city clung to the steamboat, unable or unwilling to see into the future, when river travel would be less and less important. To some observers, then, Cincinnati's relative decline among western cities suggested a character flaw, a stand-pat attitude that prevented the city from keeping pace. As Cincinnati slipped behind St. Louis and Chicago in the 1860 census and was then surpassed by Cleveland thirty years later, the myth of conservatism developed in an attempt to make sense of Cincinnati's relative decline. The myth hides much more than it reveals, however, for through the decades of relative decline Cincinnati was a *progressive* city, innovative and striving. Nowhere is this more evident than in the early twentieth-century history of its university.

The hero of the university's progressive story is Charles Dabney, who in 1904 came from the presidency of the University of Tennessee to take the same position at UC. Born and raised in rural Virginia, Dabney attended Hampden-Sydney College, near his childhood home. He earned a master's degree in chemistry at the University of Virginia and then, after trying his hand at teaching, he studied at the University of Göttingen in Germany, where he earned a PhD in chemistry. By the time he came to Cincinnati, he was well known and well regarded in higher education. He was self-assured and long-winded; he was learned and, to some, condescending. His politics were solidly progressive. Several of these traits complicated Dabney's position in Cincinnati, but he well understood the political nature of his job. He needed to gather support for the university among various constituencies—the politicians who controlled the purse strings, the residents who paid taxes and took classes, and wealthy citizens who could provide the larger gifts necessary for real institutional growth.

Charles William Dabney, circa 1909. During his sixteen years as president, Dabney transformed UC through growth and dedication to a well-articulated mission: the university should serve the city. This portrait appeared in the 1909 *Cincinnatian*. *C.U. Collection, Archives & Rare Books Library, University of Cincinnati.*

To each of these constituencies Dabney sold the university in practical terms: UC deserved support because of the services it provided to the city. In 1905, just a year after his arrival, Dabney compared UC to two of the oldest and most highly regarded universities of Europe, Bologna and Paris, which he described as "products of urban life and thought." Now, in an era of intense urban development, Dabney argued that universities needed to reconnect to their urban missions. "The problems of municipal engineering and architecture, and municipal sanitation and government, and especially the problems of municipal ownership and cooperative work on all lines—these are the greatest problems that face us today," he said at the ceremonial opening of the Teachers College. "They can only be solved through investigations, study, and experiment, and these experiments must be made through our municipal universities."[1] Nine years later, in a baccalaureate address, appropriately titled "A Gospel for Cincinnati," Dabney noted that the watchword for the age was service. "We are beginning to realize that the chief end of education is not to give a smattering of knowledge or even to develop intellectual power merely, but it is the formation of character, trained and habituated to think in terms of social obligations," he said. He encouraged the audience—graduates, alumni, faculty—to ask a unifying, guiding question: "What can we do for our city?"[2]

Under Dabney's leadership, the university became an engine of progressive change—this during an era that became identified by its remarkably broad political and social reforms. In the first two decades of the twentieth century, Americans expressed a growing faith in government to create policy solutions to a formidable range of social problems, from the promotion of human health to the improvement of the environment. At the same time, an increasingly active and powerful middle class asserted the value of professional and technical experts: physicians, engineers, and lawyers, especially. Each of these groups of experts, and many others, helped improve and implement government policies. Not surprisingly, universities were well positioned to claim special authority in training and employing experts and, in Dabney's view, lending the expertise of their faculty directly to their communities. In other words, the era's search for order broadened the role of the university.[3]

In just this way, the rising stock of expertise within American culture led to a similar rise in the value of universities, which began to lose their reputation as elite institutions, useful only for the cultivation of high culture and the conveyance of esoteric knowledge. Part of this process involved the professionalization of disciplines inside the academy, many of which created their own associations, such as the American Historical Association (1884), the American Economic Association (1885), the American Political Science Association (1903), and the American Sociological Association (1905). The creation of these and many other associations marked an important step in setting academic standards within disciplines. They established journals and held conferences, both of which helped trace the ever-evolving state of the art in knowledge, theory, and methods. While associations played a critical role in the furtherance of research, they also helped harden what critics would eventually call disciplinary "silos," which diminished the contact among the various disciplines and with the general public. In other words, the process of developing expertise created countervailing forces—one that elevated the social stature of universities and another that set them on a course that would keep them aloof from society.

University professors may have divided into increasingly distinct disciplines, but they also united into their own association, the American Association of University Professors (AAUP), in 1915. The AAUP began the process of codifying tenure and academic freedom, creating language that institutions around the nation would accept and adopt. Academic freedom—the full freedom to research and publish results, as well as independence in the classroom—became a central tenet of American higher education, and from the very beginning it was coupled with the assertion that after a probationary period, professors should be able to acquire permanent tenure in their positions, subject to removal only for adequate cause.[4] These two principles—academic freedom and the sanctity of tenure—have been at the core of faculty conceptions of higher education ever since, and they cannot be ignored in any recounting of the changing nature of a university.

All of these trends had deep implications for UC, as more people sought out college degrees in an effort to acquire expertise in any number of fields. The evolving demographics of the student body revealed the university's success in creating an institution that well served the city. Of the 1,286 students who returned a questionnaire in 1912, nearly 72 percent were legal residents of Cincinnati and another 12 percent came from the area. Only 21 percent had a parent who went to college. Twenty-two percent of the students came from "fatherless" families, and more than half were working regularly to help support themselves while they went to school. Most said they couldn't afford to go away to college. Looking at the data, Dabney concluded that while most of UC's students came from large families with modest income, "the municipal university is appreciated by all classes of the community. The moderately well-to-do, and even the wealthy send their children to the University."[5] Dabney also praised the character of UC's students. "There is a big difference, in the first place, between the boy who is sent and the one who goes, and there is a greater difference between the atmosphere of one of these Eastern cloistered colleges where young men spend their fathers' money and have a good time, and the Western college where they spend their own money and time in preparing for their life's work."[6]

UC grew in size and complexity to meet student demand. Indeed, the institutional expansion was remarkable. Under Dabney's leadership, the university created an Engineering College in 1904 and a Teacher's College a year later. The Graduate College was born in 1905, too. When the Miami Medical College joined UC in 1909, the awkwardly named Ohio-Miami Medical College of UC offered classes in the original university building on the old McMicken property. In 1912, the university organized its College of Commerce, where it taught accounting and business principles. At first those courses were offered only in the late afternoon and evening so as to cater to working men and women. In 1916, the university absorbed the School of Nursing and Health, which had resided at the city's General Hospital. In addition to a three-year nursing degree, UC began offering a five-year BS for students concentrating in nursing.[7]

This was not growth for growth's sake, but purposeful growth for the benefit of the city. From Dabney's perspective expansion was part of a sacred mission, to serve his nation by serving his community. As he wrote to Henry S. Pritchett, president of the Carnegie Foundation for Support of Education, with whom he had a long correspondence, "A great city cannot have a system of education without a college to train teachers and leaders in all lines. I believe that the university is thus the surest preventative of that wild socialism that threatens us."[8] For Dabney, there could be no greater mission for an institution.

❧ A Source of Friction and Unpleasantness

In the late 1800s, citizens of Cincinnati had not yet settled some fundamental questions about what the university should be. The most powerful constituencies—business leaders, politicians, and the faculty—all had their own opinions about whom the university should serve and how it should serve them. The lack of clarity in the institution's mission, a lack of consensus about its future development, had surely contributed to the slow growth of the university's first two decades, and the uncertainty was not assuaged by a series of less-than-ideal leaders. The lack of agreement about the university's mission also ensured that the presidency of Howard Ayers would be a difficult one. Ayers came to Cincinnati in 1899 with the primary goal of strengthening the faculty, guided by the idea that professors should be reputable researchers as well as teachers. Unfortunately, Ayers made changes in a rash and clumsy fashion. Shortly after his arrival he asked for the resignations of most of the faculty. One of those whom Ayers intended to keep, the well-regarded historian Philip Van Ness Myers, resigned in protest and in public, his open letter to the board claiming that he could not work with Ayers. "Believe me, men of the Board, a great university cannot be built upon a foundation of inhumanity, unrighteousness, and injustice," Myers wrote. Several members of the Board of Directors began to question whether the ends justified Ayers's means.[9]

Ayers came to Cincinnati with the goal of building a modern research university. While his efforts brought controversy, they also brought new professors with strong reputations, some of whom became long-time leaders at the university. Among them was Frederick Hicks, who arrived in 1900 to lead the newly created Department of Economics. Hicks later served as the president of the university.[10] Also joining the faculty: Louis T. More, a physicist who went on to be dean of the College of Liberal Arts (and brother-in-law to President William Howard Taft); Michael Guyer, a prominent biologist who served as that department's head for many years; Harris Hancock, a professor of mathematics trained at the University of Berlin; and Max Poll, a professor in Germanic literature who had previously taught at Harvard. Although Ayers almost instantly stirred enough opposition to threaten his presidency, he left UC well positioned for growth. Its Burnet Woods Campus gave it room to grow, and its new buildings had up-to-date features. Now, with a respected faculty, UC could begin to make a claim to regional significance.

Although Ayers worked to assemble an elite faculty, he hoped to attract a broad student body. He recognized that his institution's urban location provided special opportunities. Ayers wanted UC to extend its reach to "persons who have finished their school course, but desire to make further intellectual advancement." To reach these students, Ayers hoped to create self-supporting centers for "people who are too busy to go to college, or for other reasons find it inconvenient or impossible to enter as regular students."[11] In this way, Ayers anticipated extending the reach of the university, providing intellectual growth for a wide variety of citizens. Serving a range of people with a range of expectations would become a hallmark of urban institutions like UC.

The university also needed full-time students, obviously, and so it needed local high schools that could adequately prepare students for higher education. Because UC was free to city residents, higher education could be within financial reach of many Cincinnatians, but it also had to be within intellectual reach. The university pressured high schools to provide a rigorous college-prep curriculum, even offering to give "accreditation" to schools that met the standards. By early 1900, the university had accredited nearly two hundred schools in the region, from which graduates could enter without examination. This arrangement had mutual benefits. As Ayers explained, "On one hand, the University will receive recognition and support from the people represented by these schools, while on the other hand, the schools will receive stimulus and incentive to higher educational ideals and more thorough work in their educational institutions." Ayers labeled this incentive "extension work in the broadest and truest sense," since the influence of the university would be felt down the educational structure.[12]

Ayers was the first strong leader of the university, too strong in some people's estimation. It wasn't just that Ayers made enemies—anyone with authority does—but he made the wrong enemies. Among those who led the movement against Ayers was Henry M. Curtis, pastor of the Mount Auburn Presbyterian Church. Curtis found the president gruff, profane, and possibly irreligious. Ayers had been "a source of friction and unpleasantness ever since he became connected with our university some four years ago," Curtis wrote in 1903.[13] That spring Mayor Julius Fleischmann appointed Curtis to the Board of Directors, along with six other new members. Ayers's days were numbered. Curtis assumed the chair of the board's Academic Committee, and he quickly began working toward Ayers's removal and the recruitment of his replacement—awkwardly pursuing both at the same time.

Curtis approached Charles Dabney, who was both progressive and deeply religious. This second quality may have been most attractive to Curtis, and it may have most distinguished him from Ayers, for although Dabney would also have trouble with the Board of Directors, he could seek comfort and support from his church—Curtis's Mount Auburn Presbyterian Church, where Dabney eventually served as an elder.[14]

Not surprisingly, Dabney had concerns about moving to Cincinnati. He was well aware of the trials and tribulations surrounding Ayers. As Dabney surmised, "He has managed to get all of the wealthy people, the society people, the preachers, and almost all of the people of Cincinnati in fact, down upon him, and from the beginning had great difficulty with his Trustees."[15]

The fate of Ayers left Dabney uncertain about the position, but he must also have wondered if being in Cincinnati would allow him to pursue his mission. With academic interests in soil and fertilizers, Dabney's early work concerned uplifting average farmers through improved agricultural output. His later work—still focused on uplift—concerned the improvement of education in the South. At

85

Tennessee Dabney had already made great strides toward improving southern education, especially through the creation of the Summer School of the South, which, beginning in 1902, brought teachers to Knoxville for training, and his post in Knoxville left him well situated to make further strides for the region.

Before agreeing to take the UC position, Dabney consulted respected colleagues around the country, including Harvard President Charles W. Eliot, who advised Dabney to stay put in Tennessee. "I am sure that the position of President of the University of Cincinnati is insecure and, on other accounts, undesirable. The University has been unsuccessful because [it is] poor and mismanaged. Its resources are inadequate, and its government is badly constructed." Eliot admitted that Ayers was a "somewhat rough man, who has little tact and no charm of manner or address, but he is intelligent, courageous, and honest, and thoroughly deserved the support of his Board of Trustees." Here, in the end, is why Eliot didn't recommend the move: the meddling board.[16]

Eliot was not alone in his concern about the institution itself, though. Cyrus Northrop, president of the University of Minnesota, wrote flatly, "I do not think the University of Cincinnati is likely to become as large as you are."[17] Dabney replied to Northrop that he saw an opportunity "to build on the banks of the Ohio a great university." Although Dabney may have underestimated the distance from the banks of the Ohio to the university, he clearly understood Cincinnati's regional position. "With great universities to the east, north, and west of it, Cincinnati must find its chief field in Kentucky and the South and Southwest," he wrote to Northrop. To Dabney, building up the University of Cincinnati was the next best thing to building a great university in the South, and perhaps more easily done.[18] Eliot was not so sure. When he heard that Dabney had decided to take the job, he wrote a short note: "I hope your view of the present situation at the University of Cincinnati will turn out to be the true one; but the history of the University gives a distant observer no right to expect so great a reform."[19]

Dabney arrived on campus in 1904 convinced of the potential of the university or at least of his potential to change it. "I find that they are already much impressed with the idea of making an institution which will be largely attended by Southern students," he wrote to Walter Page, a prominent New York publisher with strong roots in North Carolina.[20] Over time, however, Dabney came to recognize that although Cincinnati looked south for commercial markets, it did so largely through northern eyes. Dabney found Cincinnati too German, too Catholic, and too Republican for his tastes, and despite his many accomplishments—and there were many—his tenure was a rocky one.

❦ A People's University on a Municipal Foundation

In his inaugural address in the fall of 1904, Dabney made clear his faith in God and the people. "Education is the preparation of the fully developed free man for service in his environment," he said. "It is the duty of the democracy to train its citizens to vote intelligently and to work honestly, and therefore the modern state or city must provide public schools for its children." God made every child, and so, Dabney believed, every child deserved an education. He argued that "education should include all subjects that fit men for better living and better serving."[21] Indeed, as Dabney articulated at the graduation ceremony two years later, the public nature of UC and the complexity of the city forced the creation of an ever-larger, more inclusive institution. "The University of the democracy," as he called UC, "exists by the people, of the people, and for the people. It must, therefore, be inclusive of all subjects, all methods, all men," he said; "it recognizes no classes among its students. All knowledge should be accessible to all people," he continued. "The university is, thus, the final expression of democracy; it stands for the democracy of knowledge."[22]

Dabney got to work right away, but building the university would take money. In 1906, the Board of Directors asked the citizens of the city to give more support, to increase taxes from .3 mills to .5 mills. Since the state limited the taxes that cities could levy for education, including colleges, UC lobbied the state to raise the cap. "The University of Cincinnati belongs to the people of this great and progressive City," chairman of the board Frank Jones wrote to Hamilton County delegates to the Ohio Assembly. "It deserves encouragement and liberal support and we are confident the increase in the levy we seek in its behalf will meet with public approval."[23] Tax support did increase, although the university was soon asking for even more, as rapid growth required greater investment.

Dabney envisioned an extensive building program: a new engineering building, a new medical college, a gymnasium, and a dormitory. He asked the Board of Directors to support a $1 million bond issue, which would also require the approval of city council. Board member George Guckenberger questioned the figure, claiming that taxpayers had other priorities. The *Enquirer* quoted the skeptical Guckenberger: "As a taxpayer, as a banker and a bond buyer, and as a member of this board, I do not think it is proper policy for you to go into an investment that

87

is, at best, based upon a dream, while the balance of the city is clamoring for a new sewer system, which is a thousand times more important, and a new hospital, that is delayed because the city has not the money to go ahead with it." Others on the board rose to defend the proposal, including Robert W. Stewart, who declared education to be the "salvation of all our evils," and James J. Hooker, who reminded the board that ongoing investments in elementary and high schools would soon prepare even more Cincinnatians for college.[24]

The university never got the large bond issue to expand rapidly, and instead continued to rely on large gifts from wealthy donors and smaller bonds from the city. But every time the university asked for increased public investment, controversy revived, including in 1913, when Dabney sought the issuance of more bonds. Council gave final approval without allowing a citizen vote, which only heightened the controversy. "The men who send their sons and daughters to that institution can well afford to pay for their education, and there is no reason why the public at large should be called upon to share in this burden," declared Herman Dierkes, an insurance salesman who also noted how small the student body was in comparison to the number of people who would be forced to pay back the bonds. No doubt this was a widely shared sentiment, but the university's survey of its students, produced the year before to help convince residents of UC's value, revealed that men like Dierkes significantly overstated the wealth of students' families.[25]

Dabney also pursued other avenues of funding. In the hope of securing a significant investment from the Carnegie Foundation for the Advancement of Teaching, Dabney carried on an extensive correspondence with Henry S. Pritchett, the former president of MIT who had served the same role for the foundation since 1906. Dabney worked to secure a grant to create the "Carnegie College of Engineering of the University of Cincinnati."[26] In a series of letters, Dabney sold his vision for the university and articulated the great need for further support. "I am trying to build a people's university on a municipal foundation," he told Pritchett. "The Democracy must educate itself in university, as well as in elementary school. This is the American idea, so successfully illustrated by our state universities, and I am trying to show that our great cities can build and conduct universities, as well as common schools," he wrote. He pressed Pritchett to invest in democratic institutions, not just elite schools, and he boasted, "Three-fourths of our students would never get to college, if this institution did not exist."[27] Unfortunately, a large investment from the Carnegie Foundation never came.

While Dabney's vision remained clear, he could not help but describe his deep frustrations with the Board of Directors. Writing to Francis Peabody, a distinguished professor at Harvard Divinity School, Dabney admitted that most of the board were good, college men, "but a minority are self-seeking fellows, appointed because of their service to some faction in city politics, uneducated men, manufacturers and merchants, who measure everything by commercial standards."[28] Dabney tired of explaining the value of higher education to men like Frederick Geier, of Cincinnati Milling Machine, Ernest DuBrul, manufacturer of cigar molds, and George Guckenberger, a banker. He thought they simply didn't understand either the importance of higher education or the need for society to pay for its expansion. His frustrations had a political component, too. Since Boss George Cox's Republican machine controlled the city, and the city appointed members to the board, Dabney expressed concerns about corruption. Primarily, however, he was concerned about the individuals on the board, rather than the system that put them there. "The trouble in the Board, of course, is that it is made up of men whose ideas of administering a university are those derived from stock-yards, lumber mills, and factories," he wrote to Pritchett in 1911, at a moment when it looked like the board would force him out so that the beloved and admired Herman Schneider, dean of the Engineering College, could take his place.[29]

Conflict with factions within Cincinnati kept Dabney focused on the municipal mission of his institution. He understood that UC was "a university *of* the city," rather than merely *in* the city. He argued that UC could serve as the brain of the municipal body. "When this relation is fully realized and established, boundless possibilities for service appear," he wrote in a leading national magazine. The expansion of the university had created "fresh obligation to serve the people, an obligation the University is seeking to discharge by a broad, liberal policy of co-operation with all the educational, social, and industrial interests of Cincinnati."[30] In his annual report for 1913, titled "Service of the University to the City and Its Institutions," Dabney remarked on the difficulty of selling the university to the public, claiming that "one of the most difficult things we have to do is to get the people of Cincinnati to understand what the University is and what it is actually doing for them." And, despite many attempts at reaching the public, "it still remains true that the peculiar characteristics of the University are better understood and appreciated away from Cincinnati than at home."[31]

❧ The University Will Go Radiating Out

Part of the purpose for improving the university's facilities and its faculty was to attract more students, but UC didn't just wait for them to come to campus. Even before Dabney's arrival on campus, faculty had been working on strategies to educate more students, even if it meant meeting with students off campus or setting up evening or Saturday courses to cater to full-time workers. The university's first attempt at what was known as "University Extension" began in 1890. It met with such success that UC expanded the program significantly the next year. William O. Sproull, professor of Latin and Arabic, led the effort, and he represented UC at the first national conference on University Extension later that year. Extension courses were open to anyone who could do the work, but they were intended for mature students, more than half of whom in the early years were schoolteachers. Sproull taught Latin on Saturday mornings, and he valued teaching dedicated students who had given up part of their weekend. "It acts as a mental stimulant with only good effects," he wrote of the experience. In this way, Sproull found extension work edifying for students *and* energizing for faculty.[32]

Of course the real benefit of extension was to allow citizens who entered the workforce right after high school to continue their education while maintaining their full-time jobs. Sproull thought this arrangement might also increase graduation rates, noting that a large percentage of students who started college nationwide failed to graduate, and he predicted that "the time will come when the doors of many [urban universities] will be open to students, not only the year round by day, but also the year round by night."[33] The *Times-Star* gushed at the university's newfound ability to offer instruction to working-class citizens, concluding, "In this way the influence of the University will go radiating out through the community."[34]

During the third year of extension work over two hundred students attended lectures regularly. Topics ranged from Latin and Greek to French literature, biology, and electricity.[35] While some of the courses met in the university building on Saturday mornings, others met at public buildings around the city, such as Edward M. Brown's course on Shakespeare, attended by an average of seventy-five people in East Walnut Hills. Jermain Porter, director of the observatory and professor of astronomy, taught a course at Lane Seminary in Walnut Hills. Although professors often volunteered their time to teach these courses, some received compensation, since students paid a small fee. (Students paid $2 to take the Shakespeare lecture series.) Not surprisingly, under Dabney's leadership the extension program continued to expand. By 1913, the university was holding classes at the Walnut Hills Branch Library, the Avondale Public School, the Covington Public Library, Newport High School, and other places around the city.[36]

The university tried to extend well beyond the local community—at least once even taking education on the road, on a tour through Tennessee and Georgia—but most extension work took place in the neighborhoods surrounding the university and served populations that were otherwise unlikely to seek a college degree. Perhaps the most important location for extension work was the Social Settlement, created in 1895 as part of the national settlement house movement. In Cincinnati, the movement gathered momentum in the spring of 1894, when famed Chicago reformer Jane Addams came to Cincinnati to deliver two addresses. William Sproull, who had by this point become dean of the university, introduced Addams at the College of Music's Odeon auditorium, where she spoke to a crowd composed largely of teachers. Addams described the history of settlement houses, reaching back to London and to her own Hull-House, then five years old and already engaged in a variety of work, including offering kindergarten classes and evening classes for older residents of the neighborhood. Hull-House also hosted college extension courses. Two weeks later, Addams came back to town to benefit the fledgling Cincinnati Social Settlement. This time she spoke at Sinton Hall, invited by the College Club and introduced by Philip Myers, who became the guiding force behind Cincinnati's effort.[37]

As UC's yearbook, *The Cincinnatian*, reported in 1895, Addams's visit was inspirational. "Touched by the rehearsal of her experience in this new form of University work, and stimulated by the contact with her whole-souled personality, many came to feel that 'higher education,' without such outlet and aim as Miss Addams had found, was only a kind of 'higher selfishness.'" The College Club became intimately engaged in the social settlement movement, finding a house at 88 East Third Street and making it ready for occupancy. Although some students moved into the home, the yearbook noted that the effort would be greatly improved if someone working toward a graduate degree in social science moved in. "To procure such service for the Settlement, as well as to open its advantages to a person fitted to enjoy them, the most practical method has seemed to be the endowment of scholarships by those colleges situated so near Cincinnati as to take a vital interest in her Settlement work," the yearbook lobbied, noting that such a plan had already been implemented at the Indiana University and Marietta College.[38] Among the faculty who spoke at the settlement house was Myers, who had replaced Sproull as dean of the university. He taught popular extension courses on eastern civilization in wide-ranging lectures on human history.[39]

UC's engagement in the settlement house movement took another leap forward in 1899, when students and alumni decided to form a new settlement house under the name University Settlement Association. The next year it opened in an eighteen-room house on the corner of Plum and Liberty in Over-the-Rhine, by then a very crowded neighborhood with few recreational amenities. The University Settlement was independent, with its own board, but the connections to UC were extensive. The settlement board included wealthy men such as J. G. Schmidlapp and Julius Fleischmann, but also university employees such as Dabney and Annie Laws, a founder of the Cincinnati Woman's Club and a leader in the kindergarten movement.[40]

The settlement created a library, where neighborhood children could read with tutors. It organized a kindergarten, and started a penny savings bank. A Young Woman's Club offered a variety of activities and instruction at the house, ranging from Monday night's classes on home economics—discussing how to cook for the sick, the nutritional values of foods, the chemistry of cleaning, and the like—to Saturday's class on elocution. Broadly stated, the goal of the settlement house was acculturation, steeping immigrants in American middle-class values. The year after Dabney arrived, the university described its mission "in a district where the population is almost entirely foreign." The settlement had "the opportunity of giving to these Americans their ideals of American citizenship," the report said. "In its library, its debating-clubs, where people of all classes meet on equal ground, and its social evenings, it has the opportunity to show, in a practical way, that 'plain living and high thinking' is the goal of the true American."[41] As with settlement houses around the country, most of the volunteers in Cincinnati were women, although some evening classes were taught by UC students, both male and female, who passed on what they learned at the university. Each evening, from 5:00 to 6:00, the house hosted live music, both instrumental and vocal, to which all in the neighborhood were invited.[42]

The University Settlement closed in 1911, after supporters determined that it duplicated the work of other institutions, but many of the efforts to extend the university's usefulness resulted in lasting structural changes. Perhaps this is most evident in the offering of evening classes, which expanded significantly just after the settlement house closed. In the fall of the next year, the College of Liberal Arts offered a variety of evening courses, including English composition, Latin, German, European and American history, philosophy, and psychology. The School of Commerce offered courses in accounting, banking, and commercial law, among others. The evening courses were free to all residents of Cincinnati and "to all teachers who, although non-residents, are engaged in teaching in the public schools of the city." (Students did have to pay library and lab fees.) The city appropriated $6,000 to get the classes going, and the university expected only $1,000 in tuition income from nonresident students, who paid by the credit hour. Demand for some of the classes was strong. Nearly two hundred signed up for English composition and over one hundred for English literature, psychology, and economics. Evening classes were especially attractive to women, who outnumbered enrolled men in 1914. These numbers necessitated the hiring of additional instructors, most of whom were regular faculty who taught additional classes in the evening for extra pay.[43]

The next spring, the *Enquirer* could report, "Soldiers, elevator operators, carpenters, day laborers, stenographers, merchants and collectors—such are some of the occupations of the 534 students that attend night classes of the University of Cincinnati." The *Enquirer* reported on the faculty study of the student body at length. Evening classes were part of a greater trend at the university that "has democratized the higher and professional education to an extent never done before," according to the study. Most day students came from low-income families, but the faculty study saved its highest praise for evening students, who exhibited "an earnestness of purpose" and an industriousness that carried over from their day jobs into their evening studies.[44]

❧ Learn Practice Where the Thing Is Practiced

Dabney may have been the primary architect of the university's broad outreach during the Progressive Era, but another man was responsible for its most lasting and influential component. Herman Schneider was raised in the anthracite region of eastern Pennsylvania. He graduated from Lehigh University, and after practicing for several years as an engineer, he returned to his alma mater to serve as an instructor in engineering. According to Schneider, one day he was walking through Bethlehem, listening to the blast furnaces of the massive steel mill near the university. The proximity of factory and university—combined with his experience in both industry and instruction—led him to think of the utility and feasibility of linking instruction in theory and practice by sending students into the workplace periodically during their education. As Schneider articulated years later, "Practice can be learned only where the thing is practiced." This was the origin of what became known as the cooperative system, in which engineers' regular course of study included stints in a variety of industries, where they would acquire practical knowledge, gain an understanding of the rigors of the shop floor, and, importantly, make money.[45]

As the idea formed more fully in his mind, Schneider tried to convince Lehigh to adopt this innovative system, but to no avail. In 1903, Schneider took a position at the University of Cincinnati, where at first he also could not convince the administration to adopt a comprehensive training regimen that alternated theory and practice. While he lobbied his colleagues, Schneider discussed his idea with business leaders, trying to gather support for the idea and line up industry partners who would train students once the system was in place. Cincinnati possessed a diverse economy, with dozens of suitable large and midsized firms, most of which occupied an industrial zone that nearly surrounded the university, running from the West End, north through Camp Washington and Northside, and then running east through St. Bernard, Norwood, and Oakley. Schneider soon gained the support of Ernest DuBrul and Frederick Geier, both of whom were on the Board of Directors at the time.[46]

Not until Dabney arrived in Cincinnati did Schneider break through. With the new president's support, UC's cooperative program in engineering, the first in the world, began in 1906. Twenty-eight students entered under the cooperative course, while 107 students entered the traditional program. Admission to the cooperative program was competitive, with 800 inquiries and applications coming in just the second year, but capacity expanded slowly, and the college had room for only 44 new students. In 1916, after ten years of trial, adjustment, and growth, 473 students entered the College of Engineering's cooperative program, while just 27 entered the traditional course. Shortly after World War I, the traditional course was discontinued and all students seeking an engineering degree at UC entered a cooperative program. In 1920, the first female co-op students arrived on campus. (This was also the first year most American women could exercise the right to vote.) Despite this significant advancement, the opening of engineering fields to women would be a very, very slow process.[47]

Although at the very beginning Schneider had difficulty developing relationships with Cincinnati firms with which he could place students, within a decade

(Top) Men's Co-op Class, 1906; (Above) Women's Co-Op Class, circa 1921. UC revolutionized higher education in engineering with the creation of the world's first cooperative education program. In 1920 Engineering admitted its first class of women to the program, although finding appropriate co-op positions remained a struggle for them. *Photograph files, Archives & Rare Books Library, University of Cincinnati.*

over one hundred companies were participating. By the mid-1920s more than two hundred firms were taking on students. Most of these employers were in Ohio—more than half in Cincinnati itself—but there were participating firms in all the surrounding states and Illinois. Students worked in the machine tool industry, in electrical manufacturing, for railroads, and in a remarkable range of other industries. By then the cooperative system had spread at UC, first to commerce, which added a cooperative program in 1920, and then to architecture two years later. The cooperative system had also spread beyond UC, as other institutions realized its advantages. First Northeastern adopted a co-op program in 1909, and soon thereafter so too did the University of Pittsburgh and Georgia Tech, among others. Higher education, particularly in engineering and business, was forever altered.

The cooperative program served its students well, preparing them for a productive life in industry, but the region's companies also significantly benefited. Gradually cooperative programs replaced the failing apprentice system, in which firms trained their own workers. The expense of such training had grown considerably in recent decades, given the level of education needed to properly prepare workers for fields like electrical engineering. Dabney understood the role the new College of Engineering could play in the local economy, even before the implementation of the cooperative program. He reported in 1905, "Probably nothing would do more to promote the development of the manufactures of the city than a great technical institute, which furnished facilities for scientific investigation and engineering testing, as well as the means of training great numbers of young men." Dabney envisioned the College of Engineering as an engine of economic growth in Cincinnati. "When we send our sons abroad to be educated we lose the majority of them from our home industries. The experience of other cities has been that nothing tends to diversify the manufactures of a city or to improve the existing industries like a great institute of technology."[48]

Of course, UC also benefited from this arrangement, in that it could now give its students practical training, including real experience with machinery, without having to invest in a great variety of workshops, which of course were ever-changing and expensive to create, maintain, and update. Schneider, who argued that "the funds of a university should be used for brains, and not for machines," thought one of the greatest advantages of the cooperative system was that it allowed "the elimination of the so-called 'practice shops' from the university." Instead, the university could invest in research laboratories, where real-life problems—some of them brought back into the lab by students who had been in the workplace—could be worked out for industry as a whole. In sum, Schneider devised and developed a symbiotic relationship that fed Cincinnati's industrial growth and solidified its university's utility.[49]

As much as Schneider's course of study blended theory and practice, he was clear about the separate missions of university and business. "It should be understood very clearly that the function of the school in this work is to teach the science and the art and the cultural material underlying the profession, and it is the function of the outside agencies to teach what we call the 'practice' of that profession." Schneider's broad language—"profession"—reflects his thinking of the wide applicability of the co-operative model.[50] He understood the value of learning the rigors of hard physical labor, even as students develop rigorous minds. For the deeply philosophical Schneider, part of the goal of any education was building character. The work was instructive, for what one learned about the tasks at hand, but also because of what one learned about oneself. "It is a good thing for a man to sweat his way toward the Truth."[51]

❧ In the Interest of the Patients, Science, and the City

While Herman Schneider was remaking engineering education, so too was Christian R. Holmes reconfiguring the city's health care and medical education system. After emigrating from Denmark as a young man, Holmes graduated from Miami Medical College in 1886. He interned at the City Hospital and then launched a very successful private practice, successful not least because it brought him into contact with and then marriage to one of his patients, Bettie Fleischmann. She was the daughter of Charles Fleischmann, a prominent and very wealthy Cincinnatian, and sister to Julius, who in 1900 became mayor and an active supporter of building a new general hospital. The hospital board appointed Holmes to chair a committee that would investigate where and how this hospital would be built. Holmes also used his connections (and charm) to win substantial donations to support the new hospital, including from Mary Emery.[52]

In 1903, Mayor Fleischmann hired Charles F. Walthers, from the US Engineers Office, to study a number of the sites that might be suitable for a new city hospital. Fleischmann was fully supportive of moving the hospital out of the West End, where it shared the neighborhood with breweries, stables, and other unhealthful influences. Walthers seemed intent on highlighting non-engineering concerns, including population density. He determined that putting the hospital in Inwood Park "cannot be considered seriously, as it is practically in the smoke and filth of the city even now." (Ironically, Christ Hospital would move to Mount Auburn, just above Inwood Park, the very next year.) Walthers leaned on public opinion, at least as he had gauged it, to make his final determination. "If the taxpayers had a choice in the matter," he concluded, "they would ring out emphatically 'Give us Burnet Woods' because it is a good and lasting investment, if the sick and dying were permitted to speak, they would gasp forth in feeble voice 'The Park, a breathing space,' and all of the people interested in the welfare of our University must join in the chorus 'The hospital close to our institute will give our medical department and indirectly all others such an impetus that in few years we could boast of one of the finest Universities on the globe.'"[53] Not exactly an engineering opinion, but not a bad idea.

As the conversation moved forward, a consensus developed around some fundamental principles. The hospital should be designed following the most modern doctrine, which linked healthfulness to cleanliness, sunshine, and fresh air. Once established, the hospital should gain a neighbor—the medical school. And, perhaps most important, the new hospital should be "removed from the noise and grime of the downtown district to a suitable location in the suburbs," as Holmes summarized later.[54] Right away Holmes's committee began inquiring about property in Corryville along Burnet Avenue near the Altenheim, the German home for aged men built in 1891. Other potential locations included one along Vine Street near the top of the hill at McMillan Avenue, or another near Burnet Woods and the university, the location favored by Walthers.

In typical Progressive Era fashion, Holmes turned himself into an expert, studying modern hospitals to determine the best arrangements. Holmes's research included touring hospitals in Germany, where he had begun his education. Holmes visited several cities in Germany, as well as Vienna, Paris, and London, to collect the most up-to-date ideas from the most up-to-date facilities in Europe. He was most impressed by Eppendorf Hospital in Hamburg, Germany, which featured several one-story buildings—an arrangement that greatly improved patient access to light and air. "Germany undoubtedly has the finest hospitals in the world," Holmes concluded, praising their hygienic conditions and management. Holmes learned so much from his study of modern hospitals that he spoke and published on the topic. Before an audience in Toronto he expounded on his developing theory of hospital construction: "Plenty of sunlight and pure air, various kinds of baths, health gymnastics, scientific feeding, and the best of nursing are often of much greater importance than medicines, and yet in America these modern and important adjuncts are shamefully ignored in many of our great hospitals."[55]

Holmes's ideas on hospital construction were informed not just by developments in Europe, but by the changing nature of cities, as well. "Rapid transit has entirely changed former ideas of the best location for a hospital," Holmes wrote. "It has brought the suburb, with its grass and trees and pleasant open spaces, within a few minutes' travel of the crowded city's centers of commercial and industrial activity. This allows the placing of hospitals in the most salubrious situation and does not bind them of necessity, as formerly, to nearness to the residences or work places of the hospital population."[56] As access to less dense, more "salubrious" neighborhoods improved, the contrasts with the basin became starker. Citizens got sick in the city; patients recovered in the suburbs.

Consideration of the Calhoun site, just south of the park and immediately adjacent to the university, may have been largely an endeavor to lower the price on the property near the Altenheim, which did, in fact, occur. In 1903, Holmes began assembling land between Burnet and Eden Avenues. The land was hilly, and so unevenly occupied. A total of eighteen homes were demolished. By the time the hospital was dedicated in 1915, the city had purchased sixty-five acres, following Holmes's caveat that the city should acquire enough space for expansion, "by securing enough ground to accommodate all the buildings needed for a hundred years." In addition, the extra land would serve as a buffer against undesirable neighbors and provide a park for convalescents, or perhaps provide a spot for an educational facility for tubercular children. As Holmes noted, the extra land could be used "for any purpose in the future that will promote the health and happiness of our citizens."[57]

Construction of the hospital began with the contagious wards, since those were the most inadequate downtown. Indeed, the entire design reflected the medical concerns and scientific understanding at the time. Both the removal of the hospital from the center of town and the scattered nature of the buildings reveal a predominant concern about infectious disease. The next building constructed was the Pathological Building, "with its numerous laboratories, museum, chapel, morgue, etc." This building would be, Holmes wrote, "mainly devoted to teaching and research work in the interest of the patients, science and the City."[58]

One might reflect back on Daniel Drake's complaints about the old Commercial Hospital—that it was too far from the public landing to serve accident victims well. Now, seventy years later, the removal of the hospital to Corryville reflected the most urgent medical needs of the city—the treatment of infectious diseases, not emergency care. The location also reflected the dual purpose of the municipal hospital. As Holmes noted, "The first object of a public hospital is the treatment of the sick poor." But there was a second purpose: "the training of physicians and nurses to administer to the wants of the sick in the community at large." In the fall of 1913, Holmes became dean of what was by then the city's only medical college, ensuring that the school would leave the ill-suited old university building and follow the hospital out to Corryville and into a new facility.[59]

Over President's Day weekend in 1915, perhaps 70,000 citizens filed through the new hospital buildings to see what their tax money had built. A small, invited crowd gathered for the dedication ceremony, held in the new amphitheater in the operating pavilion. At the dedication, Holmes presented Mayor Frederick Spiegel

General Hospital, circa 1931. The construction of the hospital campus followed the design artic-ulated by Christian R. Holmes, with modest-sized buildings spread over a large area to maximize exposure to sunlight and fresh air. This aerial photo shows the administration building facing Burnet Avenue at the bottom and the Medical College building in the upper right. The contagious wards sit across Eden Avenue from the college building. Children's Hospital sits to the far right. *Photograph files, Archives & Rare Books Library, University of Cincinnati.*

keys to the new hospital. "May they only be emblems of security," he said. "Let us hope the doors of this hospital will stand wide open through the coming century, welcoming all, whether sick in body or mind, who may seek shelter within its spacious portals, to receive relief, sympathy and aid at the hands of the skilled physicians, nurses, and social service workers who will minister here." Upon accepting the keys, Mayor Spiegel placed the new hospital alongside other progressive endeavors in the city. "We are a generous people. We are progressive." Those who wish to pay for services can, he said. "But those who cannot pay are equally welcome. As citizens, they have a right to hospital service without question of right."[60] The Republican mayor then touted the regulation of dairies, butcher shops, bakeries, and barbershops, all of them related to the day's events because they worked toward better public health.

The dedication also featured a speech by Dabney's friend and correspondent, Henry Pritchett, president of the Carnegie Foundation. Looking ahead to the construction of the new medical school on adjoining property, Pritchett spoke about "Democracy and Medical Education," and in general terms reflected on the value of improved medical facilities to any community. "That an American city is ready to devote such a sum for this purpose renews one's faith in our American democracy," he said, although he added, fully aware of Dabney's troubles with local politicians, "Your university has launched bravely forth upon the sea of politics." He expounded on the value of having medical students in the hospital, which he said would keep doctors on their toes. "Here education and science have joined hands with politics to serve the people and the whole people of Cincinnati; and the question is squarely up to politics as to whether it can keep step with science and education."[61]

A Useful University

Since the city owned and operated UC, it isn't surprising that university employees sought to make themselves useful to other departments of the municipal government, which itself was expanding to meet reformers' demands. At the height of the Progressive Era, in the early 1910s, the blending of education and service to the city was remarkably complete. Seemingly every academic department was searching for some tangible way to participate in the great expansion of municipal services, services that were increasingly provided by well-trained civil servants. As Dabney summarized in 1913, "The modern city is becoming more and more a great educational, engineering, and sanitary institution, as well as an agency for protecting the life and property of its citizens. For the successful conduct of its various departments, expert knowledge of many kinds is therefore required."[62]

The Progressive Era witnessed so much experimentation at the municipal level that those who sought best practices needed to gather and study information from around the country. For this reason, cities began to create municipal reference libraries, where information could be collected, digested, and distributed to lawmakers and administrators. In January 1913, the University of Cincinnati became one of the first schools in the nation to help its local government create a municipal reference library. Nearly as soon as professor of political science S. Gail Lowrie had signed on as the director of the new library, the recently elected Democratic governor, James Cox, came knocking at UC to acquire his services to run a new State Legislative Reference Library. Lowrie agreed to serve the Cox administration, but he promised to return to Cincinnati after the first legislative session. Dabney granted Lowrie a leave of absence so he could organize the state library, with the larger goal of helping create a progressive administration in Columbus.[63] Lowrie did return to UC, and by early 1915 Cincinnati's Municipal Reference Library had collected 500 books and nearly 2,000 pamphlets, all conveniently held at City Hall. Perhaps most important, it had created a clippings file filled with newspaper articles from the many local papers. In addition, two political science classes used the library twice a week as a laboratory.[64]

In search of a similar practical connection, Herman Schneider met with H. M. Wait, the city's chief engineer, to discuss how engineering faculty might aid in the testing of materials purchased by the city. "Our first idea was to have the University take over the City Testing Departments," Schneider reported to the Board of Directors. "We found, however, that there were no such Departments." And so, Schneider and Wait devised a plan to create a Bureau of City Testing and Inspection at the university. Schneider deemed it "economical and efficient to place the inspection and testing of materials used by the city under the direction of the University," because his faculty could assure scientific testing, make good use of apparatus already owned by the university, and "afford an opportunity for members of the University faculty to keep in close touch with municipal problems." This last reason is telling. The Bureau of City Tests would keep his faculty attuned to the needs and problems facing the city.[65]

Both the city and the university approved the plan, and by the end of 1912 the new Bureau of City Tests had placed a laboratory at the university, where Ellery K. Files, a professor of chemistry, analyzed a wide variety of materials purchased by the city. Assisted by cooperative students, Files tested coal, for instance, a particularly important job given the wide variability in the quality of the fuel. By 1914, every carload of coal purchased by the city was sampled and analyzed, and payments were determined based on the results. The laboratory tested all cement purchased, too, and even fire hoses. Some materials were found inferior and rejected: watery creosote, high-ash coal, high-sulfur cement, paints made with gasoline. In the end, the laboratory tests saved the city considerable money by preventing the acquisition of flawed materials.[66]

In the spring of 1914, Ralph R. Caldwell, an 1899 graduate of the university and a lawyer working downtown, praised the "usefulness of Cincinnati's university" in a paper he delivered before the Literary Club. After listing services the university provided—the Municipal Reference Library and the Bureau of City Testing among them—Caldwell also noted that "individual professors are rendering public services outside of their classroom work." Faculty members were involved in an industrial survey of the region, in the effort to control coal smoke, and in conducting a health survey. Caldwell concluded that these and many other activities outside of the classroom "go far in making the University a great asset to the community."[67]

These contributions to the community notwithstanding, Caldwell emphasized that the value of the university should be measured most directly through the creation of better citizens. Immigration had risen steadily through the Progressive Era, and the arrival of millions of Italians, Poles, Russians, and other, mostly European immigrants was transforming the nation, especially its cities. Most recent immigrants spoke little English and practiced non-Protestant religions; most were Catholic, Eastern Orthodox, or Jewish. Caldwell's growing anxiety over the influences of immigration had him fearing for America's democratic traditions. "As education is primarily for the benefit of the state and not the individual, and as the perpetuation of democratic institutions depends on it, the justice of taxation for this purpose need not be argued. Privately supported institutions of learning in this country have done great work," Caldwell admitted. "It is evident, however, that the schooling of the masses cannot be left to the caprice of private philanthropy." In other words, educating and acculturating young Americans remained the primary service the university provided to the city.[68]

❧ The Cincinnati Way

In 1917, Dabney reflected on what he and the city had accomplished in a speech delivered before the University of Cincinnati Donors' Dinner. In his address, entitled "The Cincinnati Way," Dabney boasted, "No other city owns a railroad, no other city owns an observatory, no other city owns a fully organized university, completed now by a medical department having such perfect facilities for healing, teaching, and research, as are provided in our Medical College and Hospital." Encouraging the city's wealthy citizens to pitch in, as he had throughout his presidency, he said, "Let us, then, here tonight, rededicate ourselves to the service of Cincinnati." He asked residents to seek inspiration in the work of boosters who had come before—Daniel Drake, Charles McMicken, Rufus King, Nicholas Longworth, David Sinton, and Henry Hanna, among others.[69]

The following year, Rufus Smith, prominent judge and chairman of the Board of Directors, summarized the position of the university as another school year came to a close. "The question whether we shall have in Cincinnati a municipal university is no longer open for debate," he said. "The University has come to stay and it has enthusiastic support of the great majority of our people." According to Smith, that support derived from residents' understanding of the value the institution created for the community. First and foremost was education. Smith claimed "at least 75 per cent of the students would not be able to secure a higher education if they were compelled to leave Cincinnati to secure it." What's more, "The University is becoming the head of the intellectual life of the city; and is every year becoming more valuable in advancing our industrial and commercial life."[70]

Smith's assertion accurately reflected the extraordinary growth during Dabney's administration. The university enrolled just over 800 students in 1904, over 70 percent of whom came from the city. By 1919, UC had an enrollment of nearly 3,500 students, 64 percent of whom resided in the city. The smaller percentage coming from within the city undoubtedly reflected the changing nature of the metropolis, as more Cincinnatians didn't actually live in the city, but it also reflected the growing reputation of the university. In a bit of irony, then, as the reputation of the university grew around the nation, its special relationship to the city slowly began to fade. Dabney may have exaggerated somewhat when he boasted in 1919, "The University of Cincinnati is thus becoming a great national institution and is beginning to draw from a few foreign countries," but he accurately foreshadowed the day when the city's own residents would constitute a small percentage of the study body.[71]

Still, at the end of the Progressive Era UC was the quintessential municipal university. The range of services the university provided for the city was impressive. It trained a good many of the city's doctors and nurses, its engineers and teachers. Its co-op programs were designed to meet the specific needs of the region's businesses. By the 1920s, Parke Kolbe, a well-known scholar of higher education and the president of the University of Akron, declared the University of Cincinnati "the most highly developed of all the municipal universities." It had served as an inspiration and model for Kolbe's own institution, which transitioned from the private Buchtel College to a municipal university in 1913. More Americans were seeking higher education, and most of them sought it close to home. Municipal institutions were well positioned to serve the local population, with one eye on the needs of individual students, and the other on the needs of the community.[72]

Dabney left the university in 1920 at sixty-five, the board-mandated age of retirement. Dabney departed as feisty as he arrived. In explaining the timing of his retirement to Philander Claxton, US commissioner of education, Dabney noted that the board could change its rules if it so desired. But, Dabney explained, politics were at work, driven by "a combination of Germans, beer and liquor people, and Catholics, constituting pretty much one group." He even implicated Xavier University's new campus, then under development in Avondale, in the conspiracy against the municipal university. "The Catholics have bought a large piece of ground here and are going to build a college and are determined to put a stop to this University if they can," he told Claxton.[73] In commiserating with Dabney at his forced retirement, Raymond Hughes, president of Miami University, wrote, "I can easily see how some of the complex elements in the Cincinnati municipal life could make it extremely difficult to administer your job and at the same time maintain the principles for which you so definitely have stood."[74] Dabney may not have been the most skilled navigator of choppy local waters, especially given his limited tolerance for German Catholics, but Hughes was speaking to the inevitable problem of local politics intervening in the operation of any municipal institution.

5

IN THE SERVICE OF THE NATION
The University in War and Depression

Local personalities, politics, and events shaped the early history of the University of Cincinnati, but as the twentieth century unfolded, national and international developments increasingly influenced the institution's course. From the mid-1910s through the mid-1940s, two world wars and a global depression played an outsized role in shaping the municipal university. Under Charles Dabney's guidance the University of Cincinnati had become a model urban university, but it was never a purely local institution. It sought out acclaimed professors from around the nation and Europe, and in turn the strong faculty helped draw students from well beyond the city. As important as the university was to the growth of the regional economy, many of UC's alumni pursued their careers far from their alma mater. Even the mission to serve the city could be expressed as a means of building a national reputation—as the exemplar of an urban university. Still, over the first five decades of its existence, the university mostly served Cincinnati. Then the First World War forced an abrupt departure from the school's founding mission, from which it never fully returned.

Battles had been raging in Europe for nearly three years before the United States finally joined the war in the spring of 1917. Total war devastated lives and landscapes in Europe and beyond, with more than 17 million people killed in what was the most deadly conflict to date. Not surprisingly, total war also had serious implications for higher education, as institutions reshaped themselves nearly overnight to support their nation's cause. As a symbol of this transformation, the *University of Cincinnati Record*, which under Dabney's leadership had gained the subtitle "The Service of the University to the City," included a new subtitle in 1918: "The Service of the University to the Nation." As the *Record* made clear, UC could no longer focus on purely local concerns. Some changes were temporary, designed to respond to the national emergency, but altogether the transformations pointed to a greater national engagement that merely ebbed once the war was over and surged again with each new crisis.

Just as world events were shaping the institution, so too was UC's growing appetite for raising its national and international research profile. Increasingly, universities around the nation sought talented faculty to lead research teams and train graduate students. With its constrained budget, UC was poorly positioned to compete with larger, better-endowed universities. Expanding research would require additional funding, and in an era when government grants were quite rare, faculty sought support from charitable foundations, corporations, and philanthropists. Among the latter was Anna Sinton Taft, the wife of Charles Phelps Taft and daughter of David Sinton, a successful Cincinnati industrialist. Upon her husband's death in 1929, Anna Taft set up the Charles Phelps Taft Memorial Fund "to assist, maintain, and endow the study and teaching of 'the Humanities' in the College of Liberal Arts and the Graduate School of the University of Cincinnati." Taft had a broad conception of the humanities, stipulating that her gift should support literature, language, philosophy, and history, as well as economics and mathematics. The initial $2 million gift established a transformative endowment, one that allowed UC to expand dramatically the reach of its research in these fields. Through the depression years of the mid-1930s, nearly half of the funds went to the purchase of books, allowing the library to substantially improve its collection. The fund also paid the salary of four new professors, and grants aided faculty research projects and paid for travel to conferences. Other grants provided subventions to support publications and funded graduate student fellows. Each year the Taft Fund also brought in prominent lecturers, including Joseph Schumpeter, the famed economist, and Arthur M. Schlesinger, a Harvard historian with Ohio roots, and, in 1944, the poet Robert Frost.[1] Altogether the Taft Fund represented more than the growing importance of conducting research and training graduate students. It revealed the centrality of endowments to building the institution; municipal tax money alone could not make UC visible on the national stage.

Even as international events and an expanding research profile pulled the institution in new directions, UC remained a municipal university. In his 1936 annual report, President Raymond Walters declared that UC was at the forefront of a global movement. "The economic and educational trends are toward the city university," he claimed. What's more, as "a rock-like city which has endured with courage, patience, and success the greatest of all nationwide and worldwide storms," Cincinnati was particularly well suited for this urban mission. Walters was proud that UC had trained much of the Cincinnati's civic and cultural leadership, but the university did more than train the city's elite.

A complete range of evening courses allowed it to reach working men and women, fulfilling its democratic mission. "For a municipal university to offer to adult citizens the intellectual and moral wealth of mankind is a service which cannot be measured by quantitative standards," wrote Ernest L. Talbert, supervisor of the College of Liberal Arts Evening Academic Courses. Walters agreed, and he created the Evening College in 1938 in an effort to better serve this constituency. In its first year Evening College enrolled nearly nine thousand students in courses ranging from astronomy to small house planning to real estate management. These evening students, most of them employed during the day, were on average twenty-seven years old.[2]

Undoubtedly these evening students, often taking just one or two classes a semester, were interested primarily in improving their economic lot, adding skills and credentials that would allow them to seek better jobs. For Walters, however, even in the depths of the depression the university retained its broader goal—to create better citizens. In an era when other nations had turned away from democracy toward state-controlled communism or fascism, Walters made certain that "citizenship" became the watchword of the university. "In a municipal university such as ours," he wrote in one of his early annual reports, "it is peculiarly fitting to emphasize good citizenship."[3]

❧ Responding Fully to the Call of Democracy

Just four months after the fighting began in Europe, and long before American involvement, President Dabney set the tone for the university's response to war with a lecture on "the Higher Patriotism" delivered to a group of international students in Columbus. Dabney criticized the growth of nationalism, the ultimate cause of the war, but in the process he made clear his opinion that Germany bore special responsibility for the war—and its brutality.[4] While Dabney's anti-German sentiment colored his public statements, he was even less careful in private correspondence. In early 1916, as the United States "waged neutrality" through its support of Britain, Dabney wrote to President Woodrow Wilson: "The Germans infest only three or four of our large cities and a very small portion of the county districts and when you bring your hand down upon them the great majority of them will 'shut up.'"[5] Unfortunately for Dabney, one of the cities that Germans "infested" was Cincinnati.

Upon reading about Dabney's Columbus talk in the Cincinnati papers, the German American community expressed anger and disappointment. Attorney Colon Schott wrote to Dabney to remind him that he must be more careful in public speeches, because he represented everyone in the city. "You offend grievously," he declared, before closing the letter with "A Taxpayer" above his signature.[6] After Dabney offered to meet Schott to discuss the matter and assured that he did not mean to cause offense, Schott responded with a reminder of Dabney's special place in the city. "Freedom of speech is, of course, the right of all of us," he wrote, "but those who occupy high public positions necessarily have the responsibility of being held to a higher degree of care in their public utterances than those who walk in the more humble spheres of activity."[7] Schott was not alone in his concern, and when Dabney appeared unwilling to retract his assertions about Germany, Cincinnati's German-language press encouraged a broader protest, which came in February of 1915, when the Deutsch-Amerikanischer Stadtverband resolved that Dabney should not be reappointed to his post.[8]

Dabney was retained, however, and especially after the United States officially joined the war in the spring of 1917, German Americans felt much more acutely the sting of anti-German sentiment, even in Cincinnati where the German population was large and active. Meanwhile, Dabney could declare that the university responded "fully to the call of democracy," echoing Woodrow Wilson's explanation for American involvement in the war: to make the world safe for democracy. A year into American involvement, Dabney asserted, "To this patriotic endeavor there has been no dissent from any member of the institution" and "every department and every man in the institution" had been placed "at the disposal of the country." Dabney's enthusiasm to aid in the war cause, to bring the entire institution somehow into the effort, a sentiment held broadly across the campus, was typical across the country as well. In waging the Great War, the federal government would have the unquestioning cooperation of its institutions of higher learning.[9]

With the declaration of war, UC established a Department of Military Science, and all able-bodied men began taking military drill. Some students enlisted right away and so trained at one of the many regional military camps created for the purpose, but 400 men began their training on campus. By the fall of 1917, the draft had taken some students from school, but drilling continued, as did other preparations for war. The College of Engineering offered a variety of critical courses, including topography and mapmaking, and the making of temporary bridges and makeshift structures. Most important, it dramatically increased the number of courses related to the mechanics of automobiles and trucks, the manufacture of airplanes and munitions, and the production of hydraulic systems. University-trained engineers would make and fix the machines of war.

The other colleges did their part, too. In the College of Arts & Sciences the Department of History increased offerings in the history of Germany, including evening courses, so that Cincinnatians might better understand the enemy. The Department of Botany taught a course on war gardening, and the School of Household Arts taught a course in food conservation in the expectation that the conflict would cause food shortages. Arts & Sciences also offered a War Issues course addressing the causes of the conflict. Using materials and guidance from the US War Department, the course was a required part of soldiers' training while on campus. The War Department asked that the class combine "the points of view of history, government, economics, philosophy, and modern literature"—a truly trans-disciplinary approach designed to improve the morale of the soldiers by increasing their understanding of the events in which they were swept up.[10]

Perhaps nowhere in the university was preparation for war more complete than in the medical school, where every student enrolled in the Medical Enlisted Reserve Corps. As chairman of the board Rufus Smith summarized in the summer of 1918, "During the past year the University has subordinated every activity to rendering every assistance in its power to the Government." Faculty around the country reflected on this moment, when their skills and knowledge were put toward some larger purpose beyond the walls of academe. For many it was a well-learned lesson about the power of engaging in the issues of the day, of contributing to a critical cause.[11]

In the face of growing shortage of trained technical men, the War Department created a new program to provide direct military instruction on college campuses. Secretary of War Newton Baker announced in the spring of 1918, "Military instruction under officers and non-commissioned officers of the Army will be provided in every institution of college grade, which enrolls for the instruction of 100 or more able-bodied students over the age of eighteen."[12] This program, called the Students' Army Training Corps, eventually enrolled over 140,000 men at over 500 universities and colleges. Enrollees took the War Issues course and learned military drill, marching on campus greens and athletic fields around the country. In Cincinnati, 2,000 men trained at the university, learning skills that would be useful in the war and after. Some of the training bled out into the city, as the men learned by doing. For instance, the Army Training Corps strung electrical and telephone wires around the region. The real transformation happened on campus, however, where physical changes matched those in the curriculum. UC built thirteen temporary buildings, including six sprawling barracks erected between McMicken and Baldwin Halls. By the summer of 1918, the University of Cincinnati, like many universities around the country, looked more like a military base than an institution of higher learning.[13]

Just days before the armistice in November 1918, the *Cincinnati Enquirer* offered its assessment of the university's transformation beneath photographs of the barracks at the center of campus. Dabney assured the city that some changes would be

Student Army Training Corps band, circa 1917. Preparations for war turned the campus into a "military machine," according to the *Cincinnati Enquirer*. *Photograph files, Archives & Rare Books Library, University of Cincinnati.*

World War I army barracks, circa 1918. To accommodate the students preparing for war, UC constructed a cluster of temporary barracks between the Baldwin Hall, on the right, and McMicken Hall, out of sight on the left. In the foreground is the track that encircled Carson Field, now Nippert Stadium. *Photograph files, Archives & Rare Books Library, University of Cincinnati.*

permanent, including programs to train soldiers. And the *Enquirer*, ever patriotic, encouraged all men to take military training at the university, even if they had no interest in academic credit. The newspaper concluded, "Cincinnati can be proud of the spirit which has turned in two months the academic university into a military machine, from which the finished soldier is to be turned out to help with the war for democracy."[14]

UC may have become a "military machine," as the *Enquirer* wrote, but the war did not change the fundamental purpose of higher education. Dean of McMicken College and professor of English Frank W. Chandler reminded the community that colleges "must train minds to discriminate between right and wrong, between wise and foolish policy, between ideals subversive of a hard-won freedom and those that make for the welfare, not of one people only, but of all." In the 1918 annual report for his college, Chandler pushed back against the rush to military training. Universities must make men, he argued, even as the war raged. It should be the military's job to make officers of them. "Accordingly, although the college should insist upon drill," Chandler wrote, "its chief efforts must be directed, as hitherto, towards developing the mental faculties of its students, toward giving them poise and judgment through an acquaintance with the best that has been thought and done in the world."[15]

In a thorough assessment of the war's impact on higher education, Parke Kolbe, president of the University of Akron, predicted permanent curricular changes around the nation. Classical subjects had long been in decline, and with the wartime emphasis on practical education Kolbe did not foresee a revival. The "development of science and the demands of industry" would continue to shape curricula, he thought, and the growth of "so-called vocational subjects," especially engineering, would continue. "The soldiers who return to us will be 'doers,' not theorists," Kolbe wrote. "Our education will have to offer more of the actual contact with life and the actual practice of life's activities," meaning more "field work" and "cooperative courses." Kolbe lamented the decline of classical education, but he was more supportive of another trend: the diminishment of German-language instruction. "It may be regarded as certain," he wrote, "that all foreign languages will be forever barred from our elementary schools as a result of the present war, and that neither German nor any other language will be allowed to spread insidious propaganda for any foreign system in the mind of youth at its most susceptible age." German continued to be taught in colleges, of course, but to far fewer students. As Kolbe accurately predicted, both French and Spanish surpassed German in popularity. More troubling, the overall decline in foreign language instruction at all levels of education symbolized and accelerated the American withdrawal from world affairs.[16]

In the end, the war took the lives of thirty UC students and alumni. The flu epidemic that swept through Cincinnati in the fall of 1918 took nearly as many. Twenty-four people died of the flu on campus, including several members of the Students' Army Training Corps. The epidemic became so dire that the city's Board of Health quarantined the campus for more than a month. Shortly after the war, the university also lost Christian Holmes, who had served at Camp Sherman in Chillicothe for more than a year. After he became ill, Holmes was removed to a hospital in New York City, where he died in January 1920.[17]

As the senselessness of the war and the fierce destructiveness it had unleashed began to sink in, many Americans took a more complicated view of the nation's involvement in European affairs. The United States retracted from global affairs, even refusing to join the League of Nations. Americans longed for a return to normalcy, as President Warren Harding phrased it. But the gaze of the university had been lifted by the war, if not toward international engagement then at least to national concerns. Charles Dabney stood before the graduating class of 1920 and asked them to think of the safety of their country. "What should educated young men and women be thinking of and preparing for in such a time as this, if not their duty to their country?" The war was over, but it had toppled the old order and a new tyranny—"the autocracy of the proletariat," Bolshevism—threated to replace it. "The Americanism your fathers fought for must be preserved in this land and handed down to your children," Dabney said, apparently envisioning a new, nationalistic goal for education. His primary concern was creeping socialism, with its threats from abroad and from within. "Private ownership is the condition of progress in all industry," Dabney said. "Public ownership means death to ambition, the destruction of initiative and the paralysis of all the natural energy of men." International communism loomed, but Dabney also warned against "academic cranks and 'parlor Bolshevists.'" That threat made Dabney ask, "Have we failed in educating and training [our fellow citizens]?" And reflecting the new national mission of the university, he asked, "How shall we make old-fashioned, true Americans out of our people?" Like many Americans during the first Red Scare in 1919, when the nation turned away from free speech and civil rights for all, Dabney argued that what bound Americans together was God and private property, rather than democracy and the rule of law. The "religion of justice and brotherhood," Dabney concluded, "is the essence of Americanism."[18] All this from a man who ran a large and growing municipal university.

❧ Building a Laboratory Nursery School

Dabney may have had his eyes on the creation of good Americans, but not all UC faculty were so dedicated to the cause of nationalism, and not all researchers shifted their work toward the solution of national problems. Community concerns remained central to the work of Dr. Ada Arlitt, for example, who came to Cincinnati in 1923 to serve as the psychologist at Cincinnati's new Central Clinic, a mental health facility created by the Council of Social Agencies to provide care to a previously neglected population. Originally set up in the Community Chest building downtown, Central Clinic provided "mental hygiene" services, as it was called at the time, to the entire community, but 70 percent of its patients were children, many of them referred by Cincinnati Public Schools or juvenile court.[19] Arlitt had earned her PhD in psychology from the University of Chicago and taught at Bryn Mawr before arriving in Cincinnati. In the course of her work at the clinic, Arlitt came to know faculty at the university, in both the College of Medicine and the Teachers College. In addition to giving lectures to faculty and students studying child psychology, she gave talks to mothers' clubs and civic organizations, indications that Arlitt's primary interest was in teaching.

In 1925, Arlitt joined UC's faculty to help establish the Department of Child Care and Training in the School of Household Administration. The new program focused on the care of preschool children, but it was designed to prepare college students for a range of positions. As Arlitt described it, "Our students are trained to become teachers and directors in nursery schools, leaders of parent groups or lecturers on Parent Education, teachers of Child Care and Training in colleges, universities, and high schools, social workers in the field of Child Welfare, and research assistants in Child Psychology."[20]

Arlitt's goal was to create a laboratory nursery school in which she could train students in the most effective early childhood education techniques. With the support of local philanthropists who contributed to the Mothers' Training Center Association, Arlitt opened her nursery in the Women's Building in 1926.[21] Just a decade old, the Women's Building had been constructed to house the Department of Home Economics, founded in 1908 by Annie Laws, the nationally renowned kindergarten advocate who had played a role in founding a nursing college, as well. Inside the Women's Building, Arlitt designed a nursery school with a sleeping room, a playroom, a roof garden, and an examining room for physician visits.[22] Parents and students were encouraged to observe how instructors engaged children in appropriate play.

In addition to the laboratory school, Arlitt set up dozens of mother training groups around the city, in which women could discuss child care with faculty and graduate students in the program. In addition, funding from the Mothers' Training Center Association allowed Arlitt to publish pamphlets to help guide mothers' interactions with their children, including "Toys and Occupations for Young Children," which emphasized the importance of toys to mental and physical development and included a list of appropriate toys for children under six years old. Another, more substantial pamphlet discussed "Habit Formation," which encouraged positive feedback for good behavior.[23]

By its very nature, Arlitt's program relied on community engagement. On campus, the faculty taught courses to mothers for college credit, and working through the Mothers' Pension lists, the Cincinnati Orphan Asylum, and the Babies' Milk Fund Association, among other social agencies, the program offered preschool for needy and orphaned children. Some faculty conducted "conference groups" for parents of small children at various locations throughout the city, leading discussions on topics from nutrition to discipline. Arlitt noted, "The types of mothers attending vary from members of the Junior League and the Cincinnati Woman's Club to women in the basin of the city who are employed throughout the day and can attend the conference groups only at night." In other words, the groups served women from the upper crust—those in the Woman's Club—and the working poor, many of whom lived in the dense neighborhoods of Over-the-Rhine and the West End. The program also set up exhibits of toys, books, and other educational materials with the goal of providing outreach instruction. Over 1,500 people attended these exhibits in 1927. Outreach even included taking to the airwaves, as the staff gave radio talks on various child care and training topics.[24]

Arlitt was a published researcher, and she continued her work at the university on a range of topics, but in particular on the role of race as a factor in educational performance. While at Bryn Mawr, she had conducted research on the IQ of children, and her findings suggested that racial stereotypes that rested in biology either

117

overstated or misstated the role of race. Instead, she found that social class was a larger factor in IQ disparities. Her early publications in the *Journal of Applied Psychology* on this topic become increasingly influential over time.[25]

As a means of expanding the nursery program and promoting her research, Arlitt pursued funding from the Laura Spelman Rockefeller Memorial Foundation to support fellowships for graduate students. The foundation, which already supported other experimental nurseries, may have been especially attracted to Cincinnati because of its potential to train African American women, whom Arlitt recruited in the hope of reaching underserved populations. Arlitt carefully shaped the publicity surrounding her work, however, telling the Rockefeller administrators that, "we should wish to avoid any public announcement that we are carrying on Negro education as part of the grant, inasmuch as, if this became public our classes would be swamped with colored students." Although Arlitt had no qualms about working with African Americans, she was concerned that "[s]uch a preponderance of colored students would have an unfortunate effect upon our department and upon the University as a whole." In other words, Arlitt thought training too many African Americans might adversely affect the university's reputation, a clear reflection of race relations in the city and the nation. Despite the limits imposed by racism, Arlitt's program provided an essential service for black women, some of whom became instructors themselves after earning graduate degrees from UC.[26]

In 1930, Arlitt took a leave of absence to become the director of parent education for the National Congress of Parents and Teachers in Washington, DC. By then she had long since established a national reputation for herself and for the University of Cincinnati in early childhood education—a fine example of how community-based research could elevate the institution's national profile.[27] In 1932, the many connections between the Central Clinic and the university, begun during Arlitt's tenure, were solidified when the clinic moved to the campus of the College of Medicine, where it continues to treat mental health patients, many of them children.

❀ Joys and Hardships in the Field

Arlitt was hardly the only woman to elevate UC's research profile in the first half of the twentieth century. More and more women were entering higher education and studying in a greater variety of fields. Most women who continued on to get advanced degrees and enter academia worked in fields such as education, nursing, and home economics, but some entered traditionally male disciplines in science and engineering. Among these students was Annette Braun, an entomologist who became the first women to earn a PhD from UC in 1911. Another was her younger sister, E. Lucy Braun, who earned a BA (1910), MA in geology (1912), and a PhD in botany (1914), all from UC. As late as 1900, only eight women had earned a PhD in botany in the entire nation. The low numbers of women earning doctoral degrees in the sciences assured that progress in diversifying the faculty would be very slow. Even in the 1920s and 1930s, nationally only 20 percent of doctorates in the sciences were earned by women, with some fields, such as physics, chemistry, geology, and anthropology, granting much smaller percentages.[28]

The Braun sisters, then, were unusual in their educational attainment, but even more remarkable was Lucy's career as an ecological researcher. The sisters had been raised in Walnut Hills, which at the time retained a suburban feel, and their parents took them to Rose Hill in Avondale for regular nature study outings. Both girls apparently learned well the importance of understanding how the natural world works, and their childhood investigations turned into lifelong careers.

After earning their doctorates, both Annette and Lucy taught at UC, including classes involving fieldwork. Though Annette left the teaching ranks in 1917, Lucy remained in the Department of Botany, serving first as an assistant and then as an instructor. It was not unusual for women in the sciences, even those who had a PhD, to be offered instructor roles rather than tenure-track positions. Braun finally took a regular faculty position in 1923 and earned tenure and promotion four years later. Despite her remarkable productivity, Braun remained an associate professor for twenty years, finally becoming a full professor just two years before she retired. When Braun graduated, Botany was a small program, with just one professor and an instructor. At the time of her retirement, Botany had grown to six faculty members, two of them women—Braun and fellow Cincinnati native Margaret Fulford, who had earned her BA and MA at UC working with Braun, and then returned to the department as a faculty member after earning a PhD from Yale.[29]

Braun conducted her research mainly in the field, typically accompanied by her sister, who conducted her own research on moths while remaining a companion and colleague to Lucy. (The sisters even lived together their entire lives, first in their parents' Walnut Hills home and then in Mount Washington.) Lucy published on a variety of ecosystems, but unsurprisingly much of her work focused on Ohio and Kentucky. In 1921, her article "Composition and Source of the Flora of the Cincinnati Region" appeared in *Ecology*, the journal of the Ecological Society of America founded just the year before. (Braun became the first woman president of the society in 1950.) In this first of five articles that Braun published in *Ecology*, she describes the region's deciduous forest as a meeting place to which flora had migrated from all directions. The major paths of migration were the Mississippi River and its tributaries, drawing plants up from the south, and the Appalachian Mountains, down which plants migrated from the east. Her description of plant migration echoes the story of people's movement to the Ohio Valley frontier. "The present flora of the Cincinnati Region is a result of the mingling of plants derived from various centers of dispersal," she wrote, sounding much like Daniel Drake as he described the diversity of the city's residents one hundred years earlier. Upon their arrival, plants, much like people, remained "grouped in distinct communities which exhibit marked communal relationships with the south, the west, or the north."[30]

E. Lucy Braun, circa 1940. After earning her PhD at UC, Lucy Braun became a leading researcher in the field of botany. She and her sister Annette, who was the first woman to earn her doctorate at UC, were tireless field researchers. *Photograph files, Archives & Rare Books Library, University of Cincinnati.*

Although Braun stepped away from teaching in 1948, her emeritus years were filled with research travel and publishing. Her magnum opus was *Deciduous Forests of Eastern North America*, published in 1950 to immediate acclaim. She dedicated the book to her sister Annette, who had "shared the joys and hardships in the field." Based on nearly forty years of fieldwork, the book described and mapped nine old-growth forest regions. To locate and define these "original" forests, as she called them, Braun needed to study residual fragments, undisturbed by Euro-American occupation. She was perpetually searching for the fragments of old-growth forests, and she well understood that "as the years go by, it becomes increasingly difficult to form any concept of the original forest cover. The virgin forests have been cut, the land is either cleared and farmed or is clothed with second-growth forests which may in no way suggest the original forest." To engage in this kind of work, Braun also needed to believe that forests, if left undisturbed, remained remarkably stable through time, save for the major disturbance of glaciation and periodic minor disturbances such as windstorms and fires. In essence, Braun was reconstructing the primeval eastern American forests in prose, imagining presettlement ecosystems—and in the process overlooking the significant role of Native Americans in shaping these "original" forests, a commonplace error among twentieth-century ecologists.[31]

Lucy's scientific work has remained influential, but her most lasting legacy may involve her work as an environmental activist.[32] The Braun sisters were active in the conservation movement, working to preserve patches of old-growth forests and other undisturbed fragments, especially in Kentucky and Ohio. In 1924, they helped reenergize the Wild Flower Preservation Society of America by hosting a gathering in the library of the Botany Department. Representatives from Washington, Chicago, Kentucky, and several members of the Cincinnati Chapter of the society attended. They laid out a plan for better national organization of the society and set a date for a second meeting in Washington. Lucy represented the Cincinnati chapter at that meeting and ensured that *Wild Flower*, the quarterly publication of the local chapter, would become the national organ of the society. *Wild Flower*, which began publishing just a year earlier, had featured local news and articles related to the chapter's activities. When it transitioned to its national role, *Wild Flower* published "news of more than local interest."[33] This progression certainly tracked the careers of the Braun sisters, who also sought—and gained—a national reputation for their work. Annette became the corresponding secretary of the Cincinnati Chapter, and Lucy published frequently in *Wild Flower*, where her essays combined her ecological knowledge and preservationist inclination. For instance, she ended her discussion of the migration of plants into the postglacial Ohio Valley with a denunciation of men who "thoughtlessly and ruthlessly" destroyed "what only long ages can produce." She concluded, "While a few of these remnants do still remain, let us make every effort to preserve them permanently, that we and future generations may know of the great gift bestowed upon us."[34]

For many years Lucy served on the society's board of directors, and for six years she edited *Wild Flower*. In July 1933, her last issue as editor, Braun published several historical accounts of exploring the United States, most of them from the mid-

1800s. In her introduction, Braun described the rapidity of change that had altered the environment since these pioneering accounts, lamenting that mere fragments of the original wilderness remained. "It should be our sacred duty to preserve some few remnants in every section of our country," she wrote, "to establish museums of nature—nature sanctuaries—where for all time can be maintained living examples of the original wilderness of our country." And to her fellow conservationists, she asked, "Why not concentrate your efforts on the establishment of county and state natural monuments of pioneer days, and see that they are adequately protected after being set aside?"[35] Although her work as an activist scholar is impossible to measure, in one particular place it is quite evident: the E. Lucy Braun Lynx Prairie Preserve, an undisturbed natural area in Adams County, which earned designation as a National Natural Landmark in 1967 in large part through the Braun sisters' dedication to Ohio's wild fragments.[36]

In 1935, again writing in *Wild Flower*, Braun announced to the Wild Flower Preservation Society the formation of the Wilderness Society, to which she pledged support. The article extolled the virtues of wilderness—the quiet and solitude, which she noted are "destroyed at once when the wilderness is penetrated by roads whence comes the whir of auto engines and the raucous blasts of horns to obscure by their din the calls of birds, the music of waterfalls, or the song of the rapids." Clearly the wilderness held more than scientific value to Braun.[37]

❦ A Consultant of the Corporation

The growing size and complexity of the university ensured that a diversity of opinions would develop across campus on critical topics—such as the proper role of automobiles in society. Robert Kehoe, for example, a contemporary of Lucy Braun's, had a very different relationship with automobiles, or at least with the automobile industry. In 1923, Standard Oil and General Motors created the Ethyl Corporation to produce and distribute tetraethyl lead, a highly toxic substance that reduced engine knock, increased power, and improved fuel efficiency when added to gasoline. Tetraethyl lead poisoned at least fifty men at Delco, the Dayton-based General Motors subsidiary where initial research took place, but the auto industry was keen on expanding its use. In 1924, as Ethyl attempted to increase production, five refinery workers went insane and died painful deaths after inhaling tetraethyl lead at Standard's Bayway facility in New Jersey. At the recommendation of Thomas Midgley at Delco, Ethyl hired Kehoe, already a well-known physiologist specializing in industrial hygiene, to help ensure that such industrial accidents stopped and that production could ramp up without gaining more negative publicity.[38]

In 1925, Kehoe became the medical director at Ethyl, a position he held simultaneous to being on faculty at his alma mater, UC's College of Medicine. Thereafter, Kehoe's work was largely a continual battle to make the public feel at ease with leaded gasoline in cities increasingly polluted by auto exhaust. In the process, Kehoe became one of the world's leading experts on lead toxicity, and he published widely on the risks of lead exposure. His work on laboratory animals and even, occasionally, on human subjects helped refine and standardize testing methodology. Kehoe and his employees frequently visited industrial sites working with dangerous chemicals to assess safety procedures and make recommendations. They also tested the blood of workers at local gas stations and garages, certain that if those who worked around automobiles all day showed no signs of lead poisoning then the public need not worry. Deaths and serious illness due to occupational exposure to lead plummeted due to Kehoe's work, but the broader impact was that, along with General Motors, Standard Oil, and Ethyl, the University of Cincinnati helped ensure that nearly all Americans would be lead poisoned by the 1960s.

Although Kehoe well understood lead's toxicity, and indeed spoke out against its use in paint, he also assumed that human bodies naturally—and harmlessly—contained some level of lead. A research trip to central Mexico confirmed Kehoe's assumptions about lead. Thinking the residents of a remote area would be free from industrial lead contamination, he tested urine, feces, and blood to determine "natural" levels of lead in human bodies. One of the resulting publications, "On the Normal Absorption and Excretion of Lead," which appeared in the *Journal of Industrial Hygiene* in 1933, set a paradigm that persisted for over thirty years. Kehoe concluded, "[W]e cannot doubt that the presence of lead in human excreta and human tissues, as well as in living organisms in general, is an inevitable consequence of life on a lead-bearing planet."[39] Kehoe thought that the lead he found in Mexican bodies represented a safe, background level of lead and, therefore, established the idea that non-acutely toxic levels of lead were harmless. Further work convinced him that human bodies, which had evolved in a leaded world, created a natural equilibrium by excreting lead through urine and feces. This kept lead levels in the body below toxic levels in all but the most extreme exposures, which were most likely to happen at industrial sites. This way of thinking, which turned out to be erroneous, allowed Kehoe to claim the safety of leaded gasoline even as

American cities filled with lead. As he flatly concluded in a 1934 article, "[T]here is no reason to fear the existence of danger to the public health from the distribution and use of leaded gasoline."[40]

For years much of Kehoe's work for Ethyl involved investigating complaints regarding possible lead poisonings.[41] He was also engaged in public relations as he answered the medical complaints that arose from leaded gasoline. For instance, David J. Donaldson, who pumped gas at the Atlantic Refining Company in Washington, Pennsylvania, complained of tingling in his hands, which were often covered in gas, after just a few weeks on the job. A few months later, Donaldson entered a hospital with cramps, diarrhea, general weakness, and pain in his knees and ankles. After a series of examinations, three doctors determined that he had lead poisoning. Ethyl notified Kehoe, who traveled Pennsylvania to examine Donaldson. Kehoe reported to Ethyl, "My own examination disclosed the fact that this man has certain signs and symptoms which suggest lead poisoning of a chronic type." Still, Kehoe was hesitant to call this lead poisoning, because Donaldson showed neither of the reliable signs of acute poisoning: a "lead line" on the gums and stippling of the blood. Kehoe failed to recognize that some people were more susceptible to lead poisoning than others. Instead, he determined in regard to Donaldson, "although there are certain things characteristic, or rather I should say suggestive of lead poisoning in the muscular weakness and partial paralysis," it was "much more likely that he has some other condition." He suggested three other causes: tooth infection, hysteria, or syphilis.[42]

Kehoe knew this 1926 case was a significant threat to Ethyl. He corresponded with the manager of Atlantic in Pittsburgh: "In view of the importance of this case and its relationship to the industrial and public health hazards of Ethyl gasoline, I wish to make sure that the relationships existing between this man and his physicians be maintained in the most cooperative spirit." He asked that Atlantic pay doctors' bills, regardless of the diagnosis, undoubtedly to prevent Donaldson from developing negative feelings toward his employer.[43] In the end, Kehoe wrote a report on the case, in which he emphasized the recovery and "normal" tests concerning urine and feces. Still, "It will be necessary I think to report this case along with the others to the Surgeon General, and have it considered along with a great mass of negative evidence which has accumulated for what it is worth." That "negative evidence," of course, was the growing number of people who handled leaded gasoline without getting sick.[44]

Much of Kehoe's work on lead came after 1930, when, using funds from General Motors, DuPont, and Ethyl, he founded the Kettering Laboratory at the College of Medicine. At Kettering, Kehoe and a growing number of physicians and chemists conducted a variety of research on industrial hygiene, but in the first decade the work centered on lead. His correspondence through the 1930s make it clear that the public remained concerned about the possibility of poisoning from leaded gas. Doctors suggested it to patients who exhibited certain symptoms, and many sick people assumed lead played some role in their illnesses. Kehoe was a critical part of industry's effort to absolve lead of special attention.[45]

Kehoe may have felt at ease with his dual position—academic researcher and corporate officer—but clearly the goals of these two positions came into frequent conflict. In 1937, for example, Kehoe was alerted to the case of Stanley J. Ellsworth of Churchville, New York. Ellsworth claimed that exhaust leaks in his car had given him chronic lead poisoning. Kehoe dismissed the idea, asserting as he did frequently that carbon monoxide poisoning was much more likely than lead poisoning when it came to auto exhaust and, further, "there have been no authenticated cases of lead poisoning from this source." Still, Kehoe recommended to the Socony-Vacuum Oil Company, the corporate predecessor to Mobil, that it undertake a "discreet inquiry." In this case and others, the industry goal was to prevent further suspicions of leaded gas and to avoid legal implications for companies producing and selling the product. These goals were in obvious conflict with serious, systematic investigation of complaints.[46]

In addition to handling individual cases of concern, mostly through correspondence, Kehoe also provided legal consultation for companies implicated in cases concerning leaded gasoline. For instance, in 1936, Otto Hamer, an attorney working for Packard Motors, contacted Kehoe about the case of Lloyd Banker, a Chicago man whose faulty car let gas fumes into the passenger compartment, making him sick. Banker had sued Packard. In response, Kehoe sent a lengthy letter indicating that lead exposure could not have made him sick. "There is a considerable bulk of evidence to indicate that lead intoxication of this severity would be practically impossible under the conditions described," Kehoe wrote, using language that became commonplace in his correspondence. "As a matter of fact, we have no record of any case of lead poisoning in association with contact with leaded gasoline, and there is also good evidence that no lead absorption occurs in the case of persons who have daily and regular contact with the gasoline and with the exhaust gases of motors which burn such gasoline."[47]

A month later, Kehoe encouraged Hamer to settle the Banker case. "I think it is perhaps worthwhile for you to realize that if I appear in this case, I shall not appear as a representative of the Ethyl Gasoline Corporation. I shall not conceal the fact, of course, that I have been a consultant of the latter Corporation since its origin. On the other hand my primary work is that of an investigator and teacher in the Medical School of the University of Cincinnati, and on account of the character of the work which we have been doing and the position which this laboratory occupies in this field of medicine, I shall, of course, appear in the case as a disinterested expert."[48]

Kehoe's reminder to Hamer serves as a reminder to us. Through all of this work for Ethyl, and the lead industry generally, Kehoe was first and foremost an employee of a municipal university. Kehoe's service to his field is unmistakable—even though his major conclusions about lead were mistaken. His relationships with corporations built the institution, especially through the growth of the Kettering Laboratory. Still, one would be hard pressed to make the claim that the city and its residents benefited nearly as much from this arrangement as did Ethyl, Standard Oil, and General Motors. Even as evidence mounted in the 1960s, as physicians began to get a sense of the public health disaster caused by leaded gasoline, Kehoe stuck to his position—providing a powerful cautionary tale about the influence corporate sponsorship might have over research results.[49]

🌿 The Foremost Representative of This Branch of Learning

For Kehoe entanglements beyond the university led to infamy; for Carl Blegen, they led to fame. Blegen came to UC in 1927, having been recruited by William T. Semple, head of the Department of Classics since its creation in 1920. The department brought together archaeology, history, and philology (literary and textual analysis) to study classical civilizations of the Mediterranean. This innovation allowed Semple, who came to UC in 1910 as a professor in Greek, to hire the archaeologist who would help establish the department's global reputation. Beyond his advantageous hiring, however, Semple established a strong classics program because his wife, Louise Taft Semple, dedicated her fortune to fund the study of ancient civilizations. Classical education continued to wane around the nation, but at UC the Department of Classics thrived with uncommon talent and resources.[50]

In the spring of 1927, Blegen was the acting director of the American School of Classical Studies in Athens, having stepped in for his recently fired best friend,

Bert Hill. Given the circumstances, the post was awkward and unlikely to last, despite the fact that Blegen had long served as the assistant director of the American School. Semple knew Blegen might be ready for an academic position, so he sent a letter of encouragement in which he claimed, "Interest in Classical Archaeology has so increased during the past four or five years in Cincinnati that the standard of excellence to be expected in the presentation of Archaeology in the University has risen greatly." Semple and his wife were well connected, and they had been building local interest in the classical world since their marriage in 1917. "Our supporters now demand a full time man," Semple told Blegen, "and this man they wish to be the foremost representative of this branch of learning among American scholars." Several Cincinnatians, including Semple, had already met Blegen in Athens or at his excavations in Greece, and others knew him by reputation, established through early publications, especially on Korakou.[51]

Blegen was interested in the Cincinnati job, but he wasn't interested in leaving Greece. Born and raised in Minnesota (where at age fifteen he lost his right arm in a hunting accident), Blegen had lived in Greece for most of the previous fifteen years, including years conducting research to earn a Yale PhD, which he received in 1920. Desirous of keeping his home in Athens, Blegen negotiated with Semple and Louis T. More, dean of the Graduate School, where Blegen's professorship would reside,[52] to be in Cincinnati each fall but return to Athens in January. In Blegen's mind this was a practical arrangement, since his research required him to be in Greece not just for excavations, which took place in the spring, but also so that he could clean, repair, and examine uncovered materials that needed to stay in their country of origin. Blegen made clear that the ability to live in Greece "is the determining consideration which is governing my decision." Semple and More relented, and for the next thirty years one of UC's most prominent faculty members maintained his primary residence in Athens, teaching on campus in the fall and mentoring graduate students at excavation sites in the spring. Blegen's high salary and enviable research schedule were clear indications of his stature—and of the rising importance of research and training graduate students at the university.[53]

For years after his hire, Blegen had a difficult relationship with the American School in Athens, and so he needed to develop a project outside of Greece. With Semple's encouragement, Blegen took up work in Turkey, at a site of great popular curiosity: Troy. As Semple helped make arrangements, he noted to Blegen,

"Of course, Troy would have the greatest publicity value. It would bring our undertaking to the public attention immediately."[54] Years later, Blegen called Troy "a place of unique appeal," because of Homer's account of the Trojan War in the *Iliad*.[55] Semple discussed the possibility of reopening Troy, first excavated by German archaeologists, with the US State Department and the Turkish ambassador in Washington, DC. He asked Blegen to reach out to Wilhelm Dörpfeld, the last archaeologist to work at Troy, as a courtesy. Blegen wrote to Dörpfeld soon thereafter, explaining his interest and the support of "Mrs. Semple," "a niece of William Howard Taft, former President of the United States." Blegen praised her "deep interest in archaeology," and, more important, indicated that she would "assume the entire burden of financing the campaign at Troy." Blegen would accept responsibility for the dig, if he could have Dörpfeld's "good wishes and support."[56]

Dörpfeld did indeed grant his good wishes and support, and he agreed to meet the Semples in Berlin that fall, as they made their way through Europe to Turkey where they would seek official permission to dig at Troy. Dörpfeld was pleased at the prospect of reopening Troy, noting to Blegen, "I am especially happy that you will lead the excavations because I know that it will be carried out in an exemplary manner." He also accepted the invitation to join the Cincinnati team at Troy to help orient them to the site upon their arrival in 1932.[57]

Dörpfeld even provided advice before the campaign began. "We expect to bring most of our staff from Cincinnati," Blegen told him. "Some of them are men, but there will also be several women. Do you think women will have any difficulty in superintending Turkish workmen?" Dörpfeld, who had also worked with a heterogeneous team in Turkey, responded, "Women can work very well in Troy."[58] Among the women who came from Cincinnati was Marion Rawson, a friend of the Semples who provided essential help, maintaining the field notebooks while at Troy and aiding considerably with the multivolume publication that explicated their findings. Rawson accompanied Blegen on digs through the remainder of his career, usually with her sister Dorothy. Both worked as unpaid volunteers, a luxury afforded by their family's wealth.[59] Among the other Cincinnatians at Troy were classics graduate students, including John Caskey, who later joined the faculty and led the Classics Department for two decades. Some years William and Louise Semple also visited Troy, but not everyone on site came from Cincinnati. Turkish citizens, at times dozens of men, conducted much of the work in and around the trenches.

Blegen hoped to do more at Troy than elevate public interest in classical archaeology. The goal was to connect the site to discoveries made elsewhere in the Mediterranean Bronze Age in the thirty years since Dörpfeld had left Troy. Blegen was particularly interested in locating tombs and the settlements that might have supported the citadel. In six years of work, Blegen's team established a new chronology for Troy, identifying nine distinct settlements spanning more than 3,000 years. Blegen determined that the seventh settlement was Homeric Troy, built on the ruins of a city destroyed by earthquake. News of his discoveries reverberated through the archaeological community, but they were also picked up by the popular press. The *New York Times* found something to report nearly every year from 1934 through the end of the campaigns in Troy. This coverage included the 1936 discovery of large storage jars under homes indicating that the seventh settlement may have experienced a long siege like the one Homer described in the *Iliad*. Unfortunately, Blegen found no evidence of the Trojan horse nor that Helen had been the cause of war.[60]

In 1938, UC finished its contracted work at Troy, and the next year Blegen began exploring a new site, Pylos, in the Peloponnese. This new dig, once again supported by Louise Semple, would be a UC-led campaign. "We of Cincinnati are of a provincial cast of mind," Semple explained to another prominent classicist, "and are undertaking this sort of work primarily for the promotion of the reputation and the welfare of the University of Cincinnati in the field of archaeological research. The Excavation is, therefore, to be a Cincinnati Excavation."[61] In preliminary digs that spring Blegen discovered a Mycenaean temple and hundreds of clay tablets inscribed in Linear B, a non-alphabetic script used to write an early form of Greek, which had never before been found on the mainland of Greece. This initial dig was a "huge success," Blegen noted, gaining attention in the Greek, British, and American press.[62] The discovery reshaped interpretations of Mycenaean history. Just a year later, Blegen and his Greek partner, Konstantinos Kourouniotis, were ready to identify their discoveries as the home of King Nestor, described by Homer in the *Odyssey*.[63] UC's work at Pylos suffered a long hiatus during World War II and the subsequent Greek civil war, but Blegen returned to the Palace of Nestor in 1952 and every spring for the next twelve years. Marion Rawson worked each summer, as well, and she helped write and edit *The Palace of Nestor at Pylos in Western Messenia*, a multivolume description of the work that began appearing in 1966.[64]

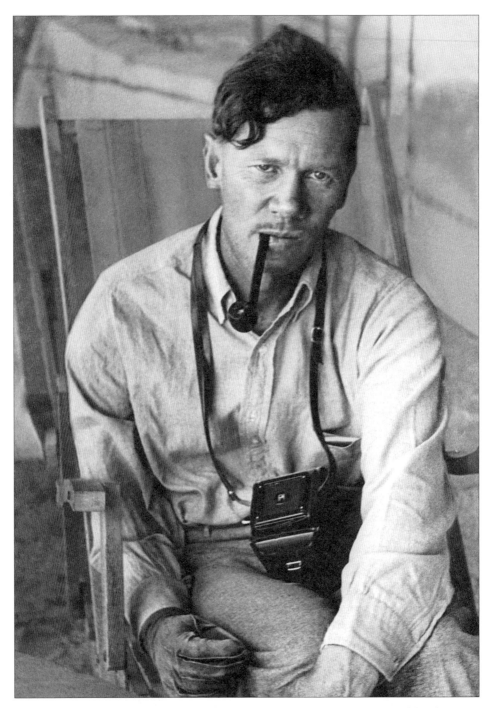

Carl Blegen, 1937. Taken at the Troy excavation, which helped make Blegen one of the "foremost representatives" of his branch of learning, this photograph captures the mix of rugged hard work and intellectual curiosity that went into producing successful archaeologists. *Courtesy of the Department of Classics Archives, University of Cincinnati.*

Carl Blegen's passport, 1933. Blegen was an international figure, his well-worn passports reflecting yearly passage to and from Greece. *Courtesy of the Department of Classics Archives, University of Cincinnati.*

By the time the Pylos publications appeared, Blegen was an emeritus professor living full time in Athens, where he died in 1971. Louise Semple had died a decade earlier, but her support of the department established by her husband, who had predeceased her, continued through a large endowment. The Semple Fund supports the study of classics in a variety of ways, including through library acquisitions, faculty research funding, and financial aid for graduate and undergraduate students.

✿ Building Bridges and Stopping Floods

Thanks to the generosity of Louise Taft Semple, UC archaeologists spent much of the 1930s exploring Troy and significantly expanding our understanding of the ancient Mediterranean. During those same years, the United States—and much of the world—was suffering through a global Great Depression. The stock market

crashed in the fall of 1929, followed by months and then years of fading economic fortunes. By the time Raymond Walters became university president in 1932,
the American economy was in a shambles. The university's budget suffered as the
city's tax base shrank, endowment returns declined, and tuition income fell along
with enrollments.[65] Budget cuts in 1932 were so steep that faculty and staff salaries
were reduced 10 percent. Around the country salary give-backs were a common
strategy in both the private and public sector, and in turn shrinking family budgets
deepened the depression as consumer spending fell. UC also tried to balance its
budget by delaying building maintenance and reducing operating costs, which undoubtedly had negative impacts on facilities. UC's famed cooperative program also
faced its most significant test, as the faltering private sector failed to provide enough
positions for students seeking practical experience. In 1932, at the nadir of the
depression, only 65 percent of the students seeking co-ops found a position. The
program adapted by allowing students to continue coursework during semesters
they were scheduled to be in industry.[66]

Despite the disruption, Walters determined not to allow the depression to re-
define his institution. He held steadfast to his philosophy that education's primary
mission was making better citizens. He allowed that economic and social achievements are "basic," but he emphasized that "the test of any nation and of any civilization is not merely its material prosperity but wealth in the things of the human
spirit: literature, art, science and religion." In other words, "The greatest duty of
a university to the nation lies in the realm we may broadly term the spiritual."[67]

If Walters refused to allow the depression to reshape the university's mission,
the Roosevelt Administration's response to the economic crisis, a constellation of
programs known as the New Deal, did allow the university to reshape its campus.
Federal dollars helped UC make several improvements, including the construction
of a regulation baseball field and tennis courts on the southern end of campus,
paid for by the Civil Works Administration. A Public Works Administration (PWA)
grant, combined with city bond funds, paid for the expansion of the Chemistry
Building, and a Works Progress Administration (WPA) grant allowed the construction of a Greek amphitheater behind the library.[68] Federal dollars also helped students directly, especially through the National Youth Administration (NYA), created in 1935 to help with the unemployment problem among young people. One of
its programs provided work-study opportunities for college students.[69] In the fall of
1936, more than five hundred UC students, both graduates and undergraduates,

were receiving support from the NYA. Undergraduate students could earn 40 cents an hour, while graduate students earned 50 cents, with the vast majority of them working on campus for professors and departments.[70]

The most visible consequence of the New Deal was at the heart of campus, where in January 1936 UC broke ground on a student union. The union replaced a parking lot just west of the stadium, nearly equidistant from the engineering building and McMicken Hall. Its central location underscored the growing importance of student life on campus, of supporting student organizations, providing meal service, and encouraging faculty community.[71] The city of Cincinnati had floated bonds in 1929 to build the union but had not raised nearly enough money. Private donors supplied some funds, but much of the cost was covered by a PWA grant—making it one of more than one thousand university or college buildings funded by that New Deal agency. According the President Walters, the new building fitted well with the university's mission. As he noted before construction began, the university "has a special obligation to provide facilities to unite its students and to supply them with gracious and civilizing influences."[72]

Prominent local architect Harry Hake and his son Harry Hake Jr. designed the union. The senior Hake had already designed several buildings on campus, including the library, completed in 1930 and named for Carl Blegen in 1979; the law school, completed in 1925 and then swallowed by a modernist shell forty years later; and Memorial Hall, a dormitory completed in 1924 and now part of the College-Conservatory of Music complex. Hake's buildings followed historic forms, including the Collegiate Gothic of Memorial Hall and the library's Greek Revival style. The Hakes used the Georgian Colonial style for the union, which featured a central clock tower and a grand two-story portico on its western facade. Construction of the building was led by Frank Messer & Sons. One of the "Sons" was Charles Messer, a 1929 graduate of UC. The construction team also included current students. Befitting the school's cooperative emphasis, engineering and architecture students helped with surveying and materials inspection.[73]

The union became the new home to the Commons cafeteria, the student dining hall, which moved out of the basement of McMicken, where it could hold just 450 students, and into the union's third floor Great Hall, which doubled as event space, accommodating dances, parties, and other student and faculty events. The union's basement held a popular soda fountain, billiards, Ping-Pong, and card tables. The second floor had space for student organizations and a paneled lounge. A faculty dining room brought together professors from around campus. Clearly this would be a social hub for the mingling of the entire university community, and spending time at the student union would quickly become essential to the college experience.[74]

As work continued on the student union, the university expanded the seating bowl of Nippert Stadium by lowering the field twelve feet. The stadium dated to 1924, when the Carson Field bleachers were replaced by a horseshoe that sat 12,000 spectators. The stadium memorialized James Gamble Nippert, who had died from an infected wound suffered during a muddy game on Carson Field the previous season.[75] (Nippert's grandfather, James Norris Gamble, a Procter & Gamble executive and inventor of Ivory soap, donated the money to complete the stadium.) Now, the once again enlarged stadium would hold 25,000 spectators, making it the second largest stadium in the state, behind Ohio Stadium in Columbus. The stadium project was funded largely by the WPA, and it employed over two hundred men for ten months.[76]

The university justified the expanded stadium partly as an effort to accommodate city residents. As the Board of Directors considered the investment, Vice President Daniel Laurence noted, "I think there has been a good deal of complaint on the part of the public because of the few desirable seats left for them after the alumni, faculty, and others have been taken care of."[77] In what the *Times-Star* called "a kind of civic event," UC played its first football game in the enlarged stadium against West Virginia at the opening of the 1936 season. Before the game, the newspaper claimed that the improved stadium gave the university "the physical basis for big time football," although the 40–6 trouncing by the Mountaineers suggested UC was not quite ready for the big time, regardless of seating capacity.[78]

UC played three games at Nippert that fall—one loss, one tie, one victory— before President Franklin Roosevelt came to Cincinnati as part of a reelection campaign swing through the Midwest. Roosevelt organized his visit around the inspection of WPA projects, with a quick stop at the Laurel Homes public housing project in the West End and a longer stop on UC's campus, where his open car entered the stadium, circled the field, and then came to a stop at the fifty-yard line. There he addressed the crowd of over fifteen thousand while remaining seated. He was welcomed with "roars of applause" and a smattering of boos from outnumbered Alf Landon supporters. Roosevelt spoke on the theme of securing the American standard of living, which meant more than survival. It meant recreation and leisure, too. "That is why projects like this stadium that serve the enjoyment of people—just for sheer good time—are just as worthwhile as building bridges and stopping floods," he said.[79]

Had Roosevelt visited Cincinnati a year later, he undoubtedly would have chosen different words. In January of 1937, heavy rains caused the worst flooding in the history of the Ohio Valley. Industry and businesses along the riverfront and in the Mill Creek Valley were inundated. Fifty thousand Cincinnatians were forced from their homes. On Sunday, January 24, Northside faced a double disaster as an expansive fire caused by leaking gasoline burned atop the floodwaters, destroying dozens of buildings. As the Black Sunday disaster unfolded, UC cancelled classes for the following week. In announcing the closure, President Walters encouraged students and employees to aid flood victims. That evening, Walters walked from his Clifton home to Mount Storm Park with his son Philip. There they overlooked the inundated neighborhood of South Cumminsville.[80] The next day the Ohio crested at 79.9 feet, the highest ever recorded in Cincinnati.

To coordinate its response, UC created a Flood Emergency Committee led by administrators. Volunteers gathered at Music Hall, where students organized the Red Cross clothing depot, sorting donations and taking orders for distribution.[81] The university community accepted donations at the YMCA on Calhoun and delivered them to Music Hall. Fifty medical students had volunteered for sanitary relief, and they were assigned to a number of posts by the city's Bureau of Sanitation.[82] Several students also provided "valiant service," using short-wave radio on the top floor of Swift Hall to communicate with people around the Ohio Valley. This service proved especially useful as the fire in the Mill Creek Valley raged; the shortwave messages were picked up by WSAI, a commercial radio station. The students, most of them electrical engineering co-op students supervised by Professor William Osterbrock, were able to communicate with stranded residents around the region, at one point directing rescues conducted by the National Guard in Portsmouth. Some of the students, including Victor Raabe, a senior, worked in Swift Hall for three days straight. The cafeteria had closed along with the rest of campus, so students took their meals at Osterbrock's home.[83] As the floodwaters receded, and the university finally reopened, the *News Record* reported that nearly fifteen hundred students, staff, and faculty had volunteered during the emergency, most of them working through the Red Cross stationed at Music Hall.[84]

Two years before the floodwaters rose, a historic university building fell. Since 1925, when the College of Law moved up to the Burnet Woods Campus, the original university building on the McMicken homestead had remained mostly vacant and neglected. The university decided that it made no financial sense to keep it. When news that the building would be demolished reached Joseph Strauss, he asked friends to collect a brick and ship it to him in California. Strauss had graduated from UC in 1892 with a degree in civil engineering. He was in the midst of a very successful career in building bridges, and he was running his own firm. When the brick arrived in San Francisco, Strauss placed it in one of the anchors of his current project—the Golden Gate Bridge. Strauss had been the chief engineer on the project since its initiation in 1929, and he saw it through to completion in 1937. Strauss described the placement of the McMicken brick as symbolic recognition of the strong foundation his alma mater had provided for his career. Thinking on a larger scale, we might describe the brick in the bridge as a symbol of UC's expanding footprint—from Troy to San Francisco—during the 1930s.[85]

A Patriotic Resolution to Keep a Stout Heart

On December 8, 1941, students gathered before radio sets in the lounges of the Student Union and the Women's Building, listening intently to President Roosevelt as he asked Congress to declare war. Japan had attacked Pearl Harbor the day before. In its first issue after the American entry into war, the *News Record* announced a new editorial policy, closing "columns to any expressions which might be deemed contrary to the successful prosecution of the war." There would be no more opinion pieces about the value of isolationism, as there had been in previous years; the peace movement would no longer gain space in the paper. Debates about the role of war and the threat of fascism were over.[86] As the shock of the Japanese attack on Pearl Harbor slowly gave way to a realization of what another world war would bring, the *News Record* reminded students, "We who are now at the University can best serve by concentrating on our academic work. It is the wish of the government that we do so."[87]

On Thursday, December 11, the men on campus gathered for a convocation in Wilson Auditorium—the largest crowd President Walters had ever seen in that building. The men were "serious and hair-trigger," Walters noted in his diary later that day. Germany and Italy had declared war on the United States that morning, and the men were focused, listening intently to a series of speakers. Walters spoke first and asked the men to think about mission, as he was apt to do. "The important thing is that you should act, not upon the spur of emotionalism, or war hysteria, but upon careful thought as to where you will be most useful to the country." Walters was undoubtedly fearful that many of his students would drop out of school and enlist immediately. He also asked the men to hold no illusions about the difficulty that lay ahead, for this war promised to be more devastating than the "War to End All Wars," concluded just twenty years earlier. "Before we leave this hall," he said, "shall we make a patriotic resolution to keep a stout heart in the dark days ahead, and, until our Government may summon us to national service, to study hard and prepare faithfully for the duties both of war and peace?"[88] After the men heard some practical information about the Selective Service, Harold Vinacke, professor of political science, gave a presentation on the strengths and weaknesses of Japan. After a week of extraordinary events, UC's nearly seven thousand male students—and a good number of its faculty—found themselves preparing for war with determination and anxiety.[89]

The women of UC held their own convocation that day, led by Dean of Women Katherine Dabney Ingle.[90] Jane Klein, president of the Women's Senate, delivered a message similar to Walters's, urging women to stay in school and prepare themselves physically and mentally for the rigors of war. "Emotional strain is the war burden of women," she said. "We must prepare to make great sacrifices for our country's sake."[91] Ingle also knew that the war would bring great changes for women. "As a college woman, you must expect to serve on a professional level in either government, industry, or civilian war work," she said the next year. Women, she thought, would have to go beyond the volunteerism and welfare work of former generations. Women would find jobs in industry, in technical work and, of course, in the military.[92]

As in the previous war, institutions of higher education changed dramatically to meet the needs of the crisis. The campus prepared in case enemy bombers made their way to southwest Ohio, creating air raid shelters in each building and establishing the lines of communication that could function during an attack. Preparations included creating a blackout mechanism at the power plant that would allow the entire campus to go dark at the flip of a switch. The libraries moved rare books to more secure locations, and the Department of Chemistry increased the protection of the most dangerous chemicals.[93] In many other ways campus swung in to action along with the rest of the community, engaging in book drives for bored soldiers and blood drives for the wounded. UC observed meatless days and organized scrap drives. Faculty even allowed students to write on both sides of the paper to reduce consumption. Campus saw campaigns to sell war bonds, and the administration encouraged car-pooling to save gas. In sum, the UC community faced constant reminders that this was total war.[94]

Campus also saw myriad enrollment and curricular changes. The ROTC program had already seen significant growth, with applications outstripping slots in 1940. Several upperclassmen applied—a new phenomenon.[95] More dramatically, the military would need thousands of nurses, and the College of Nursing and Health responded by admitting a second class of students in 1942 and accelerating the curriculum. The College of Medicine also accepted more students into its ranks, and the faculty of both colleges organized the 25th General Hospital to serve in the European theater. Eventually 600 doctors and nurses from UC served in England, Belgium, and France during the war. Back home, the College of Medicine turned to practical research questions: dysentery, gangrene, immunization.[96]

Every corner of the campus did its part. Evening College offered noncredit courses for nonmatriculated students in industry, including materials testing and inspection, and production supervision. These courses were taught by UC faculty with the help of local businessmen who would need qualified workers to ramp up production. The university prepared to train 1,000 men in diesel engines, tool engineering, safety engineering, and defense contract accounting.[97] The master's in public service expanded and the course of instruction accelerated specifically so that more women could be trained to take government jobs to replace men going off to war. Chemistry grew, pressed by student demand, with many seeking skills useful to the war effort. Many faculty and administrators took up special duties during the war, including Helen Schwartz, dean of the College of Nursing and Health, who was called to New York to oversee a national effort to reform nursing education to help hasten training.[98]

Administrators and faculty hoped that the curricula in various programs would not change radically, but rapid enrollment expansion and acceleration did require adaptation. Some colleges, including the College of Liberal Arts, passed a rule allowing drafted seniors to graduate without completing their studies, as long as they were in good standing and had the recommendation of their departments.[99] Walters was also concerned that the demands of war would diminish interest in the liberal arts, especially history, philosophy, and literature. "I believe that these departments advance our students in national preparedness by teaching them logical thinking, giving them intellectual discipline, providing historical background, and inculcating loyalty to the responsibilities of the Federal Constitution and the freedoms of the Bill of Rights," Walters noted.[100] James Vaughn, a professor of psychology, also emphasized the need for continued liberal arts education, claiming the Axis powers had been so successful because they had educated their population so well—not merely in content knowledge, but in observation, apprehension, organization, and application. "We have allowed our educational institutions to fall behind those of the fascists," he claimed. "The training of mental processes are just as valuable in time of war as in time of peace. Indeed, it is only the trained mind which is capable of switching from the chaos of war to peace."[101]

Some programs saw dramatic growth, but the overall consequence of the war was a significant decrease in enrollments. Nationwide college and university enrollments fell nearly 40 percent in the first two years of the war. At UC, enrollments decreased 17 percent in the first year of the war, as many would-be students headed into military service or directly into employment. Declines continued in the second year, with law seeing the largest percentage decrease while, not surprisingly, the College of Medicine continued to grow. By early 1944, UC had lost about half of its students, most of them called away to war through the draft or early mobilization of ROTC or other training programs, a reminder that for students and employees the most direct participation in the war came as soldiers, sailors, and flyers. By December of 1942, nearly eighteen hundred UC men had enrolled in ROTC or the reserves—55 percent of the male students. At the close of winter quarter 1944, more than one thousand men, most of them enrolled in engineering courses, headed off for further training and then the war. After the Allies had secured victory in Europe on May 8, 1945, the *News Record* listed 157 UC casualties in the European theater.[102]

❧ Echoes of War

As the Second World War drew to a close, few Americans could dream of a "return to normalcy," as they had after the First. The creation and use of nuclear weapons portended an ever more dangerous world, especially as the Soviet Union consolidated its control over Eastern Europe and invested in its own nuclear arsenal. The failure of the American isolationism in the 1920s convinced leaders in both parties that the United States would have to remain engaged in the world, through new military alliances, the United Nations, and international organizations designed to spread prosperity—and block the spread of communism. In sum, international relations and global events would retain a critical place in American politics in the postwar era, and, of course, there would be consequences for American higher education.

Domestic policy, too, suggested no return to prewar arrangements. In 1944, even before Germany and Japan had surrendered, Congress passed the Servicemen's Readjustment Act, also known as the GI Bill, as a means of preparing for the return of millions of soldiers and sailors to civilian life. The educational opportunities afforded by the bill required that universities begin preparations for an influx of students. As a hint of changes to come, ten returning soldiers found a place in the incoming College of Medicine class that fall.[103]

UC prepared for the postwar era in part by making plans to replace the antiquated McMicken Hall. The city passed a bond for the purpose in 1944. Four years later, the oldest building on campus was demolished. Many of its bricks were reused in the construction of the new McMicken Hall, designed by UC's favorite architects, Hake and Hake. The grand Georgian building, dedicated in 1950, featured a Christopher Wren tower that aligned with the tower of the nearby student union.[104] In one of the last echoes of the world war, that building gained a new name in 1966. UC alumnus and benefactor Walter W. Tangeman, an executive vice president at Cincinnati Milling Machine, died that year, and following his wishes the university renamed the student union in honor of his son, Donald Core Tangeman, who had died twenty years earlier on a PT boat in the South Pacific.[105]

6

GROWING PAINS AND OPPORTUNITIES
An Expanding Campus and Mission

The postwar decades brought a new prosperity and rapid expansion—a "golden age" in higher education. The GI Bill allowed more than 2 million former soldiers and sailors to enter college with federal tuition support. The impact was immediate and lasting. From 1946 to 1948 veterans represented more than 40 percent of the students on campuses around the country. Universities endeavored to house and educate this rush of students, but the struggle to keep pace with expanding and shifting demand did not soon subside. Growth remained the predominant theme for the next twenty-five years.

Nationally, enrollments at higher education institutions grew from just under 1.7 million in 1945 to over 3.5 million in 1960. Then in the mid-1960s, Baby Boomers, the children of the war generation, began entering college. Most of them chose public institutions. The University of Cincinnati followed these national trends. From the moment the first federally funded GI stepped on campus in 1944 through the end of the 1960s, UC rode a wave of growth that left no aspect of the institution unchanged. Both the student body and the faculty nearly doubled in the 1960s alone. The budget more than doubled in that decade. And, crucially, from 1950 to 1970, the land area owned by UC increased from 62 acres to 152 acres.[1]

The dramatic growth of higher education was part of a broader shift in the American economy, one in which the industrial jobs that had helped fuel national prosperity and the expansion of the middle class gradually gave way to service-sector jobs, many of them requiring college degrees. With this shift the fate of the national economy became ever more entangled with the health of higher education. Discussions of one bled into discussions of the other, and increasingly conversation about training the American workforce incorporated innovation on

American campuses—creating new programs, conducting new research, developing more efficient teaching strategies. More and more the discourse surrounding higher education concerned how institutions would respond to the economic needs of the nation—more science, more math, more business—and less about how universities attended to the needs of students as moral citizens.

As surely as expansion brought changes to institutional missions, it forced changes in instructional methods. In 1946, UC enrolled 16,000 students, about half of them taking evening courses, and nearly 60 percent of them veterans.[2] Twenty years later the university was struggling to accommodate new growth, as total enrollment topped 30,000 for the first time in 1968. In an attempt to stretch resources, some departments offered extremely large lecture classes. The largest met in Wilson Memorial Auditorium, which could seat 1,200. A student survey revealed that Wilson was far and away the least popular classroom, but professors expressed mixed opinions. Harold Fishbein, of psychology, went so far as to conclude that "lecture size does not matter," because "an instructor can be responsive to 800 students just as effectively as to 15." Professor of history William Aeschbacher offered more qualified support for mass teaching techniques, noting, "The use of large classes is obviously more effective in history than in some other course where it is more essential to have frequent student response or participation." Large lectures with little faculty–student interaction raised the question once again: What was the university for? Was the faculty just delivering information to the masses?[3]

After experimenting with large lectures in Wilson, the Department of Sociology decided to give up the practice. "In Wilson, students feel they are there to be acted upon, or amused," said Professor Arthur Hinman. "We want them to react." But with so many students demanding Sociology 101, the department could retreat only so far from the large-class format. In the fall of 1970, Sociology taught four classes capped at 250. Growth, it seems, required compromise. Some faculty saw the use of large lectures as a benign adoption of more efficient delivery techniques; getting information to more students was part of democratizing the university. Those who took a less sanguine view might see these developments as merely the industrial model of education reaching its apotheosis.[4]

As the scale of institutions changed, so too did the scale of national concern. Success in the Cold War was measured partly in the geopolitical influence of the super powers, but also in the ability of antithetical economic systems to produce growth and prosperity. The United States turned to universities to train the scientists

Zimmer Auditorium. Completed in 1970 as part of the Brodie Science Complex, Zimmer Hall helped UC expand the number of very large classes it offered. Pictured here in a recent photograph, Zimmer has remained an important instructional space. *Courtesy of UC Photographic Services.*

and engineers who, in turn, would help the American capitalist economy outpace the planned economies of the communist bloc. After the Soviet Union's successful launch of the *Sputnik* satellite in the fall of 1957, politicians and the press clamored for greater government investment in education, particularly in science and engineering. Cold War federal research dollars allowed medical, engineering, and science programs to expand dramatically, giving undergraduate and graduate students greater opportunities to develop research skills that would be useful in the evolving economy. Ironically, then, federal and state government involvement in higher education increased significantly in the effort to prove the superiority of free-market capitalism. As the nation waged the Cold War, government became ever more engaged in the funding and management of American higher education.[5]

University of California president Clark Kerr called the Cold War expansion "the second great transformation" in higher education, the first having taken place in the late 1800s during the rush to create new institutions that brought the University of Cincinnati into being. Kerr worried about the existential threats to universities posed by rapid growth and the nation's changing conception of higher education's fundamental mission.[6] In particular, the Cold War dramatically elevated the role of research on campuses like UC. While not all federally funded projects had direct military implications, some of them did, and many universities, including UC, found themselves reliant on Defense Department research dollars just as Vietnam War protesters demanded that higher education disentangle itself from the nation's war machine. As early as 1951, with the United States engaged in war on the Korean peninsula, University of Chicago chancellor Robert Hutchins asked the poignant question: "Why do university presidents cheerfully welcome the chance to devote their institutions to military preparations?"[7] As Hutchins pointed out, when it came to military contracts, university presidents failed to see how opportunities for growth might become threats to identity.

Classified military research had ended at UC shortly after the conclusion of World War II, but the intensifying national debate about the propriety of higher education's entanglement in the creation of the weapons of war encouraged UC to codify its policy. In May 1969, a Faculty Advisory Committee on Research affirmed the university policy of not accepting classified research from the government, and, in language that was subsequently adopted by the president, articulated a clear and simple mission for the institution: "The aim of university research is to enrich and enhance the culture and survival of the human race." The emphasis on "survival" rather than, say, "advancement," reveals just how thoroughly Cold War fears and antiwar sentiment had seeped into the debate.[8]

Despite the Cold War concerns, the UC community had good reason to be proud of its research accomplishments, especially in the College of Medicine, where Albert B. Sabin served as a professor of pediatrics. In 1939 Children's Hospital and UC recruited Sabin from the Rockefeller Institute, where the young virologist had taken up the study of polio, a crippling and sometimes deadly disease that tended to afflict young people. That work was disrupted by World War II, during which Sabin researched a variety of viruses affecting troops, including encephalitis, sandfly fever, and dengue fever. After the war, Sabin dedicated himself to understanding the polio virus and developing an effective vaccine. He determined that because infections began in the intestines, an oral live virus vaccine would be more effective than the injected vaccine developed by Jonas Salk. After successful tests on monkeys, in 1954 Sabin began a small trial in Chillicothe, Ohio. All thirty of the test subjects—male prisoners at the federal reformatory—developed antibodies, and none got sick. Sabin's live vaccine was ready for a larger test. The next significant step was the use of the vaccine on 10 million children in the Soviet Union in 1959. Once it became clear that the live vaccine did indeed produce better results than the Salk vaccine, the National Institutes of Health gave Sabin permission for use in the United States. In 1960, Salk began trials in Cincinnati, where Sabin Oral Sundays brought tens of thousands of children into schools, clinics, and hospitals to receive the vaccine. Over the course of the next decade, the Sabin vaccine was essential to the effort to eradicate polio around the globe.[9]

Sabin's international fame helped elevate Cincinnati's reputation for research, but he was hardly alone. George Rieveschl began a lifelong relationship with UC when he entered as an undergraduate student. After earning his PhD in chemistry in 1940, also at UC, he joined the faculty and continued researching methods of blocking the negative effects of histamines in humans. Rieveschl synthesized a new compound, an antihistamine with few negative side effects. Rieveschl left UC to work for Parke-Davis, a large drug manufacturer, which marketed Rieveschl's creation as Benadryl—a product that clearly fit within UC's research mission. In 1970, Rieveschl returned to UC as the vice president for research. Even the very existence of the position, created just three years earlier, reflected the growing emphasis on research at the university—and, of course, the ever-expanding ranks of administrators. In 1987, five years after Rieveschl retired, the university renamed the biology and chemistry building in his honor. Since then, Rieveschl Hall has served as a reminder of the importance of the university's research mission.[10]

🌿 Shall Burnet Woods Be a University or a Park?

With the university poised for rapid growth at the conclusion of World War II, the administration knew that campus would have to expand—again. In the 1914, the university had gained access to an additional thirteen acres of the park, and by the late 1930s its initial four buildings had grown to over twenty. UC had built a campus dense with structures, clustered in the southwest corner of the park. Still, students, faculty, and the public could easily wander into Burnet Woods. The boundary between park and campus, the winding and narrow University Avenue, was quite permeable. The lack of firm a boundary—and historical precedence— made it easy for administrators to envision further expansion into the park. Indeed, the university had drawn up plans for an additional piece of the park even before postwar growth came into view. UC was particularly keen on increasing space for the accommodation of faculty, staff, and student automobiles, the number of which expanded even more rapidly than the student population in the 1930s.[11]

In 1939, the university proposed to take park land north of University Avenue to create a 500-car parking lot, initiating a decade-long contest over the future of Burnet Woods. Cincinnati's superintendent of parks, J. W. Tait, argued that an existing lot, at the corner of Bishop and University, was sufficiently large, as was clear by how many spots remained open during the day. He also praised the park's value, noting, "Burnet Woods is one of the most intensively used of any of our larger parks." Tait reminded the city that the park had "already been greatly decreased from its original size," asserting that "the use of any part of the remaining area for any other than strictly park purposes cannot be justified."[12] With this straightforward reasoning, the Cincinnati Park Board denied the transfer of land from park to university.

As World War II came to a close, however, the university felt increasing pressure to expand its campus, and to expand its request. In 1945, UC asked the park board for twenty-two acres, to be used for more than just parking. In the same spot where the university previously envisioned a huge parking lot, it now hoped to build a women's dormitory for 400 students and a fieldhouse, where up to 5,000 fans could watch basketball and other events. That May, at a meeting between the Cincinnati Park Board and several representatives of the university, park board chairman Irwin Krohn asked a seemingly straightforward question: "Shall Burnet Woods Be a University or a Park?" With this, Krohn neatly summarized a struggle that had been ongoing since 1889, when the university prepared to move up the hill and into Burnet Woods. Behind Krohn's question was the supposition that the woods could not be a park and a university simultaneously. The city would have to choose.[13]

During the ensuing debate, opponents of campus expansion asked why the university didn't make better use of the space it already had, suggesting, for example, that it place new buildings on its expansive front lawn, which ran from McMicken Hall down to Clifton Avenue. Frank Dinsmore, UC alumnus, prominent lawyer, and current chairman of the UC Board of Directors, answered this idea with, "There is a space which has been reserved as a park space for the purpose of embellishing the whole lay-out and one which I feel sure this Board would join with the University Board in keeping in that form." In other words, Dinsmore didn't want campus to become even less parklike than it already had. Dinsmore also offered judgments about the land the university hoped to acquire. "It's part of the park that is not used for picnic purposes; in fact, I don't believe it is used very much at all for park purposes." To Dinsmore activities such as boating, playing on a playground, and picnicking counted as park purposes, but those activities occurred elsewhere in Burnet Woods. The kinds of activities that took place in this part of the park—quiet contemplation, walks in the woods—were uses that looked more like "underutilization" to Dinsmore. In this conception, park purposes required a crowd—not unlike a well-used campus.[14]

As park and university officials debated the future of these acres, their conversation often moved into assessments of the public good and the relative value of universities and parks. President Raymond Walters emphasized the singular importance of the university to city. "I think this is a matter of serving the people of the city best," he told the park board. "In coming to your decision, if you will adhere to that principle of serving the City of Cincinnati best, I would have no fear of the outcome."[15]

Krohn listened to Dinsmore and Walters and was unmoved. "It is not only the use of the land, it's what effect the use of the land will have on the entire park," he said. "It is not a question of the usefulness or the standing of the University. I think every citizen realizes what the University means, but they also realize that we must have parks for a class of people who have no other source of recreation." Here Krohn articulated his sense of the mission of city parks, which was echoed by park board member Frank Adams. "I don't think it's fair to take the park away from one class of people and give it to another," he said, in an acknowledgment that the park was largely used by poorer Cincinnatians, while the university mostly served those who were better off. "This park is centrally located in Cincinnati; it is more accessible than any other park in Cincinnati, and there are 110,000 to 135,000 people who visit it every year," he continued. This emphasis on the utility of the park indicated that the park board, as then constituted, would defend Burnet Woods from further incursion.[16]

Adams and Krohn sounded very much like the neighborhood residents who had taken up a defense of the park. Before the May 1945 meeting these activists had circulated petitions and delivered them to the park board. Those who signed, mostly residents of the neighborhoods surrounding Burnet Woods, asked that nothing "be done to curtail its beauty."[17] Another petition said, "Losing a portion of beautiful Burnet Woods" would be "an irreparable loss. We feel so strongly that we are begging you" to deny the request. That petition argued that the park was well used. In winter, visitors could sled, ice skate, even ski. In summer "innumerable groups take their evening meals to the park." Some park supporters sent the board individual "Sign and Mail" notes that praised the "wonderful old trees" and other assets.[18]

In addition to petitions, the Clifton Heights Welfare Association, which represented the interests of the neighborhoods surrounding the south end of the park and campus, had circulated a flier that listed "Reasons for Protesting." The association emphasized accessibility, noting the park could be reached by four streetcar routes and one bus route. The flier listed key attributes, including "the beauty of its many old trees" and the popular summer band concerts, which had been endowed by a "loyal, patriotic citizen." Further, the flier asserted, "The people of Cincinnati need every foot of Burnet Woods Park for Park Purposes." Higher education wasn't the only public good under stress from growing demand, it noted, concluding that, "Cincinnati should be planning more parks for its citizens rather than eliminating those we already have."[19] In a separate piece, entitled "False Plea of University of Cincinnati," the Clifton Heights group argued that the university didn't need the space at all. "The entire campus clearly shows a vast waste of space." The essay asserted that in the future universities would build up, in towers, which, of course, did become the primary means of expanding facilities in the 1960s.[20]

After the May 1945 meeting, Krohn and two other park board members sent a lengthy explanation of denial to the UC board, claiming that new buildings would "completely eliminate those park characteristics which it now possesses," because the hilly and well-wooded area would have to be graded and "all trees and other vegetation would have to be removed." Emphasizing accessibility, the explanation noted, "the park is within easy walking distance of public transportation" and is therefore "intensively used." This area also served as a buffer against "noise, confusion, and traffic hazards" along University Avenue, which separated campus and park. Because the proposed expansion would put a large fieldhouse along the redrawn park line, it "would so increase the automobile traffic over all the roads in Burnet Woods…as to make it unsafe for children to use a great part of Burnet Woods Park for play." In sum, UC could and should seek land elsewhere.[21]

Unfortunately for park supporters, the integrity of Burnet Woods lasted only as long as Irwin Krohn lived. He died in December 1948. Six months later UC advanced a new expansion proposal, one that would exchange seven acres of land owned by a trustee on the city's wealthy east side, acres that would expand Alms

Park in Mount Lookout, plus $44,000, for twenty-two acres in Burnet Woods. The proposal, stunningly lopsided from a purely monetary standpoint, sparked an even more active opposition movement, this time led by Gilbert Bettman Jr., a lawyer and long-time friend of Krohn's. Bettman, who lived in Clifton, less than a mile from the park, formed the Citizens' League to Save Burnet Woods at a meeting held in August 1949, shortly after the new plan became public. Bettman's group was joined by a new Committee for the Preservation of Public Parks of Cincinnati, headed by Ed Macke, one of the leaders of the 1945 effort.[22]

The Citizens' League to Save Burnet Woods was well organized and politically connected. Bettman set up four committees—legal, publicity, public support, and advisory. Prominent names studded the committee membership lists, as did university employees and alumni, and, of course, neighborhood residents.[23] The opponents made the same arguments that appeared in the 1945 battle, but also put forward a plan that would shift UC expansion to the east, into Corryville and onto land that the city had already purchased for the university, and would force UC to make better use of its current footprint. UC eventually did expand eastward, but it clearly expected to grow in two directions.

UC criticized the opposition plan, using the dean of the College of Applied Arts (which offered classes in community planning) to claim modern planning principles required campus expansion into the woods.[24] "The university feels its present campus is already too crowded for comfort and objects to efforts of those who would force it to create congestion and confusion in planning its front and side yards," said Dean Ernest Pickering. He added, "Good planning demands that people should be able to move easily and quickly from one spot to another by the shortest possible route. Circulation becomes one of the most important considerations of the designer."[25] This emphasis on circulation spoke less to walking around campus than to the construction of a new cross-town thoroughfare north of campus, using four of the twenty-two acres the park would shed.

The Citizens League to Save Burnet Woods lost its battle when the city council voted to transfer the land in the spring of 1950. Dense and diverse urban neighborhoods lost twenty-two acres of an accessible, forested park, and an increasingly suburban student body gained a larger campus. Although the public discourse emphasized how the city and its residents could make the best use of the land in question, the issue may have turned on *who* would use the land more than *how* they would. The discourse described two very different publics: one confined to city neighborhoods, streetcars, and shrinking urban amenities; the other upwardly mobile through higher education and spatially mobile via automobiles.

Two years after the vote, Dean Pickering moved with his college into the Alms Building, sitting on a hill overlooking the remaining fraction of Burnet Woods. Soon the Alms Building overlooked the extended St. Clair Avenue, seven lanes of pavement running across former park land, creating a new, firmer boundary between campus and park. Just as opponents had feared, it eliminated the buffer that protected the park from noise, parking, and traffic. By this point, university officials rarely used the phrase "Burnet Woods Campus," replacing it with "Clifton Campus," undoubtedly in recognition that UC was no longer a campus in a park, but a campus that had swallowed much of the woods.[26]

The university won the expansion battle, but it lost something in the process. More of its neighbors grew wary of the institution, which was still owned by the city, even though it did not always act in the best interests of the people who lived there. Among those who complained was Ella Hengehold, a widow who for more than twenty years had lived in the modest brick home at 3114 Bishop. She had raised two sons in that house, boys who no doubt made good use of the park just across the street. As the university threatened to creep closer to her home in 1949, she expressed her concern as part of a coordinated letter-writing campaign. She was disappointed in City Councilman Charles Taft's support of the expansion plan, telling him, crestfallen, "It seems to me the University of Cincinnati will never be satisfied."[27]

❧ There Is Some Divergence of Opinion at the University

As the university's research mission expanded, so too did the reach of its findings. Like Albert Sabin, researchers across the university took on projects with national or even global consequences. This included several Cincinnati researchers who took up the studies concerning health and the human environment, especially related to exposure to lead and air pollution. Not surprisingly, sometimes divergent methods or even philosophical differences among researchers led to conflict. This was the case when two Cincinnati researchers studied the deaths of twenty people in Donora, Pennsylvania. During the last week of October 1948, a temperature inversion put a lid on Donora and much of the region around, while a zinc smelter and a steel mill, both owned by American Steel and Wire, a subsidiary of US Steel, pumped emissions into the atmosphere. On Friday, October 30, dozens were sickened. By Saturday evening eighteen people had died, and firefighters were responding to distressed residents with oxygen and helping to move the stricken to the overflowing hospital. Hundreds of people fled the city, seeking relief beyond the pall. Even before the smog lifted, officials attributed the deaths to industrial emissions. "It's murder. There's nothing else you can call it," said Donora Board of Health member Dr. William Rongaus. "There's something in the air here that isn't found anywhere else."[28]

On Sunday the zinc plant shut down, rains brought relief, and the death toll rose to twenty, but observers were not any closer to understanding *exactly* what happened. Under the headline "20 Dead in Smog," the *New York Times* reported on a "mysterious air-borne plague," highlighting what was not yet known. What was that "something in the air" that was killing people?[29] This question was at the heart of several separate investigations. Two of those investigations involved the University of Cincinnati.[30]

One was led by Clarence Mills, professor of experimental medicine, who had begun researching air pollution in part because of Cincinnati's smoke shroud. The other involved Robert Kehoe, founding director of the Kettering Laboratory. These men took diametrically opposite approaches to the problem. Driven by moral outrage, Mills was eager to speak with victims and tally the human cost in prose and epidemiological data. His science was a form of activism, which he clearly hoped would translate into policy reform. Kehoe, who had become one of industry's most reliable "independent" researchers, conducted the preponderance of his work through meticulous laboratory studies. His lab contracted with dozens of companies to test a great diversity of chemicals, but the guiding question of the research was remarkably consistent: At what concentration would this chemical become toxic?[31] Kehoe developed his own precautionary principle: Government should move deliberately toward regulation, since policy grounded in a faulty understanding of the problem would not lead to the desired solution and could impede economic growth. In this way, Kehoe's science was also a form of activism, dedicated to the promotion of industrial innovation.

Mills spent much of his career studying weather and climate as factors in human culture, mostly through psychological influence, but by the early 1940s he had shifted to coal smoke and lung health. Using epidemiological methods, Mills gathered data on soot fall and deaths from lung cancer in several industrial cities. His data showed a strong correlation between polluted air and cancer, and eventually between cancer and cigarette smoking.[32] As a scholar-activist, Mills consistently took his research into the popular press and the political arena.

With his wife, Marjorie, a sometimes collaborator and coauthor, and on his own dime, Mills drove to Donora, arriving on November 6. His description of the trip appeared in *Hygeia*, a magazine published by the American Medical Association, on the one-year anniversary of the event. He narrated the last leg of the trip in detail, highlighting the strong smell of "acrid sulfur fumes" in the "fog and smog filled valleys." Although he arrived five days after the deaths had stopped, Mills wrote as if the deadly smog lingered still. They crept along, headlights on in the "valley's dismal gloom," windshield wipers pushing aside fly-ash, until they came upon "the terrible, sickening devastation wrought by the acid fumes from the large zinc smelter."[33] He assessed the health of the place before studying the health of the people, noting the dead vegetation and the dramatic erosion.

In typical Mills style, his reaction to the landscape appeared in the local newspaper two days after his arrival in a column published under his name: "The barren eroded hillsides and the devastated cemetery bear tragic witness to the presence of severe air poisoning. The remarkable thing about the Donora disaster is not that so many people should have been affected, but rather that so many should have been able to survive in the poisoned air up to now." Mills claimed the nation was eager to see what Donora would do; now was the time to press for reform. He continued, "If obstructive tactics from her giant industries are successful in preventing effective action here where a real disaster has occurred, then how can other cities with less obvious danger facing them hope for relief."[34]

After having spent just a day observing the landscape and interviewing residents, Mills spoke before the Donora Borough Council, whom he helped convince to accept a grant of $10,000 from the CIO–United Steel Workers of America. Mills asserted that industrial emissions were causing chronic public health damage.[35] He encouraged the borough council to conduct a house-to-house survey with the CIO funding. That survey found that 5,000 of the city's 13,500 residents had been affected by the smog. Mills believed that many of those who claimed no effects were merely trying to protect the industrial employers, which were essential to the city's economy.[36]

Mills had the uncanny ability to gain the attention of the press. Three weeks after the incident, the *New York Times* ran a story from Cincinnati reporting the conclusions Mills had drawn from the data collected to that point. "The Donora disaster shows how very close many of our industrialized cities have come to a kill-ing pollution level," he said. A month later, with the survey complete and the scope of the problem well established, if not the actual cause, the Associated Press pub-lished a similar story out of Cincinnati. Again Mills emphasized the development of chronic health problems in polluted atmospheres and claimed that the entire community had been at risk of death during the episode. "A slightly higher poison concentration in the air or a few hours longer time," Mills said, "and the whole community might have been left almost devoid of life."[37]

This last article drew the attention of James Crow, editor of *Chemical and En-gineering News*, the trade magazine of the American Chemical Society, with whom Kehoe had an ongoing correspondence. Crow sent along a clipping of the article and noted, "In view of your comments on the Donora situation, I was quite sur-prised to see" Mills's comments. "This seems to give the impression that there is some divergence of opinion at the University of Cincinnati." Kehoe responded immediately, noting first that he had "not questioned the seriousness of the Donora tragedy." Still, "My criticism of the things that have been said in the public press is not that they are magnifying the seriousness of the problem, but rather that they are talking about it as though they knew what to do about it, which is far from be-ing the case." Kehoe may have been embarrassed by Mills, but he noted, "Dr. Mills is entitled to his own opinions, and I am sure that he will express them where and when he wishes. He is not a member of our staff, and we are not responsible for his opinions."[38] Kehoe had reason to worry that Mills might tarnish the university's reputation for pro-industry research.

Kehoe's involvement in Donora came through his usual, formal route. American Steel and Wire hired his lab to conduct a study of its mill and smelter and determine the cause of the deaths, part of the company's preparation to defend against lawsuits.[39] Kehoe's team generated a lot of data, much of it useful only in convincing observers that their study had been exhaustive, which was undoubtedly part of the point. Kehoe's men clearly understood their role in preparing a defense for US Steel in the impending lawsuits. The first draft of their conclusions read, "The Donora disaster resulted in our opinion from a not reasonably foreseeable act of God," directly correlating findings with legal terminology. Kehoe had the good sense to make the object of the research less apparent in the conclusion. He changed it to "The Donora disaster resulted from the effects of unusual weather conditions in the Monongahela valley at

Donora upon the normal effluent of the community and the industries therein." In both articulations, the Kettering report normalized the pollution and asserted the abnormality of the weather.[40]

Kettering Lab retained the right to publish the results of its research—although frequently Kehoe chose not to. This was the case with Donora. His lab produced a seventy-page report that concluded only that more than one factor must have been at work in the disaster. Kehoe sent a copy to American Steel and Wire and kept one in his own files. The results of the research only became public insofar as they appeared in legal proceedings around lawsuits filed against the company. As those lawsuits accumulated in the spring of 1949, Kehoe wrote to Harvey Jordan, vice president at American Steel and Wire, giving his unsolicited opinion on air pollution: "Of first importance, in our opinion, is a clear understanding of the fact that there are valid hygienic, political, economic, and aesthetic considerations, which, increasingly, are focusing public attention upon the need for control of air pollution." Kehoe was fearful that bad legislation might come before researchers like him had learned precisely what the trouble was. It would serve the interest of industry to get out in front of regulation and control their emissions. "It is, and should be, we believe, the policy of industry to so establish control of air pollution as to keep it far below levels at which nuisance is evident, insofar as this achievement is commensurate with productive economy."[41]

The research of the Kettering Lab was used specifically to counteract the testimony of Clarence Mills, who had been deposed in support of the plaintiffs' cases, as lawyers negotiated a settlement for the lawsuits.[42] Given the inconclusiveness of the Kehoe report, and that of a larger study conducted by the Public Health Service, the company was able to settle the cases for a total of $265,000. Two years after the Donora disaster, industry lawyers thanked Kehoe: "Your valuable help in these cases is very much appreciated."[43]

In 1954, Mills gathered together his most recent research for a book called *Air Pollution and Community Health*. It opens with a description of the view from Mills's house in the Fairview neighborhood, "overlooking the basin area of Cincinnati 300 feet below." Clarence and Marjorie Mills had built this house themselves, a modern home with experimental technology designed to conserve energy. From it they had sweeping views of the Mill Creek Valley and the "bluish-grey heavy blanketing smog" that hid the Kentucky hills across the river. This was the scene that had helped inspire his research agenda.[44]

154

As consumers moved away from dirty coal and toward natural gas, the smoke over the basin had dissipated somewhat in recent years, but air pollution had become a more widespread and vexing problem. Mills recounted how General Hospital had moved up the hill to Avondale in the 1910s in search of a more salubrious environment. "Dr. Holmes even had every pavilion of the new hospital equipped with a roof garden for sun-bathing in the clean air and bright sunlight," Mills noted. "Perhaps it was fortunate that Dr. Holmes did not live to see his beautiful hospital engulfed in the polluted air drifting up over Avondale." The rooftop gardens, Mills pointed out, had never been used for sunbathing.[45]

Air Pollution and Community Health focused on linking air quality and disease, but Mills also commented on the behavior of his fellow scientists. "It has been most disheartening to see the country's industrial physicians subordinate community health to the financial welfare of their industrial supporters. In this they are behaving more as industrial employees than as true physicians." And, after describing his experience in Donora at length, he included sharp words about his colleague, noting that Kehoe's findings "remain unpublished and unavailable except to those interested in keeping Industry free of blame—an unusual attitude indeed for a *university's* scientist to take!"[46]

Mills raises once again the familiar question: What is a university for? UC's involvement in Donora highlighted some of the forces working against good science in the postwar era: the Cold War politics surrounding the need for economic growth; the corporate money that drove so much university research; and the increasing pressure on researchers to get good results quickly. Industry was filling the globe with dangerous chemicals—DDT, lead, beryllium, fluorine—and the most important questions had yet to be answered. What would all of these pollutants mean to human and ecological health? Despite the efforts of men such as Clarence Mills and the growth of environmental health research that encouraged community engagement and the study of the consequences of chronic exposures, real improvement in air quality was more than three decades in the future.[47]

✿ Parking for Everyone

The American economy was strong through the postwar era, but not all places thrived. Some urban neighborhoods began to show signs of deterioration as early as the late 1950s. In Cincinnati, city planners expressed concern about the Avondale-Corryville area, which showed "several strong indications" of decline, including "out-migration of original families" and the cutting up of once-fine homes into apartments to accommodate new, lower-income residents. In response, the City Planning Commission published a renewal plan designed to "stop the spread of blight," using the most popular method of the time, rehabilitation. The most important step for neighborhood renewal didn't involve buildings, however. To stop the decline of Avondale and Corryville, planners would improve connections to the rest of the city. The plan emphasized improved traffic flow, creating new east–west and north–south arteries. Not coincidentally, these changes would be critical to the University of Cincinnati and the medical complex, the former just outside the planning area, and the latter near its center.[48]

From the university's perspective, two changes stood out: the extension of St. Clair Avenue (now Martin Luther King) through Burnet Woods and its linkage west to Dixmyth and east to a widened Melish; and the widening of Jefferson to create a traffic bypass around the commercial district on Vine Street. These changes would significantly improve automobile traffic through the neighborhoods surrounding the major institutions, although they would also dramatically alter the neighborhoods themselves—making them even less attractive for middle-class residents. Among those who opposed changes to improve traffic flow was John Brady, who lived on Jefferson Avenue near St. Clair. As the city proposals developed in the mid-1950s, Brady complained, "Making Jefferson a through street to Vine would create a speedway. It would force a curtailment to parking and eventually it would hurt business in the area." Other neighborhood residents argued that creating wider streets to speed traffic would make walking to neighborhood schools, including Schiel Elementary on Vine Street, that much more dangerous.[49]

The city's plan did address schools, parks, and the conservation of housing, but the Planning Commission's primary goal was to facilitate the growth of the university and the medical complex, which included the Medical College and General, Children's, Veterans, and Jewish hospitals. The plan envisioned the hospital complex eventually swallowing the land between Goodman and Melish to the south and everything over to Harvey on the east. The plan also projected the university taking all the land east to Jefferson. Planners emphasized that the neighborhood "has value as a location for needed city-wide services, such as the university and the hospitals." Admitting that "institutional values may conflict with residential values," planners prioritized the health of the institutions. This was classic modernist thinking: people should work in one place, live in another, and shop in a third.

Planners thought that with its central location and anticipated access to planned highways, Avondale-Corryville was an ideal location for regional institutions.[50]

Expansion proceeded just as the plans anticipated, and, not surprisingly, the growth created tensions within the neighborhood. By 1961, federal grants and eminent domain powers helped UC purchase properties east to Jefferson. That year, the university agreed to the renewal plan in Corryville, claiming it would stop its eastward expansion at Jefferson, which itself would be widened by 1966. UC couldn't resist the financial incentives of building in the renewal zone, however, and over the next few years it purchased and demolished ninety-three dwelling units to build a new home for the nursing college, Procter Hall, completed in 1968. That building helped connect the medical campus to the west campus, but it also caused alarm within the community because it represented a leap outside the containment area set by Jefferson. This leap was particularly galling to a number of families that had upgraded their Corryville homes, encouraged by city policy, only to have them taken and demolished by the university.[51]

Although UC continued to grow out, in the 1960s it mostly grew up. The university followed a high-rise–low-rise concept, developed by architect John Garber, in which high-rise buildings were constructed for low-traffic uses, such as dormitories, faculty offices, and seminar rooms. New low-rise buildings would be used for high-traffic uses, such as undergraduate classrooms and laboratories.[52] Among the new low-rise buildings were Zimmer Hall, which featured a massive auditorium-style classroom, and what became known as Rieveschl Hall, which housed biology and chemistry laboratories. The third building in the Brodie Science Complex was the sixteen-story Crosley Tower, named for local inventor and businessman Powel Crosley Jr. and completed in 1969, which included faculty offices and smaller classrooms. Between 1963 and 1971, the university built seven residential towers, all on the eastern and southern edges of campus. The most prominent of the new dorms were the "Three Sisters," Sawyer, Scioto, and Morgens, constructed near the northeast corner of campus, with a large parking lot to the west and a massive new parking garage to the east, along Jefferson. Altogether the new dorms housed 5,000 students. They also helped create a barrier between campus and surrounding neighborhoods with their imposing form.

The university was making room for a seemingly ever-growing student population, but just as important, UC made room for the automobiles that would increasingly bring workers, students, and patients. Almost universally the new buildings contained new parking facilities, as garages gradually replaced surface lots. Parking posed a perennial problem for the university's commuting students, faculty, and staff, and so it garnered considerable attention from the administration—and considerable resources. The city's extensive streetcar system, which had served the Clifton area well, was entirely abandoned in the early 1950s, replaced by a bus system that experienced decades of falling ridership and curtailed service. This combination of factors ensured that parking would be a chronic problem, and by the mid-1960s, UC had determined that parking garages would be essential to the solution. Vice President Ralph Bursiek admitted, "The cost of these garages is great and amounts to $2,000 per car," but with the ever-increasing stream of cars, the investment was necessary. "The parking squeeze at UC is getting tight enough that whenever land conditions permit, garages will be built," Bursiek promised.[53]

When school opened in the fall of 1966, students found 2,206 parking spots on campus, 281 more than the year before. "Parking for Everyone," declared the *News Record* after a reporter toured the many lots and garages. Students just needed to know where to head at particular times of day.[54] Some parking required decals, purchased by students and faculty; other locations, like the CCM garage, which opened in the spring of 1967, charged by the hour for the use of its 480 spots. Despite the *News Record*'s optimism, the hunt for convenient and economical parking could be frustrating. In the winter of 1972, secretaries in the Central Clinic held a three-hour sit-in strike over parking, protesting the distance from their assigned lot to the clinic building. Many also complained that during days when they had later shifts, the lots tended to be full.[55]

By 1969 the university had 4,000 parking spaces for 27,000 main campus students, and the city was encouraging UC to triple that number by 1975 so as to alleviate problems caused by students parking in adjacent neighborhoods.[56] Parking was a constant source of frustration for those who lived in the surrounding communities. A 1972 study of the university's relationship with adjoining neighborhoods concluded flatly, "A common cause of university–community friction is the saturation of available parking space in the area by university people's cars."[57]

It wasn't just that students and employees filled neighborhood streets with parked cars. The neighbors resented the taking and demolition of buildings only to see them replaced by parking lots. This happened on the eastern edge of campus, where a series of demolitions made way for a substantial parking lot between the Three Sisters dorms and the science complex, and around the medical campus, where the city acquired property under the Avondale-Corryville Urban Renewal plan, and then allowed the university to expand its parking. This was most evident in the streets directly south of General Hospital, along Goodman and Piedmont Streets, where the university demolished homes to create parking for 270 cars.[58] The 1972 study of university–community relations included an insightful summation of neighborhood impact, correlating expansion and tension. The institution's physical influence on Corryville had been the strongest, while "there has been virtually no overt tension between the university and Fairview," the neighborhood to the southeast that had experienced no encroachment. "UC's impact on Clifton has been of a different nature," the report concluded. "Because of the heavy settlement of university people there, Clifton to a certain extent is UC."[59]

Tensions between the university and Corryville sometimes boiled up into open conflict. Student and resident interactions on occasion turned violent, and student

Cars, circa 1975. As more and more faculty, staff, and students commuted into campus by automobile, UC dedicated acres to parking, including this large surface lot across from Burnet Woods. Through the 1970s, parking created headaches for administrators and neighbors who often complained that students took valued street parking on residential streets. *Photograph files, Archives & Rare Books Library, University of Cincinnati.*

reactions were not necessarily constructive. Two incidents in the spring of 1965 drew the attention of the *News Record*. In one, neighborhood teens "launched a mortar attack ala Vietcong" on Sawyer Hall,[60] one of the three fourteen-story dormitories completed the year before. "Roman Candles and Sky Rockets" struck the building, causing little damage but some alarm. Just a few days earlier a group of UC athletes was "attacked by 10 'Rats' outside the Varsity Mug Club," a popular spot just off campus. The following week a *News Record* editorial asked "What's to be done?" Beyond referring to Corryville teenagers as "rats" and "rodents," references to the "Rat Pack," which a group of local teens had apparently called themselves, the editorial made clear—perhaps inadvertently—why neighborhood residents were wary of the university's growth. "We are fortunate in that a large portion of the University faces Clifton, and that the expansion of the school will eliminate more and more of Corryville." Meanwhile, the *News Record* recommended a greater Cincinnati police presence or the expansion of the university's police force, created that year to replace the unarmed private security guards who had formerly patrolled campus.[61] Not surprisingly the editorial didn't sit well with everyone on campus, and one response appeared in the paper the next week. Leah Aronoff, a graduate student, wrote, "the starry-eyed gaze to a future in which problems are eliminated because UC will have 'eliminated' Corryville, should be repugnant to anyone connected with the University."[62]

❦ An Image of Difference and Superiority

Growth could spark conflict, no doubt, but it also created opportunity, and not just for more students to seek an education. After the 1906 founding of what soon became known as the National Collegiate Athletic Association, college sports became more organized, competitive, and popular. In Cincinnati, athletic programs grew right along with the university. Perhaps the best sign of this growth was the completion of the 8,000-seat Armory Fieldhouse in 1954. Built just south of University Avenue, and not on the land recently acquired from Burnet Woods, the long-awaited fieldhouse allowed the men's basketball team to play before larger crowds.

The team christened the facility with a victory over Indiana, but real excitement about UC basketball arrived with Oscar Robertson, who came to Cincinnati in 1957. He played three years with the Bearcats, leading them to the NCAA Final Four twice. Robertson was a national figure, and his play elevated the profile of the basketball program. He also helped break down the color barrier on campus.

Robertson wasn't the first black player at UC, but his presence—and great suc-cess—helped ensure more opportunities for African American student athletes and non-athletes alike.

Robertson's stellar play helped UC win seventy-two home games in a row, but much of that streak occurred during the two seasons after Robertson had turned professional, while he was playing for the Cincinnati Royals of the National Bas-ketball Association. Those two Bearcat teams, 1960–61 and 1961–62, won the national championship. By the time UC made the Final Four the next season, its fifth in a row, it had established itself as the dominant team in the Missouri Val-ley Conference, which it had joined in 1957, and it was clearly among the finest basketball programs in the nation. Perhaps just as important, the successful teams helped expand the university's role within the community, as more and more city residents rooted for the teams even if they had no other connection to the school than through loyalty to the athletic program. After all, Robertson's jersey read simply "Cincinnati."[63]

While Oscar Robertson, Connie Dierking, Paul Hogue, and a host of other All-American players had helped secure a place for UC basketball among the na-tion's elite programs, football was a different story. The team had a long string of lackluster seasons, fielding only three winning teams in the 1960s. Playing in the mediocre Missouri Valley Conference with undistinguished and far-flung schools such as North Texas, Tulsa, and Wichita State, and faring poorly, UC's average attendance at home games had slid significantly since Nippert Stadium had been expanded in 1953. Sometimes fewer than half the 27,000 seats were filled, even for conference games.

Sensing the need for a new direction, athletic director George Smith tried to link changes in the football program to changes in the city itself. "We have entered a new and exciting era in the City of Cincinnati," he wrote in a preview of the 1967 season. "The area is alive with new construction and is lining up to the City's recently adopted motto of 'City on the Go.' Everywhere you look there are new campus buildings, office buildings, the Convention Hall, the underground garage, expressways—and more is in the offing, including a riverfront stadium." This last reference, to a new stadium, would be the real impetus for change, for it came in response to the promised 1968 arrival of the American Football League Bengals.[64]

The Bengals played two seasons in Nippert as the prosaically named River-front Stadium was completed. In their inaugural campaign the Bengals averaged

Oscar Robertson and teammates, 1960. Robertson, number 12, helped transform UC into one of the nation's leading basketball programs. *Photograph files, Archives & Rare Books Library, University of Cincinnati.*

more than 25,000 fans at home games. In their second season, the Bengals were led by former UC quarterback Greg Cook. They won more games at Nippert than the Bearcats that year, and they attracted many more fans. University leadership had good reason to ponder the future of their football program, then, especially since as the new stadium neared completion, and the city's football fans would redirect their gaze to the riverfront and the professional team.

The university community debated whether UC should play on the riverfront. The possibility of a move became real enough that the university undertook a study of alternative uses for the space occupied by the stadium, finding it ideal for a parking garage with classroom buildings above. *News Record* sports editor Richie Katz thought following the pro team downtown in 1970 would be a disaster. "Once they leave the comfortable confines of Nippert Stadium, UC football will go out like a light," he wrote in the spring of 1968. Katz thought too few students would make the trip downtown. Some games drew few students even on campus; only

1,683 students attended the North Texas game at Nippert in 1967. How many would have bothered to go downtown to see that game? Katz was also concerned about the possibility that the university would demolish Nippert. "A large university campus without a football stadium is not a true campus," he wrote.[65]

Undoubtedly Katz's concerns were widely shared by students, but declining attendance, poor performance, and growing competition from the Bengals indicated that something needed to change. Smith thought that if UC wanted to play in the new Riverfront Stadium, it would have to quit the Missouri Valley and join a much stronger conference, perhaps one assembled from independent schools like Pittsburgh and Penn State. If UC wanted to continue playing at Nippert, Smith concluded, it should quit the Missouri Valley and join the Mid-American Conference (MAC). In other words, regardless of where it played, UC should quit the Missouri Valley.[66]

UC did leave the conference after the spring season in 1970, choosing to become independent while it cultivated ties to the Atlantic Coast Conference and entered into discussions with other major independents about forming a new conference. This move did not end the debate about football's future, of course, and in the ensuing discussions the importance university officials attached to conference affiliation became clear. Robert H. Wessel, vice provost for graduate studies, wrote up a lengthy position paper on conference affiliation, which issued stern warnings against joining the MAC or creating a new conference that would include Miami or Ohio Universities. "Playing home-and-home games with schools in remote bucolic settings does not promise the type of financial reward that the universities of Pittsburgh, West Virginia, or Syracuse would relish," Wessel concluded. Wessel preferred that Cincinnati remain independent rather than join with other Ohio state-affiliated schools, several of which were in the MAC and none of which made money from athletics.[67] They also didn't draw well in Cincinnati. Only 9,690 people came to see the UC–OU game in 1968. "I am convinced that in the face of competition from the Bengals, a schedule consisting largely of Mid-American Conference teams would lead to financial disaster," Wessel concluded.[68]

But the issue was more than financial. Success in athletics had become an important route to building institutional prestige, which is precisely why the vice provost for graduate studies would bother to write up a position paper on the topic. "The other institutions in the Mid-American Conference are not comparable to the University of Cincinnati," Wessel noted. "With the exception of the University of Toledo, none are urban schools." Moreover, none were comprehensive universities, and, perhaps most important, none were nationally prestigious academically. "Consequently, our institutional image would not be enhanced by entering into this type of arrangement with them," Wessel wrote. Cincinnati's reputation had not been enhanced by membership in Missouri Valley Conference either, which was one of the reasons it left. "In our efforts to reaffiliate," Wessel pleaded, "we should seek to upgrade the quality of our associations rather than continuing in lackluster company." Part of that "lackluster company," in Wessel's mind, were the state schools in the MAC, including Bowling Green and Kent State. Wessel was especially concerned about state schools, because just the year before UC had accepted state affiliation in exchange for increased funding from Columbus. "Due to our affiliation with the state it is especially important that we maintain an image of difference from and superiority over the other schools in the system," Wessel wrote. "Note that Ohio State has been very careful about this."[69]

The football program remained independent until the 1990s, but the more successful basketball team became a charter member of the appropriately named Metro Conference in 1975, joining with other urban schools such as Memphis, Louisville, Tulane, St. Louis, and Georgia Tech. Football limped along as an independent in the 1970s, accumulating a record of 53–55–2. Still, if the university could not develop the fan base for football that it had hoped for, the Bearcat basketball team was a different story. The Cincinnati Royals left town in 1972, heading for Kansas City. Without an NBA team, college basketball became the only game in town.

❦ For the Enrichment of a Listening Public

Athletics helped the university build relationships with a variety of Cincinnatians, some of whom would never become students, but this was just part of UC's expanding influence in the city. After classical music fans organized a movement to get more programming on air, and a brief flirtation with the idea of bringing Ohio State University's WOSU classical music broadcasts to Cincinnati, the University of Cincinnati responded with the creation of WGUC, its own radio station. Approved in 1959 and up and running in 1960, WGUC broadcast at 90.9 FM, where it could be heard throughout the metropolitan area. The university's public radio station charter, issued by the Federal Communications Commission, described the station's purpose: "Broadcast the best in music, drama, discussion programs, and domestic and foreign news comment for the enrichment of a listening public within a radius of 50 miles of Cincinnati."[70]

From the beginning the programming was varied, with nightly news broadcasts from campus, occasional live jazz performances, and of course classical music. Initially housed in the Health Center, the station had a professional staff with student assistants.[71] The goal was not to teach students how to work in radio so much as to educate and uplift the broader public through programming. Radio promised to be an effective means of educational outreach. When the station began broadcasting, Jay C. Heinlein, a professor of political science, moderated a series called "The American President" on Sunday mornings. The program was particularly useful in the election year, during which Senator John Kennedy ran against Vice President Richard Nixon.[72]

WGUC began broadcasting with limited hours, which gradually expanded. The station broadcast BBC reports, entire operas, and lots of classical music— masterworks from Bartok to Tchaikovsky. As *News Record* reporter Rosemary Barron put it, "A world of culture has come recently to the residents of greater Cincinnati." Anyone in the metropolitan region could hear modern jazz, live drama, and Glee Club performances. As the hours of operation expanded, so did the range of broadcasts. WGUC added progressive rock in its "Full Moon Radio" program, and recordings of guest lectures and panel discussions appeared on a regular segment called "From the Campus."[73]

Even as UC experimented with radio outreach, it also attempted to educate audiences through television. At noon on Sundays, WKRC-TV briefly broadcast a program called "UC in the Home," which featured professors giving half-hour presentations. Here H. David Lipsich presented "Revolutions in Mathematics," and Peter Nash, professor of geography, hosted "Art in Society," a show that also found an audience on radio. Eventually faculty participated in WKRC-TV's "UC Folio," which featured panel conversations rather than lectures. The faculty found its way onto the local public television station, too, as WCET broadcast a variety of shows featuring academics. Alice Wood, a lecturer on home economics, for instance, moderated a series of shows on "Adventures in Home Making," and Edwin Daily, who taught in the Evening College, hosted a series of shows on "Our Physical World."[74]

In 1963, WGUC began recording Cincinnati Symphony Orchestra concerts for broadcast and distributed them nationwide via the National Educational Radio

Network. The station's connections to other public radio stations were cemented in 1971, when WGUC became one of the seventy-three stations that joined together to create National Public Radio (NPR). Membership in NPR allowed WGUC to pick up national programs, including William F. Buckley's *Firing Line* and the daily news program *All Things Considered*. By then, WGUC paid for its operations with funding from a mix of sources, including the Corporation for Public Broadcasting, the university, and donations from listeners solicited during annual fund drives.[75]

WGUC helped the university solidify connections to local institutions, especially the Cincinnati Symphony Orchestra and the Cincinnati Opera, both of which it broadcast, but also to the College-Conservatory of Music, which had been created through a merger of two much older institutions in 1955.[76] Just a year after WGUC began operations, CCM decided to merge with UC. Fundraising followed, and in the fall of 1962 CCM became the university's fourteenth college. UC acquired the school's endowment and raised additional funds to build a new facility on campus. At the time of the merger, CCM was the oldest independent music school in the nation, and it had an international reputation. It brought to UC ninety-five faculty members, most of whom were also members of the Cincinnati Symphony Orchestra. CCM also brought more than 1,700 students to the university.[77]

In 1966 CCM moved to the main campus from its home at Oak and Highland. At first CCM used a variety of spaces, including Wilson Memorial Hall for symphonic instruction and university-owned houses on the edge of campus for practice rooms. It even made use of spaces in Tangeman University Center. In March of 1967, CCM's new home opened, featuring Corbett Auditorium and Mary Emery Hall, both named for great patrons of the arts in Cincinnati. The new CCM facility featured a four-story building set atop three levels of parking. Halls of practice rooms, studios, classrooms, and a library gave CCM ample space for teaching, and a new auditorium, funded largely by private donations, provided wonderful performance space.

The absorption of CCM was part of UC's ongoing expansion by merger. The Cincinnati College of Pharmacy joined UC in 1954, nine years after the small independent college requested the merger. After it had raised a sufficient endowment, the college moved out of downtown, where it had been for 104 years, and into an addition to what was then the biology building, which eventually took the name Dyer Hall. By one measure, Pharmacy represented a small addition—just 286 students joined a university of over 13,000—but in other ways the union was a significant one. According to the *Enquirer*, at the time of the merger, 98 percent of the pharmacists in Cincinnati had graduated from the College of Pharmacy.[78]

Among the other additions was the Ohio College of Applied Science, which joined UC in 1969. That college had roots that ran back to 1828, with the founding of the Ohio Mechanics Institute. It had served the city's industrial laboring classes well for over 150 years. When it joined UC, it offered a variety of associate degrees in technology and applied sciences, including in architecture and electronics. All of OCAS's programs were vocational, training surveyors, technicians, and sales representatives, and their arrival meant a wider mission for the university. The merger with OCAS also brought UC back to the city's basin, as it acquired the Emery Building in Over-the-Rhine.

Through this merger and the others, and through all the growth in the postwar decades, and through the greater emphasis on athletics and the new outreach endeavors, the university pressed new opportunities, evolving to keep up with the quickening pace of economic and social change. Through all this change, remarkably, the questions alive at the institution's founding remained as relevant as ever. What is a university for? What does it mean to be the University of Cincinnati?

7

A UNIVERSITY AT WAR WITH ITSELF
Campus Unrest in the 1960s

In just a quarter century the old streetcar college, unified in its mission to serve the city, had metamorphosed into what Clark Kerr called a "multiversity," in which various branches served different masters and worked toward different goals. As president of the University of California, Kerr had seen firsthand how growth had riven the traditional institution. Newly established disciplines and programs vied for limited resources; new intellectual endeavors, such as Black Studies, struggled for acknowledgment and legitimacy. Writing in 1963, Kerr articulated a theme that would define this era of higher education: "The university is so many things to so many different people that it must, of necessity, be partially at war with itself." When the free speech movement demonstrations began at his own Berkeley campus a year later, Kerr's war metaphor seemed all the more appropriate.[1]

The remarkable postwar growth had helped create a new diversity among students on campus—a diversity undreamed of by nineteenth-century figures such as Charles McMicken and Alphonso Taft. The student body was increasingly diverse by race, but also by class and expectation. This last form of diversity—often overlooked—may have posed the most significant challenge for the institution as a whole. Some students came to UC to train for professional work—nursing, teaching, dancing, and designing—but others came for a traditional liberal arts education. Students sought degrees in fields as different as engineering, law, musicology, and pharmacy. Some students came to UC to train for careers as university researchers; others came merely to hone basic reading and writing skills. Some saw Cincinnati as a steppingstone toward a career as a professional athlete; others trained to become military officers. How could one university serve students with such divergent goals?

168

Since the creation of the first universities in medieval Europe, students had studied diverse subjects in relation to each other—language and literature informing natural science and mechanics. As University of Chicago chancellor Robert Hutchins summarized about the University of Paris, "The subjects that were studied were studied together. Teachers and students tried to see everything in relation to everything else."[2] That model no longer held. The multiversity was at war with itself, not just because disciplines developed ever deeper and more specialized bodies of knowledge, helping to create the "silos" that critics still find dividing universities, but also because a democratic ethos welcomed an ever-widening array of students into higher education. Universities surely split into disciplinary factions, but they also gathered to themselves a great diversity of vocational programs.

Not all conflicts on campus derived from the growing complexity of the institution. Increasingly, national debates about politics and policy—especially the United States' conduct during the Cold War—made their way into university communities. As part of commencement exercises in the spring of 1962, Class President Neal Berte's "Senior Oration" reflected on the troubled world into which he and his classmates would graduate, a world divided by the global struggle between capitalism and communism. "The cold war in which we are now engaged will be decided by *our* actions of the future," Berte said, "and, as proven in history, will be dependent upon the degree of our devotion to the principles of equality, freedom, and respect for our fellow man on which our country was founded, not the quantity of material possessions which are purely of a temporary nature."[3]

Even as the West declared it was defending democracy, however, the definition of that concept was in flux, providing an array of challenges in the United States. By the late 1960s, conflict over the civil rights movement and the war in Vietnam played out on college campuses around the nation. Years of protests around a range of issues, sometimes leading to the disruption of classes, had the nation asking a new set of questions. In the winter of 1969, before UC had witnessed any serious campus unrest, UC's first provost, the historian Tom Bonner, asked, "When will all this activism end?" He suspected that "student activism and demands for involvement" had become a permanent feature of university life. "For those of us just starting out in University administration, this is not altogether a pleasant prospect," he told his fellow administrators. "Perhaps some day we may again have the luxury of complaining about the apathy of our students! At UC, in any case,

169

I think we are experiencing the normal growing pains of a large university that is reaching out for better students, higher standards, and a better qualified faculty."[4]

To observers at the time, the tensions, conflicts, and even violence that became nearly commonplace on university campuses by the late 1960s appeared to have more to do with political differences between students and administrations than with differences among students. Still, diversity among the student body was critical to growing unrest on large campuses. In the spring of 1970, as antiwar protests spiked on campuses around the nation, Ohio Board of Regents chancellor John Millett attempted to put the unrest in perspective. "With such a large proportion of our youth enrolled in higher education," he said, "and with these youth drawn from not just the upper and middle classes of our society but also from the working class and the poverty class, we must expect considerable differences in points of view among students."[5] Universities had welcomed a broader range of young Americans into their classrooms, and now they were struggling to accept their different opinions about what the university should be.

By 1970, American universities had become essential sites of political protest, and campus unrest had become a national concern. This was particularly true at large and fast-growing institutions, like the University of Cincinnati, where after years of disturbances the entire community—administration, faculty, students, and city residents—began asking once again fundamental questions about the purpose of higher education. Baby Boomers had transformed higher education, not just through their sheer numbers, but because their generation espoused new ideas and invigorated innovation in music, fashion, literature, and politics. Academia, often derided as an ivory tower, removed from the issues of the day, retained its distinctiveness, but no one could honestly argue that it remained aloof from reality. Instead, protected by the ideals of academic freedom and free speech, faculty and students felt empowered to speak out against injustices and war. Universities became increasingly entangled in national politics. Through all of this, not surprisingly, the university community engaged in various levels of soul-searching. What was the university for?

Involved Action Is the Only Response

On the evening of Thursday March 23, 1967, three neighborhood teenagers attacked Jesse Woodman, a doctoral student at the university, as he walked from campus to his home on Ravine Street. Woodman was pushed to the ground and hit his head on the curb, fracturing his skull. He was taken to the hospital, but he died of his injuries the next night. The attack on Woodman at the corner of McMillan and Victor, just three blocks from campus, was one of a string of troubling events over the previous year, in which students were threatened or harmed by young people from the communities around the university. Some of these incidents occurred on campus, including two attempted rapes in Nippert Stadium in September 1966. In response to those attacks, the university had reviewed its security, bringing in outside consultants, and added service hours for security officers, who were hired through the Pinkerton Company. The university also improved lighting on campus. The city, too, pitched in, by increasing police patrols around campus. University assurances to students and parents that neighborhood crime had not worsened surely rang hollow after Woodman's murder. Still, because of its good relationship with Cincinnati police, UC decided not to increase its own force significantly, and a meeting between city police and university officials led to only modest changes. "We'd like to have city police cars drive through campus more often," said Vice President Ralph Bursiek, "just to show you're around."[6]

Woodman's killing and the other attacks heightened concern for safety on campus and led to some heated rhetoric about the people who lived in surrounding communities. Lynne Woodman, Jesse's widow, grew concerned about how people in the university community were talking about "them"—neighborhood residents who were to be feared or avoided. She wrote to the *News Record* in an attempt to shift the conversation, reminding students that three young people from the neighborhood had run out into traffic and carried Jesse to the sidewalk and held him until help arrived. She wondered why people didn't think of those boys as part of the community. Instead, she heard the idea that "someone must protect the University from the community." She believed, however, that the neighborhood was just as "shocked and frightened and angry" as the university community, and her response was to encourage the university to get involved in surrounding neighborhoods. "To those in the University who feel compelled to 'do something' about this death, I submit that such involved action is the only response."[7]

Increasing concern about crime, if not the actual increase in crime, did set off a series of changes beyond improved lighting and heightened policing. Richard Baker, director of community relations, a recently created position, set up an ad hoc committee designed to bring together university and community representatives to discuss a range of issues.[8] Woodman's murder kept the group's focus on crime and conflict,

171

a topic reinforced by the presence of Cincinnati's safety director and police chief on the committee. The group discussed the value of community-oriented policing and identifying problems before they evolved into criminal activity. One neighborhood representative, William Walton, executive director of the Community Health and Welfare Council, noted that some people who lived near campus felt "some hostility" toward the university, because they thought that "UC is pushing them out of their homes." The Reverend Jack Seymour, of Lutheran Church of the Cross, added that UC students could be antagonistic toward neighborhood youth.

John Winget, an associate professor of sociology, summarized the committee's discussions for President Walter Langsam, who had led UC through a decade of intense growth and now would have to guide it through years of tense conflict. Winget's report concluded, "It would appear from our meeting that tensions do exist in the surrounding area and that these can best be reduced by increasing the University's understanding of the problems created by our own growth, the changes taking place in the community and the corresponding need for an improved communication between the University and the community." Identifying the root of the problem was a necessary first step, but unfortunately the ad hoc committee was not in a position to discuss potential solutions. Instead, it merely recommended that the committee become permanent.[9]

While university officials developed a response around improved policing and committee formation, students had pursued their own approach to mend community relations: volunteering. Since the spring of 1963, the university had hosted a student volunteering program called the West End Educational Program (WEEP), which arranged tutoring for at-risk children at several neighborhood elementary schools. Under the guidance of the Reverend Stanley Holt, who directed the Westminster Foundation of the Presbyterian Church, and the YMCA/YWCA on Calhoun Street, students raised money to purchase books and brought in speakers to help inform students about social problems in the inner city. Holt, a leader of the local chapter of the Congress on Racial Equality, had moved the Westminster Foundation's campus ministry in a decidedly more activist direction. That summer, 125 students volunteered for one-on-one tutoring with fifth and sixth graders. The program was such a success that students continued fundraising in the fall and organized late afternoon and evening tutoring sessions. UC students traveled to several locations in the West End, including the Findlay Street Neighborhood House and Hayes Elementary School.[10]

The program thrived, expanding each of the next two years. In the summer of 1965, 200 UC students volunteered, some of them earning credit toward their education degrees. By the winter quarter of 1966, WEEP had expanded its tutoring to include high school students, and volunteering opportunities far outstripped leadership's ability to fill them. WEEP sent students to forty different tutoring centers, and it had branched out, offering volunteers to the senior center in Over-the-Rhine and working with children through the Cincinnati Public Schools enrichment program in activities as diverse as cooking, carpentry, and drama.[11]

Volunteering proved so attractive that later that year students from the United Campus Christian Fellowship joined with students from Xavier University and St. Xavier High School to propose the creation of a student volunteer bureau that would operate through the Community Action Council, established using federal War on Poverty funding.[12] Led by Ginny Lambert, the daughter of an accounting professor, a group of students proposed the creation of a student volunteer center even before Woodman's murder. In her proposal, Lambert emphasized UC's unique position. "As an institution it [UC] is located in the midst of urban problems and changes, and at times, through its extensive building projects, it contributes to these changes." She emphasized that UC had great resources to offer—especially the human resources represented by the students themselves. Lambert knew what she was talking about. She had volunteered for WEEP and tutored in the West End. Volunteers needed a "single channel," she thought, "to focus the student's concerns for its community, with the goal of developing within the university an interrelated total program of service, research, consultation, training, directed toward urban problems, etc. as seen in Cincinnati." A central volunteering office "would serve as a contact point within the university for all community agencies and organizations desiring the help of students, and as an office through which interested students and campus organizations would be informed of service needs and opportunities."[13] It was precisely this type of "involved action" that Lynne Woodman hoped would pull students closer to residents of the neighborhoods around campus and would build understanding across the communities.

❀ A More Relevant Education

If Woodman's death sparked concerns about the university's tense relationship with its neighbors, the death of another student spoke to a broader fissure in American society. On Monday, April 8, 1968, four days after the assassination of Martin

Luther King Jr., University of Cincinnati graduate student Noel Wright, an artist, and his wife, Lois, were driving from campus to their home in Mount Adams. That afternoon a large memorial service for King had taken place in Avondale, and emotions were high when a false rumor about a policeman killing a black teenager set off a wave of violence, mostly arson and looting along Reading Road. The disturbance centered in Avondale, but a group of angry young men and women had gathered in Mount Auburn, too, where at the corner of Dorchester and Auburn Avenues, just a block from Alphonso Taft's historic home, one of them threw a rock that hit the Wrights' car. Noel stopped. He and Lois were pulled from their car. Noel was beaten and stabbed, while Lois was held down and punched by others in the crowd. Noel died at the scene as his wife pressed on his wound, trying to stop the bleeding. A few days later the *News Record* reported that violence had "cast its long and ugly shadow over Cincinnati."[14]

Wright's murder was the most tragic outcome of rioting in Cincinnati, and, of course, the outcome that most directly affected the university community. But the riots had a more lasting effect on Avondale, the neighborhood that had become Cincinnati's largest African American neighborhood, the place that had welcomed many of the African Americans displaced by highway building and urban renewal in the urban core, especially the West End. Avondale had also become home to many of its most important black institutions, especially churches. Despite the damage, and the loss of life, the disturbance in Cincinnati was modest compared to that in many other cities, as the nation was nearly engulfed in violence after King's murder.[15]

By the time of King's assassination, the civil rights movement had forced the passage of the Civil Rights Act in 1964 and the Voting Rights Act in 1965, but conditions in inner-city neighborhoods had only continued to deteriorate. Segregation had hemmed in growing African American populations throughout urban America. Even as the national economy continued to boom, unemployment grew among African Americans, especially young black men. Schools attended by blacks tended to be overcrowded and understaffed. Crowded housing contributed to sanitation problems and public health concerns, while neglect from absentee landlords and poor city services fed a growing rage about conditions in what were increasingly called "ghettos." The lack of progress toward social and economic equality helped fuel the growth of a more assertive movement, one based in the idea of Black Power and a more expansive definition of rights. Beginning in 1964, a series of "long hot summers"—months when teenagers were out of school and sweltering conditions kept people outside—turned some black neighborhoods into war zones. By 1968, Americans came to expect scenes of arson, looting, gun battles, and National Guard patrols in its most troubled urban neighborhoods. In this way, the violence that led to Woodman's death was part of a well-known narrative of racial conflict in inner-city America.[16]

Two weeks after King's assassination, Cincinnati city councilman Myron Bush, a UC alumnus, came to campus to speak on "U.C.'s Role in the Urban Crisis." Like most people in the city, Bush was trying to find a way forward after tension had turned to violence, and thus far he had been unimpressed by what he had heard. "I am alarmed when I hear prominent members of the business community, some of whom are U.C. graduates, express surprise and unawareness of social conditions in the minority community and seem apparently ignorant as to the fact that established and respected business practices have brought about these conditions just as surely as 1 plus 1 makes 2." In other words, Bush wondered why people educated by UC didn't understand the role racism played in keeping the black community impoverished. "For some time U.C.'s business college would not accept Negro students," he continued. "Now, I understand they do, however more must be done to encourage Negroes to enter into this field of knowledge so they will become able to manage and enter into business activity." More broadly, Bush thought students must be taught about the world they live in. He even suggested that "the freshmen classes, as required course material, could be oriented in a class on discrimination and its techniques, and how it affects the society in which we live. It is high time that the university forthrightly approaches this problem from the standpoint of its effect on our day to day lives."[17]

Bush wasn't the only one thinking about the university's role in the urban crisis or the civil rights movement, of course. A number of African American students came together to create the United Black Association (UBA) in the spring of 1968. The UBA quickly became an important voice for change on campus and in the neighborhoods around. The increasingly active UBA was not distracted by the outbreaks of violence and instead focused on the broad goals of the civil rights movement. In mid-May, shortly after it had gained university recognition as a student organization, the UBA issued a list of demands to President Langsam. The students wanted the university to break down the barriers that kept campus segregated, demanding that black students be admitted to all-white organizations and that the university abolish "customs, traditions, and subtle forms of discrimination and de facto segregation." The language of the demands, which appeared on the front page of the *News Record*, revealed just how excluded African American students felt from most university events and organizations.[18]

Curricular changes were at the heart of the UBA demands. The group wanted new English courses in African American literature and poetry, and courses in black history. The UBA made clear that such courses would not be designed especially for black students, but should, in fact, be required for all students. While it never became a required course, the Department of English did offer American Black Poetry, Prose, and Drama the next fall, attracting nearly one hundred students. Offering the course, taught by two doctoral students, continued an expansion that was under way even before UBA sent its list to Langsam. As the Department Head James K. Robinson said, "[T]he Department is reacting to a national situation in stressing the contribution of the Negro to American culture." In another curricular addition, the Department of History began offering a survey of black history, taught by Herbert Shapiro, which fulfilled a university distribution requirement, and in its first semester it attracted forty students, about a third of them African American. Within a year the Department of Geography also began offering a survey of modern Africa.[19]

Such curricular changes served two purposes. First, as had been suggested by Bush, the courses educated all students about black culture and the long history of racism. Second, courses in black and African culture were critical to attracting more African American students to the university—and retaining them. Beyond the creation of individual courses, UBA wanted the university to establish a Black Studies program, a demand that was growing, not just at UC, but at universities around the country. Despite the progress, the UBA kept up the pressure for curricular change and for the hiring of more black faculty. As UBA vice president Bob Merriweather pointed out, none of the new courses in black studies offered in the fall of 1968 were taught by black faculty.[20]

Black faculty also demanded changes, including the establishment of a Department of Black Studies in the College of Arts and Sciences. A lengthy 1970 proposal for the new program clearly articulated the political and social role for Black Studies. The new course of study could "provide Black students with a more relevant education than they are currently receiving." Minority students would find a place in the university and find empowerment, according to the proposal, most probably written by W. David Smith, an assistant professor of psychology who had become the director of Black Studies Program Development. The proposal also spoke to a growing rift among supporters of Black Studies, with some, like Smith, asserting that the program be staffed only by black faculty, and others, like Shapiro, a left-leaning historian who had been active in the civil rights movement, defending the contributions of white allies like himself. The proposal reflected Smith's position: "The establishing of new black courses, evaluating existing black courses, planning, staffing and directing the proposed 'Department of Black Studies' must be done by Black people."[21]

In the fall of 1970, the university began advertising a program in Afro-American Studies, the change in name representing the rapidly evolving nature of the field and the rapidly changing racial politics in the nation. By the fall of 1971 the Department of Afro-American Studies was up and running, with Smith serving as the first head. The department offered courses in racism, Pan-Africanism, African history, and Swahili, along with several other classes that explored the African American experience.[22]

Beyond the diversification of the curriculum and the faculty, black students demanded changes in the way the university interacted with the community. Most concretely, the UBA demanded the creation of a new office that would monitor housing in the neighborhoods around campus. On May 1, 1968, UBA officers, including Tony Jackson and Dwight Tillery, sent a letter to President Langsam concerning discrimination in off-campus housing. The letter reveals just how thoroughly the civil rights movement influenced activism on campus, as students worked to integrate the neighborhoods around UC. The UBA claimed that many students were living in unapproved housing, meaning that their landlords were not necessarily renting to African Americans, which was the policy of the university. Providing open housing—units that landlords would lease to a renter of any race—was still a major concern in the city, and the neighborhoods around UC were no exception. The UBA recommended that UC expand its list of approved landlords while enforcing its non-discrimination policy through a formal pledge process. "With the increasing number of students coming to this University who are not living with their parents, and with the urban crisis surrounding us, we feel that it is imperative that the University make a firm commitment on housing immediately," the UBA wrote.[23]

Not surprisingly, the university responded by creating a new committee. The day after receiving the letter from the UBA, Langsam wrote to William Jenike, assistant vice president for planning, asking him to chair what became known as the

University Housing Registry Committee. The committee, composed of a variety of staff, administrators, and students, including Tillery, began meeting two weeks later. Seeking the advice of experts in Cincinnati housing issues, the committee invited representatives from Housing Opportunities Made Equal (HOME), a non-profit organization dedicated to open housing. Martha Smudski said that the university should recognize that it represented "authority" in Clifton, and it should be able to make better inroads in the community than HOME would alone. Smudski trained the committee on the techniques they had developed to secure open housing. The committee came to realize, however, that discrimination compounded a problem that affected all students: apartments were in very short supply.[24]

The housing committee met through the summer, implementing in its entirety the plan of action proposed by the UBA. It sent letters to all students, asking them to encourage their landlords to participate in the program by signing a nondiscrimination pledge. The committee soon discovered, however, that some of the 125 registered landlords were renting out apartments that were in very poor condition. Officials quickly became troubled by the idea of creating an approved list of landlords using just one criterion: willingness to sign the nondiscrimination agreement. Still, by the time school opened, the university had created an Off-Campus Housing Office in Beecher Hall, headed by Hershell Hardy, charged with helping students find suitable—and open—housing in neighborhoods around campus. In just a matter of months, student activism had made a structural change in the university and fundamentally changed its sense of responsibility for students living off campus.[25]

Through all of these efforts, UBA achieved a considerable degree of legitimacy, moving into its own office space, helping create a center for black student activities, and gaining representation on the Undergraduate Advisory Council.[26] And the UBA kept up the pressure by issuing a new list of demands in the spring of 1969. After meeting in a closed-door session on May 20, UBA members gathered on the student union bridge to explain their demands to anyone who would listen as they passed by. And many people would, because the bridge connected several important parts of campus, particularly the Tangeman Union Center, McMicken Hall, and the library. Long the place where student organizations publicized events and gathered support, "the Bridge" had evolved into the University of Cincinnati's most important political space as campus activism increased. Between classes students funneled through, reading signs hanging from the railings, pausing at tables set up to educate and politicize.[27]

The Bridge, circa 1985. Connecting the Tangeman University Center, in the background, with the western part of campus, including McMicken Hall and Teachers College, the bridge became the university's most important political space during the late 1960s and early 1970s. The buildings to the left, Old Tech and Tanner's Lab, and the bridge itself were demolished in the 1990s. *Photograph files, Archives & Rare Books Library, University of Cincinnati.*

On this particular day, UBA leaders used a bullhorn to announce eighteen demands. The gathered, perhaps as many as 150 students, black and white, moved to the Van Wormer administration building to present Langsam with the demands and to call on him to respond within twenty-four hours and cancel classes until he had. Langsam refused to cancel classes, and protests escalated quickly. Some students, including the radical activists of Students for a Democratic Society (SDS), called for an immediate boycott of classes, which they decided to enforce by entering McMicken Hall and disrupting classes already in session. Protesters threw desks and chairs out of the windows of one room, and even started a small fire, all in the hope of forcing students out of their classes. The third floor, home to the Department of History, received considerable damage, mostly in the form of broken windows and furniture. The protest gathered momentum and participants, moving to Wilson Auditorium, the physics and chemistry building, and Teachers College. In the last, students opposed to the cancelling of classes forced the protesters out. Those protesters seemed to have lost some of their energy after the walk back across campus. The protest ended as it had begun, on the student union bridge, with discussion and debate.[28]

Debate about protest tactics, especially those that disrupted classes, did not prevent a thorough discussion about the UBA's eighteen demands. Langsam responded to each of the demands, mostly pointing to progress already made. In addition to demanding more black faculty and increased offerings in Black Studies, the students demanded better wages for non-academic employees. Langsam replied that they were above prevailing wages in the area. The UBA demanded an increase in the number of blacks employed in non-academic positions, including the business office. They also expressed concern about the university's expansion into the neighborhoods. Regarding community relations, Langsam assured, "The building plans of the University do not contemplate main-campus expansion into adjoining neighborhoods. Evidence of this policy may be found in the increasing number of high-rise structures on campus." He also promised to create a new position, dean of community programs, which would be staffed by a black educator.[29]

Although the UBA remained frustrated by the slow pace of change, the university's response to student demands was comprehensive and meaningful. Curricular changes were most apparent, undoubtedly because faculty could implement most changes relatively quickly, but these weren't the only obvious results of black protests at UC or around the nation. Enrollment of blacks in colleges and universities rose sharply in the late 1960s. In 1971, 11 percent of college-age Americans were black, and they constituted 6.6 percent of the college population.[30] This was almost exactly the percentage of black students at UC. In total 1,407 of the 22,389 fulltime students were black, although the percentage varied considerably across the campus. About 7 percent of those enrolled in the business school were black, whereas at University College, the two-year access college created in 1960, the percentage was nearly 20 percent. Engineering had among the lowest percentage of African American enrollees—just 1.5 percent of the 659 full-time students. Enrollments at the graduate level lagged considerably. Only one African American was pursuing a graduate degree in engineering, and even in Arts & Sciences fewer than 4 percent of the graduate students were black.[31] Still, the administration pointed to improvements in undergraduate enrollment. At the same time, the percentages and real dollar amounts of financial aid awarded to nonwhite students continued to grow. In 1967, roughly 20 percent of financial aid went to nonwhite students. By 1970, that figure had grown to 30 percent. Over that same period, the percentage of financial aid awards to nonwhites went from 14 percent to 22 percent.[32] As real as the improvements were, the figures indicated that the university could not change as rapidly as the city it served. By 1970 nearly 28 percent of Cincinnati's population was African American.

🌺 One Solidified University Community

United Black Association activism coincided with the antiwar movement, which became increasingly organized and assertive as the war in Vietnam dragged on and casualties increased. On campuses both of these movements were influenced by another growing movement—the New Left, led by SDS. Beyond civil rights and an end to the war in Vietnam, the New Left agenda included an end to the Cold War and the initiation of broad antipoverty programs. The radical democratic thinking of SDS informed student activism through the second half of the decade, as all kinds of student efforts—local and national—included public demonstrations, rallies, and teach-ins. The growing influence of SDS, along with several outbursts of violence on campuses around the nation, convinced the administration that unrest would eventually come to UC.[33]

In February 1969, Provost Bonner provided a report to the President's Advisory Council, emphasizing that UC should learn from other campuses and refrain from overreacting to student protests. Bonner assessed three potential sources of unrest at UC. He was least concerned about black student activists, with whom the administration had an excellent relationship, or so he thought, because communication channels were open. "But," Bonner added, "remember—and this is the real powder keg—we have more Black students than Wisconsin, Duke, Brandeis, Swarthmore, and Columbia *combined*—and all of the issues that have torn those campuses apart are present here." Still, Bonner thought that the most immediate threat of disruption came not from black activists or from the antiwar movement. Rather, he was most concerned about the Campus Reformation Council, a loosely organized group consisting of perhaps 500 students, led by sociology graduate student David Altman. Bonner saw Altman as a moderating force of a potentially radical movement. Of the more militant faction within the Campus Reformation Council, Bonner reported, "They are usually white, frequently from middle-class families, often broken families; they lack firm religious or moral codes in their background; they are intelligent, sensitive, often artistically inclined; and they are attracted to romantic conceptions of 'participatory democracy' and the writings of Herbert Marcuse." Clearly the administration was trying to make sense of the broad student movement through a close analysis of demography and behavior.[34]

The Campus Reformation Council had made a series of proposals to increase the role of students in university governance, including the election of student representatives to the Board of Directors, the creation of an open forum for the discussion of campus issues, and the establishment of an ombudsman, to whom students could convey concerns on any issue. Altman, who was heavily involved in environmental issues, hoped that the council would be a temporary organization, one that helped students engage and create new democratic structures. "As citizens of a campus they have a right to be heard and a right to know," he told the *News Record*, where he had served as editor-in-chief the previous year.[35] As was the case with several of the UBA demands, many of the council's ideas quickly became reality. When it met on March 4, the Board of Directors welcomed a student and a faculty representative to the table, to add their voices, though not their votes, to the proceedings. Although it took a little longer, the university also created an ombudsman's office in September 1970.[36]

What troubled Bonner about the council was not these modest proposals for a more democratic institution, but the opinions of some of the students who began to engage in participatory democracy. The council held a series of forums, at which the initial conversation revolved around abolishing the current Student Senate. As Altman had hoped, a great range of opinions found voice, and as the administration feared, some of these voices expressed radical democratic ideas. Among the radicals were Jack Reinbach and James Finger.[37] Reinbach and Finger were both active members in UC's chapter of Students for a Democratic Society, which had been initiated by antiwar students in the fall of 1966. The group was unified in its opposition to having ROTC on campus, because it cemented a relationship between the university and the military. UC's SDS chapter was not particularly active until the spring of 1969, when Reinbach, a senior in the College of Arts & Sciences, called a (re)organizational meeting. Approximately seventy students attended, and the newly energized group decided that their first activity would be to disrupt military recruiting on campus by signing up for slots with recruiters, thereby wasting their time.[38]

A month later, demonstrations became more confrontational, as protesters disrupted the president's review of the university's ROTC students. Carrying white crosses representing the war dead, about one hundred protesters occupied the stands in the Armory Fieldhouse, and then walked across the court before Langsam could review the cadets, dropping the crosses on the floor as they moved past Langsam. Neither the cadets nor the SDS protesters engaged the other. After the demonstration, Langsam, himself an ROTC graduate, asserted that the protesters misunderstood the program and, echoing a common critique of war protesters, he claimed, "ROTC and the military protect the freedom of the critic's right to criticize."[39]

SDS protests in Cincinnati and elsewhere encouraged a national debate about the relationship between the military and higher education. UC had two ROTC programs, the Army cadets numbering 300 and the Air Force cadets numbering 350. In May 1969, a formal debate about the appropriateness of military training on UC's campus took place in Wilson Memorial Hall, where philosophy student Earl Maxwell argued that the university should stop saying ROTC was apolitical and acknowledge its "complicity in this crime against mankind," by which he meant the war in Vietnam. English Professor William Hamrick wondered why the program was controlled by military officers. Without faculty control, Hamrick thought, ROTC should operate as an extracurricular activity—off campus. Dan Beaver, a professor of history, argued just the opposite. Keeping ROTC on campus was the best way to ensure that officers received the civilizing influences of a liberal education.[40]

SDS made itself known through its ROTC demonstrations, but its influence over campus protests became clearer on May 20, following the UBA's presentation of demands. Hundreds of students participated in the following "boycott," and thousands were out of their classes milling about, but interestingly only nine students faced disciplinary action in the aftermath. Charges were dismissed in six cases due to insufficient or conflicting information, and two of the three who actually received discipline were SDS leaders Reinbach and Finger, who had led the charge through McMicken Hall. Reinbach carried a squirt gun that looked like a rifle; Finger beat on a "cigarette urn" as he marched. Both were suspended for a year.[41]

Campus cooled down over the summer of 1969, since few students were around, but protests picked up again in the fall—to no one's surprise. On October 2, 1969, student body president Mark Painter and the Student Senate requested that the university cancel classes so that students might have an educational program on Vietnam—a teach-in—on October 15, National Moratorium on the War in Vietnam Day. Langsam responded, "The idea of special education programs is commendable, but there is no justification for depriving all students of their right to attend the classes for which they registered." Painter was disheartened by the response but even more disturbed that the Faculty Executive Committee and University Cabinet voted not to cancel classes without allowing students to contribute to the debate. When October 15 arrived, however, hundreds of students and faculty participated in the day's events. Painter and other student leaders organized a teach-in on campus, during which speakers presented "both sides" to the war. The *Cincinnati Post* estimated that half the student body skipped classes. After the teach-in, about two thousand protesters marched from UC to Fountain Square, where they gathered with hundreds who had arrived from other places, including Xavier University, which had cancelled classes that day so that students could participate in "Community Awareness on Vietnam."[42]Antiwar protests became more insistent after April 30, 1970, when President Richard Nixon announced that American troops had entered Cambodia in an effort to disrupt North Vietnamese supply lines. Within an hour hundreds of students had gathered at the student union bridge, the political epicenter of campus, to protest the war. Soon the gathering turned into a march, heading up Clifton Avenue to Hebrew Union College. After a crowd roamed around campus and Calhoun Street and Clifton Avenue until three in the morning, the protest ended peacefully, with just a few windows broken in McMicken and Beecher Halls.[43] Another protest gathered the next morning, again at the bridge. This time the demonstrators, perhaps 800 of them, marched down the hill to Fountain Square. As the morning march gave way to a noon-time sit-in at the intersection of Walnut and Fifth Streets, the crowd dwindled to a stalwart group, all of whom sat peacefully while they were arrested for blocking traffic. In total 114 students and 3 faculty were detained, including Herb Shapiro of the Department of History.

After the arrests, the central administration (without Langsam, who was out of town and would not return for over a week) gathered in an emergency meeting to discuss the possibility that students might be forced to go to the Hamilton County Workhouse for want of $40—the amount of the threatened fine plus court costs. Although several people expressed concern about allowing students to go to jail, the administration decided not to use university funds or even serve as a conduit for donated money, for fear of a public backlash. Instead, private money, including faculty donations, made its way to court to keep students out of jail. Provost Bonner himself went downtown to bail out Shapiro, the only faculty member who had refused to post his own bail.[44] After that crisis had been averted, UC's campus remained peaceful. "By May 1," Provost Tom Bonner reflected with pride three weeks later, "we were the only large university in Ohio that had not experienced a shutdown or been forced to use police or guardsmen to preserve order."[45]

The situation changed dramatically on May 4, when four students were shot and killed by National Guardsmen on the campus of Kent State University. Massive demonstrations and the fear of more violence caused many campuses around the nation to close. This was the case at UC, which cancelled classes the next day. In calling for calm, Provost Bonner ask that "instead of individual students, faculty, and administration, we must think of ourselves as one solidified University community trying to show our concern over the senseless violence that is so prevalent in this nation today."[46] Although the community and the nation had been divided on the war in Southeast Asia, Bonner hoped that his diverse and fragmented campus might come together around the idea that students should not be dying here at home.

In lieu of attending classes, many students participated in a "Day of Commitment," a demonstration against violence. After gathering at the bridge, from which hung a huge banner reading "Peace Now," as many as 5,000 students and faculty marched once again down to Fountain Square. About the same number gathered that evening at Nippert Stadium for a vigil, capping a day filled with somber and often silent reflection. Administrators expected the university to re-open the next day, but student leaders called for a three-day strike, and on May 6 student strikers began blocking doors to McMicken and Beecher Halls, eventually moving to occupy the administration building. There they issued a list of demands, including that UC condemn Ohio governor Jim Rhodes "and the murders at Kent State." The students also demanded that the university "condemn the Nixon Administration's invasion of Cambodia" and "American Imperialism in Asia, the world, and in the national black communities." Other demands spoke to long-simmering issues related to the war, such as the presence of ROTC on campus. But the list speaks to the students' social consciousness far beyond Vietnam, including the demand the university divest its endowment holdings in polluting industries, and that it "provide a co-operative or other form of day-care for the community and the students," and that "the university actively seek housing for the 245 families displaced when 70 acres of land were acquired in Corryville for establishing an environmental health center."[47]

185

Fountain Square protest, 1970. Students and faculty marched downtown to protest the United States' invasion of Cambodia in the spring of 1970. Soon after this photo was taken, 114 students, and 1 faculty member, were arrested for blocking traffic. *Photo by Jack Klumpe, provided by Kevin Grace.*

On May 7, the University Senate passed a series of resolutions, expressing sorrow about the deaths in Kent and opposition to bringing the National Guard to UC. And, in a vote that clearly revealed whom the faculty blamed for the violence in Kent, the senate voted to rename Rhodes Hall, the engineering building then under construction, "Peace Hall." By May 8, it was clear that student demonstrations would not ease, and in the interest of public safety Langsam officially closed the school. Plans to reopen classes after a cooling-off period were dashed when two more students were killed at Jackson State in Mississippi on May 15. Black students on campus demanded that the university honor the Jackson dead, both of whom were African American, just as it had honored the Kent dead. On May 17, the University Senate met to discuss the killings in Mississippi. As Senate chairman Gene Lewis described, "The gallery was jammed with at least 1,000 people, many of them students who had just returned to the university in the expectation of the resumption of classes on Monday, May 18." Following the precedent of allowing those present to speak during the meeting, the Senate listened to "a combination of Black and White activists" who demanded that the university close. The Senate responded by voting to close for the remainder of the quarter. "I am convinced," Lewis wrote four days later, "that the Senate acted essentially as a buffer for hostility, possibly of a violent nature, against the President and the Board of Directors."[48] The administration agreed that the university should not reopen, and it worked out guidelines by which students would receive grades and seniors would graduate. Students who were passing their classes as of May 5 were given an "S," while those who were failing received an "N."[49]

Although some commenters continued to talk of student protesters as a distinct and privileged group—sheltered from war and the rigors of the workplace—the campus unrest around the war and civil rights reflected just how connected students were to the world around them. As the Faculty Senate Steering Committee asserted during the turmoil, "The membrane separating the university from its environment, always a permeable one, has been rent recently on scores of the nation's campuses." The image of the ivory tower, always an imperfect metaphor at an institution like the University of Cincinnati, was now all the more inappropriate. After paraphrasing Charles Dabney's goal of making the university not just *in* the city but *of* the city, the University Senate noted, "It is now even more clear than in President Dabney's time that universities cannot remain isolated from the burning issues of our time."[50] Or, as a *News Record* editorial put it just two days after the killings in Kent: "It has become readily apparent that the American University has become a decidedly political force in the nation."[51]

None of Us Has Lost Faith in the Young People

Summer break allowed the nation to pause and reflect on the killings at Kent State and Jackson State and the protests that had the forced the closure of dozens of universities. Michael Dale, outgoing student body president in 1970, noted that the university's failure to reopen "resulted in the most extensive soul-searching ever carried out by this institution."[52] Many Cincinnatians were disgusted by the protests on campus and just as concerned that Langsam had capitulated to the protesters by closing the university. A WKRC editorial on May 20, 1970, admitted that closing school allowed for a necessary cooling-off period, but it asserted that disruptive protests could no longer be tolerated. "Indeed it probably will not be tolerated by the long-suffering majority of our citizens who have had a bellyful of turmoil and anarchy," said WKRC. "It will not be tolerated by the millions who have toiled to provide their children an education only to see the educational machinery destroyed by mindless radicals." To some Americans, college campuses had been tarnished by protests and radical ideas.[53]

After the administration worked out how the closure would work, it created a Presidential Task Force to plan the reopening in the fall, hoping to avoid the chaos of the previous spring. Historian and AAUP president Arnold Schrier issued a statement to the group: "To give expression to the moral discontent, even outrage, that has welled up on our campus, we need imaginative new approaches to our traditional curriculum," he said, pressing a common approach to meeting the needs of a changing world: adjust the curriculum. "As a member of the faculty I would urge the Task Force to consider the varieties of ways in which the University may provide constructive means for engaging both faculty and students in the social concerns of the wider community. Among these might be programs of community involvement that would carry academic credit."[54]

Faculty and administrators had plenty of models for constructive engagement, including the nationwide teach-in on environmental issues held just two weeks before the Kent State shootings. The event, held on April 22, was called Earth Day, during which millions of people heard speeches, participated in clean-ups, and engaged in political activism, such as letter-writing and marching. On UC's campus, Earth Day activities focused on the student union bridge, not surprisingly, but events were held around campus, including the engineering quad, which filled with booths, most of them designed to teach students about aspects of pollution. Both students and faculty engaged in teaching. Alex Fraser, a professor of biology, spoke on "Urban Ecology" in the Kehoe Auditorium of Kettering Lab. Students also heard from guest speakers, including a physician who spoke on black lung among coal miners. Business student John Schneider, who became the university's first ombudsman later that year, spoke on "The Economic Aspects of Pollution Problems," and medical student Sue Linkhorn spoke on birth control.[55]

Despite the positive model of Earth Day demonstrations, the protests surrounding the Vietnam War, the killings at Kent State and Jackson State, and the closing of universities around the nation, all helped widen the generational divide that had opened between the Baby Boomers and older Americans. At the same time, campus antiwar activism exacerbated the always evident cultural divide between those who attended college and those who did not. Public suspicions of universities grew even as their centrality to the nation's economy became manifest, trends that might have been more interrelated than contemporaries noticed. In Cincinnati, as in other parts of the country, residents expressed concern about the radicalization of students, the violence of protests, and losing sight of the purpose of higher education. Anderson Township resident Mrs. J. R. Larkin wrote to Mayor Eugene P. Ruehlmann, "As a citizen who has paid taxes, supported and attended the university, I think some firm measures should be taken before we have a state of riot control at U.C., so common now on other campuses." Clearly the national context mattered. "I really think the time is now to find out who these students are and make sure that our school does not become another Berkeley." Larkin was so disturbed that she began "to wonder at the wisdom of so called higher education."[56] A number of citizens wrote a joint letter to Langsam after hearing that the university would remain closed, protesting that a "group of radicals" had forced the university to act. That action would in turn ensure future disturbances. They concluded, "[Y]ou are rapidly losing esteem in the eyes of the student body and in the eyes of all the interested citizens of the community who support the university through their tax dollars."[57]

If many in the broader community had lost faith in higher education, and perhaps even in the younger generation that attended the nation's universities, UC's University Senate, well aware of the deep fissures and strong emotions that were running through campus, affirmed its positive stance at the height of the unrest:

"None of us has lost faith in the young people who are the brightest hope of the future," wrote the Senate steering committee. "For all their passionate intensity, they have not really lost faith in the American experience or the values that guided it. They are simply more insistent, more demanding, less experienced perhaps, in drawing the attention of all of us to the darker lining of the American Dream."[58]

After receiving the report from the Presidential Task Force on Campus Unrest, which had met over the summer, Langsam issued a new policy on political protest. "The life of a university is rooted in freedom, mutual respect, and trust," Langsam opened. (That Daniel Drake and Alphonso Taft undoubtedly would have found this statement perplexing gives an indication of how much the institution had changed.) Langsam then issued a hard line: "The Board will permit no moratorium, shut-down, schedule alterations to enable members of the University Community to express or reflect political, social, or philosophical opinions, or to carry on political activity, or to manifest mass sympathy or grief—except when such a manifestation is requested by the President of the United States or the Governor of Ohio." The statement stipulated that disruptive demonstrations would not be permitted: no excessive noise, no blocking of buildings, no occupation of buildings. In essence, the tactics of the civil rights movement were declared off-limits. In an attempt to tamp down activism on the campus, Langsam declared, "One man's 'right to dissent peaceably' must not be permitted to interfere with the equal right of another not to dissent, but to continue his lawful duties and activities." Even faculty members were admonished to keep their lectures and discussions "germane to the specialty they have been appointed to teach." Most remarkably, "Peaceful meetings to register dissent may be held on campus only on the University Center Bridge, the plaza atop Building A-4 [Zimmer], or, in the event of inclement weather, in the main lobby of the old section of the University Center."[59] While it was considerate of Langsam to allow free speech to continue even during foul weather, the statement struck many students and faculty as unnecessarily restrictive of fundamental rights of assembly and free speech on campus—all of which was publicly owned.

Despite national concerns about the direction of higher education in light of campus unrest, student activism helped create a cohort of socially engaged leaders for the city of Cincinnati. After earning his undergraduate degree, Mark Painter attended UC's law school and eventually became a long-serving judge. David Altman also attended UC Law and became a prominent environmental lawyer. Dwight

Tillery, who led the United Black Association as a student, became a prominent local politician, serving as mayor in the 1990s. For some students, however, activism clearly interfered with their educational goals. In the summer of 1970, Reinbach and Finger, both of whom had occupied the administration building after the Kent State shootings despite their suspensions a year earlier, learned that they would not be permitted to return to UC. Finger remained dedicated to the antiwar movement, although it had cost him personally. In 1971 he was found guilty of throwing a brick at a police van during protests surrounding the visit of General William Westmoreland to UC's campus. A year later, Finger was still trying to find his way. Having been denied admission to other universities, he petitioned President Warren Bennis for readmission to UC or, at least, a declaration that he was innocent of throwing the brick. Bennis granted neither.[60]

To the Suburbs

Political protests on and around campus in the late 1960s helped contribute to the sense of disorder at the heart of the city. Through the 1960s, rising crime rates, persistent racial conflict, a deteriorating environment, and concerns about the quality of city schools all contributed to this sense of urban chaos and decline. Americans with the means—mostly white, upper- and middle-class residents—fled the city in increasingly large numbers. The construction of highways and subdivisions filled with single-family homes facilitated a dramatic physical expansion of American metropolises. In Greater Cincinnati, most of this new construction took place on former farms well outside the central city, where land was cheaper and taxes were lower. Residents sought larger homes, larger yards, and quieter neighborhoods, all of which became easier to find after the completion of Interstate 75 in the early 1960s. By 1974, suburban commuters could reach downtown on the newly completed Interstate 71, and the pattern of suburban growth and urban depopulation was well established by the time the workers completed I-275, the circle freeway designed to divert traffic around downtown Cincinnati, in 1979.

Suburban growth forced university leadership to reconsider its relationship to the city. While neighborhoods around the university became increasingly poor and African American, city and state planners anticipated that jobs and retail would follow wealthier residents into the suburbs. With traffic jams an increasing concern, even as the region completed its major highways, the university sought new ways to reach its increasingly distant market, the students who would graduate from suburban high schools. Reaching out to potential students now meant reaching *way* out. University extension efforts included offering classes at Princeton High School, twelve miles north of the main campus. The Princeton Center offered a variety of courses designed to provide worker training, including architectural drawing and industrial management. All of the courses offered at Princeton were to be similar to those offered at the main campus, and so were provided merely for the convenience of students.[61]

The popularity of the Princeton extension encouraged a larger investment in suburban higher education. With the backing of Republican governor Jim Rhodes, who had committed the state to a major new investment in higher education, the University of Cincinnati planned to build two new suburban campuses, one to the north and another to the east. The first, located in Blue Ash, was to be operated by University College, the two-year school that had begun operating on main campus earlier in the decade. Initially called the Raymond Walters Branch of the University of Cincinnati, it opened for business in the fall of 1967. In its first semester, the branch received just over 600 students. The new facility, paid for by the state, featured twenty-two classrooms, an auditorium-lecture hall with seating for 450, five laborato-

Raymond Walters College, circa 1976. Completion of a two-year college in suburban Blue Ash in 1967 represented the shift in the university's mission. State support helped the University of Cincinnati better serve distant suburbs. This photograph shows Muntz Hall, expanded in 1976 to meet growing demand. *Photograph files, Archives & Rare Books Library, University of Cincinnati.*

ries, a small library, a bookstore, and a restaurant. But the most prominent feature of "the 122-acre campus," as the *Cincinnati Enquirer* reported, was the "adequate room for student and faculty parking." Indeed, with nearly 700 parking spaces, the Blue Ash facility took the name "campus," but retained none of its historic associations.[62]

The construction of the Raymond Walters Branch was part of a major investment of state monies in education as a means of improving Ohio's economy. Governor Rhodes had declared that Ohio would provide convenient access to higher education throughout the state. Some of this investment occurred in cities, including the creation of Cleveland State University, but much of it was in rural counties, where economic opportunities were limited. Although the Blue Ash campus was set in the center of the city's growing northern suburbs, the other two-year campus would be better situated to serve both suburban and rural students. Clermont County was the rapidly growing, increasingly suburban county to the east of Cincinnati. With the planned construction of I-275 and the seemingly continuous investment in State Route 32, now known as the James A. Rhodes Appalachian Highway, Clermont County appeared poised for growth. Clermont County had fewer than 40,000 residents in 1940. By 1960 it had a population of more than 80,000, and it was approaching 100,000 as university officials debated the creation of a technical college in the late 1960s.

The new and improved roads, along with the obvious suburbanizing trend, inspired developers to create ambitious plans for the urban fringe. Clermont Industrial Parks, Inc., for example, incorporated in 1966 "for the purposes of acquiring, subdividing, developing and selling real estate, created a proposal for a "New Town," which it called Grant Park, just south of Route 32 near Batavia. The town would be based around industry, as the company's name suggested, but the goal was to create a complete community, with affordable housing, public lands, a new airport, and a new college campus. The plan envisioned a population of 30,000 people by 1975, living in a mixed-race, largely working-class community, where the technical college trained workers for local industrial jobs. Indeed, the technical college, and the state funds that would build it, was the linchpin of the plan.[63]

After months of searching and competing proposals, UC recommended and the Ohio Board of Regents approved the construction of a Clermont campus in the fall of 1969. The branch would be built near the Clermont County Airport on a piece of land referred to as "the Johnson Farm," part of the property Clermont Industrial Parks had proposed for its new town. Siting the new campus near the airport was a coup for Batavia, and the airport was integral to the forward-looking mission of the school from the start, as students would be trained for various jobs in the aviation industry, from mechanics to pilots. The other eastern suburban communities that had lobbied for the campus, including Milford and Bethel, could not match Batavia's advantages, especially, as the *News Record* reported, "access to the new Appalachian Highway."[64] In the spring of 1970, Walter Langsam joined Governor Rhodes at the Clermont County Land Presentation Banquet, to celebrate the transfer over sixty acres of land, which had been purchased by local businesses for donation to the university. Langsam spoke about the state's plan "to provide an institution of higher learning within some thirty miles of every community" in Ohio. "The University of Cincinnati is very happy to help implement that plan in Clermont County, now also *our* County," Langsam said, emphasizing the university's expanding mission. Langsam made clear that with the state's support, the municipal university was more than willing to take up the task of educating its distant suburban neighbors.[65]

The Clermont branch campus would meet a variety of educational needs, offering two-year degrees in education, business administration, and liberal arts, which were still the most common areas of concentration in higher education, but the school would emphasize career-oriented programs, including secretarial training, industrial and retail management, and aviation technology. "In this way," Langsam noted, "the University hopefully can repay local business and industry and the tax-paying public by supplying an educated and well-trained employee and managerial force." Langsam continued: "It is our hope, too, that the branch campus eventually will be a community center for the performing arts, drama, and lectures."[66]

The mission, then, for the Clermont branch would reflect that of the main campus, although it would grant only two-year degrees. Still, we should pause to reflect on the meaning of the college's creation—a manifestation of the reshaped metropolis, one in which suburban children would be raised in a world of automobiles, indeed in a world inconceivable without them. Many of these suburban children would also come to think of the city as a place of noise and pollution, conflict and chaos. It was the place where students protested, where the races clashed. Writing to Langsam as part of the lobbying effort to locate the Clermont branch in Batavia, Mary K. Branch, a counselor at Batavia High School, captured these two realities. "The new Appalachian Highway that is being constructed through here will make this spot easily accessible to almost anyone from any direction," she wrote, echoing one of the central factors in the branch location. "Moreover, the fact that it is far removed from the hectic traffic situation of downtown Cincinnati will make it very appealing to prospective students from our county as well as adjacent counties."[67]

Expansion in the suburbs didn't mean that the Clifton Campus would stop growing. In the fall of 1969, UC's total enrollment topped 35,000 for the first time. The growth came across the board, with the College of Arts & Sciences growing by 16 percent in one year. Nearly 11,000 students were enrolled in evening programs, most of them at the Clifton campus's Evening College. Raymond Walters College in Blue Ash and a third suburban location, the Tri-County Academic Center in Brown County, also grew. In sum, the university, like the city that it served, remained dense and conflicted at its core, even as it sprawled outward. In the decade that lay ahead, the problems of managing the expanding multiversity would only become more complex.[68]

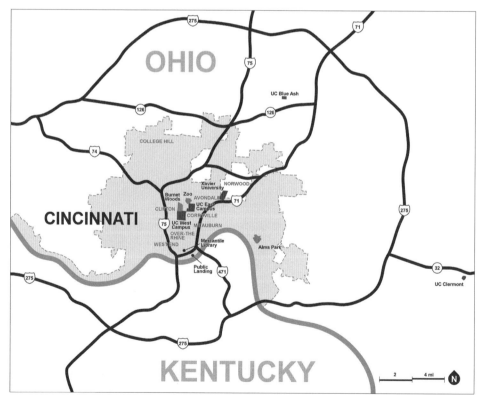

By the end of the 1970s, highways had helped transform metropolitan Cincinnati, allowing residents to commute farther and farther to work—and school. The distant Blue Ash and Clermont campuses reflect the changing scale of the university's mission. *Map by Conrad Kickert.*

8

A UNIVERSITY WITHOUT WALLS
The Urban Crisis and the End of the Municipal University

As Walter Langsam left office in 1971, the university community had every reason to hope that the worst had passed. The vast majority of students had tired of the protests, and they were eager to see a return to normalcy. Administrators and faculty wanted to get back to the work of educating. Investigations into the nation's explosion of campus protest and violence had drawn a variety of conclusions, one of which—that the violence of the previous few years correlated strongly with school size—threw into doubt the wisdom of higher education's growth strategy. Large, impersonal schools were more likely to see disruption than were smaller schools, where students knew administrators and felt real attachment to their institutions.[1]

The disaffection of students was just one of many consequences of growth. The next president of the University of Cincinnati would be called upon to manage a multiversity that seemed too unwieldy for efficient administration. Who better to hire than the provost of the State University of New York at Buffalo, Warren Bennis, a former management professor at MIT who had become famous for his writings on leadership? Upon arriving in Cincinnati, Bennis articulated a broad strategy. "We have to be our own unique kind of university, one that develops and uses the resources, the people, and the history within which it can flourish." Bennis believed that UC should not simply emulate other schools. Instead, it should be an exemplary *urban* university, because no other institution had taken up that challenge. His prime task was to make UC "the greatest urban university in the nation," one dedicated to the study of urban problems and the development of their solutions. Ironically, Bennis would rededicate UC to community engagement at a time when Cincinnati could no longer afford to support its own university, and as UC's status as a municipal university was drawing to a close.[2]

Public universities around the nation had experienced an explosion in the number of students, faculty, course offerings, and programs in the boom decades after World War II. When Bennis arrived, UC enrolled over 22,000 full-time students working toward degrees in more than eighty graduate and even more undergraduate programs scattered across seventeen colleges and two branch campuses. Approximately 1,600 full-time and 1,200 part-time faculty taught everything from modern dance to gross anatomy. Perhaps most remarkably, universities, UC among them, had created new layers of administration in an attempt to manage incredibly complex institutions. At the close of World War II, UC had just fifteen administrators: a president, vice president, an assistant dean of the university, and twelve deans, one each for the ten colleges along with a dean of women and a dean of men. As the 1960s came to a close, the president was joined by five vice presidents, a provost and four vice provosts, nineteen deans, and dozens of associate deans.[3]

The proliferation of administrators reflected the growing complexity of the multiversity, but it didn't necessarily lead to better management. Indeed, the modern university posed management problems unlike any seen in the business world, for no reasonable business would take on so many disparate tasks, and certainly not with such a diffuse power structure. Bennis called the modern university "society's closest realization of the pure model of anarchy." Individual faculty had remarkable control over their labor, setting their own research agendas and, often, determining which courses they would teach—traditions created in the name of academic freedom. Under these conditions, getting the university to move in any particular direction would be very difficult.[4]

But this is precisely what universities had to do, not just to meet the shifting needs of the economy, but also to keep pace with social changes. Among these were dramatic technological developments that fundamentally altered curricula in a variety of fields. Indeed, important new areas of study emerged in the postwar decades, including nuclear physics and computer science. New technologies revolutionized the practice of medicine and pharmacy, and altered basic research in chemistry, biology, and physics, just to name a few. The dramatic growth of understanding in these fields, along with mathematics, ecology, psychology, etcetera, required the continual revision of curricula. At the same time, the rights revolution was still working its way through society, which also had curricular consequences, especially in English, history, sociology, philosophy, and political science. And outside the classroom, the university was still trying to become as inclusive as it should be, trying to create a more welcoming and useful place for all individuals, regardless of race, class, gender, and sexual orientation. As Bennis reminded the university, "It was students who exposed the multiversity for the unresponsive machine it had become." The institution's primary challenge in the 1970s was to make the multiversity responsive—to its students and the evolving world in which they lived.[5]

Responsiveness can appear to be mere reaction, especially if the responses are halting and modest—something university leadership hoped to avoid. On the other hand, in attempting to be proactive the university could put itself in the position of predicting the future. For instance, Bennis described the great potential of "new instructional media," video and television, predicting a revolution that never came. Large, underfunded institutions like UC were especially attracted to "interactive television, television instruction, self-teaching and self-evaluating devices," as Bennis described them, because they promised to cut costs dramatically by allowing an undersized faculty to instruct the growing number of students. To facilitate the revolution, UC created a new University Media Services Center, which helped professors show films and record lectures for television instruction. "Within the next decade," Bennis wrote in 1973, "the use of the new instructional media on all levels of education will be very extensive, so that it is necessary to acquaint future teachers and instructors with the tools of their profession."[6]

Of course instructors had been experimenting with new media technologies in the classroom for some time. In 1970, Professor Jack Gottschang taught Biology 101 to 1,450 students, with 1,200 attending lectures in Wilson Auditorium and another 250 watching on a television in the Brodie Science Complex. Even the labs were presented to students on tape. "If TV teaching is done properly," Gottschang said, "it will increase the quality of education, not detract from it." A year earlier, Assistant Professor of History Dabney Park opened his Western Civilization survey class with a slideshow synchronized to modern music. Students watched images of historical figures on a screen—Louis IV, Martin Luther, Napoleon—as Earl Scruggs played banjo and the Cowsills sang about the glories of "Hair." "You can teach so much, so fast with the media," Park told the *News Record*. Perhaps inadvertently, staff reporter Tom Frame threw some doubt on the technique, putting "education" in quotation marks when referring to the ten-minute section of the slideshow concerning war. As Frame noted, "The show is fast enough and the connections between the music and the slides so subtle that it presents a kind of total experience that is not translatable into writing or speaking." Park asserted that "the media increased the students' capacity to learn." He intended to expand his use of the technique, preparing a series of "canned lectures that combined movies and tapes." Students could then watch the "lectures" in the language lab when they wanted to, helping to solve the problem of large classes. As for the students, immediate reactions were enthusiastic: "tremendous," "out of sight." But beyond the novelty and obvious entertainment value of the slideshow, what students learned about the relevance and meaning of the past was, apparently, "not translatable into writing or speaking."[7]

In addition to keeping the university up with new trends in pedagogy and emerging areas of research, Bennis would have to repair the university's relationship with the broader community. Vice Provost William Nester warned Bennis even before his arrival that the number-one priority of his administration would have to be "restoring the confidence the public once had in UC and higher education in general." This would require more than savvy public relations. Confidence would only come through good works. "Since we depend so heavily on public as well as private support, we need to involve many more faculty and students in an organized fashion," Nester wrote. "We will have to *demonstrate* our intent to serve the public in concrete ways. The variance in life styles between the U.C. subculture and the 'real world' is a definite hurdle since so few persons have represented U.C. on an official basis with the community centers of power in the past."[8] Bennis understood the importance of city-university relations. As Executive Vice-President Ralph Bursiek had warned him, "The influence of the citizens of the community on University affairs cannot be underestimated." To improve the university's reputation, Bennis would have to attend to the board of directors, and to "city fathers and pivotal community groups."[9]

Bennis tried to instill a new ethos of community engagement in an environment of new fiscal restraints. The 1970s ushered in an era of federal government cutbacks, especially in funding science research. Around the nation, the rapid deceleration of growth in higher education meant decreasing opportunities for graduate students in a wide variety of fields, from the sciences to the humanities. The Baby Boom had waned in the mid-1960s, and forecasts no longer projected perpetual growth in the number of school-aged children. Institutions accustomed to expansion now began planning for a future of intense competition for students. Many universities responded by cutting requirements, continuing the movement away from a classical liberal arts education, toward what Bennis called "a 'pragmatic' model," one that anticipated rapid curricular changes designed to keep pace with workforce demands. The College of Arts & Sciences and Evening College also created majors in "General Studies," individualized degrees with essentially no structure. Students had remarkable freedom in determining their course of study, and in the end, Bennis hoped, "the selection of courses, though personal, will have the coherence which general education demands." By offering more and more degrees and majors, the university could attract more students, which it did. Even as universities around the nation saw a drop in enrollments, UC continued its steady growth in the early 1970s, expanding by 3 percent in each of the first two years of the decade.[10]

All of this change took place inside the university as the urban crisis took hold in the neighborhoods around it—and around the nation. Like most older American cities, Cincinnati experienced continued white flight in the 1970s. The city had over 450,000 residents in 1970, down 10 percent from its peak twenty years earlier. By the end of the 1970s, the city had shed another 15 percent of its population, losing another 67,000 residents. Once the sixth largest city in the United States, it was now thirty-second. The declining population had financial consequences for the city, largely because those who remained were poorer than those who left. Inner-city poverty rates soared, as was especially evident in Avondale and other neighborhoods around UC's campus.[11] Jobs fled the city, too, and as was the case in many American cities, especially in the Midwest, Cincinnati's tax base shrank, even as increasing social problems put more pressure on municipal budgets.

❧ A Command Post to Revitalize the City

In November of 1971, the *News Record* reported hopefully on Bennis's official inauguration. Held in Armory Fieldhouse with state and city officials, the ceremony had a prominent theme: "Let the Sun Shine In," played by the UC Philharmonic Orchestra, and sung by a student chorus. A new day had arrived, promising an end to turmoil and conflict. Still, "No time is quiet for universities," Bennis reminded his audience. "They are always in turmoil." Conflict was built into the nature of universities. "No struggles are more anguished than those between ideas, between opposing views of the world, of reality, and such clashes occur every day on this campus, on every good campus in the country." This, after all, was one of the primary purposes of a university.[12]

Bennis had graduated from Antioch College in Yellow Springs, Ohio, where he learned the importance of social engagement. He believed "the University should

201

be, along with City Hall, the command post of all the operations to reclaim, renew, rebuild, revitalize the city." Sounding much like Charles Dabney, Bennis hoped to recommit the university to community engagement. But Dabney arrived in a thriving city made chaotic by growth and dynamism; Bennis arrived in a shrinking city made chaotic by decay and conflict. While Dabney had hoped that faculty expertise could bring order and efficiency to an industrial city, Bennis thought the troubled city could serve as a laboratory, in which his faculty and students could explore new approaches to social ills. "The city around us is itself a university without walls," he wrote in his first mid-year report, using a metaphor that described the city as a place to learn rather than instruct. This philosophy—that the university could learn from the community as much as the community could learn from the university—reflected the more democratic tenor of the times.[13]

In 1972, the Carnegie Commission on Higher Education published *The Campus and the City*, a book-length report on higher education's response to the urban crisis. It noted that Americans had created most of their universities outside of cities, in the British tradition, and that some had fortified themselves against encroaching urbanity in an effort to secure their remove from the problems of everyday life. Still, there was a short list of institutions, including City College in New York and Temple University in Philadelphia, which had "long been not only *in* but *of* and *for* their cities." The University of Cincinnati was on that list. Bennis understood that this oft-overlooked, perpetually struggling, midwestern university could best secure a national reputation by pressing this connection to the city.[14]

Although he was new to Cincinnati, Bennis understood the seriousness of the urban crisis, how the problems of poverty, poor education, racism, crime, and limited access to health care had compounding consequences for inner-city residents. In the face of such a crisis, UC could only do so much. "If all our faculty and students gave up their educational pursuits and their research and devoted all their time to community service, they would still not solve the major problems," Bennis wrote. "They would, however, undoubtedly end up destroying the educational system that, hopefully, will produce the ideas and people on which a better community and future can be built. That is the idea of university, nothing short of that will do."[15]

Even as Bennis articulated the limits of what a university could do for its surroundings, he highlighted paths forward. One such path was the "expanded classroom," in which students could receive course credit for selected volunteer assignments. In this regard, Bennis articulated a vision that tapped into deep roots and followed the lead of students. In 1969, in partial response to African American student demands, the university had created Able Students Perform Ingenious Roles in Education (ASPIRE), a program run through the Student Community Involvement Program,[16] which itself had been created only in 1967 as students sought more volunteering opportunities, such as the West End Educational Program. By the time Bennis came into office, ASPIRE sponsored several ongoing programs, including tutoring in South Avondale, which had grown with the help of the UC chapter of Delta Sigma Theta, a national black sorority. The program bounced around among various sites in Avondale, eventually moving to Carmel Presbyterian Church, a grand edifice in the center of the community. As ASPIRE director Dorothy Hardy summarized, "This program gives an opportunity to the Black student wanting to contribute his time and skills to help his fellow Black children in a low income neighborhood, who need tutoring in school subjects." By the fall of 1972, 125 students were engaged in ASPIRE activities; 95 percent of these students were black.[17]

Hardy hoped to engage students in all underserved communities. "An aggressive program that meets the needs of Appalachian migrants in the Over-the-Rhine or other such neighborhoods is needed," Hardy wrote. To reach that growing community, she helped devise the Appalachian Thrust Program. Befitting her understanding of how volunteering empowered students as well as the communities they served, in advertising for students Hardy wrote, "Ideally Appalachian students would participate in and coordinate this program under the guidance of the University Coordinator."[18]

Under Hardy's leadership, ASPIRE set up volunteer programs in Millvale and Mount Auburn, too, and for years she was among those who hoped that UC students could volunteer at the Cincinnati Workhouse, the large county jail in Camp Washington, less than two miles from campus. In 1974, when administration suggested merging ASPIRE with the larger Student Community Involvement Program, which performed a similar task but worked through existing organizations, Hardy noted that ASPIRE had a distinct mission. Not only did the program provide much needed service to disadvantaged communities, but it also encouraged black leadership and self-determination, since ASPIRE required students to organize their own engagement.[19]

Hardy's expansive vision for community engagement—in which students earned course credit—elicited concern from some quarters of the university. Even the president's staff expressed suspicion about these programs and noted that it wasn't surprising that some colleges didn't recognize the credits, given the vagueness of the training and oversight. Beyond questions of the specific educational value, two broader concerns about service learning developed. First, and most obviously, urban America had overlapping and reinforcing problems that would overmatch the most dedicated college student or program. This, in a nutshell, was Bennis's warning: The university could not solve the city's problems, and so it should be careful about raising expectations about its role in ending the urban crisis. Second, a focus on service could very quickly engulf the educational mission of the university, replacing it with social activism.[20]

❦ Metropolitan Affairs

If UC was ill prepared to solve the city's problems through direct engagement, it might at least improve access to higher education by increasing the recruitment and retention of black students, faculty, and administrators. UC struggled to diversify its community, and like many institutions around the nation it realized that simply removing barriers to participation would not suffice. It would have to take what became known as "affirmative action." In 1972, the University Senate helped craft and codify an Affirmative Action Statement: "The University of Cincinnati reaffirms its policy that discrimination on the basis of race, color, religion, national origin or sex will not be practiced in any of its activities. Furthermore, where past or present discrimination continues to have an adverse effect upon members of minority groups and women, the University will take affirmative action to eliminate that effect." For instance, UC hoped to increase the percentage of women and minorities receiving degrees in areas where they had been traditionally underrepresented. As for hiring faculty, UC hoped to reach a level at minimum equal to the percentage receiving PhDs nationally. Fearing a backlash from conservatives, the Senate was careful to note that these were not quotas. They were goals.[21]

Black students and faculty clamored for the hiring of more black administrators, with the expectation that greater diversity at decision-making tables would positively influence university policy. Unfortunately, this goal was easier to agree with than to accomplish, in part because qualified black administrators were in high demand around the nation, and in part because UC was new to minority recruitment. Bennis took a common approach to hiring a black administrator: the creation of new positions. UC hired an administrator to oversee the institution's progress in recruiting and retaining black students and faculty, and created a new vice presidential position for Urban Affairs. Some faculty objected to the hiring of new administrators to solve ongoing problems, and even the title of the new VP position raised concerns. Bennis took this as a sign that faculty didn't understand well exactly what the new VP for Urban Affairs would do. In his first report to the university community, Bennis wrote, "The chief task of the Vice President for Urban Affairs will be to link the wide range of urban expertise available at the University to the metropolis and to anticipate, interpret, and funnel the varying calls of the community to the appropriate University office."[22]

Charles Johnson of the Harvard Business School was among the sixty applicants for the Urban Affairs position. As he corresponded with UC about the job, he noted that the phrasing of the position, "urban affairs," might be inappropriate since it "conjures in the mind of many people, both in the business and academic community, a lot of activities that have mostly to do with 'Black people' in 'inner city ghettoes,' and the problems they generate for institutions in or near such an environment." Johnson had a broader vision, incorporating the entanglement of urban problems and suburban growth. "Metropolitan Affairs" would be a more appropriate title for this position, he thought.[23] Urban historian Zane L. Miller, who chaired the search committee, agreed, advising Bennis that the title of vice president for metropolitan affairs would "more accurately reflect our concern with the quality of life for all and with the total environment in large population centers."[24]

Johnson became the first black vice president at UC in May 1972. Not surprisingly, he was highly supportive of the university-without-walls concept, both for teaching and research. "The once popular notion of not dirtying academic hands with what might be termed 'on-location' research is inadequate today," he noted in a published interview.[25] But Johnson also pushed for reform on campus, becoming an advocate for improvements to University College. Johnson pointed out that the city had "no community college operating that answers the needs of the black community." Although Cincinnati Technical Institute was evolving and growing just two miles away, along the border of Clifton and Northside, Johnson believed University College was better positioned to serve Avondale and other large black neighborhoods. He recommended that UC create a remedial program to improve access and success at University College.[26]

At the time Johnson arrived, University College was clearly failing to recruit and retain black students. When it had opened a decade earlier, none of University

College's students were black, and all of its growth in minority enrollment had taken place in the last couple of years. Still, in 1971, only 20 percent of the students in University College were black, below the 27 percent in the city and well below the percentage in neighborhoods closest to UC. Just as problematic, the high attrition rate meant that few blacks were actually acquiring degrees. In the fall of 1972, United Black Association and the Black Student Caucus asserted that "University College has proven itself to be a farce, into which many black students, after high school, are encouraged to enter. Lack of good counseling and administration in this college has been the downfall of too many black students enrolled there. We want the appointment of black counselors and black administrators to University College." In early 1972, only six of the ninety-five full-time instructors were black. No administrators were.[27]

The response from Hilmar C. Krueger, vice president for university branches and community and technical programs, suggested the limits to which UC could go to serve those who were inadequately prepared for higher education. "I doubt that the lack of good counseling and administration has been the downfall of many black students," Krueger wrote. Instead, Krueger suspected that the students who left without degrees—both white and black—had "inadequate academic preparation" and that the university had failed "to recognize the corollaries of an open door policy of admissions," by which he meant that higher attrition was to be expected. Far from giving up on his students, Krueger agreed with Johnson and recommended "more and different remedial courses in English and mathematics" and the creation of a new "office of academic and career counseling not only in the University College, but in all two-year colleges." Better advising, he thought, would be critical to broader student success.[28]

After two years of little progress, Johnson resigned, citing lack of support from the president and disrespect for his office and his work from other administrators. In his letter of resignation, Johnson referenced "micro- and macro-aggressions" by colleagues that affirmed to him that while serving as a vice president, he was not really part of the decision-making team. The *News Record* quoted Johnson as he speculated on why Bennis would have been unsupportive of the Office of Metropolitan Affairs, given that it was his creation. "I don't really know why Bennis was so non-supportive," Johnson said. "I will point out that he never really had faculty consensus that the OMA is a good idea." In other words, not everyone believed that the university should invest its faculty talents and limited financial resources in solving the problems of urban America. More generally, Johnson speculated that the university was simply too large to manage effectively.[29] Johnson, who returned to the East Coast and served in a series of administrative posts, also expressed concern about Cincinnati Public Schools. He had three children at North Avondale Elementary, which was in the throes of serious changes brought on by conflict surrounding racial integration and persistent budgetary problems. Of course, these complaints about the racial climate—both inside the university and in the city itself—persisted long after Johnson's departure.[30]

Johnson's resignation was deeply disturbing, especially to black students and faculty. Melvin Posey, a sociologist who taught in Afro-American Studies and served as president of the United Black Faculty Association, circulated an appraisal of the resignation, making certain that it made it to Mayor Ted Berry, who had become Cincinnati's first black mayor just two years earlier. Posey's blunt assessment of institutional racism at UC included a sober conclusion: "What is most unfortunate about the resignation of Dr. Johnson is that the top leadership within both the University of Cincinnati and the city of Cincinnati does not recognize the price that whites pay when a man such as Dr. Johnson is forced to leave the city."[31]

Johnson's resignation created a new opportunity for Lawrence C. Hawkins, a UC alumnus who had joined the faculty in 1967 and had become its first African American dean in 1969, leading the new College of Community Services. One of the famed Tuskegee Airmen during World War II, Hawkins spent a career in education, mostly with Cincinnati Public Schools, before returning to his alma mater. He taught in and later became dean of Continuing Education, which included summer school and the Evening College. With Johnson's departure, Hawkins became vice president of continuing education and metropolitan affairs and eventually a senior vice president.[32] As Johnson prepared to leave campus, the university also hired Dwight Tillery, former president of the United Black Association, who had gone on to earn a JD at Michigan. Tillery, hired away from the city's Solicitor's Office, became assistant executive vice president of administration and associate university counsel, a new position.

Despite the promotion of Hawkins and the arrival of Tillery, the university struggled to keep pace with the changing demographics of the city, especially within the faculty and administration. One could argue that the university simply no longer served the city in which it sat, despite Bennis's rhetoric about the role of an urban university. Increasingly poor and black, the neighborhoods around the university—the West End, Over-the-Rhine, Mount Auburn, Walnut Hills, Avondale, Corryville—became the kinds of places in which academics might find social problems worthy of study, but these were not the kinds of neighborhoods from which the university hoped to draw students. In the era of the urban crisis, the university's municipal mission shifted.

✻ A People's Hospital?

The university's efforts to serve the city faced special challenges at General Hospital, which was owned by the city but had been managed by UC since 1962. During that time, Medicare and Medicaid, both created in 1965, had revolutionized health care access for the elderly and the poor. At the same time, these programs helped elevate expectations regarding health care among all Americans. Health care spending as a percentage of the national economy rose dramatically in the decade after 1965, but citizens expressed growing dissatisfaction with the delivery system, especially as hospitals and clinics struggled to care for the previously underserved. Health care facilities simply could not grow fast enough.[33]

To meet demand, the city made massive investments in General Hospital. With the aid of local taxes and federal grants, the expansion came in three phases. In the first, the city constructed a new Emergency Unit, completed in 1965, designed to see about 275 patients a day. The second phase, completed in 1969, was a new hospital building with inpatient care facilities. The last aspect of the hospital to receive attention was the outpatient clinic, in which non-emergency patients sought care. But even as the new hospital neared completion, outpatient facilities were scattered, inconvenient, and cramped. A facilities assessment made as the university and hospital lobbied for phase III funding, described a clinic operation housed in four separate buildings. Some clinic patients were "seen in basement areas of hospital pavilions which were formerly used for maintenance purposes and have been converted, out of necessity, to patient care areas. They are also serviced by damp, dark, hot corridors which depict medical care provided in charity institutions around the turn of the century."[34]

Dissatisfaction among the poorer patients—those who were most likely to use the clinics at General—peaked in the late 1960s and early 1970s, as advocates for the poor, the women's health movement, and a consumer movement combined to pressure healthcare providers to restructure services. General had a huge staff—over two hundred interns and residents. It was also training some four hundred medical students and hundreds of nursing students every year. As was common around the nation, Cincinnati's largest teaching hospital had primary responsibility for treating the poor, many of whose access to health care was via the emergency room, an inefficient and frustrating arrangement for everyone involved. Care of indigent patients was paid for in part by city and county taxes, but altogether the hospital operated at a loss—with the university paying for deficits in the early 1970s as the city struggled to find a solution. In sum, even as the city made major investments in General Hospital, it could neither cover actual costs nor provide satisfactory outpatient care.[35]

On April 8, 1970, about seventy-five concerned citizens, many of them taking special buses from Over-the-Rhine and English Woods, an expansive public housing project on the city's near west side, gathered for an evening meeting at Christ Church downtown. Social worker Ron Arundell, who had developed the East End Clinic, called the meeting to discuss access to health care for people in Over-the-Rhine and other underserved neighborhoods. To advertise the meeting, organizers had created a flyer with the headline, "Cincinnati General, People's Hospital?" It read, it part, "Many people are upset about the long waiting periods, seeing a different doctor each visit, and being treated unkindly." Among those who attended that evening was Peggy Chenault, coordinator of patient and community relations for General Hospital, who later reported on the meeting to the hospital administrator, noting that Arundell "is supposed to be a student of Saul Alinsky," the Chicago-based community organizer—a reference that suggested how unsettling the gathering was for the hospital.[36]

Bishop Roger Blanchard of the Episcopal Diocese in Southern Ohio attended the meeting and praised Arundell for his work at the East End Clinic, which served a largely Appalachian community that lived far from the services provided at General. Arundell played the banjo and sang a song he wrote about the hospital, with lyrics about people tired of waiting. Chenault summarized additional complaints. Instead of praising the care, those who attended feared "they are being used solely for experimental purposes," a reference to growing concern that the poor were being subjected to medical research without their consent. After attendees aired their grievances, the gathered made plans to picket General Hospital on April 23, 1970.[37]

Calls for reform continued, and by early spring 1971 a diverse group of citizens joined together to create the People's Health Movement (PHM), which grew to 400 participants within a year. "Membership includes quite a mixture of people," the *Cincinnati Post* reported, "many persons from the poverty neighborhoods, doctors and nurses, including about a dozen who work at General, young left-wing intellectuals, suburban housewives and even five Dominican Sisters of the Sick Poor." In other words, a wide range of people were working to improve health care for the poor.[38] As complaints about General grew, along with its annual deficits, the university debated the future of its relationship with the hospital. Some called for complete university ownership and management, since the facility was central to medical school training, but William Meyers, assistant to the president, warned Bennis about the gathering storm. "The General Hospital seems likely to become a focus for racial problems to an increasing extent as the central city becomes more heavily black," Meyers wrote. "It is thus something of a political liability." Meyers recommended against the university taking over the hospital, "unless some overriding reasons for doing so can be shown."[39]

Even as Meyers expressed caution, the university was investigating total-body radiation experiments that a university physician and several of his colleagues had conducted on General Hospital patients since 1960. Patients thought they were receiving radiation in the hopes of curing late-stage cancers, but funding for the work came from the Department of Defense, which thought the data might be useful in preparing for nuclear war. Because the majority of the patients were African American, and most had since died, the university was concerned about implications for race relations and future federal funding of medical research. In the fall of 1971, after the testing had stopped, the Medical School tried to keep a lid on "the Radiation problem," fearing adverse publicity and a congressional hearing.[40] The lid came off on January 26, 1972, when the *Washington Post* ran an article under the headline "Faculty Study Hits Whole-Body Radiation Plan," describing the findings of the Junior Faculty Association (JFA), which had gathered information on all eighty-seven patients who had been tested. Many of them died within weeks of the radiation treatment. The report cast doubt on the value of the study to cancer research. Instead, the JFA concluded that, although the patients were unaware of it, the study was really concerned with damage caused by radiation rather than its therapeutic potential. All of the patients had incurable cancer, but there was no doubt that the radiation hastened death in many instances.[41]

Although the news about the radiation experiments was shocking, and certainly tainted the reputation of General Hospital and its relationship to the College of Medicine, the People's Health Movement remained focused on more mundane concerns. It took on Cincinnati's Department of Health, which it found unresponsive and inept, and successfully lobbied for the creation of a larger Board of Health with citizen representation to oversee the department. The PHM was able to add two new members, who encouraged the Board of Health to request public hearings on the state of General Hospital. Meanwhile, city council member Bobbie Sterne took up the issue, visiting the Medical Center Advisory Committee to express PHM concerns in person. University administrators knew that the emergency room was overloaded, which greatly exacerbated problems, but it was also not well managed. Despite the management problem, Sterne and the PHM saw a university role in the solution: opening neighborhood clinics staffed by university physicians and students. (As much as reformers expressed concern about the university, they much preferred UC to the Department of Health.) Charles Barrett, a member of the Advisory Committee, responded that university physicians were overworked as it was and couldn't be expected to take on the work of a clinic, too.[42]

In April 1972, hoping to head off a public hearing, a Medical School faculty forum focused on the "delivery of health care to the community." Dr. James Agna, a professor of medicine, noted that "improvement in ambulatory care for the sick poor was of prime importance," while admitting that it was currently unsatisfactory. Of the 134,000 expected emergency room visits, most would be made up of sick poor, transients, and patients with accidents that were not severe. Like many observers, Agna understood that improvement in service had to be coupled with the creation of ambulatory neighborhood clinics. Dr. William Elsea, Cincinnati health commissioner, attended the faculty forum and noted that most of the sick poor actually lived near General, in areas that had a high infant mortality rate, suggesting that neighborhood clinics might not be the solution, since the hospital was well located to treat the residents of Mount Auburn, Walnut Hills, Corryville, and Avondale.[43]

Chair of the People's Health Movement Yvonne Mayes also addressed the Medical School faculty, offering a lay opinion on how health care access might be improved. She asked that medical students get involved in community health care, noting that their services at clinics would control costs and provide excellent training opportunities. She hoped that these hospital-operated clinics would be twenty-four-hour facilities. Echoing a philosophy built into the Great Society programs of the 1960s—of maximum feasible participation—she also argued that neighborhoods should have a say in formulating some clinic policies, including what they should treat. Mayes believed that doctors should make use of local knowledge about neighborhood health problems.[44]

In May 1972, the city and the UC Board worked out an agreement concerning reforms. The city would approve $1,500,000 in construction and equipment funding and provide $140,000 for the psychiatric outpatient department, along with some additional spending. The university would increase its funding for physicians in the Emergency Unit and fund a team of physicians for a new clinic unit. City Councilwoman Bobbie Sterne took the lead for the city, no doubt because her own experience as a nurse had elevated her concern for adequate health care. Sterne expressed apprehension about the level of supervision provided by resident physicians, especially because the College of Medicine had plans to expand. She asked, "How can the size of the medical class be doubled without almost doubling the faculty? Without this, the possibility of improved supervision is dim indeed." Sterne proposed the creation of a separate hospital board: "I think General Hospital could only benefit by having some community leaders turn their attention to the problems—as well as supplying a means for some representation to the patients who use the center. The overall problems of the University are so demanding that it is difficult to see how the same Board which deals with them can have sufficient time and energy to serve the Medical Center properly." Here was the management problem again. In essence Sterne was asking how the multiversity could run a hospital too.[45]

Although the university had become proactive in seeking a solution to the problems at General, in June 1972 the city council conducted hearings, listening to poor citizens. The testimony confirmed that many people came to General's overcrowded emergency room because they had no better option. After the hearings, city council summarized the complaints, which included "long waiting periods, insensitivity in the attitude toward patients and families . . . inadequate supervision of medical students, failure to admit patients who should be admitted . . . police and security guards are unnecessarily rough in carrying out their responsibilities."[46] In response to the hearings, the People's Health Movement began a petition drive to remove the University Board of Directors from control of General Hospital. The goal was a charter amendment that would mean, according to the PHM, "that the people who make decisions at General Hospital will now be directly accountable to the people who are served by the hospital." That petition drive ultimately failed, however, and the effort sapped the energy from the organization.[47]

In the fall of 1974, the university celebrated the completion of a new ten-story building at the College of Medicine. The new Medical Sciences Building was part of a major expansion of the school itself, with the expectation that the incoming class would reach 192, up from 120. New leadership hoped to change the reputation of the hospital—still largely seen as a hospital for the poor, despite the skilled medical staff and the use of the most advanced equipment and techniques, including organ transplants. The federal government had helped finance the new building, and Health, Education, and Welfare Secretary Caspar Weinberger attended the ceremonial opening. About thirty demonstrators held a protest outside the building, some representing the Revolutionary Students Brigade, others the People's Health Movement. The PHM's Carol Steinery was there to express continued concern about patient care—"long waits and high prices." But now, after a great deal of publicity concerning the radiation experiments and the physical linking of the medical school and the hospital, she added another concern: "More people will be used as guinea pigs."[48]

Despite these ongoing concerns, the university continued to manage the hospital, which became known as the University of Cincinnati Hospital in 1982. In the interim its reputation within the community improved significantly, partly because care of the poor improved, but also because of its role as the region's primary trauma center, attending to heart attacks, gunshot wounds, and automobile accidents, each representative of a deep public health problem in American society. Ironically, a hospital that had been located to serve patients with contagious disease, removed from the bustle of the city, was now closer to the sprawling metropolis's center, and thus well located for emergency care. The emergency room, the focus of years of social justice protest, became the locus of the hospital's most important service to the metropolis. Highways and thoroughfares funneled ambulances from around the region, and, starting in 1984, helicopters began delivering patients from even more distant suburbs. The rooftop helipad was just the latest architectural adaptation to reflect the changing nature of medical treatment, and the changing nature of society, too.

❦ You Deserve a Break Today

The permeability of the boundaries around campus—the university without walls— ensured that in addition to students and faculty reaching out into the city, the realities of the world continued to seep onto campus. In 1972, the employees of the on-campus food contractor, Canteen, issued a number of complaints, most of them related to job insecurity, low wages, and racial discrimination. Canteen employed just over 100 workers on campus, 80 percent of them African American. Canteen workers sent a lengthy letter to the editor of the *News Record* about broken promises from their employer, which had signed a one-year contract to provide food services in TUC after the university gave up on Saga, the previous contractor. Employee morale deteriorated after the dismissal of some well-liked managers and with the growing expectation that Canteen, which was losing money, would not renew its contract. This fueled concern about job security. The workers' letter to the editor was designed to rally the support of faculty and students. The workers also sought cooperation in case they organized a strike, although they were careful not to use that word. As the workers concluded, "[W]e hope to appeal to your senses of justice, responsibility, and fair-play" and we "wish to avoid unnecessary confrontations at this time of year."[49]

Three faculty members—Larry Jost, assistant professor of philosophy; Paul Kaplan, assistant professor of sociology; and Glen Whaley, instructor of sociology—reached out to the Canteen Workers Committee to offer support and guidance. They hoped to help organize the workers into a union, a process that was also under way among faculty, who voted to allow the AAUP to negotiate a binding contract in 1974. Working with a group that they referred to as the Canteen Workers Grievance Committee, Jost and the other active faculty developed a list of demands for the administration. The most important demand concerned rehiring workers after the usual summer slump, during which many workers were laid off. Workers were also concerned about raises, especially important in this inflationary era, and the promotion of African Americans to management positions. Negotiations led to some promises, and affirmation that Canteen and UC were equal opportunity employers, but promises about raises remained vague. When Canteen did fail to renew its contract, the workers were rehired by the new contractors, but not necessarily in similar positions or for more pay, as they had demanded. Richard Towner, director of Tangeman, responded to the demands with considerable sympathy for the workers, although perhaps less for the faculty involved, whom he described as troublemakers, and he assured those involved that African Americans had and would continue to experience fair treatment. He also noted that fifty-nine out of sixty of the employees seeking to be rehired at the end of the summer found positions. In communication with President Bennis about the complaints, Towner made two assertions. First, and most apparent, food service was a low-wage industry. Second, and perhaps less apparent, the university could not do much about that. Still, a very modest hourly raise was enough to end concerted unionization efforts.[50]

Canteen workers gained faculty support, and the interest of some dedicated students, but by and large the student body appears not to have taken up their cause. While workers' grievances failed to impassion students, the poor quality of the food did. Complaints about food on campus were perennial, of course, but they had grown more insistent in the early 1970s. The administration responded with a dramatic reconfiguration of Tangeman University Center. The new strategy brought independently operated restaurants to campus. In the spring of 1973, LaRosa's Pizza and Mr. Jim's Steakhouse opened in TUC and immediately began operating at a profit and returning money to the university. Students and other customers expressed greater satisfaction with the food and prices, as well. Richard Towner had found a way to turn a money-losing service provided to students into a profit center for the university: invite private food vendors to campus under a contract that charged rent or a percentage of the profits or both. Towner thought Tangeman would become a model for student unions across the country, as old-style cafeterias would be replaced by familiar restaurant brands.[51] Tangeman took another major step in this new direction when McDonald's opened its first restaurant on a college campus in TUC's Columbia Room in October 1973. With a long service counter and large eating area, it was the restaurant chain's largest facility yet.

McDonald's was a popular choice among students in a hurry and interested in a predictable, inexpensive meal. The campus setting seemed ideal for the fast-food model, but McDonald's management may not have been entirely prepared for all the implications of being on a college campus. As soon as McDonald's opened, students complained about "discriminatory hiring policies," not involving race, but hair length. According to the corporate employee handbook, men "must have clean hair, trimmed to a length that will not be objectionable to our customers." Clearly the generational and cultural divides so apparent in the 1960s had not closed.[52]

Protests, such as they were, worked through formal channels, involving student government, lawyers for the school, and McDonald's. McDonald's manager Ed Cummings worked with student government to find a compromise, which was announced just three days later. Essentially the corporate code would remain unchanged—employees would wear clean, pressed McDonald's uniform shirts, dark, pressed pants, polished shoes, and "clean, neat, and moderate length hair."

215

Tangeman University Center McDonald's, 1980. The McDonald's on UC's campus was a first for the rapidly expanding company. *Photo by Sandy Underwood. Photograph files, Archives & Rare Books Library, University of Cincinnati.*

Sideburns would be no longer than the base of the ear. The area of compromise involved the ability of men to pull their hair up if it was long enough to touch their collars. Student government attorney general, Dale Sugarman, put a happy face on the modest achievement. "McDonald's is cooperating with us."[53]

The right of men to wear facial hair at work struck some observers as not quite so noble a cause as those that had recently inspired student activism, but the issue highlighted how corporations would have to adjust their cultures to find a comfortable home on campuses, where inclusion and acceptance of diversity had become central to institutional missions. And there were other concerns, as well, especially surrounding McDonald's exclusive use of disposable packaging. Unlike the cafeterias it largely replaced, students walked away from the McDonald's counter with handfuls of disposable containers, including paper cups. People noticed an immediate uptick in litter, since many students carried their food away from TUC, and trash built up around campus. "While the campus was never the cleanest place," wrote student Mark Fingerman in a letter to the *News Record*, since McDonald's opened "litter on campus has increased, or so it seems, a thousand-fold." Even when disposed of properly, the waste from McDonald's posed a problem, as "garbage cans are full to the point of overflowing."[54]

Fingerman asked merely that TUC empty the cans more regularly; no one wondered, at least not in the pages of the *News Record*, if the university should rely on a business that generated so much trash as a matter of course. The piles of waste were a reminder that campuses would have to adjust just as companies would. The presence of national companies on campus—with their brands, trademarks, and marketing—helped erode the sense of difference, of remove from the surrounding society. Students were learning how to participate in the burgeoning consumer culture right in the middle of campus.

Just a little more than a year after the restaurant had opened, CCM student Joel Mitchell borrowed a McDonald's uniform, put on tap shoes, and hopped up on the counter, where he sang "You Deserve a Break Today," the infectious McDonald's jingle, while performing what the *News Record* called "an original tap dance number." His dance was so enthusiastic that he broke a light cover, sending broken glass onto the counter, into the french fry bin, and onto the floor. The manager pulled Mitchell off the counter, ending the show. Campus security arrived with "nightsticks drawn," but Mitchell avoided arrest for his performance art by saying he did it "just for a laugh" and agreeing to pay for the damage.[55]

Intentionally or not, Mitchell's dance well represented the uncomfortable relationship between the critical and questioning culture of a college campus and the single-minded pursuit of profit inherent in corporate commercialism. Protest may have devolved into mere commentary, but Mitchell had at least reminded students to ask questions about what they were doing, and his actions challenged the *News Record* headline which appeared in 1971 over an Associated Press piece on colleges: "Activism Gone: Students Today Concerned with Careers."[56] Indeed, student protests had diminished significantly after spring 1970. Antiwar protests waned as Nixon pulled troops out of South Asia, with the withdrawal of the last combat troops from Vietnam coming in March 1973. But even protests related to social justice and racial inequality faded, despite the fact that those problems obviously persisted.

❧ UC Women Are Organizing

Mass protests on college campuses may have faded after the eruptions in the spring of 1970, but the Associated Press greatly exaggerated the disappearance of activism. Women on campuses around the nation were still gathering momentum around their own movement for inclusion, curricular innovation, and improved campus services. Feminist activism at UC did not focus on admitting female students, since women had been on the university's campus since day one. Rather, women demanded that the university improve female representation on the faculty and in leadership. In the fall of 1970, just 300 of the 1,630 faculty members were female, only a slightly higher percentage of women than two years earlier, even though UC had added nearly 200 new positions since 1968. As women demanded changes to hiring practices, the growing influence of feminist thinking pushed a variety of other issues onto the administration's agenda, including women's health and day care.[57]

In 1972 Congress amended the Higher Education Act by adding language that prohibited "discrimination on the basis of sex in any federally funded education program or activity." Known simply as "Title IX," the amendment is usually associated with equity in college athletics, where it has had a clear impact, but the changes for institutions like UC ran much deeper.[58] Despite the new federal protection, however, most changes on campus came from the bottom up. Months before Congress passed Title IX, students concerned with the myriad implications of sexism on campus created the Women's Center, which opened an office in TUC. Staffed by volunteers, including Joan Rothberg, an Arts & Sciences undergraduate, and Trudy Weber, a graduate student in community health, the Women's Center distributed birth control information and made healthcare and legal aid referrals. The center also provided information about safe housing and set up a self-defense program.[59]

The Women's Center was hardly an apolitical organization. In April, the center's steering committee crafted a "Statement on General Hospital to City Council," which it copied to various city and university leaders. The statement expressed support for the People's Health Movement. "Women often wait six or more hours to be treated and then we are degraded and humiliated by a bunch of aloof-know-it-all arrogant doctors who treat us as if we were children," it read. Using language articulated in the growing women's health movement, the committee noted that doctors don't teach patients, but rather condescend to them. All of this spoke to the continuing influence of the student democracy movement, but also, clearly, to the gathering momentum of the women's movement, which would have consequences for campus life and all of American society. As the young women declared in 1972, "Good health care is a right and not a privilege!!"—an assertion that echoes to this day.[60]

The growing influence of feminism can also be seen in the movement for day care on campus. Although men were engaged in the effort, many female students—and would-be students—saw day care as essential to the achievement of women's professional goals. In May, students participated in a mass rally at the Brodie Plaza and marched up to the president's office in Van Wormer. The demonstration had been organized by Students and Parents United for Day Care (SPUD), which had supporters among students, faculty, and administrators—anyone who understood that the lack of reliable day care prevented many women from attending college. SPUD asked the university to provide space for a day care center and a subsidy for women who couldn't afford the entire cost. Student volunteers also became involved in the effort through the Student Community Involvement Program.[61]

The university had taken some positive steps, including extending its commitment to nursery school in 1969, when the Ada Hart Arlitt Child Development Center opened in a building on Dennis Street. The preschool had briefly borrowed space in the nearby Saint George's School, but now had its own space, which included five playrooms and specially designed observation areas for parents. After receiving a grant from the Andrew Jergens Foundation, Arlitt added an evening day care service to allow women with small children to enroll in Evening College classes. But as valuable as the Arlitt Center was, it was not designed to provide day care for all university students and employees, many of whom struggled to find appropriate places for their young children. Private day care facilities were simply too expensive for most UC students. As late as the fall of 1973, a year after the SPUD rally, Arlitt staff member Cynthia Harris complained that the university did not do enough to help mothers. At the time of Harris's complaint, the university had formed a Child Care Council, with representatives from a variety of groups, which was working to secure space on campus. By the end of the fall quarter, the council had created the UC Child Care Co-operative and with the help of the College of Education was engaged in fund raising, but frustrations persisted given space constraints at the university.[62]

In the spring of 1975, Linda Langmeyer, a doctoral student in business and a Child Care Committee dropout, well described what was at stake. "Affirmative Action means more than just hiring women for faculty positions, accepting women graduate students, and opening previously closed doors to women generally," she wrote in a letter to the editor of the *News Record*. "It also means providing services that will enable women to participate in all phases of academic life without causing undue psychological and economic hardships." These structural changes were much more difficult for the university to make, in part because they required resources—space and money—but also because leadership often did not fully appreciate how important they were. "It is about time the University recognizes that it has opened the doors only partially to equal rights and opportunities," Langmeyer wrote.[63]

As was the case around the nation, many men at UC were slow to recognize the strength and implications of the women's movement. In January 1974, the *News Record* finally took notice of the activism on campus, describing the work of the Women's Affairs Council under a front-page headline: "UC Women Are Organizing." The Women's Affairs Council, which had become active in 1971 and worked cooperatively with the Women's Center, sponsored alternative educational programs, including "Our Bodies and Our Selves," a health course that tackled issues related to pregnancy and birth control. In 1973, the council started "Women Helping Women," a telephone counseling service that allowed women to speak with other women who had been trained to answer a range of questions and address a range of problems. Organizers were shocked to find that a substantial percentage of callers had been raped and were seeking guidance. Linda Sattem, one of the most active students, helped create an antirape squad, specially trained women who could counsel assaulted women. As Sattem told the *News Record*, "We will tell her what she can expect, whether or not she decides to report the incident."[64]

Not surprisingly, the women's movement brought changes to the curriculum, as well. Women's Studies organized in 1974, when the administration appointed Dana Hiller, an assistant professor of sociology, as the first director. UC's nondegree program was part of an explosion in Women's Studies programs across the nation—eighty had been created since 1968. Hiller had the goal of working with other colleges in the region to expand opportunities and "take advantage of the wider resources of the community." Hiller also noted, "It seems especially important to me that a major urban university such as UC have such a program." The program opened with courses drawn from eight different departments, including Afro-American studies, English, history, psychology, and sociology. Courses were taught by eighteen different faculty members, many of them men. Early offerings included "Human Sexuality" and "Women in Asia," reflecting the research specialties of the faculty involved. The program grew quickly in its early years as more and more departments added courses that analyzed women in society.[65]

The creation and expansion of Women's Studies was part of the curricular adaptation to the democratic revolution of the 1960s, which itself was a small part of the university's effort to keep pace with the changing nature of the society it served. Afro-American Studies continued to grow in the 1970s, and in 1975 Judaic Studies became a degree program that linked the study of Hebrew with Jewish history and literature. It also rekindled the historic relationship with Hebrew Union College, which offered several courses that counted toward the degree. The rights revolution also included the creation of the UC Gay Society in 1973, although the intensity of homophobia impeded the organization's activism, as many would-be participants were fearful of the consequences of being openly gay. Some students did speak out, including Powell Grant, a graduate student in piano at CCM. "Our educational system, our family structure, our entire society has failed drastically in preparing our people to deal with their sexuality honestly and openly," he wrote in the *News Record* in 1974. Still, it would take many more years before Queer Studies would find a place in the curriculum at UC and around the county.[66]

The proliferation of new programs dedicated to the study of formerly neglected groups had little impact on overall enrollments. Arts & Sciences, home to these new programs, served roughly the same number of students—6,000—through the 1970s. The three two-year colleges continued to grow, however, in large part by serving the expanding suburban population. And, in the turbulent economy of the 1970s, more and more students chose preprofessional degrees, especially in the College of Business.[67]

❧ A University Island

As much as UC tried to reach out to the city, to engage in urban problem solving, it could not prevent the continued decline of the urban core. Intellectually the university remained engaged in the city; physically, it continued to disengage. By the end of the 1970s, the main campus would occupy a "Superblock" surrounded by easily identifiable boundaries, creating what planners in the 1960s had called "a university island." If Cincinnati was a university without walls, as Bennis proposed, the institution was building the next best thing: definite campus boundaries, secured by thoroughfares that made the university physically distinct and separated from surrounding neighborhoods and even Burnet Woods. In 1964, the dramatically widened and extended St. Clair Avenue became part of an important east–west commuting corridor and simultaneously created a firm boundary to the north. At seven lanes, the road provided a considerable physical and visual barrier to the park on the other side—a virtual moat that made the park seem distant and unapproachable.[68] In 1972 researchers concluded, "There has apparently been a continuously held assumption among university development and planning officials that major arteries make good borders, and in any event are hard to cross."[69]

University planners ignored the neighboring park entirely. New buildings on the north side of campus turned their backs to Burnet Woods, facing inward, away from the traffic on St. Clair. Crosley Tower, completed in 1969 as part of the Brodie Science Complex, was the university building closest to the park, but it could have been built anywhere. Its base was surrounded by a short concrete wall, and its only ground-level access faced the parking garage to which it was attached. The same number of windows faced each direction, regardless whether the view was a parking lot or a park. Burnet Woods, across the street, played no role in the building's design. Just fifty years earlier campus and park had blended seamlessly, with students wandering the woods, picnicking in groves, and playing on the fields. Now, after decades of remarkable growth, the green of the park had been banished by buildings and pavement.

A new master plan for Burnet Woods, completed for the city in 1972, revealed just how much thinking about the park—and the city generally—had changed as the urban crisis deepened. The plan came as the city contemplated a permanent fix for a problematic sewer that ran under the park's lake. The plan considered the university, of course, which was at that point filling out its Superblock toward the widened Jefferson Avenue. The plan also addressed the new federal environmental research facility to the east.[70] Oddly, however, planners did not attempt to improve park access for either of these institutions. Instead, the plan's centerpiece was a new building that would contain a warming house for ice skaters, whom they thought would make use of an expanded lake in the wintertime. More important, the new building, set near the southeast corner of the park, would contain a restaurant. To accommodate customers for this new facility, the plan called for two new parking lots. One would sit on property acquired at the south end of Bishop Street, which would be dead-ended. The other would occupy the corner of Lakeside Drive and St. Clair. Planners knew that approximately 300 cars parked in the park during school hours, and they rightly assumed that the university would never be able to supply enough parking for its students. "It is well established that Burnet Woods is a major parking lot for the University of Cincinnati," the plan noted, "and if there is an agreement negotiated whereby a restaurant would be located on the site, it would necessarily be mandatory that the university students do not encroach upon the parking privileges set aside for the restaurant operation."[71] The restaurant—potentially a Frisch's—would eventually be the plan's undoing. Clifton residents, supported by Councilman David Mann, who lived in the neighborhood, questioned the need to introduce surface parking and a new building in the city's limited green space.[72]

The same year Clifton residents defeated the restaurant-in-the-park idea, the university proposed to build a new home for its basketball team. College athletics continued to gain in popularity and with its success under Coach Gale Catlett the men's basketball team had outgrown Armory Fieldhouse. But UC planners proposed building a new arena at a time when the entire institution was under intense budget pressure. What's more, the proposed building would sit on the university's largest parking lot, meaning that additional expense would come from having to build a garage. Beyond the budgetary constraints, the timing of the proposal could hardly be worse, since the newly opened Riverfront Coliseum could hold over 16,000 fans, more than twice as many as the Fieldhouse. Recognizing the value of using the larger facility, in 1976 the Bearcats moved their games to the riverfront, three miles from campus. Playing games downtown only intensified lobbying for a new arena on campus.[73]

In the fall of 1977, the Board of Trustees voted to pursue construction of a campus arena, although it would be housed in a mixed-use building so as to make it eligible for state funding. Board chairman Charles Barrett claimed, "The Multi-Purpose Center is basically an academic building and must be so to qualify for capital improvements consideration." Addressing concerns about the Riverfront Coliseum, board member Ambrose Lindhorst said the campus center wouldn't be a threat to the downtown arena. "Any suggestion that this facility is primarily designed as an arena is totally erroneous," Lindhorst said. "We don't intend to compete with any private coliseum." The *Cincinnati Post* clearly didn't believe this position, and it immediately began attacking the "All-Wrong Arena." The *Post* editorial board was concerned not just about the finances but was also dismayed "at the way in which this whole project was hatched, in closed-door discussions by law-makers and UC officials." Why would the university spend money on an arena when it had trouble keeping the grass cut, the *Post* wondered. Barrett did admit that a new arena would probably operate at a loss. But in his defense he noted that this would not be unusual at the university. As he told the *Post*, many university facilities—for example, libraries—operated at a loss.[74]

Libraries might not be profitable, but most people understood that they were essential to a successful university, which is why in April 1979 UC dedicated a new central library, which was later named for long-time president Walter Langsam. The dedication celebration lasted three days, befitting the importance of the building to campus. The celebration featured some musical selections and speeches from various deans and professors and distinguished visitors, including the historian William McNeill from the University of Chicago. Like many of the other speakers, McNeill addressed the theme of universities adjusting to the "ever altering circumstances" in society and the academy.[75] This theme was suggested not just by the rapidly evolving world of higher education, but by the building itself. Like most recently constructed campus buildings, Langsam sat atop a parking garage. Its three floors covered five acres and provided open and flexible space, much of it for stacks, obviously, but also for study carrels and other places for students to sit, read, and converse.

Langsam Library was built amid growing concern about the future of libraries. Microforms and computer files were revolutionizing data storage, and telecommunications were transforming information transfer, promising the creation of vast information systems. Futurists were beginning to imagine a world without books and hence without a need for libraries. Still, over the following decades the university's collection continued to expand to match the growth of knowledge. University president Henry Winkler, who had succeeded Bennis in 1977, expressed great faith in the continuing relevance of libraries. "A library collection is more than books," he said. "It is, in the truest sense, a collection of knowledge that is waiting to aid students by liberating their minds from preconceived notions and challenging their comfortable assumptions." As Winkler concluded, "the library symbolizes the very purpose of a university."[76] No one could say that about the proposed arena, which may be why its construction was delayed until 1987.

❧ We Feel Powerless to Preserve This Relationship

By the early 1960s it was clear that the city could no longer support the growing university by itself. The state began providing financial aid after the passage of a major bond for higher education in 1963, and in 1967 the city and state negoti-ated an arrangement by which the University of Cincinnati became a "munici-pally-sponsored, state-affiliated institution of higher education." This was a new category of institution and, it turned out, an unsustainable one. The University of Akron and the University of Toledo, the other two large municipal universi-ties, joined the state system earlier in 1967, but Cincinnatians were not yet ready to give up their city-owned school. The intermediate state-affiliated status gar-nered wide backing, however. City residents had to pass a charter amendment in order to change the university's status. The amendment gained the support of Democrats, Republicans, and Charterites, as well as that of both major newspa-pers. In its endorsement, the *Cincinnati Enquirer* called the amendment "perhaps the least controversial item on the November 7 ballot." Not surprisingly, the issue passed easily.[77]

The state agreed to give support to UC because it wanted to expand oppor-tunities within Ohio for its still growing college-age population. State officials were especially interested in expanding educational opportunities in the areas of engineering and law, both of which UC was well positioned to provide. In ex-change for state support, all Ohio residents received a lower tuition bill, although Cincinnati residents still got a special tuition break. Cincinnati retained control of the board, appointing five members, while the state would now appoint four. Most important, state funding shored up the university's finances, and continued state and federal aid for new buildings facilitated continued growth. Still, these investments did nothing to improve the city's ability to support higher education. Cincinnati's portion of funding for the university continued to erode, dropping from 5 percent of the budget in 1968 to 3.2 percent in 1972. Over those same years, the state proportion of funding went from 15 percent to 17 percent. Tui-tion continued to cover a larger share of the university's budget, rising from 20 percent to 24 percent.[78]

By 1975, budget pressures had increased despite the millions flowing in from the state, and solutions were limited. UC students already paid higher tuition and the faculty already had lower salaries than those at state schools. The budget was already bare-bones. The city was not in a position to increase its property tax. Pres-ident Bennis lobbied the state to simply increase its support, to alter the existing contract to allow more state money to flow to UC. Not surprisingly, support outside the city for this option was essentially nil. As public debate continued, it became

Becoming a state university, 1977. President Warren Bennis and Governor Jim Rhodes sign the papers that ended UC's municipal status. Note the flags in the background: the American flag on the left and the flag of the City of Cincinnati on the right. *Photograph files, Archives & Rare Books Library, University of Cincinnati.*

clear that UC would have to change its municipal status in order to receive more state support. This prospect raised questions in the city. What would happen to General Hospital? Who would pay the debt the city had taken on to build university buildings? What would happen to the city tax levy? Would city residents still give generously to the school despite its state status? Councilman Charles P. Taft also expressed concern about giving up a municipal asset, one built up through a century of local investments. "It would be pure nonsense to give UC to the state for nothing and I'm not about to let this city do it," Taft said. "The price for UC is $300 million, but it's not for sale." Councilman Tom Brush expressed what by then had become widespread resignation: "We prefer to have UC remain a municipal university, obviously. However, we feel powerless to preserve this relationship."[79]

Opponents to UC's becoming part of the state system made an emotional argument about the end of a special relationship. In a very real sense the city would lose its university. Its mission would change, its constituency, its board, its student body. In 1973, more than 34,000 of UC's 79,000 living alumni lived in Cincinnati; almost 20 percent of the region's college graduates had their degrees from their hometown university. In 1975, more than a third of UC's students came from the city; more than two-thirds came from Hamilton County. Clearly, despite persistent financial limitations, the university had long served its city well. Still, as B. Kesterson Dietrich noted in a lengthy *Cincinnati Magazine* article, "Tradition and municipal control are fine, but they won't save the university."[80]

After the state passed legislation to change UC's status, the issue came before Cincinnati voters in June 1976. In a series of WKRC editorials Bennis lobbied for approval by stressing financial realities and offering reassurances. "We do not intend to stop being the University of Cincinnati in every implication of that name," he said. "We are and will continue to be a University *of* the City, regardless of the source of our funding." Cincinnati voters overwhelmingly approved the measure. The change in status had broad support in the faculty and among current students and clearly, with the lopsided vote, with alumni and the general public. UC became a state school in the summer of 1977, when Ohio, once home to several of the nation's municipal universities, lost its last.[81]

9

TOWARD A THIRD CENTURY
Competing on the National and International Stage

July 1, 1977, was a momentous day in UC's history. At 10:00 A.M., Charles Barrett, chair of the Board of Trustees,[1] signed the agreement that made UC a state university. In the same sitting, the board voted to accept the immediate resignation of Warren Bennis and to elevate Henry Winkler from executive vice president to interim president. The *News Record* headline describing the board actions—"Winkler Named Acting President"—gives a good indication of modest student reaction to the events of the day. For most observers the final step in the transition from municipal to state university was essentially a transfer of assets. "UC now belongs to the state in the physical sense," the *Post* wrote, but "it will always be the Queen City's in spirit." At the lunch following the board meeting, Governor Jim Rhodes said UC's fate now depended on "the people in Columbus too"; university officials would have to build relationships with Ohio legislators and the state education bureaucracy, particularly the Ohio Board of Regents, which gained oversight of UC policies. Despite all the bureaucratic change, most students probably sensed no difference on a daily basis. There was no fundamental shift in identity. After all, as Bennis promised, UC was still the University *of* Cincinnati, even though the "of" lost some of its meaning. Indeed, many students might not have paid any attention to the transition, given that the issues of the day remained, as they had been before, tight budgets and contract negotiations between the administration and the local chapter of the American Association of University Professors (AAUP).[2]

The other question of the day: how would Henry Winkler handle the many problems the institution faced? After a chaotic decade, the university community sought a sense of stability, and in Winkler, an alumnus and prominent historian with a kindly demeanor, UC found a leader who instilled confidence and serenity.

Unfortunately for him, and the university, state affiliation did not usher in a period of calm. The era of rapid growth came to a close and student activism waned, but the urban crisis did not end. The chaos of the 1960s gave way to disinvestment, persistent crime, and concentrated poverty. The city's population continued to fall, from 385,457 in 1980 to 364,040 in 1990, even as its suburbs continued to grow. Cincinnati's metropolitan area added more than 300,000 people in the last three decades of the twentieth century. By the turn of the century, the City of Cincinnati had just over 330,000 residents, meaning it had lost 35 percent of its population in the previous fifty years, and the city now constituted less than 20 percent of the metropolitan region's total population. At the same time, concern about university enrollments shifted from rapid growth to gradual shrinkage. UC's enrollment peaked at just under 40,000 in 1980 and then fell slowly over the next twenty years to just over 33,000. UC administrators and faculty began to wonder if an urban university could thrive in a declining city.[3]

The changing nature of the city also posed challenges to the university's mission. What role should an urban-serving university play in a disappearing city? After two decades in which urban and university decline appeared to be causally linked, dean of University College John Bryan wrote to President Joseph Steger to recommend the university "become much more aggressive in regularly getting the suburban target populations to campus so that they can see for themselves that it is green, pleasant, interesting, and safe." Bryan's encouragement was telling in two ways. Most obviously Bryan recognized that to flourish UC would have to better serve the suburbs, the "target populations" that continued to grow. Second, Bryan's description of the campus—"green, pleasant, interesting, and safe"—read more like a wish list than a reality. Echoing statements that he had heard Steger make many times, Bryan asserted that the campus and the surrounding neighborhoods would have to change if the university wanted to attract suburban students. In essence, UC, no longer a municipal university in fact or in mission, would have to evolve to become a better suburban-serving university.[4]

Cincinnatians did not necessarily equate suburbanization with the failure of the central city, which maintained many pleasant and attractive neighborhoods and remained home to several prominent corporations. But for many people in the region a new sense of crisis developed in April 2001, when violence erupted after a Cincinnati police officer shot and killed Timothy Thomas, a young, unarmed African American man. Protests in Over-the-Rhine, where Thomas had been killed,

led to conflicts with police in riot gear. Some protesters smashed windows and set fires; others attacked white motorists who were passing through. After four nights of violence, most of it well away from campus, the mayor issued a curfew for all Cincinnati neighborhoods, and the entire region had a moment to reflect on the state of the city. In some way or another, the violence—both between police and African American men and during the protests—indicated the seriousness of the problems that ran through the city. Persistent poverty and racism had created and maintained a deeply divided metropolis—that much was clear—but beyond that there were only questions. In what direction was Cincinnati headed? What might be done to diminish the divisions of race and class? At UC, administrators and faculty asked a more pointed question: What role should the university play in fixing this place?

The civil unrest of 2001 sped Cincinnati's depopulation, especially in Over-the-Rhine, and reporting about the string of police killings that led to the unrest tarnished the city's reputation around the nation.[5] Administrators fretted about the university's future. They also became proactive, setting priorities and creating policies that greatly increased UC's role in the city's economic development, planning, and public safety, especially in the half dozen neighborhoods surrounding campus. The city no longer owned the university, but that in no way diminished the importance of local politics to the operations of the institution. Indeed, one might easily conclude that UC's entanglement in the city's governance only became more complex and fraught in the four decades following 1977.

Although local conditions may have been foremost in administrators' minds, national trends in higher education were equally important to guiding the university's trajectory. Most evident among these was the diminishment of faculty power in institutional governance in the face of the dramatically expanding ranks of administrators, what the AAUP called "administrative bloat." This long-term trend continued in part because administrators had trouble conceiving of problems that couldn't be solved by hiring more administrators. Nationally, in the thirty-five years after 1975, executive positions within university administrations increased by nearly 150 percent, while tenure-track faculty positions increased by only 23 percent. At the same time, employee rosters became ever more complex, with research universities adding lawyers, planners, accountants, financial administrators, and an explosion of vice presidents, vice provosts, and associate deans. At UC and universities around the nation, administrations increasingly followed a corporate model, meaning that faculty were less and less likely to be at the table when executives set hiring and spending priorities.[6]

Beginning in the late twentieth century, UC was led by two very strong presidents, Joseph Steger, who steered the university from 1984 to 2003 with an empire builder's vision and a business manager's efficiency, and Nancy Zimpher, who became UC's first woman president, taking over for Steger with the confidence and skill to sweep up some of the messes Steger had made while transforming the university. Both were served by a veritable army of administrators, some of them occupying relatively new or newly powerful positions. Most important among them were Ronald Kull, who headed the University Architect's Office; and in the Office of Finance, Dale McGirr, followed by Monica Rimai, who served under Zimpher. Together these offices charted a path forward using tools, metrics, and language borrowed from the business world.

Another national trend—the dramatic rise in the cost of health care and a spike in competition among hospitals in the 1990s—led to the most significant structural change at the university in the late twentieth century. In October 1996, the Board of Trustees voted to lease University Hospital to a private corporation for $1. Privatization, supporters argued, would allow the hospital to cut costs. University Hospital had already joined the Health Alliance with three other hospitals: Christ, Jewish, and Saint Luke's—all of them private. University Hospital became private in 1997, but only after considerable debate and complaint, much of it derived from rising health-insurance rates and the increasing burden of uninsured Americans in need of care, but at least part of it due to the secretive nature of the university's privatization plan and the administration's clumsy handling of public relations generally. "I think it's a grave mistake in public policy," said Tyrone Yates, a city council member, UC alumnus, and leading skeptic about the change. "It's bad on its face. It's against the public's interest." After privatization, advocates for the poor challenged the university's right to make the change, especially since it appeared that the new entity might step back from its traditional role as the city's primary center for indigent care.[7]

As the vagaries of the healthcare industry forced a reorganization of East Campus, myriad other pressures forced changes at UC and in American higher education generally. Perhaps most dramatic, universities significantly stepped up investments in athletics. Some institutions hoped that the investments would lead directly to profits through television and ticket revenue or indirectly through

231

improved fundraising facilitated by the creation of a vertical community of alumni engaged in their alma mater. In this way, alumni increasingly shaped higher education—and not without raising some concern on campus. As early as 1951, University of Chicago Chancellor Robert Hutchins asked, "Why are the alumni organizations of the country, except that of Chicago, dedicated to the affectionate perpetuation of all the wrong things about their universities?" Athletics, according to Hutchins, was one of those wrong things, since it moved institutions further from their mission. Hutchins was anticipating a growing concern, and by the turn of the twenty-first century very few administrators were willing to suggest that their institutions might be spending too much money on athletics, lest they lose the support of powerful alumni.[8]

The spread of the corporate model of administration, the increasing importance of athletics, and the growing influence of alumni were national trends that had clear consequences for UC. But perhaps the most evident transition in higher education was the growing intensity of competition in attracting students and faculty. The "Golden Era" of the 1960s and early 1970s gave way to what Clark Kerr called "the Great Academic Depression" of the 1980s and 1990s, when institutions, some of them quite new and others newly enlarged, needed to find new markets from which to draw students. For some universities, including UC, South and East Asia became important sources of students, and for nearly all institutions marketing became an essential component of higher education administration. The search for more and better students encouraged marketing departments to create new "brands" that competed with historical identities that had evolved over time. Marketing departments also emphasized national or international rankings in which their institutions showed well, creating a feedback loop of using rankings to sell the university while selling the university to improve rankings. By the early twenty-first century, *Forbes*, the *US News & World Report*, and any number of websites issued rankings of all kinds, including overall institutional quality, individual program quality, endowment size, percentage of students passing the bar exam, campus beauty, and return on investment.[9]

Institutional competition and an increasingly global economy and culture heightened internationalizing impulses. Beyond recruiting international students, universities created partnerships with foreign institutions in the hope of linking students and faculty in research and teaching, but ultimately for the purpose of raising institutional profiles. Universities also added a raft of study abroad programs, especially by looking beyond Europe, a long-term trend that gave students intensive cross-cultural educational experiences and gave institutions attractive images for marketing purposes. The number and quality of study abroad opportunities became yet another measure of comparison for prospective students.

The internationalizing impulses of higher education were evident in a trip taken by Patricia Hill Collins in the summer of 2001. Collins, head of the Department of African American Studies, visited South Africa to attend a seminar on nation-building.[10] The trip was part of her department's effort "to bring a global perspective to our curriculum," as she phrased it in an email to Steger. While in South Africa, Collins visited Robben Island, where Nelson Mandela had been imprisoned, and Winnie Mandela's home in Soweto. At the second stop, she flipped through two notebooks filled with letters from universities that wished Mr. Mandela well upon his release from prison. "There in the book was a letter from you signed in 1990," Collins reported to Steger. "What a jolt—out of hundreds of U.S. colleges and universities, there was the University of Cincinnati represented among the many schools that spoke out against apartheid."[11]

Collins's email is instructive for two reasons. Most obvious is her clear articulation of the increasingly international mission of the university. But perhaps more interesting is her pleasant surprise at the presence of Steger's letter in Mandela's home. Collins had no expectation that her institution would work for social justice—that UC would be a positive force as it raised its global profile. In this way, the presence in Mandela's home of both Steger's letter and Patricia Hill Collins raises once again the persistent question: What is the university for?

❧ A Campus of Distinction

Construction on UC's campus has been nearly continuous since the university moved to Burnet Woods, but it has ebbed and flowed. For example, the wave of construction of the 1960s and 1970s was followed by a brief hiatus as enrollments declined, but shifting research and pedagogical demands, along with cultural pressures, left UC with a long list of building needs by the mid-1980s. In addition, President Steger and his cabinet desired a greener, more inviting campus. In 1988 the proposed replacement of a large surface parking lot on West Campus, between Langsam Library and the Three Sisters dorms, sparked a comprehensive planning effort.[12] A new master plan, published in 1991 and updated in 1995 and 2000, helped guide a vigorous construction schedule. The swift appearance of updates reflected "the rapidly evolving needs of the university," as the 2000 update noted.[13] The pace of updating also mirrored the pace of construction. Indeed, the intensity and ubiquity of the work on campus led to a common joke: UC stands for "Under Construction." The pace and degree of change was dizzying.

To create the master plan, the university hired George Hargreaves and Mary Margaret Jones, who had an international reputation in planning but no experience in campus design. The Hargreaves plan had a broad goal: "to create an identity (image) and establish a 'place' for the University of Cincinnati as an international leader in education and research." Hargreaves studied the campus and its history and concluded that the rapid growth of the postwar era, with its Brutalist science buildings and towering dorms, had taken place with little concern for how the pieces would work together. Buildings no longer gathered around traditional quads. The ultimate goal of the plan was to attract and retain students by providing a "college experience," a phrase that appeared in quotation marks in the plan, too. Although the plan did not well define the phrase, clearly a college experience was one that increased the distinctiveness of campus. It would be detached from the surrounding neighborhoods, separated from the traffic of surrounding streets. In short, students would feel as though they were on a campus and not in a city.[14]

The Hargreaves plan would achieve this goal by considering new construction in relation to old, beginning with the mapping of "force fields"—geometric planes created by buildings, topography, and vegetation. UC had three sets of these force fields, none of which dominated, a situation that helped create a chaotic feel on campus. One force field followed the buildings on the ridge above Clifton Avenue, a north–south line repeated on the other side of campus with the Three Sisters dorms. A second force field, at approximately a forty-five-degree angle, ran through Nippert Stadium and aligned with the ravine that ran through that part of campus. The third force field had been created by the placement of the engineering quad along another ridge.

The Hargreaves plan proposed to utilize and amplify these force fields in future construction and landscape design to help advance connectivity, drawing together an expansive campus with design themes and improved circulation. The greatest challenge would be to connect East and West Campuses, a goal complicated by the busy intersection of Jefferson, Vine, and Martin Luther King (MLK). In a first step, the university purchased properties around Procter Hall, with the critical acquisition coming in 1995, when UC made a deal with the

University of Cincinnati Master Plan, 1991. The Hargreaves plan emphasized the creation of new green spaces to create a better "college experience." Most important was the construction of the campus green, which replaced a large surface parking lot.

Corryville Community Council and the City of Cincinnati to buy the recreation center that was on the north side of MLK. In exchange, the university built a new rec center in the heart of the neighborhood, completed in 1999.[15] This win-win arrangement provided the neighborhood with a more accessible and useful recreation center while allowing the university to continue expanding its East Campus, making room for the Vontz Center for Molecular Studies, a conference hotel, and University Hall, a large administrative building completed in 1999 to house increasingly important administrative divisions, including the University Architect's office, the UC Foundation, and several offices that report to the vice president for finance. The University Commons, a green space that runs between

Procter Hall and the Vontz Center, was converted from ball fields to a decorative fountain, which served a largely visual purpose for occupants of the hotel and motorists on MLK. Combined with the subsequent reskinning of Procter Hall, completed in 2012, these changes dramatically improved views of the university from the edge of campus.

Although University Commons was mostly seen rather than occupied, overall the master plan's great success derived from its emphasis on open spaces where students and faculty could meet, mix, and exchange ideas. Hargreaves thought that casual, serendipitous contact made a campus an interesting place to be, especially given the diversity of people these spaces could bring together. Indeed, these new outdoor spaces would create a sense of "community," a word that referred to something distinct from the city itself. On West Campus, the plan created three new green spaces. The first, already under development, was a large McMicken Commons, a useful (and used) lawn that also opened vistas from the student union to McMicken Hall and from the new University Pavilion to Braunstein Hall. Creating the expansive McMicken Commons required the demolition of four buildings, Old Commons, Basic Science, Old Tech, and Tanners Hall. Few lamented the loss of these structures, even though Old Tech was the second oldest building on campus when it fell.[16] The largest new green space, the area that sparked the planning, replaced the sprawling surface parking lot between the Three Sisters and the College of Business, one of the few buildings completed in the mid-1980s, with a new, highly designed Campus Green, with braided paths, landforms, and plantings that created a sense of distance and seclusion. A third major new green space, Jefferson Quad, was to help form a gateway on the east side of campus, just in front of Edwards Center, a nondescript but essential "swing" building that provided temporary space during the years of construction and renovation.[17]

Beyond creating new open spaces, the plan used two additional strategies to distinguish the campus from the surrounding city. Since "the presence of through traffic conflicts with any attempts to create a true campus atmosphere," the plan largely removed automobiles from campus—perhaps the single most important step in creating a distinctive campus feel. The centerpiece of the plan was a braided path that replaced a through street and helped connect the lower campus and the new Campus Green with McMicken Commons. This braided path was eventually designed as a single hardscape slope called "MainStreet," to be distinguished from an actual street, apparently, by the lack of a space between the two words. The curvilinear pedestrian way created a service corridor, linking the student union with a greatly expanded recreation center and a new student life building, which appropriately took Joseph Steger's name. MainStreet helped create a social core for the community, although it could not quite replace the energy of the student union bridge, the former political and cultural center of student life, demolished with the reconstruction of surrounding buildings. The other strategy for emphasizing the distinctiveness of the campus was the creation of gateways that marked entrances to campus, using sandstone pylons and signage that clearly announced arrival on campus and departure from the city. These gateways also helped connect east and west, at least thematically, since similar entranceways welcomed people to both campuses.[18]

Removing roads and adding gateways were important to the plan, but the university needed buildings. Working with the University Architect's office, Jay Chatterjee, dean of the College of Design, Architecture, Art & Planning (DAAP), argued that new buildings should be landmark structures designed by the world's leading architects. With Chatterjee's guidance, most of the new buildings on campus were developed under what came known as the "Signature Architect Program." Perhaps the most universally praised of the buildings designed under the program was the first: Michael Graves's $37 million Engineering Research Center, completed in 1995. Graves, who earned his undergraduate degree at Cincinnati in 1958, used his familiar postmodern design and familiar materials to create an evocative building. Connected to the engineering buildings to the west, the Graves building provided a grand focal point for the end of University Avenue, the street that once served as the northern boundary of campus.

The second building completed under the program expanded the home for Chatterjee's DAAP. After seeking presentations from nearly a dozen leading architects, UC selected the design from Peter Eisenman, whose philosophy of architecture prized form over function. His building, completed in 1996, provided inspiring and challenging spaces while honoring the slope down which the building gradually falls. The design nearly engulfed the unattractive 1976 Wolfson addition and added new entrances to the older Alms building. Eisenman's Aronoff Center for Design and Art cost $35 million to build and then another $20 million to reskin just fifteen years later, an indication that Eisenman's philosophy of impermanence did not fully fit the university's needs. The Aronoff addition gained international attention because it purposefully disoriented occupants with slanted walls and odd angles. Eisenman even used the word "displace" to describe his unsettling intentions, a word that also perfectly captures what the new campus was designed to do—to make the university less *of* Cincinnati. As new buildings accumulated, it became increasingly clear that the Signature Architect Program sought to create a global university, one that was pulled into the wider world through inspiring design.[19]

Eisenman's building earned nearly as much criticism as praise, but it found a significant fan in Herbert Muschamp, the *New York Times* architecture critic. "Cheerful, bewildering, generous, controlling: this is not a building one simply walks through. One works through it, as if it were an emotional problem." This was a building that made its occupants think, and that, Muschamp reminded the building's many critics, was the point of a university. Muschamp praised Chatterjee, calling him "one of the century's most enlightened patrons" of architecture, and concluding that UC "has risen to one of the major challenges of the contemporary city. Show us something new. Give us big, urban objects that we can look at, discuss, love or despise." The Signature Architect Program was off to a rousing start.[20]

In quick succession other new buildings and major renovations followed. UC hired Frank Gehry, whose Vontz Center for Molecular Studies was completed in 1999 at the cost of $46 million. It used the curved walls made famous by Gehry's Guggenheim Museum in Bilbao, Spain, completed just two years before. The Vontz Center employed complicated brick panels instead of Gehry's more familiar metallic skin, which allowed the unusual form to fit with the other buildings around the new East Campus quad. (A $17 million "renovation" just twenty years after the building's completion suggested one doesn't pay for innovative architecture just once.) Also in 1999, UC unveiled the reconstructed College-Conservatory of Music, designed by architect Henry Cobb, of New York's famed Pei Cobb Freed & Partners. Cobb created a stunning "village" of repurposed historic buildings and a significantly renovated Mary Emery Hall.[21]

In 2004, the mixed-use Steger Student Life Center opened on MainStreet, becoming home to several student organizations, including the Women's Center, and providing retail space—most significantly Starbucks, whose arrival on campus was as meaningful as McDonald's was two generations earlier. The curving Steger building successfully wove together old and new materials to create a transition between the traditional engineering quad and the contemporary MainStreet. Two years later, Bernard Tschumi's $116 million Richard E. Lindner Center opened at the core of a new "Varsity Village." Wedged between the Shoemaker Center and Nippert Stadium, the Lindner Center mostly serves the athletic department.

Also in 2006, UC opened an impressive new recreation center designed by Thom Mayne's Los Angeles design firm Morphosis, which was in the process of remaking university architecture around the country. Cincinnati's $111 million recreation center was just one of several imposing campus buildings coming out of the firm, each emphasizing mixed use. At UC, the building mixed classrooms with recreational spaces, retail, and a four-story dormitory (which unfortunately echoed the downtown jail, with its horizontal slit windows). Morphosis strove to design urban spaces that heightened energy and created community. This was to be innovative architecture designed to inspire innovative thinking, much as Eisenman hoped his building would do.[22]

By the time construction slowed on UC's new campus, it had attracted considerable attention, earning the praise of students and helping UC to appear in rankings of most beautiful campuses.[23] In the fall of 2015 the *New York Times* published a special magazine on American colleges, with stunning photographs of Cincinnati's remade campus accompanying an essay titled "If You Build It." A twilight image taken from atop Rieveschl Hall featured several of the recent buildings, including the 2015 Nippert Stadium expansion, the recreation center, and the Richard E. Lindner Center—all three of which are dedicated to athletics. If the images were flattering, the prose was not. Hiring "starchitects" to engage in "daring, up-to-date work" had become a national trend in higher education, but author Nikil Saval wrote that at UC "a murderers' row of architects—Frank Gehry, of course, along with Michael Graves, Peter Eisenman, Bernard Tschumi, and Thom Mayne—has been involved with the most ambitious campus-design program in the country, a decades-long bid to turn a quiet commuter school into one with a global reputation." Saval might have overestimated the university's pre-building-boom quietude, but the global ambitions were clear enough. While Saval suggested the strategy had paid dividends, with UC's first appearance on the *US News & World Report* list of top global universities in 2011 and moving up to 129th by 2015, it was hard to miss the connection between campus construction and the university's increasing selectivity. The days of admitting anyone who graduated from a city high school were long gone.[24]

Saval pointed to the university's greatly expanded $1.1 billion debt, calling the building boom a financial gamble. Indeed, the explosion of the debt was one of the messes Zimpher and Rimai were forced to clean up. But, according to Saval, the real risk was existential: "that the university will turn into a luxury brand, its image unmoored from its educational mission—a campus that could be anywhere and no-

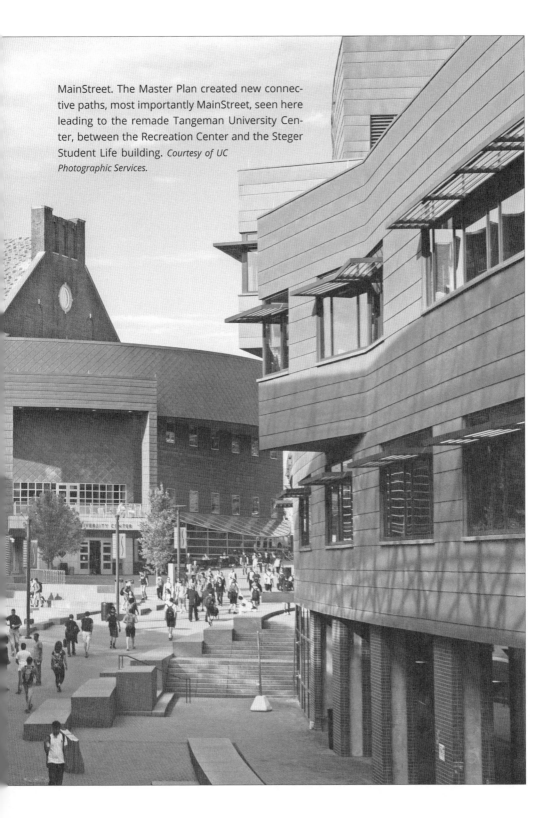

MainStreet. The Master Plan created new connective paths, most importantly MainStreet, seen here leading to the remade Tangeman University Center, between the Recreation Center and the Steger Student Life building. *Courtesy of UC Photographic Services.*

where." In other words, with the turn toward internationally known architects, the campus had lost part of its Cincinnati-ness. The new buildings had achieved their goal, but taken together the message was unmistakable: Local is parochial. Using unfamiliar forms and often unfamiliar materials, the buildings connected UC's campus with global trends and disconnected it from local culture and the local environment. Perhaps the Rec Center's gray metallic skin would sparkle in the Los Angeles sun; in frequently overcast Cincinnati it often simply looks gray. Inside, too, a cavernous gymnasium, mostly clad in gray metal and dimly lit, was perforated by skylights, a design feature that could only have been imagined by someone who had never played basketball and a mistake so egregious as to make some people long for the "plain, but neat" buildings Charles McMicken had requested in his will.[25]

More to Saval's point, the university ended the tradition of using local architectural firms. The campus had been dotted by the works of Samuel Hannaford, Hake and Hake, Garber and Woodward, each of whom had created iconic Cincinnati buildings, on campus and off. In other words, the architecture of campus had echoed through the city. And with the great transformation, each time an older building gave way to a new one, a physical connection to the university's deep history was lost. Beecher Hall fell to make way for University Pavilion; Wilson Memorial Hall fell to make way for temporary trailers; and in 2017 the Alumni Center and Faculty Club were carted away to make room for a new Lindner Business College building.

At the heart of campus, Tangeman University Center was gutted, with a mall-style food court replacing the old-style cafeterias that had served students for decades. McDonald's too was demolished. By the time the renovations were complete in 2004, the grand Georgian building was nearly encircled by a gray metallic skin, its grand copper tower made to hover menacingly over a large skylight. Altered nearly beyond recognition, Tangeman provides perhaps the most fitting symbol of the remade university, and a fine place to contemplate whether or not the university knew where it was headed.[26]

❧ Transformation of the Neighborhood Was Necessary

The changes on campus were matched by those in the surrounding neighborhoods. One of the driving forces of the work, Dale McGirr, vice president for planning, finance, and community development, summarized later, "When we became dedicated to the transformation of the campus in 1990, we immediately said the transformation of the neighborhood was necessary as well."[27] To effect change the university purchased some land, including the parcels north and east of Procter Hall, but most of the change happened without direct acquisition. Rather, UC created a number of Community Development Corporations (CDCs) in partnership with surrounding business leaders, through which changes could be planned, financed, and implemented. The CDCs and the Uptown Consortium, a collaborative non-profit created by the major employers in the area, allowed UC to be more nimble, often avoiding the slow and conflicted politics that are inevitable with government action. As UC's Community Development coordinator Scott Enns summarized, "Quietly, without fanfare, UC has partnered with local businesses, investors, and community leaders to establish six non-profit development corporations in Corryville, CUF,[28] and the Heights to address neighborhood revitalization issues."[29] Altogether the impact of the CDCs would be dramatic and obvious, while the role of UC remained somewhat obscured—by design.[30]

The university's goals were straightforward. As they existed, the surrounding neighborhoods, especially Clifton Heights and Corryville, were largely unappealing and frequently dangerous, and these qualities greatly inhibited UC's ability to attract quality students—the "target populations" of suburbia. So, UC set out to do nothing less than transform uptown, focusing on key thoroughfares and business strips: Martin Luther King, Calhoun, McMillan, and Short Vine.[31] The CDCs encouraged the development of attractive, secure off-campus housing and new commercial and social spaces that reflected New Urbanist ideals of walkability and mixed use. The nineteenth-century booster paradigm of building institutions to make the city more attractive to prospective residents had flipped. Now the institution sought to rebuild the city to make itself more attractive to prospective students.

At the time the transformation began, Calhoun Street, the major route to campus from Interstate 71 and the prosperous east side suburbs, was little more than a row of fast-food restaurants—McDonald's, Hardee's, Arby's, Kentucky Fried Chicken[32]—most of them featuring litter-strewn parking lots. UC hoped to replace this drive-thru landscape with an appealing, walkable district. Elsewhere, heavy commuter traffic reduced pedestrian comfort levels, especially at the intersection of Martin Luther King and Jefferson, through which more than 70,000 cars passed each day by the year 2000. Decades of urban planning featuring thoroughfares and parking rather than public transit and housing had created a cityscape that challenged the revival of a pedestrian-centered street culture.[33]

UC wanted to create physically attractive surroundings for students and employees, but the primary concern was safety. As UC alumnus Andy Morgan articulated to President Zimpher in 2004, the university needed to stem the bad publicity created by crime in the neighborhoods around campus. He told Zimpher, "The secret is to get rid of the trash and get rid of the people in the area who are not there for any academic reasons, or are not productive members of society. This may sound harsh…But it is the truth." These changes wouldn't just make students feel more comfortable. "I have had hundreds of contacts over the years with parents, both black and white," Morgan wrote, "and the number 1 issue is their children's safety." In other words, if UC wanted to grow, it needed to control the area around campus, which in turn meant controlling, at least to some degree, who lived in and visited these neighborhoods.[34]

The rapid change off campus began with the same critical move that initiated the dramatic changes on campus: the deal with the Corryville Community Council in 1995 that allowed UC to acquire land around Procter Hall and relocate the Corryville Recreation Center, a building around which that neighborhood could be transformed. But the real turning point came when UC began to create the CDCs, beginning with the Corryville Community Development Corporation, also in 1995. Four years later, UC created the Clifton Heights Community Urban Redevelopment Corporation (CHCURC), and shortly thereafter the University Heights Community Urban Redevelopment Corporation. In each instance UC was careful to keep controlling votes with community members, but the redevelopment goals were clearly set by the university. UC paid for staff and rent and, more important, it committed $75 million for use as long-term loans, in essence financing much of the development that would take place around campus. This "endowment funding" represented a real risk, but one that administrators thought was necessary. In an early success story, UC provided a $3.3 million loan for the redevelopment of a church so that it could accommodate Urban Outfitters in 2001.[35] Next, another modest step, UC helped develop Bellevue Gardens, a forty-apartment project along Martin Luther King across from the Medical School campus. It opened in 2002.[36]

The most anticipated transformation took place south of campus, in the blocks between Calhoun and McMillan, the area occupied largely by fast-food restaurants and poorly kept apartments. All of the blocks between Ohio Avenue and Clifton Avenue became the target of CHCURC, which with the help of the city declared the area "blighted" and thereby subject to eminent domain acquisition for redevelopment into a massive mixed-use development called McMillan Park. This three-block development would be anchored by a new condominium tower and a small park. Eleven property owners sold their land to the city, which handled the assembly of parcels. The buildings were cleared as the property changed hands, the newly empty lots making the area even less attractive. Two small businesses, Acropolis Chili and Inn the Wood, joined forces with a company that owned two of the fast-food restaurants to resist the city's attempt to take their properties. In defending his business, Acropolis Chili owner Joe Kennedy said, "I wasn't a blight for 17 years while I was paying my taxes. The blight is what the city's creating up here," he said, referring to the newly emptied lots. "I'm in a panic. I haven't slept a decent night in two damn years. I'm not looking to start over again from a brand new spot." Dan Deering, CHCURC's executive director, took a different view. "This is not some private developer trying to make something happen without community consensus. We have to re-invest in ourselves if we want to be competitive in the future. If we don't, we'll continue to experience population decline."[37]

Despite the fact that the redevelopment had been backed by loans from UC's endowment, the university managed to keep the long battle to acquire the properties at arm's length. The city and CHCURC played the roles of bureaucratic villains, and Deering, who owned rental properties in the area and was not a UC employee, became the face of the redevelopers, and his rhetoric focused on community need rather than institutional growth. Because the protracted conflict was waged by proxies, most of the university community simply looked forward to the day when the project would be complete and ignored the consequences of the redevelopment on Kennedy and Bill and Diana Wood, owners of Inn the Wood. After five years of failed negotiations, the eminent domain case came to trial. In early 2005, Hamilton County Common Pleas Judge Thomas Crush upheld the city's right to take the restaurants through eminent domain. "There can be no doubt that a public purpose is served by this urban renewal plan designed to revitalize a declining, deteriorating neighborhood," he wrote. Within months the city came to terms with the Woods, paying $1.6 million for their corner lot. Kennedy settled too.[38]

In 2007, Ohio's First District Court of Appeals overturned the city's use of eminent domain against the owner of the Hardee's and Arby's lots, Clif-Cor Corporation—the last holdout between Calhoun and McMillan. Soon after winning its case, Clif-Cor settled, and the boarded-up buildings came down. By then University Park Apartments had opened atop a $40 million parking garage on the north side of Calhoun and a completely remade Clifton Heights seemed possible. Towne Properties, a prominent regional developer, agreed to take on the long-stalled project, and after some significant reconfigurations—including moving the parking structures aboveground and replacing the high-end condominiums with moderately priced apartments—the massive U Square at the Loop, a mix of apartments, office space, shops, bars, and restaurants, was born between two new, hulking parking garages.[39]

On the west side of campus, UC used its own funding and the University Heights Community Urban Redevelopment Corporation to create the Stratford Heights development, completed in 2005 with less conflict and much less bad publicity. Designed to provide safer, more up-to-date housing for student groups, including fraternities and sororities, the development represented a significant leap of the university across Clifton Avenue. This development was made possible because it was controlled by the CDC, which allowed UC to claim this was not an expansion of the campus across Clifton, even though the university funded Stratford

U Square. By 2013, the acres between Calhoun and McMillan, once occupied mostly by fast-food restaurants, had been transformed into U Square, a New Urbanist, mixed-use complex catering to the university community. *Courtesy of UC Photographic Services.*

Heights, helped design it, and ensured that it would serve only its students. The secretary of the CUF Neighborhood Association, Linda Ziegler, summarized the strategy in reflecting on the Calhoun project: "What UC has done is fund all these mini-redevelopment corporations, which I see as a kind of money-laundering, so then they can say, 'It's not us, it's them.'"[40] Dale McGirr confirmed the mistrust but asserted that UC did not control the decisions. "People don't trust us," he said in 2006, "[so] we specifically put these [CDCs] in the control of business associations and community association members. They're in control of their agenda."[41]

As it turned out, the work of the CDCs was prelude to a more organized intervention through the Uptown Consortium, formed in 2004 by UC in partnership with the other major players in the area: Children's Hospital, Cincinnati Zoo & Botanical Garden, the Health Alliance of Greater Cincinnati (which later changed its name to UC Health), and TriHealth, a hospital group that included Good Samaritan on Clifton Avenue. Collaboration with the other major employers created possibilities for even more dramatic transformations. Uptown Consortium instantly became a significant lobbying force, at the local, state, and federal levels. It also became a financial fulcrum, from which the university could further leverage its surroundings. In explaining the advantages of Uptown Consortium over CDCs, also called neighborhood development corporations (NDCs), Vice President for Finance Monica Rimai noted that beyond the gathering of financial might and the improved coordination of efforts, "UC really must look to UpCo, because the organizational limits of the neighborhood specific NDC(s) create constant conflict of interest problems that get in the way of really efficient development."[42]

The great potential was not lost on John Linser, a UC alumnus who grew up in Corryville in the 1950s. Upon reading about Uptown Consortium, he wrote to President Zimpher in early 2004: "I am both excited and a little nervous about the work of the Uptown Consortium." The nervousness concerned "displacement and gentrification," which seemed inevitable, especially in the neighborhood south of the hospitals. He reminisced about the vibrancy of the community in the 1950s, and he hoped there were "specific goals about the development in the area. Not just to make it more attractive to the professionals who work nearby, but to be respectful of the historical context of the community."[43]

To ensure the effectiveness of the Uptown Consortium, the partners brought in Tony Brown, an expert in community development financing, and paid him $204,000 a year (plus a $17,000 signing bonus and potentially $50,000 in additional bonuses for good performance). His extraordinary salary reveals just how important redevelopment had become to the member institutions. The city had deteriorated for fifty years, and this new structure would facilitate public–private partnerships that brought together entrepreneurial initiative with government tools, such as eminent domain. Neighbors could only hope their vision for the area aligned with that of the major institutions.[44]

Uptown focused its attention on two areas of significant interest to the university: Short Vine and the MLK corridor east of University Hospital. "Today, Short Vine is largely barber shops, beauty salons, and tattoo parlors," concluded Brown, as he worked on redevelopment plans. "We think we can make it substantially more than that, with restaurants, clothing stores, and things that will be more attractive to those who come through the neighborhood every day." In addition to encouraging private-sector student apartment development, planning hinged on redeveloping University Plaza, a tired retail area that featured a rundown Kroger grocery store. The plaza occupied a prominent location, where Vine Street had been cut off and traffic redirected onto Jefferson. Uptown encouraged development by leveraging New Market Tax Credits, a federal program designed to encourage investment in impoverished areas by making them more profitable.[45] Brown also helped the university lobby in Washington, DC, for regional development support, and in an effort to attract the National Institute of Occupational Safety and Health to the MLK corridor. And, after years of lobbying, federal support also came in the form of transportation funds to add an interchange at MLK and Interstate 71, a major development that greatly improved access to East Campus and surrounding development lots. As Zimpher phrased it in her own lobbying effort with federal administrators, "We are working to create a critical mass of technology resources in Uptown that will catapult this area into national and international prominence." Her language revealed how much university goals for their neighborhood echoed the goals for the institution: "national and international prominence."[46]

Not surprisingly, UC's intervention in surrounding neighborhoods continued to cause friction, with critics expressing concern that gentrification meant a loss of community, that the construction of characterless buildings meant a loss of identity, and that demolition of older buildings meant a loss of history. Neighborhoods did lose some historic, even iconic buildings—Inn the Wood in 2005, the Friars Club on the corner of McMillan and Ohio in 2010, the Schiel School on Short Vine in 2011, and the Goetz House on McMillan in 2014. On the other hand, even where the new architecture was uninspiring, it was mostly an improvement over what it replaced. All the same, the mere pace of the change ensured that community complaints about UC's extraordinary influence in Uptown would persist. Indeed, the role of large institutions in remaking their neighborhoods remains a national issue. As historian LaDale Winling concludes in his study of universities and urban planning, "The expanding city of knowledge remains a highly contested form." Still, UC's expansion by other means has been successful, especially when measured by enrollment growth, the primary goal of the intervention. UC broke enrollment records for the fourth consecutive year in 2016, with the student body rising above 44,000.[47]

🌿 A Change in Focus

In his 1998 annual report, President Steger succinctly articulated the new mission of the university. "To succeed, a university must act globally and interact where knowledge is being explored. Today that means everywhere in the world. The University of Cincinnati is projecting itself worldwide and participating in the global community. Our connections are formal, personal, and electronic." Steger selected data to illustrate how UC participated in this global community. It attracted students from more than 80 countries. Its faculty were "involved in more than 105 countries," both in conducting research and leading study-abroad trips. "The university is truly an international enterprise," he concluded.[48]

Perhaps too much like an enterprise for some faculty, who expressed concern that the university was being run like a corporation, with too much authority concentrated within a cadre of administrators. Steger had spent his career in management, bouncing between higher education and business, and he arrived at UC from Colt Industries. His experience taught him the importance of bold leadership. The rapid change on and off campus was evidence enough of the effectiveness of his approach, but even if most observers applauded Steger's ability to move the unwieldy institution, there were grumblings about the direction the institution was headed. The grumbling bubbled to the surface when UC's physical rebranding effort reached into collegiate structures and threatened the existence of programs and a fundamental reshaping of the university's democratic mission.

In the fall of 2001, Provost Tony Perzigian created a Collegiate Structures Committee to consider the future of three colleges: Arts & Sciences, Evening and Continuing Education, and University College. Together these colleges enrolled more than a quarter of all UC students. They were all located on West Campus, and they taught in many of the same disciplines. Perzigian charged the twelve-member committee with considering "possible reconfiguration or consolidation of those colleges' administrations, programs, and curricula in order to improve delivery of undergraduate instruction." The committee was chaired by Vice Provost Kristi Nelson, and only four of its members were from the UC faculty. The three colleges under consideration had a total of six representatives.[49]

Five months after its creation, the Collegiate Structures Committee issued its final report. The twenty-seven-page document described a number of potential paths forward, but it was mostly a compendium of data concerning duplication of courses and preparedness of students. It also contained statements of principles: that the university should maintain its access mission; that duplicated efforts should be diminished; that advising and guidance should be improved. Significantly, as if the conclusions had been preordained, the report was clear only about the future of one of the three colleges: UC "needs a strong College of Arts & Sciences." Duplication would be diminished by collapsing the other two colleges. The only question was how.[50]

The first step in restructuring came just three months later with the dissolution of the Evening College, effective June 2002. As had been the case before the creation of a separate Evening College in the 1930s, evening students would now take classes in the various other colleges, particularly Arts & Sciences and Business. This shift reflected new thinking about nontraditional students and how the university could best serve them. "English literature shouldn't be any different at 8 P.M. than it is at 8 A.M.," Perzigian said, "because the students have the same capabilities and goals." Steger echoed this sentiment, although putting it in business terms: "When shopping at night, we don't call it evening Kroger." In the short term, the dissolution of Evening College meant considerable stress for faculty, staff, and students, as they adjusted to the new structure, but in the long term it also meant a diminishing focus on offering courses in the evening, since no single unit maintained this distinct mission. Over time, however, in parts of the university evening and weekend courses for working students were gradually replaced by online courses that allowed students to pursue their education flexibly.[51]

In September of 2002, as the consequences of Evening College's dissolution were moving through the university, faculty and staff in University College assumed they would be next. Diane Mankin, a professor of art history in University College, voiced her concern directly to the provost. She, like many of her colleagues, thought the administration had been starving the college for years, failing to provide consistent leadership, shrinking the number of full-time faculty, and thereby making it difficult for the college to succeed.[52] That November, as news spread that one of their major classroom buildings would be demolished to make way for new construction, Mankin noted a general dismay at how restructuring had taken place, with too little input from those who would be most affected. "Evening College was dissolved very quickly right out from under us, literally," she complained. Perzigian tried to assuage her by describing the goals of the restructuring process. "Let me assure you that the agenda is very simple: attracting, better serving and retaining more students," he said, adding, more ominously, "Few UC colleges should have any bragging rights or interest in preserving the status quo."[53]

Perzigian heard so many complaints that he sent all University College faculty an email to address "misunderstandings and misinformation." Calling the imperative behind restructuring "obvious and compelling," he reminded the faculty that the university's enrollment had been declining, leading to the state's decision to roll back the university's subsidy by $3 million. As Perzigian put it, "We must do better in serving our diverse mix of students." Then, in language the faculty could not have found reassuring, Perzigian wrote, "I envision that University College will continue to exist, with a different and more focused identity, and thus a different name to mark the change in focus." Perzigian's phrasing confirmed the University College faculty's suspicion that their mission had been pared down to one line: admit "underprepared students" and try to prepare them to transfer into a four-year degree in another college.[54] Not surprisingly, this didn't sit well with the faculty, who thought associate degrees were useful and worth offering on the main campus.

The administration, including Perzigian, understood that dissolving University College would have political ramifications, since many people believed it provided the best route to a college degree for African Americans living in the neighborhoods surrounding UC. "In the context of our urban mission and in the light of our social responsibilities to the wider Cincinnati community, it is essential that we continue to offer, on the West Campus, the experience of a major university to a wide and diverse array of students," Perzigian wrote. In other words, UC wouldn't stop serving African American students. But the poor performance of University College in graduating students with associate degrees or successfully moving them into baccalaureate programs suggested that it needed to find a better way of doing so.[55]

Within a year of Perzigian's clearing up "misunderstandings and misinformation," University College was dissolved. Perzigian defended the choice by suggesting that it is better for students to get four-year degrees (although at UC bachelor's degrees were more likely to be five- or six-year degrees). With the dissolution, students seeking associate degrees would go to Blue Ash or Clermont, and students needing additional preparation for college-level work would be assigned to a new—and short-lived—unit, the Center for Access and Transition. With racial tensions in the city still high after the Timothy Thomas shooting, the closure of University College raised eyebrows and ire in the African American community. "There are still serious unanswered questions as to the implications these changes will have for African-American students," the NAACP said in a statement as the main campus access college disappeared.[56]

A second wave of collegiate restructuring led to the dissolution of the College of Applied Sciences (CAS) in 2010. Upon its closure, much of its faculty and some of its signature programs moved to the College of Engineering, which changed its name to the College of Engineering and Applied Science. As with University College and Evening College, CAS was more likely to serve first-generation college students, some of whom needed more support, especially in advising and financial aid. The evolving mission of the university—with its rhetoric about being "world class" and building international relationships—clearly didn't speak to the missions of these colleges. Perhaps just as important, in the competitive world of higher education, numbers matter, including graduation and retention rates, as well as average SAT and ACT scores. University College in particular had low retention numbers—not surprising given the population it served—and this made it an easy target for restructuring. UC was striving to rise in national rankings, and admitting fewer at-risk students was an easy way to get results.[57] In the effort to create a global institution, some aspects of the old municipal university were bound to fall away.

🎋 The Big Gamble on Big-Time Sports

Perhaps UC's most protracted effort to raise its national profile came in the area of athletics. From 1975 to 1991, UC was a member of the Metro Conference, composed of several universities with similar profiles, including the University of Louisville and Memphis State University. The Metro did not sponsor football, and so UC and the other football schools played that sport as independents. This arrangement became increasingly unsatisfactory given the growing potential of football television revenue to shore up athletic department budgets. When attempts to expand the Metro Conference and add football failed, South Carolina and Florida State departed to other conferences, while Cincinnati and Memphis split to found the Great Midwest Conference. The Great Midwest was no solution, as it also did not sponsor football, and it lasted only until 1995, when the realignment of conferences intensified. A great reshuffling began, as NCAA Division I sports moved toward super-conference configurations and a formal designation of "power conferences" with automatic bids to football bowls. UC was determined to create or join one of these elite conferences, ostensibly because these could assure appropriate competition for its athletes and put Cincinnati in league with schools with academic reputations that matched—or exceeded—its own. Over the next decade plus, the conference shuffle proved highly disruptive for universities such as Cincinnati, but few institutions had so much at stake.

UC joined forces with other striving universities, many of them urban institutions, including Louisville, Houston, and Memphis, in an effort to create a conference that could make claims to elite status. In February of 1995, athletic directors and university presidents were working toward the union of the Metro, which had regrouped by adding replacements for its departed members, and the Great Midwest. Many details remained unsettled, including the new conference name, but the organizers were ready to put out a brief marketing piece with relevant data. "The formation of the Super Conference," as it was briefly called, "will enable the new league to soundly begin the tradition of intercollegiate competition. Our mission is to commit and ensure the growth and success of the Super Conference and its member institutions. A high level of consistency by the Super Conference will provide success and solid symmetry between academics and athletics." The vague and awkward language suggested the pace at which organizers were working. A new structure for competition, new legal documents, new TV deals, all needed to be in place before the next football season. The group eventually decided on a new, patriotic name befitting the lack of geographical concentration of its membership: Conference USA.[58]

Although athletic directors tended not to discuss openly why the conference scramble was taking place, the public knew the process was being driven by money, which meant that the fate of all Division I collegiate athletes was being determined by football and its great revenue potential. The new Conference USA included some familiar foes, such as Louisville, Tulane, Houston, and Southern Mississippi, but it also incorporated several non-football schools, including DePaul, St. Louis, and Marquette. Because football playoff appearances and television deals were driving the realignment, Conference USA was flawed from the outset. The new conference also failed to raise UC's football profile, which could hardly be lower. From 1989 to 1993, attendance of Cincinnati home football games averaged just over 15,000, making UC the lowest drawing of the six football teams joining Conference USA. (The highest drawing team was long-time rival Louisville.) During those same, lowest-drawing seasons, UC won 17 games and lost 37.

Fortunately for Cincinnati, conferences shuffled again in 2005, when the Big East Conference lost prominent football members Virginia Tech, University of Miami, and Boston College and decided to rebuild its football profile by adding new schools, including UC. After decades of work, UC had finally reached an elite conference, one that seemed to match its own strengths, since UC would now play men's basketball—where it had a long tradition of success—with other perennial powers, such as Georgetown, Connecticut, and Providence. President Zimpher did not exaggerate when she said, "Entry into the Big East is just about as big as it gets."[59] Membership in the Big East in many ways marked the final step in the transition from municipal streetcar college to national research university.

Just when the good feeling about entering the Big East had settled in, and before students had arrived on campus in the fall of 2005, President Zimpher gave an ultimatum to extraordinarily popular (and successful) sixteen-year head basketball coach Bob Huggins: quit or be fired. The ultimatum came after a string of bad publicity for the program, much of it surrounding the off-court behavior of UC's players—one assaulted a roommate, another assaulted his girlfriend and police officers, and still another assaulted a police horse. The bad behavior culminated in a drunken driving incident involving Huggins himself. The removal of Huggins that fall caused a tremendous uproar in the city, and in part revealed how little progress had been made in women's equality, given the gendered nature of the attacks on Zimpher. In some circles, however, especially within the faculty, Zimpher had made a bold statement about the university's expectations about behavior. Athletics had to be more than about winning. ESPN's Pat Forde noted that because so many Cincinnatians were calling for her removal, "Nancy Zimpher might have started the clock on herself." "But," he concluded, "she showed the toughness, leadership, and authority that a president should when dealing with the athletic fiefdom. Score this one a victory for the eggheads."[60]

Even without Huggins, entry into the Big East promised higher visibility for the school, especially in eastern markets that had not historically sent many students to UC. Better television contracts and gate receipts promised some financial reward as well, but entry into an elite conference did not come cheap. To match conference expectations, UC made a cluster of investments in "Varsity Village," including the Lindner Center, a new track encircling a new soccer field, tennis courts, and improvements to Nippert Stadium. And there were opportunity costs that came with the university's prioritization of athletics fundraising, as the UC Foundation dedicated time and money to encourage donors to fund the construction of athletic facilities instead of investing in the core mission.

If the cost of entering the Big East had been steep, remaining competitive would require continuous investment. In the fall of 2010, UC inflated a bubble over a new full-sized football field. The indoor facility replaced the never-developed Jefferson Quad, designed to be one of the gateways in the original Hargreaves plan. The bubble was part of a $15 million project to improve practice fields to be used by a number of teams, but driven by the needs of football. "UC was the only school in the Big East Conference, other than the University of South Florida in Tampa, Fla., without an indoor practice facility," a UC news release explained.[61] Calling the bubble a "necessity," Athletic Director Mike Thomas said, "This facility will allow us to recruit and retain the best student athletes." Clearly, entering the Big East had created pressure on UC to finance further improvements. "I see this not only being the difference maker for us but eliminating the disparity between us and those we compete against in the Big East Conference."[62]

In 2012 and 2013 the Big East fell apart. Several prominent members—West Virginia, Syracuse, Pittsburgh, and Notre Dame—departed for conferences that featured football, and the seven non-football-playing universities of the Big East fled as a group, eventually taking the name of the conference with them. The remaining schools, including UC, scrambled to fill vacancies and reformulated as the American Athletic Conference, a Conference USA reboot but without powerhouse Louisville, which landed in the Atlantic Coast Conference in 2014. This dramatic realignment caused yet another round of hand-wringing, as UC found itself once again in league with urban schools of modest academic and athletic reputations, such as Memphis, Temple, Tulsa, and Houston. As the dust from the NCAA realignment began to settle, observers identified Cincinnati as one of the biggest losers, its long struggle for premier conference membership thwarted after less than a decade in the big leagues.[63]

The Bearcat at Nippert Stadium. UC invested heavily in Division I athletics as it attempted to raise its national and international profile. Its football team met with considerable success during an eight-year stint in the Big East. *Photo by Joseph Fuqua II. Courtesy of UC Photographic Services.*

UC administrators and athletic directors did not give up. Cincinnati began a multiyear pitch to secure an offer to join the Big 12, the last of the major conferences that seemed prepared to add members. Part of the effort involved two big-ticket facility improvements. First, UC upgraded and expanded Nippert Stadium in time for the opening of the 2015 football season. The $86 million investment added 1,100 seats and 53 luxury suites, with most of the improvements coming in a towering glass pavilion that replaced the press box on the west side of the stadium. Second, UC committed $87 million for basketball with a redesign of Fifth/Third Arena, a facility that had sufficient capacity but never functioned well. Hired in 2014, Athletic Director Mike Bohn was confident that the investment in athletics would pay dividends. "It's a strategic investment with a high return," he said.[64] In speaking specifically about the $87 million upgrade to the basketball court, Board of Trustees member Rob Richardson noted, "It's a calculated risk, frankly. We have to make investments in order to become competitive."[65]

Perhaps the Board of Trustees and the athletic director felt compelled to continually invest in new facilities because of the university 100 miles up Interstate 71.

Ohio State University had one of the very few athletic programs in the nation that turned a profit. A member of the Big Ten since 1912, Ohio State never struggled for a place at the big table, and its fans rewarded success with loyalty. Like UC, Ohio State has made a series of investments in its stadium, increasing capacity to over 104,000 at the time Nippert renovations brought Cincinnati's capacity to about 40,000. Buckeye football games consistently draw more than 100,000 fans to Ohio Stadium, more than twice the largest crowds at Nippert.

Ohio State is an anomaly and a very poor model for the other public universities in the state. Most university athletic departments generate annual deficits, and continuously upgraded athletic facilities generate debts. Indeed, because UC athletics do not break even, the athletic department requires significant subsidy from the general fund, most of which comes from tuition. As a 2015 student-researched and -written exposé that appeared in *City Beat* made clear, most students were unaware how much of their tuition paid for the athletic subsidy. In the seven years between 2007 and 2014, student fees and general fund money covered $127 million of the athletic department budget, the only way the university could prevent the accrual of annual deficits. According to the exposé, that meant the average undergraduate student paid $4,000 to support athletics while pursuing a degree. For many undergrads this translated into a greater student loan burden upon graduation.[66] Not only did spending on athletics generate debt for students, it clearly required the university to move limited funds away from academics. According to the Knight Commission, formed by the John S. and James L. Knight Foundation to ensure that athletics programs operate in accordance with the educational missions of their institutions, from 2005 to 2015 Cincinnati's funding for athletics per athlete increased 265 percent when adjusted for inflation, reflecting investments made to remain competitive in the Big East. Meanwhile, UC's academic spending per full-time student fell 21 percent when adjusted for inflation.[67]

Despite the *City Beat* exposé and perennial newspaper articles about the salaries of football and basketball coaches outpacing those of university presidents (true at UC, Ohio State, and most Division I schools) and all other state employees, the public remained largely unconcerned about athletic spending. In defending the high salary of football coach Tommy Tuberville (more than $2 million per year), Bohn said, "The University of Cincinnati is a nationally respected leader in research, academics, and medicine and we are committed to ensure we match that standard with our coaches."[68] Clearly the desire to be competitive, easily measured in sports in wins and losses; the desire for national rankings, published throughout each football and basketball season; and the desire for national exposure, easily quantified in appearances on ESPN or other cable networks, all added up to a rationalization for a dramatically revised university mission, one that placed success in athletics alongside success in "research, academics, and medicine."[69]

In noting the national trend toward increased athletic spending as instructional spending stagnated, the American Association of University Professors asked in 2014, "Is there an athletics 'arms race' under way?" As UC accumulated even more debt in the hunt for that white whale—the profitable athletic department—it is hard to avoid concluding that there surely was.[70]

❧ Seeing It Realized

While striving for national rankings and an international profile, UC did not abandon its tradition of community engagement. Faculty in one of the university's most prestigious colleges, Design, Architecture, Art & Planning (DAAP), emphasized the value of linking students to real-life clients with real needs, particularly in Cincinnati. In 2002, DAAP's Community Design Center, organized to provide technical and research services to community groups and city departments working to improve the environment in underserved neighborhoods, added a new instructional component: the Niehoff Urban Studio. Funded by a gift from Buck Niehoff, a UC alumnus and trustee, the Niehoff Studio brought together planning and architecture students with students of other disciplines to work on broad societal problems in specific settings.[71]

Initially the studio occupied space in the first floor of the Emery building, the former home of the College of Applied Sciences in Over-the-Rhine, owned by the university since 1969. Food became the first two-year research topic as a response to the 2001 civil unrest after the death of Timothy Thomas. Faculty of the studio, along with studio director Frank Russell, believed that food could serve as a bridge between different cultures and provide a unifying theme in a divided city. Students investigated urban food availability, asking fundamental questions: Where should new stores be built? What role should public markets and street vending play? Can urban markets connect to small, regional farms?[72]

In its first year the studio gained co-sponsorship and specific site concerns from Kroger, which was in need of fresh ideas for urban markets generally and for its Corryville store specifically. Among the student projects was a "Super Kroger" designed by Jay Blackburn and Mark Siwek. They imagined a mixed-use development pedestrian-accessible from multiple angles, including from William Howard Taft, the busy thoroughfare ignored by the existing Corryville store. Hoping to illustrate how green technology could transform the traditional big-box store, Blackburn and Siwek created a two-story model, borrowing from designs that had worked in other places. The Niehoff design had no direct connection to the rebuilt (two-story) Kroger in Corryville, completed in 2017, but Russell later called this the most important urban grocery project designed at the studio.[73]

In 2004, the Niehoff students turned their attention to Over-the-Rhine, the long-troubled neighborhood that had been the epicenter of civil unrest three years earlier. The projects began with extensive research on the needs of the neighborhood's residents, identifying key constituents as African American single mothers, African American males, "Bohemian Artists," the homeless, young urban professionals, small business owners, and the police. Although the projects in Over-the-Rhine varied considerably, one gained special attention from thirty studio students. The Dominican Sisters of Hope and the Sisters of Notre Dame de Namur jointly

The Niehoff Urban Studio, 2015. Frank Russell (standing to the right), working with students in this photograph, led community-focused, interdisciplinary studios, reviving a vision for the university first articulated by Charles Dabney. *Photo by Joseph Fuqua II. Courtesy of UC Photographic Services.*

operated a job training program at Venice Pizza, where low-income residents learned the skills necessary to enter the workforce. Originally on McMicken Avenue in University Heights, Venice Pizza had been evicted for failure to pay rent and was in need of a new location. UC students joined with others from Miami University, which maintained a Center for Community Engagement in Over-the-Rhine, to design and build a new restaurant and training facility on Vine Street. After two years of work, Venice on Vine opened in what one nun called "a work of art," a beautiful nineteenth-century building in the heart of what was soon to become a remade neighborhood. According to UC architecture student Emily Wray, "The best part is seeing it all get built. So many projects we might do in school don't get built. That's the best part of this project and seeing it realized. It's real, and it all shows real hard work and individual care."[74]

After two years of working on—and in—Over-the-Rhine, the Niehoff Center moved up the hill to the old Turner Hall on Short Vine, purchased and renovated by Short Vine Development Company, another CDC funded by UC. Niehoff students, including some from departments outside DAAP, such as anthropology and civil engineering, took up a variety of themes that had them engaged around the city. For two years the studio addressed housing and community development in Uptown, a timely topic, and workshopped ideas for senior housing for emeriti and alumni desirous of staying connected to the university in retirement, and affordable housing for service workers employed in the area. In subsequent years the studio addressed streetscapes and "gateways," as well as transportation and mobility.[75]

The studio encouraged students to apply the theory they had acquired in coursework to actual locations. At times student work remained fanciful, unconcerned with political and economic realities, but in some instances students developed workable solutions for ongoing urban problems. In the fall of 2009, for instance, Alissa Weaver developed an urban agriculture project for Avondale. "Many Avondale residents do not have local access to fresh produce," wrote Weaver in describing the "food desert" concept. She proposed a community garden that could provide residents with an option for local fresh food. The garden would work in conjunction with a proposed Avondale Community Culinary Center, where residents could learn how best to prepare the produce and about its nutritional value. Weaver also imagined a job training program at the Culinary Center, allowing the project to work on multiple neighborhood problems at once. This vision became reality at Gabriel's Place, which opened in 2011 with design work contributed by the studio.[76]

Not unlike the faculty and students at Charles Dabney's Progressive Era UC, the Niehoff Studio took up timely issues, hoping to influence ongoing public discourse, to offer innovative paths forward. In 2014, for instance, at the request of the nonprofit Queen City Bike, several students considered Wasson Way, an underutilized rail corridor that connected the Little Miami Valley with Walnut Hills. Some students imagined a commuter rail line that would connect suburbs, including Mariemont, with urban destinations along the route, such as the busy Rookwood Commons shopping plaza and Xavier University. Other students worked on a rails-to-trails project, imagining a recreational corridor that would better connect Evanston, an oft-overlooked neighborhood, with assets enjoyed by its more prosperous neighbors. Students explored the potential economic impact of a new bike trail, including new investments in commercial spaces along the route, as well as potential downsides, such as rapid gentrification. The studio produced considerable research on the value of green infrastructure to both human and economic health in cities, and suggested ways in which both visions—commuter rail and bike trail—could coexist.[77]

Over the course of its first fourteen years, the Niehoff Studio served 160 community-based groups, but this was hardly the only avenue for UC's continued community engagement.[78] The theme appeared in university plans and in its marketing campaigns. In yet another instance of attempting to valorize community engagement—which is rarely a priority among faculty—in 2006 Zimpher created the Center for the City, a new office to help connect faculty with local organizations in need of support in the form of research or advice. The center also provided grants to faculty engaged in locally oriented research. This "city fellows" program did not outlive Zimpher's administration, a common fate for innovations initiated within the central administration.[79] Still, the Niehoff Studio and the Center for the City serve as reminders that regardless of how much the university worked to improve international connections and create an international profile, its best connections were nearby, where the University of Cincinnati already held considerable clout. It also reminds us that at least part of the university's mission continued to be providing service to the city.

Epilogue

We Will Be *in* Cincinnati

The University of Cincinnati approaches its bicentennial at a moment of high anxiety in higher education. The cost of a college degree and the excessive debts students carry upon graduation have put pressure on universities to seek efficiencies and defend their value to society. Around the nation, state support for higher education has fallen, and Ohio is no exception. State funding per student has shrunk consistently since the mid-1980s, with a growing percentage of the cost of education being covered by tuition. In 2016, Ohio's per-student spending was 15 percent lower than it had been before the Great Recession began in 2007.[1] At the same time, universities have found it harder and harder to maintain their research budgets. Since 2010, federal spending on research has fallen, after sixty years of expansion, a trend that threatens funding paradigms from medicine to engineering.[2]

In addition, parental and student demands for a practical education—one with direct and predictable implications for employment—have encouraged the continued movement away from the study of the humanities and toward business and engineering, a shift that has strained faculty and resources. Increasingly, the metric by which society assesses institutions of higher learning is "return on investment," usually measured by comparing starting salaries with average debt loads upon graduation. State legislatures, including Ohio's, have capped tuition increases on state universities and have sought ways to shorten the amount of time and money students need to spend on campus to earn a degree. High school students now routinely enter college with many requirements already fulfilled, through advanced placement exams and College Credit Plus courses. Designed to speed students toward degrees and control costs, these policies also diminish faculty control over curriculum, and in the long term they will no doubt change the meaning and value of an undergraduate degree.

Even beyond cost and return-on-investment concerns, the national discourse suggests the system is broken. From critics largely outside higher education, we hear that campuses are too politically charged, with teachers who are much more "liberal" than average Americans. And, some complain, faculties are too dedicated to research and spend too little time and effort on teaching.[3] From within academia, critics condemn the size of athletics budgets and criticize the adoption of a corporate model of management, with centralized administrations setting new priorities, encouraging perpetual innovation, and demanding improved efficiency and growth through the development of new markets. As a result, institutional goals often sound strikingly like those of for-profit corporations, much to the dismay of faculty in traditional arts and sciences disciplines.

Perhaps the troubling national discourse about higher education would be less disquieting at UC if the university had stable leadership. After Nancy Zimpher left in 2009 to become chancellor of the State University of New York, UC witnessed five presidential transitions in less than a decade and experienced nearly as much turnover in the provost's office. Many of the important players—including briefly serving presidents Gregory Williams and Santa Ono—came from outside Cincinnati and spent their short stays learning about the institution as much as leading it. Consider this: during the century from 1904, when Charles Dabney came to lead UC, through 2003, when Joseph Steger retired, UC had eight presidents—a remarkable period of stability at the helm. Steady leadership saw the university through changes wrought by two world wars, the Cold War, Vietnam protests, the civil rights movement, the women's rights revolution, and dramatic shifts in the acceptance of the LGBTQ community, not to mention experiments with and adaptation to new communication technologies: radio, television, the Internet.

In the fifteen years after Steger retired, UC had five presidents. As had become the norm in higher education, corporate search firms brought in career administrators, often in expensive and not entirely public processes that resulted in hiring candidates who had no real connection to the institution and who didn't stay long enough to develop one. When leaders serve for an average of just three years, concerns about mission and vision can become acute. At a meeting of administrators I attended in 2016, an associate dean indicated that colleagues in his college had become confused about the university's identity. Some faculty and administrators behaved as though UC were a community college, thinking only about teaching undergraduate students, since enrollments were the primary driver in the budget model. At the same time, some faculty thought UC should function like MIT, where training graduate students and landing large research grants are paramount. With so little clarity or consistency in the articulation of the university's mission, no wonder many faculty and administrators pondered the future with trepidation.

As Clark Kerr pointed out, however, there is "a tendency in higher education to view the future with alarm and the past with appreciation." A vast literature describing a crisis in higher education has been accumulating since the 1960s, although the explanation of what is causing the crisis has shifted over time—from rapid growth to stagnation, from diffuse, chaotic management to concentrated power.[4] One might even read the history of UC as two hundred years of near continuous crisis, given chronic budget concerns and the constant pressure to evolve to meet societal demands.

Yet despite the national discourse questioning the value of higher education and the accumulation of state and federal policies adverse to higher education, there is good reason to look to the future with hope, especially in Cincinnati. UC found great success in the early twenty-first century, particularly when measured by the number and quality of students it enrolled. And UC appears better prepared than many institutions to weather anticipated disruptions to higher education. Investments in the campus and in surrounding neighborhoods have paid off, the university's debt notwithstanding. Just as important, a national trend toward urban living, especially in dense, walkable neighborhoods, has led to pockets of revitalization in long-declining neighborhoods in every direction from the university. The improved reputation of the central city and investments in new housing and retail can only help boost an urban university.

And there are many reasons to believe that higher education is healthier than the negative rhetoric from without and the hand-wringing within would have you believe. A variety of data reveal just how vital higher education remains in the United States. The income disparity between college graduates and those with only a high school diploma continued to widen in the early twenty-first century. A 2011 Georgetown University study estimated lifetime incomes at an average 84 percent higher for Americans with bachelor's degrees.[5] Add to this the remarkable research achievements coming out of American universities, from biomedical engineering to sustainable design, and the incredible value that institutions of higher education add to the national economy becomes clear. Each year colleges and universities in the United States attract hundreds of thousands of international students from all corners of the globe. In 2015 UC alone enrolled students from 114 countries.[6] The accessibility and quality of higher education in the United States is the envy of the world.

Still, UC celebrates its bicentennial at a time when its administration feels pressure from the state—and society more broadly—to grow and generate profits in research and teaching. "What the state needs from the University of Cincinnati is to become even more productive as a driver of our state's economy," the chancellor of the Ohio Board of Regents, Eric Fingerhut, said in 2009. "I'm not saying UC hasn't been doing this well," Fingerhut assured the readers of the *Enquirer*. "But we've got to get to another level because the future of our economy is going to come out of the relationship between universities and the private sector."[7] We can hear in Fingerhut's demand echoes of the nineteenth-century booster Daniel Drake, who well understood that institutions of higher learning provide more to their communities than an education to their citizens. As the history of UC makes clear, universities contribute to their localities in myriad ways, from enlightening political discourse to expanding cultural opportunities to offering solutions to social problems. But in the early twenty-first century the purely economic calculation—"as a driver of our state's economy"—appeared to have overshadowed everything else.

Unfortunately, discussion of the broader purpose of higher education has fallen out of vogue. The national discourse scorns idealistic articulations of university missions. In an era focused on return-on-investment calculations, assertions about the essential role of higher education in nurturing democracy can seem quaint. Inspiring active and engaged citizens, improving the spiritual lives of students and the aesthetics of communities; these aspects of higher education are too vague and unquantifiable for today's data-driven rankings. However, as philosopher Martha Nussbaum noted in an influential defense of the humanities, "[W]e are not forced to choose between a form of education that promotes profit and a form of education that promotes good citizenship."[8] We can have both. We just have to tell people this is the mission.

History is nonlinear, and one can easily imagine events that would spark national soul-searching about the health of our democracy and, inevitably, about what institutions of higher education might do to revive it. If the history of UC tells us anything, it's that we've been here before, at a challenging moment for a nation in need of solutions supplied by its universities.

✿ The University of Everywhere?

Perhaps the greatest challenge facing higher education in the early twenty-first century came from the disruptive force of the Internet. Smart technology and online communication threatened to upend entire sectors of employment—from journalism to retail to long-haul trucking—and in higher education administrators rushed to adopt new technologies, fearing competitors would beat them to it. In the short term, online classes and online degrees held out the promise of increasing access for students and increasing markets for institutions. In the long term, however, they may be laying the groundwork for a radical transformation of higher education.

For a relatively brief moment, massive, and free, online courses (called MOOCs) promised a path to a dramatic democratization of higher education and the possibility that only the very best institutions would survive to deliver content at scale. With ventures like Coursera and edX offering free or inexpensive courses in cooperation with some of the world's leading universities, some observers of higher education predicted the revolution was near. In 2015, Kevin Carey predicted *The End of College* and the beginning of what he called "The University of Everywhere," a future in which the disruptive power of the Internet has made higher education truly democratic—cheaper and available anywhere with telecommunications. But Carey's predictions were based as much on his understanding of the flaws of the current system as on the advantages of online delivery. Carey claimed that research universities weren't good at teaching undergraduates, because faculty aren't trained to teach and don't care for it. "All available evidence suggests undergraduates simply aren't learning very much," he concluded.[9]

This doesn't strike me as true in the least. Part of what Carey is missing, and part of what has slowed the revolution, despite the popularity of online classes, are the unquantifiable aspects of what higher education gives—has always given—to its students: the "college experience"—the very thing the Hargreaves plan hoped to accentuate on Cincinnati's campus. At its heart, education is about human relationships created through the discovery, articulation, and debate of new knowledge and understanding, in class and out. As Abraham Flexner scolded in 1930 as Columbia University experimented with large correspondence courses, "The whole thing is business, not education." Correspondence courses eventually found a niche market, as universities with good reputations shied away from "home study" courses. Similar experiences attended innovations in the use of radio and television to deliver content for college credit. That these technologies failed to disrupt the development of large, centralized research universities serves as a reminder that higher education is not mainly about transmitting information.[10]

Online teaching and learning are in their infancy and may yet dramatically alter the landscape of higher education, but meanwhile applications to and attendance of traditional colleges and universities continue to rise. UC's record enrollments, combined with the explosion of on- and off-campus housing, suggest an ongoing demand to be *at* college, to experience what it has to offer—in person. Certainly UC is building as if the campus will continue to draw students well into the future. In 2017, UC listed twelve major construction projects, from a new business college to a new dormitory. In total, over half a billion dollars in construction was under way or proposed. In other words, Carey's University of Everywhere may eventually appear, but the university in Cincinnati will persist nonetheless.

✿ Please Join In

On July 19, 2015, a University of Cincinnati police officer shot and killed Samuel DuBose during a traffic stop in Mount Auburn. The following months on campus were difficult, especially for African American students, staff, and faculty, who expressed grave concern for their own safety and for the safety of others in surrounding communities. Students formed a new group—the Irate8, the name capturing their mood while reminding everyone of the very small percentage of students on campus who were African American, a percentage that had actually declined since peaking in the late 1970s. The Black Faculty Association also became an important voice in the aftermath, taking the opportunity to teach about racism and white privilege while advocating for social justice on campus and off.

For everyone associated with the university, this was a time to assess the institution's relationship to the African

Ashley Nkadi, co-founder of the Irate8 (2016). In the fall of 2016, Nkadi led an Irate8 boot camp, training fellow students in the techniques of activism. Sparked by the shooting death of Samuel DuBose, student and community activism forced the university to make changes, much as it had in the 1960s and 1970s. *Photo by N. C. Brown. Courtesy of* The News Record.

American community, its efforts to provide a safe, diverse learning environment, and the persistence of structural racism in the United States. Students organized protests and a teach-in; faculty organized public forums, in which panels of experts and community members discussed the issues; administrators, fearing lawsuits and bad publicity, engaged outside consultants to analyze the problem, hired additional administrators to implement the solutions, and created committees for oversight. In other words, everyone behaved as expected, in a city—and country—where racial inequality, concentrated poverty, and community–police relations seemed to be the only constants in a world otherwise in constant flux. The campus had been transformed, the surrounding neighborhoods improved, and the university's mission updated, but suddenly it felt like 1968 again.

The officer who shot DuBose lost his job soon thereafter.[11] It took much longer for the UC police chief to lose his, even though data revealed a dramatic and inexplicable rise in traffic stops under his leadership, with much of the growth coming through an obvious tendency to target African Americans at a much higher rate than whites. In sum, the data revealed an unannounced effort to exert police influence in the neighborhoods around the university, especially Clifton Heights and Mount Auburn. In 2016, the outside consultants issued a major report and suggested a variety of reforms, most of them internal to police operations and reporting. The chair of the Board of Trustees, Rob Richardson Jr., announced satisfaction with the progress in the year after the shooting. "We want to be a world-class example for what policing is and how it should be done," he said in a UC press release. Even police reform was to be spoken of in terms of international prestige.[12]

The shooting of Sam DuBose was just one of a string of similar killings around the country that had heightened awareness of the unequal treatment of African American men by police. Many in the university community supported the growing Black Lives Matter movement, designed to keep attention focused on the problem and force changes to police training, encourage prosecution of bad actors, and heighten media coverage of violence involving black victims. The shooting also happened in a local context of university expansion by proxy. The university had gained permission from the city to police well beyond its campus, and it had done so with vigor. Policing had become another means by which the university could control space, with the ultimate goal of making students—at least white students—feel more secure in the surrounding neighborhoods.

On the one-year anniversary of DuBose's death, the university came together for a prayer vigil on the Campus Green. Since it took place in the summer, when few students and faculty were around, the event was attended mostly by administrators, clergy, and the family of Sam Dubose. While several speakers spoke movingly about DuBose and the need for racial reconciliation and for social justice, the most moving words came from his mother, Audrey DuBose, who said she had been awakened to injustice by the killing of her son. She asked everyone: "Please join in." Movements need heroes, and sometimes martyrs, but mostly they need commitment from a great number of people.

❀ The Heart of This Region

On April 5, 2017, recently hired President Neville Pinto addressed an All-Faculty Meeting in the Great Hall of TUC. For more than twenty years, Pinto had been a faculty member in chemical engineering and then dean of the Graduate School at UC, but he had left to become the dean of Engineering at the University of Louisville in 2011. He then served as provost and interim president in Louisville before returning to the institution where his career began. Much had changed during his six-year absence, but as he addressed the faculty he looked out on many familiar faces. The faculty and staff had seen too much instability in recent years, Pinto knew. He also knew there had been plans and revised plans, visions and re-visions.

Sensing the exhaustion from transitions of all types, Pinto announced his theme would be continuity, reconnecting the university to its historical mission. UC's third century will be much like its second, he said; UC will remain "student-centered, faculty-driven, and urban-serving." Significantly, the continuity Pinto described centered on Cincinnati itself. "We are at the heart of this region," he said. Engagement in the city would come through service and through research, and, he emphasized, it could be mutually beneficial. The future of the nation and the world would be urban, Pinto said, and then, sounding very much like Charles Dabney a century earlier, he hoped Cincinnati would define "the urban research university of the future." The university has more than a teaching and research mission, however, and Pinto emphasized, "We must fulfill every aspect of our mission." To fulfill its democratic mission, to provide access to education to the community it serves, UC must be inclusive. With more than a gesture toward the killing of Sam DuBose, Pinto affirmed that the university must work for social justice.[13]

J. Martin Klotsche noted the potential of urban universities in the mid-1960s, when urban growth combined with urban problems positioned schools such as UC for important work. "If diversity is the dominant characteristic of American higher education," he wrote, "then the urban university should embrace its special location. If it finds strength in its urban setting, and capitalizes on it, then its true mission can be accomplished." Historian Thomas Bender has made the case that the city is the most likely location for the creation of a truly open, multicultural society, since it is in cities where diversity mingles. Clearly Cincinnati, like all American cities, has failed in fundamental ways, most evident in the consequences of racism, but one need only revisit Drake's passage about Cincinnati's diversity to be reminded that this city was built by and for a pluralistic population. Diversity has been part of our urban identity, and now we are challenged to create truly inclusive communities. The University of Cincinnati appears well positioned for the task.[14]

President Pinto made no promises about growth or greatness or being world-class at this or that. Some things about the future we can only guess. However, he was certain of one thing: "We will be *in* Cincinnati for all of our third century." This phrase seems a fitting way to end this story. I have written about the university and about Cincinnati, but mostly this book has concerned the preposition that unites them in the title *University of Cincinnati*. For some time the "of" indicated ownership; UC was a municipally owned and operated university. But mostly it has indicated a service obligation, a mission to provide higher education to as broad a constituency as it could through as many avenues as necessary. Only time will tell precisely how this university will be *of* Cincinnati in its third century.

ABBREVIATIONS

ARB   Archives & Rare Books, University of Cincinnati
BCA   Bettman Center Archives, Cincinnati Parks
CHLA   Cincinnati History Library and Archives
FHS   Filson Historical Society, Louisville, Kentucky
ML   Mercantile Library
MUSC   Miami University Special Collections
RAC   Rockefeller Archive Center
UNC   University of North Carolina Archives
WCA   Winkler Center Archives, University of Cincinnati

Notes

Introduction The University *in* Cincinnati

1. Robert M. Hutchins, *Freedom, Education, and the Fund: Essays and Addresses, 1946–1956* (New York: Meridian Books, 1956), 178.
2. Abraham Flexner, *Universities: American, English, German* (New York: Oxford University Press, 1930), 5.
3. Ibid., 44.
4. Matthew Arnold, *Culture and Anarchy: An Essay in Political and Social Criticism* (London: Smith, Elder & Co., 1869), viii.
5. David Star Jordan, *The Voice of the Scholar: With Other Addresses on the Problems of Higher Education* (San Francisco: Paul Elder and Company, 1903), 190.
6. The US Census Bureau calculated that the nation's demographic center in 1870 was in Highland County, Ohio. Ten years later it was in Boone County, Kentucky. See US Census Bureau, *Centers of Population Computation for the United States, 1950–2010* (Washington, DC, March 2011), 4.
7. See, for example, John R. Thelin's *A History of American Higher Education* (Baltimore: Johns Hopkins University Press, 2004), which does not mention UC, although it does mention the Cincinnati College of Agriculture, by which I think Thelin means Farmers' College in College Hill. See also Maurice Berube's *The Urban University in America* (Westport, CT: Greenwood Press, 1978), which manages to tell the history of *urban* universities without mentioning UC.
8. Steven J. Diner, *Universities and Their Cities: Urban Higher Education in America* (Baltimore: Johns Hopkins University Press, 2017), 41.
9. Ibid., 74–75.
10. Charles Franklin Thwing, *The American College in American Life* (New York: G. P. Putnam's Sons, 1897), 63.

Chapter 1 A Frontier Institution

1. Daniel Drake, *Anniversary Address Delivered to the School of Literature and the Arts* (Cincinnati: Locker and Wallace, 1814), 4–5, 7. For more on Daniel Drake see, Henry D. Shapiro and Zane L. Miller, eds., *Physician to the West: Selected Writings of Daniel Drake on Science and Society* (Lexington: University Press of Kentucky, 1970), a collection of some of Drake's most important writings, which also includes two fine biographical pieces, one each by the two editors.
2. Drake was apparently uninterested in the diversity represented by the small African American population in Cincinnati.

3. In 1801, Athens, Georgia, became the literal Athens of the South, and home to the University of Georgia. In 1804, Athens, Ohio, became the home to Ohio University, theoretically precluding Cincinnati from claiming the title of "Athens of the West," although that term had already been widely applied to Lexington, Kentucky.

4. Oliver Farnsworth, *The Cincinnati Directory* (Cincinnati: Morgan, Lodge and Co., 1819), 30.

5. On the creation of urban institutions in the West, see Richard C. Wade's classic, *The Urban Frontier: The Rise of Western Cities, 1790–1830* (Cambridge, MA: Harvard University Press, 1959); on the creation of a distinctive western culture see Wendy Jean Katz, *Regionalism and Reform: Art and Class Formation in Antebellum Cincinnati* (Columbus: Ohio State University Press, 2002), 1–26.

6. Peale quoted in Howard Ensign Evans, *The Natural History of the Long Expedition to the Rocky Mountains, 1819–1820* (New York: Oxford University Press, 1997), 31.

7. Daniel Drake, *A Natural and Statistical View, or Picture of Cincinnati and the Miami Country* (Cincinnati: Looker and Wallace, 1815), 155–57. On very early educational efforts in Cincinnati see Daniel Aaron, *Cincinnati: Queen City of the West, 1819–1838* (Columbus: Ohio State University Press, 1992), 202–27.

8. Daniel Drake to Samuel Brown, February 14, 1819, Samuel Brown Papers, 1817–1825, folder 3, FHS.

9. Baum eventually lost the house due to the financial crisis, but it was lived in by a number of prominent citizens, including Nicholas Longworth, Anna Sinton Taft, and Charles Phelps Taft, before becoming the Taft Museum in 1932. http://www.taftmuseum.org/museumhistory.

10. "Act to Incorporate the Cincinnati College, January 2, 1819," Cincinnati College Records, box 1, folder 57, ARB.

11. *Laws and Regulations of the Cincinnati College* (Cincinnati: Cooke, Powers, and Penney, 1819), 15.

12. Farnsworth, *Cincinnati Directory*, 39.

13. Transylvania has roots back to 1780, but it became a university at this later date. Indeed, even then it only slowly evolved into an actual university. See Wade, *The Urban Frontier*, 233–43. On the creation of "Booster Colleges" designed to lay claim to real urbanity, see Daniel J. Boorstin, *The Americans: The National Experience* (New York: Random House, 1965), 152–61.

14. Daniel Drake to Samuel Brown, February 14, 1819, Samuel Brown Papers, 1817–1825, folder 3, FHS.

15. John Hough James Diary, vol. 1, John Hough James Collection, Diaries and Family Correspondence, box 1, MUSC.

16. "Cincinnati College," *Western Spy*, September 28, 1821, and "Cincinnati College," *Cincinnati Gazette*, as found in John Hough James Diary, vol. 1, John Hough James Collection, Diaries and Family Correspondence, box 1, MUSC.

17. John Hough James Diary, vol. 1, John Hough James Collection, Diaries and Family Correspondence, box 1, MUSC.

18. W. N. Blane, *An Excursion Through the United States and Canada during the Years 1822–23* (London: Baldwin, Cradock, and Joy, 1824), 124, 127.

19. Ben Drake and E. D. Mansfield, *Cincinnati in 1826* (Cincinnati: Morgan, Lodge, and Fisher, 1827), 46.

20. Daniel Drake, *An Anniversary Discourse on the State and Prospects of the Western Museum Society* (Cincinnati: Looker, Palmer and Reynolds, 1820), 18–19.

21. Ibid., 21.

22. Ibid., 7.

23. "Western Museum," *Liberty Hall*, June 17, 1820; Robert Todd to William Lytle, February 12, 1820, Lytle Papers, box 12, folder 10, CHLA.

24. "Western Museum," *Liberty Hall,* June 17, 1820; Drake, *Anniversary Discourse,* 24.

25. William Henry Venable, *Beginnings of Literary Culture in the Ohio Valley: Historical and Biographical Sketches* (Cincinnati: Robert Clarke & Co., 1891), 310–11; Drake, *Anniversary Discourse,* 25, 26; "Lectures before the Western Museum Society," *Liberty Hall,* December 14, 1819.

26. Drake, *Anniversary Discourse,* 26, 27.

27. Blane, *Excursion,* 126.

28. Drake and Mansfield, *Cincinnati in 1826,* 45, 46. On the longer story of the Western Museum see Louis Leonard Tucker, "'Ohio Show-Shop': The Western Museum of Cincinnati, 1820–1867," in *A Cabinet of Curiosities* (Charlottesville: University Press of Virginia, 1967).

29. Daniel Drake to Samuel Brown, November 3, 1818, Samuel Brown Papers, 1817–1825, folder 3, FHS. Drake summarized the early history of the college in *Proceedings and Correspondence of the Third District Medical Society of the State of Ohio in Reference to the Medical College of Ohio* (December 1832), 4–9.

30. Drake to Brown, November 3, 1818, Samuel Brown Papers, 1817–1825, folder 3, FHS.

31. Ibid.

32. Drake to Brown, November 17, 1818, Samuel Brown Papers, 1817–1825, folder 3, FHS.

33. Ibid.

34. Coleman Rogers to Samuel Brown, November 3, 1818, Samuel Brown Papers, 1817–1825, folder 3, FHS.

35. Drake to Brown, February 14, 1819, Samuel Brown Papers, 1817–1825, folder 4, FHS.

36. Coleman Rogers to Samuel Brown, December 2, 1819, Samuel Brown Papers, 1817–1825, folder 5, FHS.

37. Daniel Drake, "Circular: Medical College of Ohio," August 20, 1820, Daniel Drake Collection, box 3, WCA.

38. Drake to Brown, February 14, 1819; Drake, "Circular: Medical College of Ohio."

39. Drake to Brown, November 3, 1818, Samuel Brown Papers, 1817–1825, folder 3, FHS; Drake, *Proceedings and Correspondence of the Third District Medical Society,* 6.

40. Charles Fenno Hoffman, *A Winter in the Far West* (London: Richard Bentley, 1835), 126, 128; Report on the College, March 28, 1873, Cincinnati College Records, box 5, folder 294, ARB.

41. "Cincinnati College," *Western Spy,* September 28, 1821, as found in John Hough James Diary, vol. 1.

42. Miami didn't begin instructing students until 1824, after years of gathering momentum to actually build the school and fending off an attempt by Cincinnati to move it from Oxford to the larger city on the river.

43. Drake and Mansfield, *Cincinnati in 1826,* 41–42. On the "mortality rate" of booster colleges see Boorstin, *The Americans,* 158. On the proliferation of antebellum colleges and the difficulty of even determining how many there were (what counts?), see James Axtell, *Wisdom's Workshop: The Rise of the Modern University* (Princeton: Princeton University Press, 2016), 160–62.

44. "Law Department of the Cincinnati College," *Western Law Journal* (October 1843): 1; Irvin C. Rutter and Samuel S. Wilson, "The College of Law: An Overview, 1833–1983," *University of Cincinnati Law Review* 52, no. 311 (1983); Reginald McGrane, *The University of Cincinnati: A Success Story in Urban Higher Education* (New York: Harper & Row, 1963), 26–27.

45. Daniel Drake to Board of Trustees, August 27, 1839, Cincinnati College Records, box 1, folder 45, ARB; Report of the Building Committee to the Board of Trustees, March 22, 1836, Cincinnati College Records, box 1, folder 43, ARB.

46. North Wing Stock Account, Cincinnati College Records, box 1, folder 15, ARB; "General Meeting of the Corporators and other Contributors, of the Cincinnati College," March 8, 1836, Daniel Drake Collection, box 5, folder 1, WCA.

47. "Duty of Resident Physician and Surgeon," Cincinnati College Records, box 1, folder 18, ARB.

48. Daniel Drake, "Marine Hospitals in the West," 24th Congress, 1st session, House of Representatives (Doc. no. 264), May 31, 1836.

49. Ibid.

50. Drake to Levi Woodbury, September 6, 1836, Cincinnati College Records, box 2, folder 93, ARB.

51. Faculty Meeting Notes, September 19, 1836, Cincinnati College Records, box 1, folder 26, ARB.

52. L. C. Rives to the President of the Board of Trustees of the Cincinnati College, April 4, 1838, Cincinnati College Records, box 2, folder 86, ARB.

53. Drake to James Whitcomb, January 15, 1838, Cincinnati College Records, box 1, folder 55, ARB.

54. Drake to Whitcomb, April 23, 1838, Cincinnati College Records, box 1, folder 62, ARB.

55. Robert Punshon, Surveyor, to Levi Woodbury, Secretary of the Treasury, November 24, 1837, Cincinnati College Records, box 1, folder 63, ARB.

56. Affidavit (copy) Edward Kimball, Resident Physician of the Marine Hospital, January 13, 1838, Cincinnati College Records, box 1, folder 103, ARB.

57. Joseph Pierce et al. to Punshon, October 1837, Cincinnati College Records, box 2, folder 99, ARB.

58. Testimonial, April 24, 1838, Cincinnati College Records, box 2, folder 102, ARB.

59. Drake to Whitcomb, April 23, 1838.

60. Report of Committee, April 7, 1838, Cincinnati College Records, box 1, folder 70, ARB.

61. Whitcomb to Drake, October 23, 1838, Cincinnati College Records, box 1, folder 61, ARB.

62. Joshua Martin to Drake, July 25, 1839, Cincinnati College Records, box 1, folder 14, ARB. By "abroad" Martin meant not local, not necessarily from outside the United States.

63. "Cincinnati College August 26, 1839," Cincinnati College Records, box 1, folder 31, ARB.

64. Articles of Agreement for Dissolution of the Property of the Med Faculty of Cincinnati College, August 28, 1839, Cincinnati College Records, box 1, folder 10, ARB.

65. "General Meeting of the Corporators and other Contributors, of the Cincinnati College," March 8, 1836, Daniel Drake Collection, box 5, folder 1, WCA.

66. "New Stock Book of the Cincinnati College," Cincinnati College Records, box 3, folder 138, ARB.

67. Daniel Drake to William McGuffey, August 19, 1836, William Holmes McGuffey Papers, Miami University, Digital Collection.

68. Board of Trustees Address the Public, March 2, 1837, Cincinnati College Records, box 3, folder 176, ARB; List of Students Enrolled during 1837, Cincinnati College Records, box 3, folder 181, ARB.

69. E. D. Mansfield to McGuffey, January 29, 1840, William Holmes McGuffey Papers, Miami University, Digital Collection.

70. Mansfield to McGuffey, March 2, 1840, William Holmes McGuffey Papers, Miami University, Digital Collection.

71. E. D. Mansfield, *Memoirs of the Life and Services of Daniel Drake, M.D., Physician, Professor, and Author* (Cincinnati: Applegate & Co., 1855), 290.

72. Mercantile Library, "1847 Twelfth Annual Report," 23, Annual Reports, 1847–1860, ML.

73. "Report on the Cincinnati College Academical Department" (first Draft, 1846), 40–41, Cincinnati College Records, box 3, folder 158, ARB.

74. Mercantile Library, "1847 Twelfth Annual Report"; "Opinion on the question of whether the Cincinnati College Building and Grounds in Cincinnati are Subject to Taxation," November 28, 1849, box 1, folder 78, Cincinnati College Records, ARB.

75. Mercantile Library, "1847 Twelfth Annual Report," 10, 11, 14.

76. This language comes from the rules of the Chamber, which appeared in each annual report through the mid-century. "Annual Report of the Cincinnati Chamber of Commerce and Merchant's Exchange for the Commercial Year Ending August 31, 1868," Chamber of Commerce Materials, CHLA.

77. See the various annual reports in Box Annual Reports, 1847–1860, ML.

78. On the secularization on American higher education in the 1800s see Julie A. Reuben, *The Making of the Modern University: Intellectual Transformation and* the *Marginalization of Morality* (Chicago: University of Chicago Press, 1996). Although from a later era, perhaps the best example of an elite family sending its children east for an education comes from Alphonso Taft, who sent all of his well-known sons Charles Phelps, Peter, William Howard, Henry, and Horace to Yale University.

79. Mercantile Library, "1850, Fifteenth Annual Report," Annual Reports, 1847–1860, ML.

Chapter 2 Shall It All Be in One Place?

1. "Our City's Pride," *Cincinnati Enquirer*, June 19, 1880.

2. *Belatrasco*, September 1880.

3. McMicken freed his slaves in his will and set aside funds to send them to Liberia, should they choose to go. See *The Will of Charles McMicken of Cincinnati, Ohio* (Cincinnati, 1858), 18, https://www.libraries.uc.edu/content/dam/libraries/arb/docs/university-archives/mcmicken-will.pdf.

4. The published will of Charles McMicken includes a useful, brief biography. See ibid. Reginald McGrane includes a more extensive biography in *The University of Cincinnati: A Success Story in Higher Education* (New York: Harper & Row, 1963). See 46–53.

5. McMicken did have at least one child outside of marriage who did not appear in the will. John McMicken was born to one of Charles's slaves and lived as a black man in Cincinnati. Their familial relationship was an open secret in town. John B. Shotwell, *A History of the Schools of Cincinnati* (Cincinnati: School Life Company, 1902), 448.

6. *Board of Directors Minutes* (1859–1876, vol. 1), ARB.

7. On African American schools in Cincinnati see Nikki M. Taylor, *Frontiers of Freedom: Cincinnati's Black Community, 1802–1868* (Athens: Ohio University Press, 2005), 161–74. Griffin's thesis is held at ARB.

8. *The Will of Charles McMicken*, 19.

9. Ibid., 23–24.

10. Alexander McGuffey and Cornelius Comegys complained about the failure to teach the Bible after the first three years of the university's instruction. See "Report of Committee on University on the Bible," June 19, 1876, *Board of Directors Minutes* (1859–1876, vol. 1), 587–88. For the fuller Bible War story see Steven K. Green, *The Bible, the School, and the Constitution: The Clash That Shaped Modern Church-State Doctrine* (New York: Oxford University Press, 2012).

11. *The Will of Charles McMicken*, 21, 22.

12. Edwin G. Burrows and Mike Wallace, *Gotham: A History of New York City to 1898* (New York: Oxford University Press, 1999), 781. A brief history of municipal universities can be found in William Carlson's *The Municipal University* (Washington, DC: Center for Applied Research in Education, 1962).

13. Annual Report, *Board of Directors Minutes* (1859–1876, vol. 1), 195.

14. On land-grant universities see the comprehensive but somewhat dated *Colleges for Our Land and Time: The Land-Grant Idea in American Education* by Edward Danforth Eddy Jr. (Westport, CT: Greenwood Press, 1956).

15. On the development of American anthropology see Tracy Teslow, *Constructing Race: The Science of Bodies and Cultures in American Anthropology* (New York: Cambridge University Press, 2014); on the development of sociology, economics, and political science see Dorothy Ross, *The Origins of American Social Science* (New York: Cambridge University Press, 1991).

16. On the rise of science and the fracturing of classical education, see Julie A. Reuben, *The Making of the Modern University: Intellectual Transformation and the Marginalization of Morality* (Chicago: University of Chicago Press, 1995), and Laurence R. Veysey, *The Emergence of the American University* (Chicago: University of Chicago Press, 1965). Among the new universities were several that served African Americans, including Fisk, Morehouse (originally called Augusta Institute), and Howard, all founded in the late 1860s.

17. The Literary Club was formed in 1849 by some of the city's intellectual elite. An all-male, exclusive organization, in every era its membership list read like a Who's Who of Cincinnati. In addition to the Tafts, members included Judge Stallo, Cornelius Comegys, and, over the years, many men with connections to the university. The club has published a series of anniversary volumes, each of which contains useful information about membership and papers delivered, among other details. See, for instance, *The Literary Club of Cincinnati, 1849–1999: One Hundred and Fiftieth Anniversary Volume* (Cincinnati: The Club, 2001).

18. Charles Phelps Taft, "The German University and the American College," an essay delivered before the Cincinnati Literary Club, January 7, 1871 (Cincinnati: Robert Clarke & Co, 1871), 4. On Germany as a model for American institutions see James Axtell, *Wisdom's Workshop: The Rise of the Modern University* (Princeton: Princeton University Press, 2016), 221–75. For more on Americans studying in Germany see Anja Werner, *The Transatlantic World of Higher Education: Americans at German Universities, 1776–1914* (New York: Berghahn Books, 2013).

19. Taft, "The German University and the American College," 21–22.

20. Ibid., 25.

21. Ibid., 20.

22. Ibid., 27.

23. Louisiana courts denied the transfer of real estate in that state to the city of Cincinnati. See *Perin v. McMicken's Heirs*, 15 La. Ann. 154, 1860 La. LEXIS 574 (1860).

24. For a good recounting of this story see Cincinnati Museum Association, *Third Annual Report, 1884* (Cincinnati: Robert Clarke & Co., 1884), 23–37.

25. "Rules of the School of Drawing and Design, McMicken University," "A Circular: The School of Drawing and Design," *Board of Directors Minutes* (1859–1876, vol. 1), 194, 202. For a good, brief biography see James D. Birchfield, Albert Biome, and William J. Hennessey, *Thomas Satterwhite Noble, 1835–1907* (Lexington: University of Kentucky Art Museum, 1988).

26. In 1868, the second iteration of the Cincinnati Academy of Fine Arts sponsored its first exhibition at a gallery on Fourth Street. Among the works of prominent artists, Asher B. Durand, Mary Pope, Sanford Gifford, and George Innes, was a study Noble had done in preparation for *Margaret Garner*. See *Cincinnati Academy of Fine Arts Catalogue of the First Exhibition at Wiswell's Gallery* (Cincinnati: Robert Clarke & Co. Printers, 1868).

27. "A Circular: The School of Drawing and Design," *Board of Directors Minutes* (1859–1876, vol. 1), 202; "Meeting of the University Board," *Cincinnati Enquirer*, October 18, 1872.

28. "University Project: Report of Special Committee," Board of Education (Cincinnati, June 30, 1869), Cincinnati Observatory Collection, box 8, folder 8, ARB.

29. Ibid.

30. *Common Schools of Cincinnati 39th Annual Report* (Cincinnati: Times Steam Book and Job Printing Establishment, 1868), 77.

31. *Board of Directors Minutes* (1859–1876, vol. 1), 304.

32. Alphonso Taft, "A Lecture on the University of Cincinnati: Its Aims, Needs, and Resources, Delivered before the Young Men's Mercantile Library Association, May 9, 1872" (Cincinnati: Robert Clarke & Co, 1872), 14.

33. The creation of this new board marks the official founding of the University of Cincinnati, which is why the university used 1870 as its founding date for many years. The names of everyone who has served on the Board of Directors and the dates of their service can be found at https://www.libraries.uc.edu/content/dam/libraries/arb/docs/university-archives/boardmembers.pdf.

34. Taft, "A Lecture on the University of Cincinnati," 14.

35. March 30, 1871, *Board of Directors Minutes* (1859–1876, vol. 1), 312.

36. May 4, 1871, *Board of Directors Minutes* (1859–1876, vol. 1), 318.

37. Taft, "A Lecture on the University of Cincinnati," 36, 43, 44.

38. Ibid., 57; *Common Schools of Cincinnati 41st Annual Report* (Cincinnati: Wilstach, Baldwin & Co., Printers, 1870), 61. This sentiment echoed that of Thomas Huxley, who in 1875 visited the recently founded Johns Hopkins in Baltimore and declared that universities do not need an architect, but just "an honest bricklayer." Paul Venable Turner, *Campus: An American Planning Tradition* (Cambridge, MA: MIT Press, 1984), 163.

39. Isaac M. Wise, *Baccalaureate Address, Delivered at the Commencement of the Cincinnati University, June 19, 1884*, 10; "Report of Special Committee," February 1, 1884, *Board of Directors Minutes* (1883–1891, vol. 3), 42. Longworth initiated the transfer of the McMicken School to the Cincinnati Art Museum to honor his father, who died in 1883. Joseph Longworth had desired the creation of a joint art school and art museum. Cincinnati Museum Association, *Third Annual Report, 1884* (Cincinnati: Robert Clarke & Co., 1884), 23–37.

40. Circular from President J. D. Cox, May 17, 1886, *Board of Directors Minutes* (1883–1891, vol. 3), 256–57. For a history of St. Xavier College see Roger Fortin, *To See Great Wonders: A History of Xavier University, 1831–2006* (Scranton: University of Scranton Press, 2006).

41. The dental college closed in 1926.

42. Taft, "The German University and the American College," 7.

43. Shotwell, *A History of the Schools of Cincinnati*, 187.

44. *Annual Report of the Directors of the University of the City of Cincinnati for the Year Ending December 31, 1879* (Cincinnati: Times Book and Job Printing Establishment, 1880), 17.

45. *Annual Report of the Directors of the University of the City of Cincinnati for the Year Ending December 31, 1878* (Cincinnati: Times Book and Job Printing Establishment, 1879), 11.

46. Ibid., 8–9. For more on Hawthorne see Greg Hand, "UC Seeks Photo of First Woman Graduate," http://www.uc.edu/news/NR.aspx?id=19482. For a history of Hebrew Union College see Michael A. Meyer, *Hebrew Union College–Jewish Institute of Religion: A Centennial History, 1875–1975* (1976; rpt. Cincinnati: Hebrew Union College Press, 1992).

47. *Annual Report of the Directors of the University of the City of Cincinnati For the Year Ending December 31, 1879*, 13–14.

Chapter 3 To the Woods

1. Despite the proliferation of universities, enrollments in higher education around the nation grew only slowly in these decades. Demand for education was not driving the creation of

these institutions. See Laurence R. Veysey, *The Emergence of the American University* (Chicago: University of Chicago Press, 1965), 16.

2. "Report of the Minority of the Committee Appointed to Investigate the Charges against Thomas Vickers, Rector of the University of Cincinnati," June 19, 1882, *Board of Directors Minutes* (1877–1883, vol. 2), 521, ARB. Vickers survived the challenge and the Board of Directors' investigation. On Cincinnati's economic strength see Philip Scranton, "Diversified Industrialization and Economic Success: Understanding Cincinnati's Manufacturing Development, 1850–1925," *Ohio Valley History* (Spring 2005): 5–22.

3. Steven K. Green, *The Bible, the School, and the Constitution: The Clash That Shaped Modern Church-State Doctrine* (New York: Oxford University Press, 2012), 93–135; George Augustine Thayer, *The First Congregationalist Church of Cincinnati (Unitarian): A History* (Cincinnati, 1917), 34–37.

4. The city grew to 325,000 by 1900, but Cincinnati's national rank fell to tenth. Cincinnati was no longer the largest city in the West. (It wasn't even in the West any longer!) This decline in the city's rank among the nation's urban centers would have significant and lasting consequences for the city and for the fledgling university. For the context of industrializing Cincinnati see Zane L. Miller's *Boss Cox's Cincinnati: Urban Politics in the Progressive Era* (Chicago: University of Chicago Press, 1968) and Steven J. Ross's *Workers on the Edge: Work, Leisure, and Politics in Industrializing Cincinnati, 1788–1890* (New York: Columbia University Press, 1985).

5. John H. White Jr., *Cincinnati, City of Seven Hills and Five Inclines* (Cincinnati: Cincinnati Railroad Club, 2001).

6. Special meeting of the board after the morning fire, November 7, 1885, *Board of Directors Minutes* (1883–1891, vol. 3), 210–11; *Academica*, November 1885.

7. Special meeting of the board after the morning fire, November 7, 1885, 210–11. For more on Hebrew Union College, see Michael A. Meyer, *Hebrew Union College–Jewish Institute of Religion: A Centennial History, 1875–1975* (1976; rpt. Cincinnati: Hebrew Union College Press, 1992)

8. "McMicken University Damage Resulting from Yesterday Morning's Fire," *Cincinnati Enquirer*, November 8, 1885.

9. The *Cincinnati Times-Star* editorial was reprinted in *Academica*, November 1885.

10. November 16, 1885, *Board of Directors Minutes* (1883–1891, vol. 3), 215, 218.

11. July 9, 1872, *Board of Directors Minutes* (1859–1876, vol. 1), 372.

12. Circuit Court of Hamilton County, Ohio, No. 1136, Transcript and Original Papers filed May 19, 1891, as found in *The University Case: Records, Briefs, and Decisions*, 71,185, ARB.

13. *The University Case: Records, Briefs, and Decisions*, 106, ARB.

14. *The University Case: Records, Briefs, and Decisions*, 71, ARB.

15. *Academica*, December 1885. The Moerlein and Jackson breweries were especially close to the university.

16. "The McMicken Trust," *Cincinnati Enquirer*, January 25, 1886.

17. *Academica*, December 1885.

18. Circuit Court of Hamilton County, Ohio, No. 1136.

19. This first petition, from Walter Logan and twenty-one other students, asked, rather improbably, that an unused room on the fourth floor be used for a gymnasium. "From Students for Gymnasium," October 18, 1875, *Board of Directors Minutes* (1859–1876, vol. 1), 530. For a later petition see, "Communications," *Belatrasco*, October 1880.

20. W. Stecher, "A Word in the Interest of Physical Culture in Our Schools," *Academia*, February 1884. The idea that athletics were an integral part of training a complete person became widespread in the late 1800s. See, for example, Charles Franklin Thwing, president of Western Reserve University, who wrote, "athletics represent the training of an important part

of the whole man for life's service." Charles Franklin Thwing, *The American College in American Life* (New York: G. P. Putnam's Sons, 1897), 27.

21. *McMicken Review*, May 1887.

22. *McMicken Review*, June 1887.

23. Editorial, *Belatrasco*, October 1880.

24. "A Student's Complaint," *McMicken Review*, April 1890.

25. *McMicken Review*, November 1891.

26. *McMicken Review*, December 1891.

27. Committee of Law Report, November 19, 1888, *Board of Directors Minutes* (1883–1891, vol. 3), 400.

28. Ward Baldwin, C. G. Comegys, L. M. Hadden, "Why the University of Cincinnati should be moved from its present site to the south part of Burnet Woods Park" (n.d., probably 1889), 3–4, CHLA.

29. The ordinance appears in the *Annual Report of the Directors of the University of Cincinnati, 1889* (Cincinnati: Commercial Gazette Job Print, 1890), 24–26.

30. Circuit Court of Hamilton County, Ohio, No. 1136.

31. This area is now part of Clifton Heights.

32. Circuit Court of Hamilton County, Ohio, No. 1136.

33. "To Burnet Woods," *Cincinnati Enquirer*, March 8, 1893; Circuit Court of Hamilton County, Ohio, No. 1136. The University of Cincinnati is not alone in having moved farther from the center of the city in which it was founded. Perhaps most famously, Columbia University moved twice, once from its lower Broadway location to Madison Avenue in Midtown and then to Morningside Heights in 1897. See Steven J. Diner, *Universities and Their Cities: Urban Higher Education in America* (Baltimore: Johns Hopkins University Press, 2017), 4–5.

34. *Burnet Woods Lease*, MSS VF 86, CHLA.

35. *Annual Report of the Board of Park Commissioners for the Year Ending December 31, 1891* (Cincinnati: Commercial Gazette Job Print, 1892), 6; *Annual Report of the Board of Park Commissioners for the Year Ending December 31, 1892* (Cincinnati: Commercial Gazette Job Print, 1893), 6.

36. October 17, 1892, *Board of Directors Minutes* (1892–1898, vol. 4), 39. "The University Will Be Built in Burnet Woods," *Cincinnati Enquirer*, October 18, 1892.

37. Report from Committee investigating relations between YMMLA and Cincinnati College to the Board of Directors of the YMMLA (undated), Exhibit 1, as found in Supreme Court of the State of Ohio, *Emerson E. White et al. v. William Howard Neff et al., Record* (Cincinnati: Robert Clarke & Co., 1894), 143, Cincinnati College Records, box 5, folder 355, ARB.

38. Report from Committee investigating relations between YMMLA and Cincinnati College, 146, 147.

39. *Emerson E. White et al. v. William Howard Neff et al.*, 7, Cincinnati College Records, box 5, folder 355, ARB.

40. Jacob D. Cox to E. W. Kittridge, April 27, 1897, Cincinnati College Records, box 5, folder 298, ARB; "Consolidation Now All But Effected," *Cincinnati Enquirer*, May 26, 1897.

41. "In Burnet Woods the New Varsity Will Open," *Cincinnati Enquirer*, September 21, 1895.

42. "Danced in the New Gymnasium," *Cincinnati Enquirer*, October 5, 1895.

43. *The Cincinnatian, 1896* (University of Cincinnati, 1896), 11.

44. "City Hall Pick-Ups," *Cincinnati Enquirer*, November 7, 1896.

45. *Burnet Woods Echo*, March 31, 1896.

46. "Mayor Donates $2,000 for University Athletic Field," *Cincinnati Enquirer*, February 6, 1901.

47. Editorial, *University Weekly News*, October 2, 1902.

48. "Fence or No Fence, the Question," *Cincinnati Enquirer*, July 1, 1902.
49. "Fence Around Athletic Field," *Cincinnati Enquirer*, June 26, 1902; "Fence About Athletic Field," *Cincinnati Enquirer*, November 7, 1902.
50. Ayers Report, September 15, 1902, *Board of Directors Minutes* (1898–1902, vol. 5), 462.
51. "Split Over University Fence," *Cincinnati Enquirer*, November 5, 1902.
52. "Fence," *University Weekly News*, November 11, 1902.
53. "Fence Matter Again Bobs Up," *Cincinnati Enquirer*, November 27, 1902; "University Fence," *Cincinnati Enquirer*, June 3, 1903. *University of Cincinnati v. Cincinnati*, 13 Ohio Dec. 741; 1903 Ohio Misc. LEXIS 54; 1 Ohio N.P. (n.s.) 105. LexisNexis Academic.
54. German immigrants created Turner Societies, where they practiced gymnastics and espoused liberal politics. The movement was especially strong in Cincinnati. See Dann Woellert, *Cincinnati Turner Societies: The Cradle of an American Movement* (Charleston, SC: History Press, 2012).
55. "Divided," *Cincinnati Enquirer*, June 27, 1902.
56. Committee on College Property Report to E. W. Kittredge, March 1900, Cincinnati College Records, box 5, folder 304, ARB.
57. "Emery Buys College Building," *Cincinnati Enquirer*, December 17, 1901.
58. "Trustees of Cincinnati College," *Cincinnati Enquirer*, January 17, 1902; Handwritten deed, Cincinnati College Records, box 3, folder 201, ARB.
59. Howard Ayers to E. W. Kittredge, February 7, 1902, Cincinnati College Records, box 5, folder 293, ARB. McKim, Mead & White had designed many famed buildings, but they had also completed campus plans for Columbia University (1894) and New York University (1892). On the former see Andrew S. Dolkart, *Morningside Heights: A History of Its Architecture and Development* (New York: Columbia University Press, 1998), especially 115–36.
60. "Favors Burnet Woods as Site," *Cincinnati Enquirer*, March 11, 1902. The Ninth Street building was demolished in 1982, along with the Baptist church next door, to make way for a city-owned parking garage. The Law School had long since moved up to Burnet Woods, when it occupied Taft Hall in 1925.
61. W. O. Sproull, "The University of Cincinnati" (November 30, 1895), 168, 178, Literary Club Papers, vol. 18. Emphasis in the original.
62. Ibid.
63. Comegys report, June 26, 1895, *Board of Directors Minutes* (1892–1898, vol. 4), 296.
64. "Magnificent Gift of Henry Hanna," *Cincinnati Enquirer*, June 27, 1895. For a hagiography of Comegys, which includes several documents about his life and death, see Charles George Comegys, *Cornelius George Comegys, M.D., His Life and Career in the Development of Cincinnati for Nearly Half a Century* (Cincinnati, 1899).

Chapter 4 A Progressive Institution

1. "University Day, November 21, 1905," 6–7, Charles William Dabney Papers, 1905–1918, folder 2, CHLA.
2. Charles Dabney, "A Gospel for Cincinnati," June 7, 1914, Charles W. Dabney Papers, box 29, folder 355, UNC. Note that despite the fact that the nation was urbanizing rapidly in the late 1800s and early 1900s, not all institutions of higher learning turned their attention toward municipal affairs. Merle Curti and Vernon Carstensen managed to write 600 pages about the University of Wisconsin during the Progressive Era without saying much about Madison at all. Like many state land-grant schools, Wisconsin focused its attention more on agricultural than urban questions. See Curti and Carstensen, *The University of Wisconsin: A History* (Madison: University of Wisconsin Press, 1949), vol. 2.

3. On the development of progressive social policies see with Daniel T. Rodgers, *Atlantic Crossings: Social Politics in a Progressive Age* (Cambridge, MA: Belknap Press of Harvard University Press, 1998). On the role of urbanization in the creation of progressive reform see Robert H. Wiebe, *The Search for Order, 1877–1920* (New York: Hill and Wang, 1967).

4. On the creation of the AAUP see the classic text, Richard Hofstadter and Walter P. Metzer, *The Development of Academic Freedom in the United States* (New York: Columbia University Press, 1955), especially 468–90.

5. Charles Dabney, "The Municipal University: Its Ideals, Methods, and Work," December 7, 1912, Charles William Dabney Papers, folder 11, CHLA; "Some Inside Statistics as to University Students," *Cincinnati Enquirer*, March 1, 1913.

6. "Meeting of the Association of Collegiate Alumnae, University of Cincinnati," October 28, 1909, 5, Charles William Dabney Papers, 1905–1918, folder 8, CHLA.

7. "Courses in Nursing Are Added at University," *Cincinnati Enquirer*, July 10, 1916. Steven Diner calls Dabney's collaboration with city schools to educate new teachers and provide continuing education for current teachers "uniquely successful." Steven J. Diner, *Universities and Their Cities: Urban Higher Education in America* (Baltimore: Johns Hopkins University Press, 2017), 39.

8. Charles Dabney to Henry S. Pritchett, December 5, 1908, Charles W. Dabney Papers, box 7, folder 113, UNC.

9. See Reginald McGrane, *The University of Cincinnati* (New York: Harper & Row, 1963), 177–79, 186–92. See also "Final Report of the Citizens' Committee on University Affairs" (Cincinnati, 1900), which recounts the episode in great detail.

10. "Prof. F. C. Hicks Is to Be University Head," *Cincinnati Enquirer*, May 27, 1920.

11. Ayers Report, February 19, 1900, *Board of Directors Minutes* (1898–1902, vol. 5), 176–77.

12. Ibid.

13. Henry Curtis to Charles Dabney, October 20, 1903, Charles W. Dabney Papers, box 7, folder 100, UNC.

14. "Summons Comes to H. M. Curtis," *Cincinnati Enquirer*, September 7, 1915.

15. Charles Dabney to Dr. Walter H. Page, December 16, 1903, Charles W. Dabney Papers, box 7, folder 102, UNC.

16. Charles W. Eliot to Dabney, December 22, 1903, Charles W. Dabney Papers, box 7, folder 102, UNC.

17. Cyrus Northrop to Dabney, December 30, 1903, Charles W. Dabney Papers, box 7, folder 102, UNC.

18. Dabney to Northrop, January 22, 1904, Charles W. Dabney Papers, box 7, folder 104, UNC.

19. Eliot to Dabney, January 8, 1904, Charles W. Dabney Papers, box 7, folder 103, UNC.

20. Charles Dabney to Dr. Walter H. Page, December 16, 1903, Charles W. Dabney Papers, box 7, folder 102, UNC.

21. "President Dabney's Inaugural Address," *Cincinnati Enquirer*, November 17, 1904.

22. "First United Commencement of the University" (n.d.), 16, 18, Charles William Dabney Papers, 1905–1918, folder 1, CHLA.

23. Frank J. Jones to Hamilton County Delegation, January 19, 1906, Charles W. Dabney Papers, box 7, folder 112, UNC.

24. "Trouble in University Board," *Cincinnati Enquirer*, December 2, 1908.

25. "Opposition to Bonds for University," *Cincinnati Enquirer*, May 24, 1913.

26. Dabney to Henry Curtis, June 11, 1908, Charles W. Dabney Papers, box 7, folder 113, UNC.

27. Dabney to Henry S. Pritchett, December 15, 1908, Charles W. Dabney Papers, box 7, folder 113, UNC.

28. Dabney to Francis Peabody, March 10, 1909, Charles W. Dabney Papers, box 8, folder 114, UNC.

29. Dabney to Pritchett, May 13, 1911, Charles W. Dabney Papers, box 8, folder 117, UNC.

30. Charles Dabney, "The University and the City in Co-Operation," *Outlook* (July 25, 1908), 655.

31. Charles Dabney, "Service of the University to the City and Its Institutions" (December 20, 1913), 5, Cincinnati Observatory Collection, box 7, folder 21, ARB.

32. W. O. Sproull, "University Extension in Cincinnati," *The Proceedings of the First Annual Meeting of the National Conference on University Extension* (Philadelphia: J. B. Lippincott, 1892), 146.

33. Ibid., 151.

34. As quoted in ibid., 146.

35. "University Extension Courses," *The Cincinnatian* (University of Cincinnati, 1895), 23–24.

36. Dabney, "Service of the University to the City and Its Institutions," 11.

37. *Annual Report of the Directors of the University of Cincinnati for the Year Ending December 31, 1896* (Cincinnati: Commercial Gazette Print Job, 1897), 62–63; "Miss Addams of Hull House— The Most Famous Social Settlement," *Cincinnati Enquirer*, April 24, 1894; "Greeted by a Large Audience Was Miss Addams Yesterday at Sinton Hall," *Cincinnati Enquirer*, May 12, 1894; "Miss Jane Addams of Chicago, Explains the Socialistic Settlement Idea," *Cincinnati Enquirer*, May 19, 1894. For the context of the social settlement movement see Judith Ann Trolander, *Professionalism and Social Change: From the Settlement House Movement to Neighborhood Centers, 1886 to the Present* (New York: Columbia University Press, 1987).

38. "College Settlement," *The Cincinnatian, 1895* (University of Cincinnati, 1895), 117–18.

39. "Prof. Myers Delivers the First of His Lectures on Eastern Civilization," *Cincinnati Enquirer*, January 29, 1897.

40. "Representatives: Elected to University Settlement Board of Directors," *Cincinnati Enquirer*, December 11, 1901; "Settlement: Protests against the Dropping of Prof. from the Pay Roll," *Cincinnati Enquirer*, April 4, 1907.

41. *University of Cincinnati Record, Annual Reports, 1904* (University of Cincinnati, 1905), 92.

42. "Cincinnati's Social Settlement," *Commercial Tribune*, December 10, 1900.

43. Report on Evening Classes, September 10, 1912; October 1, 1912, *Board of Directors Minutes* (May 1910–December 1913, vol. 8), 450; "A Municipal University," *Cincinnati Enquirer*, April 12, 1914.

44. "Some Inside Statistics as to University Students," *Cincinnati Enquirer*, March 1, 1913.

45. "Dr. Schneider, 67, Cincinnati Dean: Ex-Head of University Dies," *New York Times*, March 29, 1939; Herman Schneider, "Thirty Years of Educational Pioneering: The Philosophy of the Cooperative System and Its Practical Test" (University of Cincinnati, 1935), 16. For a more complete biography see Clyde W. Park, *Ambassador to Industry: The Idea and Life of Herman Schneider* (New York: Bobbs-Merrill, 1943).

46. Graham Taylor, *Satellite Cities: A Study of Industrial Suburbs* (New York: D. Appleton and Company, 1915), 91–126.

47. Clyde W. Park, *The Co-Operative System of Education: A Reprint of Bulletin No 37, Series of 1916. U.S. Bureau of Education, with Additions* (University of Cincinnati, 1925), 43. On women in the co-op program see M. B. Reilly, *The Ivory Tower and the Smokestack: 100 Years of Cooperative Education at the University of Cincinnati* (University of Cincinnati, 2006), 41–45.

48. *University of Cincinnati Record, Annual Reports, 1904* (University of Cincinnati, 1905), 28.

49. Herman Schneider, "Three Years of the Cooperative Courses," *American Machinist* (September 9, 1909), 444.

50. Park, *Co-Operative System*, 52.

51. Herman Schneider, "Thirty Years of Educational Pioneering: The Philosophy of the Cooperative System and Its Practical Test" (University of Cincinnati, 1935), 16.

52. "Dr. Holmes Is Unanimously Chosen Dean of Medical College," *Cincinnati Enquirer*, October 8, 1913.

53. Charles F. Walthers to Julius Fleischmann, February 10, 1903, Christian R. Holmes Papers, box 1, folder 29, WCA.

54. "Dedicatory Exercises, Cincinnati New General Hospital," February 20, 1915, 2, Christian R. Holmes Collection, box 1, folder 34, WCA.

55. "Hospitals Studied by Dr. Holmes," *Cincinnati Enquirer*, April 20, 1903; Christian R. Holmes, "The Hospital or Ward Unit, An Address Delivered before the Canadian Hospital Association at the Royal Victoria Hospital, Montreal, March 29, 1910" (Toronto: William Briggs, 1918), 7.

56. Christian R. Holmes, "The Planning of a Modern Hospital, An Address Delivered before the Department of Nursing and Health, Teachers' College, Columbia University, February 21, 1911" (Detroit: National Hospital Record Publishing Company), 5.

57. "Hospital Site Purchased by City," *Cincinnati Enquirer*, March 1, 1903; Christian R. Holmes, "Modern Hospitals, With Special Reference to Our New Municipal Hospital and Its Relation to Medical Education in Cincinnati," Lecture delivered at UC, January 9, 1908, Christian R. Holmes Collection, box 1, folder 30, WCA.

58. "Dedicatory Exercises, Cincinnati New General Hospital," February 20, 1915, 7, Christian R. Holmes Collection, box 1, folder 34, WCA.

59. Christian R. Holmes, "Modern Hospitals"; "Proposed Medical College," *Cincinnati Enquirer*, January 16, 1914.

60. "Dedicatory Exercises."

61. Ibid.

62. Dabney, "Service of the University to the City and its Institutions."

63. "Prof. Lowrie Picked by Governor for Director," *Cincinnati Enquirer*, January 18, 1913; "Heads: State Research Bureau," *Cincinnati Enquirer*, January 21, 1913.

64. "Research Bureau," *Cincinnati Enquirer*, January 8, 1915. For Lowrie's description of the value of the library during World War I, see *University of Cincinnati Studies, The Service of the University to the City and the Annual Reports of Officers for 1917*, ser. 1, vol. 14, no. 4 (University of Cincinnati, 1918).

65. Plan for Bureau for Testing and Inspection, College of Engineering, February 6, 1912, *Board of Directors Minutes* (1910–1913, vol. 8), 327–28.

66. *Annual Reports of the City Departments*, 1914, 749.

67. Ralph R. Caldwell, "The Municipal University: An Inevitable Development of the Times," May 16, 1914, Literary Club Papers, vol. 36, 583–601, Literary Club of Cincinnati.

68. Ibid.

69. Charles Dabney, "The Cincinnati Way," March 10, 1917, folder 15, Charles William Dabney Papers, 1905–1918, CHS. On Dabney's vision see Gene D. Lewis and Zane L. Miller, "Charles W. Dabney and the Urban University: An Institution in Search of a Mission, 1904–1914," *Cincinnati Historical Society Bulletin* 1980 (38): 150–79. See also "Endowments of Local University Have Increased from $813,000 in 1905 to $1,586,513 Now," *Cincinnati Enquirer*, January 14, 1915.

70. *University of Cincinnati Record, Commencement Exercises, June 1918*, ser. 1, vol. 14, no. 3 (University of Cincinnati, 1918), 20.

71. Charles Dabney, "President's Report," *University of Cincinnati Record, Annual Reports for 1919 and Progress of the University in Fifteen Years, 1904 to 1919*, 13.

72. Parke Rexford Kolbe, *Urban Influences on Higher Education in England and the United States* (New York: Macmillan, 1928), 153, 48.

73. Dabney to P. P. Claxton, March 6, 1920, Charles W. Dabney Papers, box 10, folder 139, UNC.

74. R. M. Hughes to Dabney, February 25, 1920, Charles W. Dabney Papers, box 10, folder 139, UNC.

Chapter 5 In the Service of the Nation

1. *The University of Cincinnati Report of the President, 1932–34*, 170–72; *The University of Cincinnati Report of the President, 1934–35*, 19, 144–45. On Frost's relationship to UC see Dale Patrick Brown, *Literary Cincinnati: The Missing Chapter* (Athens: Ohio University Press, 2011), 121–31.

2. *The University of Cincinnati Report of the President, 1935–36*, 5–6, 93–94; *The University of Cincinnati Report of the President, 1937–38*, 106–7, 110–11.

3. *The University of Cincinnati Report of the President, 1934–35*, 6.

4. This lecture appeared in print five years later as part of a collection of Dabney's essays: *Fighting for a New World* (New York: Abingdon Press, 1919).

5. Charles Dabney to Woodrow Wilson, January 8, 1916, Charles W. Dabney Papers, box 9, folder 128, UNC.

6. Colon Schott to Dabney, December 29, 1914, Charles W. Dabney Papers, box 8, folder 123, UNC.

7. Schott to Dabney, January 4, 1915, Charles W. Dabney Papers, box 8, folder 124, UNC.

8. On Germans in Cincinnati during the war and after see Don Heinrich Tolzmann, *The Cincinnati Germans after the Great War* (New York: Peter Lang, 1987).

9. *War Bulletin*, March 1918 (University of Cincinnati, 1918), 3. For the national context of enthusiasm see Carol S. Gruber, *Mars and Minerva: World War I and the Uses of the Higher Learning in America* (Baton Rouge: Louisiana State University Press, 1975), especially 99–100. For a summary of the war's impact on higher education see Parke Rexford Kolbe, *The Colleges in War Time and After* (New York: D. Appleton and Company, 1919). The best book on America during the war remains David M. Kennedy's *Over Here: The First World War and American Society* (New York: Oxford University Press, 2004).

10. Kennedy, *Over Here*, especially 57–58, where Kennedy emphasizes the propaganda purpose of the War Issues course. Frank Aydelotte, *Final Report of the War Issues Course of the Students' Army Training Corps* (Washington, DC: War Department, 1919), 15.

11. *University of Cincinnati Record, Commencement Exercises, June 1918*, ser. 1, vol. 14, no. 3 (University of Cincinnati, 1918), 14. On the war making faculty feel useful, see Gruber, *Mars and Minerva*, 114–116.

12. Committee on Education and Special Training, *A Review of Its Work during 1918* (War Department, 1919), 57.

13. For the national context of the Students' Army Training Corps, see Gruber, *Mars and Minerva*, 213–52.

14. *Cincinnati Enquirer*, October 27, 1918.

15. *University of Cincinnati Studies, The Service of the University to the City and the Annual Reports of Officers for 1917*, ser. 1, vol. 14, no. 4 (University of Cincinnati, 1918), 20–21.

16. Kolbe, *Colleges in War Time and After*, 197, 101, 102. The University of Wisconsin, also located in a heavily German region, saw a significant drop in demand for its German courses during and after the war. See Merle Curti and Vernon Carstensen, *The University of Wisconsin: A History* (Madison: University of Wisconsin Press, 1949), 2:324.

17. *University of Cincinnati Record, The Service of the University to the Nation and the Annual Reports of Officers for 1918*, ser. 1, vol. 15, no. 3 (University of Cincinnati, 1919), 10, 149; "Active Life of Physician Ends," *Cincinnati Enquirer*, January 10, 1920.

18. *University of Cincinnati Record, Commencement Exercises*, ser. 1, vol. 16, no. 4, June 1920 (University of Cincinnati, 1920), 7–15.

19. *Four Year Report (1923 to 1926 inclusive) of the Central Clinic* (Cincinnati, 1929), available online via Hathi Trust.

20. Ada Arlitt to Beardsley Ruml, January 10, 1928, LSRM, Series III–5, box 44, folder 456, RAC. Courtesy of Kathy Milar.

21. In the 1959, the university changed the name of this building to Beecher Hall in honor of former Cincinnati resident Catharine Beecher, sister to Harriet Beecher Stowe and supporter of women's education. Beecher Hall was demolished in 2000. See "UC Is Given $440,000 for Research, Training," *Cincinnati Enquirer*, November 4, 1959.

22. "Authority on Child Care at U.C.," *Cincinnati Times-Star*, May 25, 1925. For a short description of the nursery see *The Twenty-Eighth Yearbook of the National Society for the Study of Education* (Bloomington, IL: Public School Publishing Company, 1929), 390–91.

23. Ada Hart Arlitt, "Toys and Occupations for Young Children" (Department of Child Care and Training School of Household Administration and the Mothers' Training Center Association of Cincinnati, n.d.); Ada Hart Arlitt, "Habit Formation" (Department of Child Care and Training School of Household Administration and the Mothers' Training Center Association of Cincinnati, 1929).

24. Ada Arlitt to Beardsley Ruml, January 10, 1928, LSRM, Series III–5, box 44, folder 456, RAC.

25. Carl N. Degler, *In Search of Human Nature: The Decline and Revival of Darwinism in American Social Thought* (New York: Oxford University Press, 1991), 172–73. See also Ada Arlitt, "On the Need for Caution in Establishing Race Norms," *Journal of Applied Psychology* (June 1921): 179–83.

26. Ada Arlitt to Beardsley Ruml, January 18, 1928, LSRM, Series III–5, box 44, folder 456, RAC. For a fuller analysis of Arlitt's relationship with Rockefeller see Katharine S. Milar, "A Special Relationship: Race, Child Study, and Rockefeller Philanthropy," *Journal of the History of the Behavioral Sciences* (Fall 2010): 394–411.

27. "Unusual Honor for Professor at U.C.," *Cincinnati Times-Star*, June 6, 1930.

28. Margaret Rossiter, *Women Scientists in America: Struggles and Strategies to 1940* (Baltimore: Johns Hopkins University Press, 1984), 36, 172, 270.

29. Faculty are listed in the annual university catalogues. Fulford, for whom the university herbarium is named, taught at UC for forty-seven years.

30. "Composition and Source of the Flora of the Cincinnati Region," *Ecology* 2, no. 3 (July 1921): 162, 165, 178. Braun even described the use of railway roadbeds, well-drained gravel beds—"artificially constructed pathways"—that had gained in importance as a means of plant migration from the arid West.

31. E. Lucy Braun, *Deciduous Forests of Eastern North America* (Philadelphia: Blakiston, 1950), vii. Among the best descriptions of Native American interventions in pre-European settlement forests can be found in William Cronon, *Changes in the Land: Indians, Colonists, and the Ecology of New England* (New York: Hill & Wang, 1983).

32. James M. Dyer, "Revisiting the *Deciduous Forests of Eastern North America*," *BioScience* 56, no. 4 (2006): 341–52.

33. *Wild Flower* 1, no. 3 (July 1, 1924): 18; "'Wild Flower' the National Organ," *Wild Flower* 2, no. 2 (April 1925): 1.

34. E. Lucy Braun, "Through the Long Ages," *Wild Flower* 2, no. 3 (July 1, 1925): 3–4.

35. E. Lucy Braun, "Then and Now," *Wild Flower* 10, no. 3 (July 1, 1933): 26.

36. Lynx Prairie is part of the Cincinnati Museum Center's 16,000 Edge of Appalachia Preserve. See http://www.cincymuseum.org/nature.

37. E. Lucy Braun, "The Wilderness Society," *Wild Flower* 12, no. 4 (October 1, 1935): 38. On the formation of the Wilderness Society see Paul Sutter, *Driven Wild: How the Fight against Automobiles Launched the Modern Wilderness Movement* (Seattle: University of Washington Press, 2005).

38. In 1923, Dayton became the first place in the world where motorists could fill their tanks with leaded gasoline. Dayton was the epicenter for experimentation because of Thomas Midgley, the imaginative engineer who helped make Delco a center of automobile innovation. For the broader context of the leaded gasoline story, see Christian Warren, *Brush with Death: A Social History of Lead Poisoning* (Baltimore: Johns Hopkins University Press, 2000), 116–33. See also Gerald Markowitz and David Rosner, *Deceit and Denial: The Deadly Politics of Industrial Pollution* (Berkeley: University of California Press, 2002).

39. Robert Kehoe, "On the Normal Absorption and Excretion of Lead," *Journal of Industrial Hygiene* (September 1933): 271.

40. Robert Kehoe, Frederick Thamann, and Jacob Cholak, "An Appraisal of the Lead Hazards Associated with the Distribution and Use of Gasoline Containing Tetraethyl Lead, Part 1," *Journal of Industrial Hygiene* (March 1934): 127.

41. He describes his job clearly in a letter to W. V. Hartmann, May 20, 1931, Kehoe Papers, box 10, folder 2, WCA.

42. Kehoe to E. W. Webb, Ethyl Gas Corp, New York, NY, November 10, 1926, Kehoe Papers, box 10, folder 4, WCA.

43. Meanwhile, Donaldson's primary physician, John Johnson, responded briefly to Kehoe's diagnosis. A chest x-ray had already ruled out syphilis, and one abscessed tooth seemed an unlikely culprit given the range of symptoms. "As for hysteria being considered I cannot agree with you," Johnson wrote. "Of course I took care of him through his illness. You saw him when he was convalescent." See John Alton Johnson to Kehoe, November 24, 1926, Kehoe Papers, box 10, folder 4, WCA.

44. Kehoe report, December 7, 1926, Kehoe Papers, box 10, folder 4, WCA.

45. See Kehoe Papers, box 10, WCA.

46. Kehoe to J. B. Rather, Socony-Vacuum Oil Co. Inc., November 15, 1937, Kehoe Papers, box 10, folder 5, WCA. See also E. R. Alden, Socony-Vacuum Oil Co. to Kehoe, November 23, 1937, in which Alden notes that a quiet investigation would be impossible in a small town like Churchville. Kehoe Papers, box 10, folder 5, WCA.

47. Kehoe to Otto M. Hamer, Attorney at Law, April 25, 1936, Kehoe Papers, box 10, folder 3, WCA.

48. Kehoe to Hamer, Chicago, May 15, 1936, Kehoe Papers, box 10, folder 3, WCA.

49. Despite ongoing concern of the public, Kehoe concluded in 1939, "All of the experimental and clinical evidence of the past fifteen years indicates that there is no greater danger associated with the handling of leaded gasoline than in handling of ordinary gasoline of similar quality." Kehoe to Ralph Greene, April 14, 1939, Kehoe Papers, box 10, folder 25, WCA.

50. Jack L. Davis and Evi Gorogianni, "Embedding Aegean Prehistory in Institutional Practice: A View from One of Its North American Centers," in *Prehistorians Round the Pond: Reflections on Aegean Prehistory*, edited by John F. Cherry, Despina Margomenou, and Lauren E. Talalay (Ann Arbor, MI: Kelsey Museum Publication 2, 2005), 95. See also Natalia Vogelkoff-Brogan,

Jack L. Davis, and Vasiliki Florou, eds., *Carl W. Blegen: Personal and Archaeological Narratives* (Atlanta: Lockwood Press, 2015).

51. William T. Semple to Carl Blegen, March 2, 1927, Carl W. Blegen Papers, box 1, folder 10, ARB.

52. Semple indicated that the professorship would be in the Graduate School rather than the College of Liberal Arts because "the main justification for such an expenditure on the part of the University is the high quality of your attainments in scholarship and research." Semple to Blegen, March 2, 1927, Carl W. Blegen Papers, box 1, folder 10, ARB.

53. Blegen to Semple, March 25, 1927, Carl W. Blegen Papers, box 1, folder 15, ARB.

54. William Semple to Carl Blegen, June 5, 1931, Troy (Blegen) Excavation Records, box 1, folder 2, Classics Department Archives.

55. Carl W. Blegen, John L. Caskey, Marion Rawson, and Jerome Sperling, *Troy: General Introduction, The First and Second Settlements* Vol. 1, Part 1: *Text* (Princeton: Princeton University Press, 1950), 5.

56. Blegen to Wilhelm Dörpfeld, August 18, 1931, Troy (Blegen) Excavation Records, box 1, folder 2, Classics Department Archives.

57. Dörpfeld to Blegen, September 2, 1931 (translated from German by Sarah Stradling), Troy (Blegen) Excavation Records, box 1, folder 2, Classics Department Archives.

58. Carl Blegen to Dörpfeld, December 7, 1931; Dörpfeld to Blegen, December 19, 1931 (translated from German by Sarah Stradling), Troy (Blegen) Excavation Records, box 1, folder 2, Classics Department Archives; Dörpfeld noted that Heinrich Schliemann's wife had worked at Troy without trouble. Blegen, Caskey, Rawson, and Sperling, *Troy: General Introduction*.

59. Robert D. Blegen, *Carl W. Blegen: His Letters Home, Book II—From Distant Fields* (N.p., 1995), xvii–xix. The Rawson fortune had been made in the pork packing business.

60. "Trojan Cemetery Yields Treasures," *New York Times*, August 12, 1934; "Hold Homer's Troy Site of Nine Cities," *New York Times*, December 27, 1935; "Troy Excavations Back Homer's Epic," *New York Times*, December 28, 1936; "Gate of Old Troy Found on Plain," *New York Times*, December 29, 1937.

61. William Semple to Edward Capps, April 23, 1938, Troy (Blegen) Excavation Records, box 1, folder 5, Classics Department Archives.

62. Robert D. Blegen, *Carl W. Blegen: His Letters Home*, 20–21. The very first trench at Pylos eventually revealed 600 tablets and fragments of tablets.

63. K. Kourouniotis and Carl W. Blegen, "Excavations at Pylos, 1939," *American Journal of Archaeology* (1939): 557–76.

64. Carl W. Blegen and Marion Rawson, *The Palace of Nestor at Pylos in Western Messenia*, Vol. 1, *The Buildings and Their Contents* (Princeton: Princeton University Press, 1966), 5–8.

65. Nationally college and university enrollment fell nearly 10 percent from 1931 to 1933, according to LaDale C. Winling. See *Building the Ivory Tower: Universities and Metropolitan Development in the Twentieth Century* (Philadelphia: University of Pennsylvania Press, 2017), 60.

66. *The University of Cincinnati Report of the President, 1935–36*, 44.

67. *The University of Cincinnati Report of the President, 1934–35*, 6.

68. *The University of Cincinnati Report of the President, 1932–34*, 16–17, 21; *The University of Cincinnati Bulletin, Report of the President, 1937–38 and 1938–39*, 7.

69. Kevin P. Bower, "'A Favored Child of the State': Federal Student Aid at Ohio College and Universities, 1934–1943," *History of Education Quarterly* (September 2004): 364–87.

70. "N.Y.A. Finances 500 Students in University," *News Record*, October 10, 1936.

71. Cincinnati's Student Union was not among the nation's first. The state's first student union, at Ohio State, Enarson Hall, was completed in 1910. https://ohiounion.osu.edu/about_the_union/history.

72. *The University of Cincinnati Report of the President, 1934–35*, 22–23; Winling, *Building the Ivory Tower*, 4.

73. "Old Library Renamed for UC Archeologist," *News Record*, November 2, 1979; "Students Help to Construct Latest Building," *Cincinnati News Record*, September 26, 1936; "Student Union to Be Completed for September Use," *Cincinnati Bearcat*, March 29, 1936. For an exploration of architecture on campus see Paul Bennett, *The University of Cincinnati: An Architectural Tour* (New York: Princeton Architectural Press, 2001).

74. "New Deal Officials Grant Appropriation Funds Requested for Student Services Building on University Campus," *Cincinnati Bearcat*, October 5, 1935; "Student Union Building Open to Evening School," *Cincinnati Bearcat*, October 2, 1937; *University of Cincinnati Bulletin Report of the President, 1937–38 and 1938–39*, 225–28.

75. Barbara Blum, "Naming Nippert," *UC Magazine*, http://magazine.uc.edu/issues/0413/ jimmy_nippert.html.

76. "Ground Broken for Student Union Building, Making $750,000 in U.C. Projects Under Way," *Cincinnati Enquirer*, January 14, 1936; "24,000 Expected to See U.C. Dedication Game," *Cincinnati Post*, September 24, 1936.

77. "Board Approves Proposed W.P.A. Stadium Project," *Cincinnati Bearcat*, November 9, 1935.

78. "A Dedication at U.C.," *Cincinnati Times-Star*, September 26, 1936.

79. "President Roosevelt to Address Students," *News Record*, October 14, 1936; "Pres. Roosevelt Greets Students and Citizens Amid Rain and Cheers," *News Record*, October 21, 1936. Student Dick Powell used his regular *News Record* column, "The Soap Box," to mock both Roosevelt, whose visit he chalked up as a win for "Moscow and Lenin," and the football team, noting that the president had put the stadium "to better use than the football team has been in the habit of doing." Dick Powell, "The Soap Box," *Cincinnati News Record*, October 17, 1936.

80. "U.C. Students Asked to Help," *Cincinnati Post*, January 25, 1937; Raymond Walters Diary, January 24, 1937, Raymond Walters Collection, UA-73-20, box 2, ARB.

81. "U.C. Co-eds 'Behind Scenes' at Music Hall Clothing Depot," *Cincinnati Times-Star*, January 28, 1937.

82. "U.C. Medical Students Aid," *Cincinnati Post*, January 29, 1937.

83. "U.C. Maintains Short Wave on 24-Hour Flood Service," *Cincinnati Enquirer*, January 26, 1937.

84. "Workers Lauded by Administration, Classes Resumed," *News Record*, February 13, 1937.

85. "University of Cincinnati Razes Its Original Home," *Cincinnati Enquirer*, September 24, 1935; *A Golden Gate Bridge Jubilee, 1937–1987* (University of Cincinnati, 1987). See also Joseph B. Strauss, *The Golden Gate Bridge: Report of the Chief Engineer, September 1937* (San Francisco: Golden Gate Bridge and Highway District, 1938).

86. "An Editorial," *News Record*, December 10, 1941; "War Casts Gloom on U.C. Campus," *Cincinnati News Record*, December 10, 1941.

87. "Ability to Live Ordinary Life Needed in Emergency," *News Record*, December 10, 1941.

88. Raymond Walters Diary, December 11, 1941, Raymond Walters Collection, UA-73-20, box 2, ARB; "Men's Convocation," December 11, 1941, Raymond Walters Records, UA-73-20 box 6, folder 16, ARB.

89. "Convocations Stress Continued College Preparation during War," *News Record*, December 13, 1941.

90. Ingle was the daughter of President Charles Dabney.

91. "Convocations Stress Continued College Preparation during War."

92. "U.C. Expects to Train More Women," *News Record*, April 25, 1942; "Department Largest Ever, 92. Produces Successful Grads," *News Record*, December 12, 1942; "'Women Must

Expect to Take Part in War Effort,' States Dean," *News Record*, December 12, 1942; *University of Cincinnati Report of the President for 1941–1942 and 1942–1943*, 60–61.

93. "If Bombs Should Fall on University Campus…," *News Record*, April 25, 1942; "Areas Chosen in All U.C. Buildings as Possible Air Raid Shelters," *News Record*, March 21, 1942.

94. "U.C. Civilian Defense Corps Progresses on Three Fronts," *News Record*, January 10, 1942; "Four Divisions Set Up for Campus Defense," *News Record*, April 4, 1942; "UC Raid Protection to Cost at Least $2,000," *News Record*, April 8, 1942; "If Bombs Should Fall on University Campus. . . . "

95. "Large ROTC Enrollment Exceeds Government Quota," *News Record*, September 28, 1940.

96. Winkler Center for the History of the Health Professions, "25th General Hospital," http://digital.libraries.uc.edu/exhibits/winkler/25thGeneralHospital/index.html. On the consequences of the war for higher education generally, see Willis Rudy, *Total War and Twentieth-Century Higher Learning: Universities of the Western World in the First and Second World Wars* (Madison, NJ: Fairleigh Dickinson University Press, 1991).

97. "Evening College Aids in Uncle Sam's Defense Plan," *News Record*, January 18, 1941; "U.C. Prepares to Train 1,000 for Defense," *News Record*, October 25, 1941.

98. "Nursing Dean Obtains Leave for New Job," *News Record*, March 6, 1943; "U.C. Expects to Train More Women"; "Department Largest Ever, Produces Successful Grads."

99. "U.C. Rule Aids Drafted Students," *Cincinnati Post*, January 10, 1942.

100. *University of Cincinnati Bulletin Report of the President, 1939–1940 and 1940–1941*, 7.

101. "Students Perform Duty by Remaining in School," *News Record*, December 20, 1941.

102. "Attendance Decreases 17%," *News Record*, February 18, 1942; "Enrollment at U.C. Decreasing, But Not as Much as Expected," *News Record*, February 27, 1943; "1800 U.C. Men Enroll in Reserve," *News Record*, December 12, 1942; "Departure of 1,000 Soldiers to Deplete Student Body," *News Record*, March 8, 1944.

103. "Bond Issues Win," *News Record*, November 9, 1944; "Veterans Begin Training under GI Bill of Rights," *News Record*, September 21, 1944.

104. "Dedication of McMicken Hall and Spring Homecoming," April 28, 1950, Raymond Walters Collection, box 17, folder 12, ARB.

105. Donald Tangeman had not attended UC, but both of his parents were alumni and significant benefactors to their alma mater. For a history of TUC see Tangeman University Center Records, box 1, folder 1, ARB.

Chapter 6 Growing Pains and Opportunities

1. Keith W. Olson, *The G.I. Bill, the Veterans, and the Colleges* (Lexington: University Press of Kentucky, 1974), 44; *University–Community Tension and Urban Campus Form*, Vol. 1 (1972), 29, 32. The rapid increase in students led to the creation of many new institutions, including many in cities, such as the University of Wisconsin–Milwaukee, opened in 1956, and the University of Illinois Chicago Circle, opened in 1965. See J. Martin Klotsche's *The University of Wisconsin–Milwaukee: An Urban University* (Milwaukee: University of Wisconsin–Milwaukee, 1972), and Sharon Haar, *The City as Campus: Urbanism and Higher Education in Chicago* (Minneapolis: University of Minnesota Press, 2011).

2. *University of Cincinnati—Report of the President, 1945–1947*, 6. The university anticipated so many returning servicemen to apply to college that it instituted preferential admissions— accepting all former students returning from duty, admitting qualified residents of Cincinnati, and taking only nonresidents with "superior academic records." See "University of Cincinnati Office of the President: Admission Procedure for 1947," November 15, 1946, Raymond Walters Papers, box 16, folder 4, ARB.

3. *Report of the President, University of Cincinnati, 1967 to 1969,* 7; "Profs. Divided over Teaching in Wilson," *News Record,* April 24, 1970.

4. "Profs. Divided over Teaching in Wilson."

5. See Yanek Mieczkowski, *Eisenhower's Sputnik Moment: The Race for Space and World Prestige* (Ithaca, NY: Cornell University Press, 2013), especially 20–26, 68–70.

6. Clark Kerr, *The Uses of the University* (1963; rpt. Cambridge, MA: Harvard University Press, 1995), 86.

7. Robert M. Hutchins, *Freedom, Education, and the Fund: Essays and Addresses, 1946–1956* (New York: Meridian Books, 1956), 80.

8. The Research Office reported that classified research of a military nature ended at UC shortly after World War II. See University Senate Steering Committee, "The University and the World Beyond the Campus," n.d. (May 1970), 12, Campus Unrest Files, box 1, folder 10, ARB.

9. A good, short biography of Sabin can be found at http://www.sabin.org/legacy-albert-b-sabin. For a fuller telling of the vaccine story see David M. Oshinsky, *Polio: An American Story* (New York: Oxford University Press, 2005).

10. "George Rieveschl, 91, Allergy Reliever, Dies," *New York Times,* September 29, 2007. The first vice president for research was Hoke Greene, who served in a series of administrative posts.

11. The city also constructed University Avenue in 1914 as a new boundary between UC and Burnet Woods. See "An Ordinance—Number 206–1914," as found in Raymond Walters Papers, box 16, folder 2, ARB.

12. Report of the Superintendent, Mr. Tait (J. W. Tait) Re: Proposed Parking Facilities in Burnet Woods North of University Avenue (October 25, 1939), Burnet Woods File, 5410–181E549e, BCA.

13. "Memorandum Re: Meeting of Park Board and University Committee at the Offices of the Board of Park Commissioners," May 4, 1945, 7, Burnet Woods File, 5410–181E549e, BCA.

14. Ibid., 7.

15. Ibid., 9.

16. Ibid., 7, 9.

17. Petition to Board of Park Commissioners, April 18, 1945, Burnet Woods File, 5410–181E549c, BCA.

18. Petition to Board of Park Commissioners, n.d. (1945), Burnet Woods File, 5410–181E549c, BCA; "Please Sign and Mail," 6–6–1945, Burnet Woods File, 5410–181E549c, BCA.

19. Clifton Heights Welfare Association, "Should the University of Cincinnati Be Granted an Additional 19 Acres of Burnet Woods Park for Their Campus Expansion?" n.d., Burnet Woods File, 5410–18 1E549e, BCA.

20. Clifton Heights Welfare Association, "False Plea of University of Cincinnati," n.d., BCA.

21. Board of Park Commissioners to Board of Directors, UC, May 21, 1945, Charles P. Taft Papers, box 25, folder 2, CHLA.

22. Ed Macke to Members of City Council, n.d. (1949), Charles P. Taft Papers, box 25, folder 1, CHLA.

23. The committee lists appear on the letterhead. See Gilbert Bettman to Charles P. Taft, January 17, 1950, Charles P. Taft Papers, box 25, folder 2, CHLA.

24. The College of Applied Arts became the College of Design, Architecture & Art in 1961. The Department of Architecture offered planning courses through the 1960s, before the creation of a separate planning department. The city of Cincinnati had been a national leader in community and metropolitan planning, but faculty played no significant role in city planning

while UC was a municipal university. Planning did not become a school, and the college did not become DAAP, until 1982.

25. "UC Plan Is Defended by Dean," *Cincinnati Enquirer*, January 5, 1950.

26. Interestingly, no part of campus was actually in Clifton.

27. Mrs. E. Hengehold to Charles Taft, December 21, 1949, Charles P. Taft Papers, box 25, folder 1, CHLA.

28. "20 Dead in Smog," *New York Times*, November 1, 1948; "'Smog' Linked to 18 Deaths in Day and Hospital Jam in Donora, PA," *New York Times*, October 31, 1948. The most complete study of Donora is Lynne Page Snyder, "The Death-Dealing Smog over Donora, Pennsylvania: Industrial Air Pollution, Public Health, and Federal Policy, 1915–1963" (PhD diss., University of Pennsylvania, 1994). Snyder published synopses of her work, including "Revisiting Donora, Pennsylvania's 1948 Air Pollution Disaster," in *Devastation and Renewal: An Environmental History of Pittsburgh and Its Region* edited by Joel A. Tarr (Pittsburgh: University of Pittsburgh Press, 2003).

29. "20 Dead in Smog."

30. The most important study came from the US Public Health Service, which concluded that no *single* substance could have caused the deaths, and so some "combination of substances" must have caused the "clinical syndrome." H. H. Schrenk, et al., "Air Pollution in Donora, Pa.: Epidemiology of the Unusual Smog Episode of October 1948," *Public Health Bulletin No. 306* (Washington, DC: Public Health Service, 1949).

31. Kehoe had made his career through contracts with industry, of course, and Donora posed an opportunity to develop a new relationship with US Steel.

32. Mills noticed that white men in polluted areas were much more likely to die of lung cancer than either black men or women of any race. They were also much more likely to smoke.

33. Clarence A. Mills, "The Donora Smog Disaster," *Hygeia* (October 1949): 684–86. See also Mills, *Air Pollution and Community Health* (Boston: Christopher Publishing House, 1954), 29–43.

34. Clarence Mills, "Nation's Spotlight Focused on Donora," *Herald-American* (Donora), November 8, 1948.

35. "Borough Council Ready to Launch Smog Investigation," *Herald-American* (Donora), November 8, 1948; "Nation's Spotlight Focused on Donora," *Herald-American* (Donora), November 8, 1948.

36. In addition to the human deaths, 800 animals also perished, most of them on farms.

37. "Smog Called Threat to Many Communities," *New York Times*, November 20, 1948; "Donora Smog Held Near Catastrophe," *New York Times*, December 25, 1948.

38. James M. Crowe to Kehoe, January 24, 1949; Kehoe to James Crowe, January 27, 1949, Kehoe Papers, box 5.3, folder 5, WCA. In other correspondence a Kettering employee noted, "Dr. Clarence Mills, who has been doing some unwarranted writing for the public press, is not associated with us and does not have access to our data." William F. Ashe to Dr. Kintner, Illinois Institute of Technology, January 6, 1949, Kehoe Papers, box 5.3, folder 4, WCA.

39. Kehoe appears not to have visited Donora personally, instead sending two trusted laboratory researchers. Much of their work consisted of medical exams of 215 workers at the two plants. About 40 percent of the men volunteered that they had experienced symptoms during the episode. Kehoe did not conduct community surveys, but he did send Ed Largent, an expert on fluoride testing, who took samples of vegetation around the city. These samples, along with those taken from the men, the industrial plants, and the atmosphere, were sent back to Kettering for analysis. See Medical Exams, Draft Report, Kehoe Papers, box 5, folder 2, WCA. Much of the correspondence in the Kehoe Papers is between the lab and Reed,

Smith, Shaw & McClay, the Pittsburgh law firm of American Steel and Wire. Jacob Cholak, Kettering's chief analyst, was in charge of research.

40. Early draft of the Health Survey—Between May 30, 1949 and July 2, 1949, Kehoe Papers, box 5.1, folder 2, WCA.

41. Kehoe to Harvey Jordan, May 24, 1949, Kehoe Papers, box 5.3, folder 5, WCA.

42. "Donora Smog Cases: Evidence of Foreseeability" [n.d., circa 1950], Kehoe Papers, box 5, folder 3, WCA. This undated and unattributed document was undoubtedly prepared for (and perhaps by) Reed, Smith, Shaw & McClay, the Pittsburgh law firm of American Steel and Wire. It contains a section titled "Clarence Mills." It reads in part, "Plaintiffs' expert, Mills, has been agitating for some years that 'smoke' affects health. His theory is based on statistical correlation on respiratory morbidity and mortality with soot-fall. Mills' publications both before and after the smog have been collected. His deposition was taken and much of his recent newspaper publicity has been collected. Any first-hand knowledge of his pronouncements, public or private, should be contributed. It is important that we be prepared to rebut Mills' testimony."

43. Carl Glock (sp?) to Kehoe, April 19, 1951, Kehoe Papers, box 5.3, folder 5, WCA. [$265,000 is approximately $2.6 million in today's dollars.]

44. Mills, *Air Pollution and Community Health*, 13.

45. Ibid., 119.

46. Ibid., 15, 53.

47. For a broader assessment of postwar science and the effort to blunt regulation see Naomi Oreskes and Erik Conway, *Merchants of Doubt: How a Handful of Scientists Obscured the Truth on Issues from Tobacco Smoke to Global Warming* (New York: Bloomsbury, 2011). Interestingly this wonderful book does not address Robert Kehoe, one of the greatest of his generation of merchants of doubt.

48. City Planning Commission, *Report on the Avondale-Corryville General Neighborhood Renewal Plan* (Cincinnati, 1959).

49. "Corryville Residents Protest Jefferson Avenue Extension," *Cincinnati Post,* June 16, 1956; City Planning Commission, *Report on the Avondale-Corryville General Neighborhood Renewal Plan,* 4. The final plan, published a year later, clearly took into account community concerns about the emphasis on blight, and instead it emphasized conserving the "old values" of the neighborhoods. See City Planning Commission, *Avondale-Corryville General Neighborhood Renewal Plan* (December 1960), 9.

50. City Planning Commission, *Report on the Avondale-Corryville General Neighborhood Renewal Plan* (1959), 4. The importance of the hospitals to the planning process became even clearer when the City Planning Commission published a separate *Plan for the Hospital Complex: A Part of the Avondale-Corryville Urban Renewal Area* (December 1963).

51. "Rebuilt Jefferson Ave Reopens," *Cincinnati Post-Times Star,* May 3, 1966; *University–Community Tension and Urban Campus Form,* Vol. 1 (1972), 29.

52. "Science Complex–Engineering Complex," May 23, 1964 (No author), Walter C. Langsam Papers, box 3, folder 6, ARB.

53. "Decal Holders Guaranteed Parking Places!" *News Record,* October 6, 1966; "UC Goal: Garages under New Buildings," *Cincinnati Enquirer,* Feb 8, 1969.

54. "Decal Holders Guaranteed Parking Places!"

55. "Minutes of the Medical Center Parking Committee Meeting," February 7, 1972, Warren Bennis Papers, UA-78-2, box 3, folder 15A, ARB.

56. "UC Goal: Garages under New Buildings."

57. *University–Community Tension and Urban Campus Form*, Vol. 1 (1972), 32, 33.

58. Robert Carroll, Hayden May, and Samuel Noe, *University–Community Tension and Urban Campus Form* (University of Cincinnati, October 1972), 41. "City May Sell Two Land Tracts for Hospital Lot," *Cincinnati Enquirer,* September 23, 1970. Other urban universities have also had long-running conflicts with neighbors, including Columbia and the University of Pennsylvania. See special issue of *Planning Perspectives*.

59. *University–Community Tension and Urban Campus Form*, Vol. 1 (1972), 34.

60. Sawyer Hall was demolished in 2006. In subsequent years its sisters, Morgens and Scioto, were completely refurbished into glass towers.

61. "Wipe Out UC's Rodents," *News Record*, April 15, 1965. The shift from private security guards to trained university police occurred with little fanfare. See Edward R. Bridgeman, "Today's Campus Cop Wears a Different Cap," *Cincinnati Horizons* (December 1979), 15, 18.

62. Letter to the Editor, *News Record*, April 29, 1965.

63. For more on the basketball program see *Bearcats! The Story of Basketball at the University of Cincinnati* (Louisville: Harmony House Publishers, 1998), by Kevin Grace, Greg Hand, Tom Hathaway, and Carey Hoffman. See also Oscar Robertson's autobiography, *The Big O: My Life, My Times, My Game* (New York: Rodale, 2003).

64. Statement of George Smith, Athletic Director, "UC Football '67," Walter C. Langsam Papers, box 23, folder 8, ARB.

65. "Use of Nippert Undetermined," *News Record*, May 16, 1969; "Death of the Bearcats," *News Record*, April 19, 1968.

66. Sports Reference—College Football, http://www.sports-reference.com/cfb/schools/cincinnati/; George Smith to William Nester, February 28, 1969, Walter C. Langsam Papers, box 23, folder 8, ARB.

67. In 1970 the MAC consisted of Toledo, Miami, Ohio University, Western Michigan, Kent State, and Bowling Green.

68. Robert H. Wessel to William Nester, August 12, 1969, Walter C. Langsam Papers, box 23, folder 7, ARB.

69. Ibid.

70. "Memo: WGUC Purpose and Activities April 1979," WGUC Files, box 1, folder—WGUC History, ARB. For the founding story see Bruce I. Petrie, "Station WGUC: From Sputnik to NPR Satellite," *Cincinnati Historical Society Bulletin* (Summer 1981): 86–108.

71. "WGUC Makes Debut," *News Record,* September 19, 1960.

72. "Dialing U.C., Radio and T.V.," *News Record,* October 6, 1960.

73. "WGUC Airs Educational Programing," *News Record*, October 19, 1961.

74. "Weekly TV-Radio AM Schedule," *News Record*, December 15, 1960; "Dialing U.C., Radio and T.V."; "Radio-TV," *News Record*, March 23, 1961. In the early 1960s, the *News Record* published WGUC's music schedule, so that listeners could anticipate upcoming symphonies and operas.

75. "A Brief History of WGUC-FM 90.9," WGUC Files, box 1, folder—WGUC History, ARB; "WGUC Turns to Listeners for Support, Expansion," *News Record*, October 30, 1973.

76. The conservatory was founded in 1867 by Clara Baur; the college was formed in 1878 by Reuben Springer.

77. "City College-Conservatory Becomes UC's 14th College," *News Record*, September 17, 1962.

78. "University Becomes Home," *Cincinnati Enquirer*, November 28, 1954; "Ground Broken for UC Building," *Cincinnati Enquirer*, March 11, 1954; "Formal Merger Sunday of UC, Pharmacy College," *Cincinnati Enquirer*, November 21, 1954.

Chapter 7 A University at War with Itself

1. Clark Kerr, *The Uses of the University* (1963; rpt. Cambridge, MA: Harvard University Press, 2001), 7.

2. Robert M. Hutchins, *Freedom, Education, and the Fund: Essays and Addresses, 1946–1956* (New York: Meridian Books, 1956), 145, 147.

3. Neal Berte, "Senior Oration," June 10, 1962, Walter C. Langsam Papers, box 30, folder 5, ARB.

4. Remarks by Dr. Bonner, Provost, to Advisory Council, February 17, 1969, Walter C. Langsam Papers, box 2, folder 2, ARB.

5. John D. Millett, "Observations on Student Disruption," [circa 1970], Campus Unrest Files, box 1, folder 4, ARB.

6. "UC Student Jumped, Killed in Latest Clifton Incident," *News Record*, March 30, 1967; "What Protection for Coeds? Administration States Policies," *News Record*, October 1966; "UC Student Dies Following Beating," *Cincinnati Enquirer*, March 25, 1967; "UC Slaying Triggers Police, Dog Patrols," *Cincinnati Enquirer*, March 28, 1967.

7. Letter to the Editor, *News Record*, April 6, 1967.

8. Interestingly, Baker lived in Madeira, at the time an essentially all-white and distant suburb.

9. John Winget to Walter Langsam, April 27, 1967, Walter C. Langsam Papers, box 23, folder 9, ARB.

10. "West End Ed. Project Sponsors Tutor Program," *News Record*, April 4, 1963; "W.E.E.P. Earns $75 for Tutor Program," *News Record*, April 4, 1963; "Folk Singer, Sheila McKenzie to Give Concert Friday, Oct. 18," *News Record*, October 17, 1963; "W.E.E.P.—Just One Case in Many," *News Record*, October 24, 1963; "Presbyterians Obtain Home for Westminster Foundation," *Cincinnati Enquirer*, November 26, 1952; "Holt Leaving to Accept Chicago Post," *Cincinnati Enquirer*, December 15, 1967.

11. "WEEP Seeks Additional Tutors," *News Record*, May 28, 1964; "WEEP Fall Series Needs Five Hundred Coed Tutors," *News Record*, September 30, 1965; "WEEP Offers Opportunities in Volunteer Tutorial Work," *News Record*, January 13, 1966.

12. "Proposal for a Student Volunteer Bureau," Myron Bush Papers, box 10, folder 5, ARB.

13. [Ginny Lambert], "Proposal for a Student Volunteer Center," March 6, 1967, Walter C. Langsam Papers, box 23, folder 9, ARB.

14. "Violence Strikes Down UC Grad," *News Record*, April 12, 1968.

15. "Guard Moves on Rioters; Curfew Slapped on City," *Cincinnati Enquirer*, April 9, 1968. On the transformation of Avondale see Charles F. Casey-Leininger, "Making the Second Ghetto in Cincinnati: Avondale, 1925–70," in *Race and the City: Work, Community, and Protest in Cincinnati, 1820–1970*, edited by Henry Louis Taylor Jr. (Urbana: University of Illinois Press, 1993), 232–57.

16. For broader context of the 1968 riots see Thomas J. Sugrue, *Sweet Land of Liberty: The Forgotten Struggle for Civil Rights in the North* (New York: Random House, 2008).

17. "U.C.'s Role in the Urban Crisis," April 18, 1968, Myron Bush Papers, box 3, folder 20, ARB.

18. "UBA Submits Demands; To Meet with Langsam," *News Record*, May 21, 1968. On the importance of black student activism around the country see Martha Biondi, *The Black Revolution on Campus* (Berkeley: University of California Press, 2012).

19. "UBA Submits Demands; To Meet with Langsam"; "Another Black Course Offered; UBA VP Comments on Others," *News Record*, October 15, 1968.

20. "UBA Submits Demands; To Meet with Langsam"; "Another Black Course Offered." To improve black student recruitment, Admissions hired its first fulltime black officer in September 1968.

21. The Establishment of a Department of Black Studies in the College of Arts and Sciences" (January 1970), 3, 10, box 9, folder 156—UBFA, UBA, etc. (1), Office of the President—Warren Bennis, UA-78-2, ARB.

22. *University of Cincinnati Catalog, 1971–1972.* On the evolution of Black Studies see Biondi, *Black Revolution on Campus*, 241–67.

23. Letter from UBA to Langsam, May 1, 1968, box 20, folder 2, Office of the President—Walter C. Langsam, UA-87-9, ARB.

24. Minutes of the University Housing Registry Committee Meeting, June 4, 1968; Minutes of University Housing Registry Committee Meeting, November 25, 1968, box 20, folder 2, Office of the President—Walter C. Langsam, UA-87-9, ARB.

25. Minutes of the University Housing Registry Committee Meeting, September 19, 1968, box 20, folder 2, Office of the President—Walter C. Langsam, UA-87-9, ARB; "Housing Registry Established as Campus Makes Racial Strides," *News Record*, October 4, 1968.

26. Thomas Bonner to Students and Colleagues at the University of Cincinnati, May 21, 1969, box 1, folder 9, Campus Unrest Files, ARB; "Housing Registry Established as Campus Makes Racial Strides"

27. The *News Record* acknowledged the importance of the bridge by granting it a capital B by 1969.

28. "Student Disorders Unfurl on Campus Community," *News Record*, May 23, 1969.

29. Walter Langsam, "Response to the Central Committee of the United Black Association," May 27, 1969, box 1, folder 9, Campus Unrest Files, UA-04-012, ARB.

30. "Black Enrollment Rising Sharply, U.S. Data Show," *Chronicle of Higher Education* (October 4, 1971).

31. Garland G. Parker to Bennis, November 16, 1971, box 9, folder 156—UBFA, UBA, etc. (1), Office of the President—Warren Bennis, UA-78-2, ARB.

32. G. E. Mitchell to Mary Woelfel, November 18, 1971, box 9, folder 156—UBFA, UBA, etc. (1), Office of the President—Warren Bennis, UA-78-2, ARB.

33. On 1960s activism more broadly see Todd Gitlin, *The Sixties: Years of Hope, Days of Rage* (New York: Bantam Books, 1987).

34. Remarks by Dr. Bonner, Provost, to Advisory Council, February 17, 1969, box 2, folder 2, Office of the President—Walter C. Langsam, UA-87-9, ARB.

35. "Students Propose Changes to Langsam," *News Record,* January 14, 1969. Altman earned a JD from the College of Law in 1974.

36. *Board of Directors Minutes*, March 4, 1969, 38.

37. "First Forum Draws Cross-Section, Dissolving, Restructuring Discussed," *News Record*, January 21, 1969.

38. "SDS Members Discuss Issues; Reveal Philosophy, Objectives," *News Record*, November 23, 1966; "SDS Structures Campus Chapter," *News Record*, April 4, 1969. On SDS as a national movement see Kirkpatrick Sale, *SDS: The Rise and Development of the Students for a Democratic Society* (New York: Random House, 1973).

39. "Demonstrators Interrupt ROTC Review," *News Record*, May 13, 1969.

40. "ROTC Debate Draws Comment," *News Record*, May 13, 1969. For a description of the ROTC programs as they existed in 1970 see University Senate Steering Committee, "The University and the World Beyond the Campus," n.d. (May 1970), 6–11, box 1, folder 10, Campus Unrest Files, ARB.

41. William Nester to Walter Langsam, July 17, 1969, box 6, folder 1, Office of the President—Walter C. Langsam, UA-87-9, ARB; "UC Students Suspended for May Protest Roles," *Cincinnati Enquirer,* July 25, 1969.

42. *Cincinnati Post & Times Star*, October 16, 1969; "Painter, Kornick Praise Student Conduct," *News Record*, October 17, 1969; "Cincinnati Students Join in Moratorium," *Cincinnati Post & Times Star*, October 15, 1969.

43. President's Administrative Council, Special Meeting May 1, 1970, box 1, folder 20, Campus Unrest Files, UA-04-012, ARB.

44. Ibid.; author's correspondence with Gene Lewis, June 1, 2016.

45. Tom Bonner, "An Open Letter to the Faculty," May 21, 1970, box 155, folder 5, Theodore M. Berry Papers, US-93-03, ARB.

46. "Action without Violence," *News Record*, May 6, 1970.

47. "The Strike Demands of May 6, 1970," box 1, folder 4, Campus Unrest Files, UA-04-012, ARB.

48. Gene D. Lewis to University Faculty, May 21, 1970, box 1, folder 9, Campus Unrest Files, UA-04-012, ARB.

49. Bonner, "An Open Letter to the Faculty"; "University Grading Policy Approved by Academic Cabinet and President," May 19, 1970, box 1, folder 4, Campus Unrest Files, UA-04-012, ARB.

50. University Senate Steering Committee, "The University and the World Beyond the Campus," n.d. (May 1970), box 1, folder 10, Campus Unrest Files, ARB.

51. "The Vocal Majority," *News Record*, May 6, 1970.

52. Michael Dale speech, box 1, folder 4, Campus Unrest Files, UA-04-012, ARB.

53. WKRC Editorial, May 20, 1970, box 62, folder 14, Eugene P. Ruehlmann Papers, US-74-02, ARB.

54. "AAUP Statement before Hearings Subcommittee of the UC Presidential Task Force by President Arnold Schrier," July 7, 1970, box 62, folder 15, Eugene P. Ruehlmann Papers, US-74-02, ARB.

55. "Environmental Teach-in Begins Tomorrow, Week-Long Program Highlighted by Earth Day," *News Record*, April 21, 1970.

56. Mrs. J. R. Larkin to Ruehlmann, no date [February 1969], box 62, folder 13, Eugene P. Ruehlmann Papers, US-74-02, ARB.

57. Harold and Sue Snyder et al., to Walter Langsam, May 19, 1970, box 1, folder 9, Campus Unrest, UA-04-012. ARB.

58. University Senate Steering Committee, "The University and the World Beyond the Campus."

59. Walter Langsam to Board of Directors, September 21, 1970, box 1, folder 11, Campus Unrest Files, ARB.

60. Documents related to Finger and Reinbach can be found in box 1, folder 10 of the Campus Unrest Files, ARB; "Jury Finds James Finger Guilty," *Cincinnati Enquirer*, May 26, 1971; James Finger to Warren Bennis, February 26, 1972, box 3, folder 8D, Office of the President—Warren Bennis, UA-78-2, ARB.

61. "Two Year College to Expand," *News Record*, April 6, 1961.

62. "Branch of UC to Be Built by 1967," *Cincinnati Post Times-Star*, February 16, 1966; "New Blue Ash Scene," *Cincinnati Enquirer*, February 16, 1966; "Blue Ash Extension to Open Sept., '67," *News Record*, February 17, 1966; "Walter's Extension Planning Open House This Sunday," *News Record*, November 3, 1967.

63. "A Proposal to Develop a New Community in the Cincinnati Metropolitan Area," (n.d., circa 1968), box 4, folder 21A, Office of the President—Warren Bennis, UA-78-2, ARB.

64. "Board of Regents Approves Branch School in Clermont," *News Record*, October 21, 1969.

65. Walter Langsam, "Clermont County Land Presentation Banquet," April 15, 1970, box 4, folder 21A, Office of the President—Warren Bennis, UA-78-2, ARB.

66. Ibid.

67. Mary K. Branch to Walter Langsam, October 9, 1969, box 4, folder 21A, Office of the President—Warren Bennis, UA-78-2, ARB.

68. "UC's Enrollment Passes 35,000; A&S Increases by 16 Per Cent," *News Record*, October 21, 1969.

Chapter 8 A University without Walls

1. *The Report of the President's Commission on Campus Unrest* (Washington, DC: US Gov't. Printing Office, 1970).

2. Warren Bennis, "Teach or Travel," in *Today, Tomorrow . . . and the Day After* (University of Cincinnati, 1972), 9; "Mid-Year Report: University of Cincinnati, Warren Bennis, President, September, 1971–March, 1972," 4, box 1, folder 6, Office of the President—Warren Bennis, UA-78-2, ARB.

3. *University of Cincinnati Bulletin: Annual Catalog of All Colleges, 1945–46*; *University of Cincinnati Bulletin: Annual Catalog of All Colleges, 1969–70*.

4. Warren Bennis, *The Unconscious Conspiracy: Why Leaders Can't Lead* (New York: Amacon, 1976), 26.

5. Warren Bennis, "Report of the President, University of Cincinnati, 1971–1973" (Pamphlet held at ARB), 1.

6. Ibid., 8, 9.

7. "Profs. Divided over Teaching in Wilson," *News-Record*, April 24, 1970; "History Prof Introduces Exciting New Method of Teaching with Films, Music," *News Record*, October 21, 1969.

8. William Nester to Warren Bennis, July 22, 1971, box 4, folder "Univ. Problems and Priorities ('71)," Office of the President, Warren Bennis, UA-77-10, ARB.

9. Warren Bennis, Rough Draft of Midyear Report (March 1972), 2, box 1, folder 6, Office of the President—Warren Bennis, UA-78-2, ARB.

10. Ibid., 17; Bennis, "Report of the President, University of Cincinnati, 1971–1973," 6; Stanley Aronowitz, *The Knowledge Factory: Dismantling the Corporate University and Creating True Higher Learning* (Boston: Beacon Press, 2000), 132–33.

11. Charles F. Casey-Leininger, "Making the Second Ghetto in Cincinnati: Avondale, 1925–70," in *Race and the City: Work, Community, and Protest in Cincinnati, 1820–1970*, edited by Henry Louis Taylor Jr. (Urbana: University of Illinois Press, 1993), 232–57.

12. "'Let the Sun Shine In—Theme," *News Record*, November 9, 1971.

13. "Mid-Year Report: University of Cincinnati, Warren Bennis, President, September, 1971–March, 1972," 4, box 1, folder 6, Office of the President—Warren Bennis, UA-78-2, ARB.

14. Carnegie Commission on Higher Education, *The Campus and the City: Maximizing Assets and Reducing Liabilities* (New York: McGraw-Hill, 1972), 4.

15. Bennis, Rough Draft of Midyear Report (March 1972), 18–19.

16. In 1969 the Student Volunteer Center became the Student Community Involvement Program. See "SCIP Involves Students in Community Relations," *News Record*, October 7, 1969.

17. "Synopsis of Programs" (n.d., circa 1972), box 2, folder 8-D, Office of the President—Warren Bennis, UA-78-2, ARB. See also the administration responses to "Grievances Presented to President Bennis by the Black Student Government Caucus and the United Black Association," November 22, 1972, box 2, folder—Johnson Advisory Comm. on Black Concerns—1, Office of the President—Warren Bennis, UA-77-10, ARB.

18. "Synopsis of Programs" (n.d., circa 1972).

19. "ASPIRE, SCIP Merger Suggested," *News Record*, April 19, 1974.

20. John Schneider to Bennis, December 19, 1972, box 2, folder 8-D, Office of the President—Warren Bennis, UA-78-2, ARB.

21. "Affirmative Action," *Candid Campus* (December 4, 1972), 1. For the national context see Terry Anderson, *The Pursuit of Fairness: A History of Affirmative Action* (New York: Oxford University Press, 2004).

22. "Mid-Year Report: University of Cincinnati, Warren Bennis President, September, 1971–March, 1972," 27.

23. See box 1, folder 6, Office of the President—Warren Bennis, UA-78-2, ARB.

24. Zane Miller to Members of the Advisory Committee, Vice President for Urban Affairs, March 15, 1972, box 2, folder—VP for Urban Affairs—Search Com. (2), Office of the President—Warren Bennis, UA-78-2, ARB.

25. "Dr. Charles Johnson Named New Vice President for Metropolitan Studies," *Candid Campus*, May 24, 1972; "Johnson Opens Up," *Candid Campus,* December 8, 1972.

26. Johnson Memo to Advisory Committee on Black Concerns, January 22, 1973, box 2, folder–Johnson Advisory Comm. on Black Concerns—2, Office of the President—Warren Bennis, UA-78-2, ARB. For a short history of Cincinnati State University see http://www.cincinnatistate.edu/about-cs/cincinnati-state-history.

27. "Grievances Presented to President Bennis by the Black Student Government Caucus and the United Black Association," November 22, 1972, box 2, folder—Johnson Advisory Comm. on Black Concerns—1, Office of the President, Warren Bennis, UA-77-10, ARB; Advisory Committee the President, January 23, 1973, box 2, folder—Johnson Advisory on Comm. on Black Concerns—2, Office of the President, Warren Bennis, UA-77-10, ARB.

28. "Grievances Presented to President Bennis by the Black Student Government Caucus and the United Black Association."

29. "Johnson Cites Bennis' 'Non-Support' as Reason for Resignation," *News Record*, August 7, 1974.

30. Charles Johnson to Warren Bennis, June 23, 1974, box 156, folder 3, Theodore M. Berry Papers, ARB.

31. Melvin Posey, "The Resignation of Dr. Charles Johnson: An Appraisal," box 156, folder 3, Theodore M. Berry Papers, ARB.

32. University of Cincinnati Press Release, October 1, 1974, box 156, folder 3, Theodore M. Berry Papers, ARB.

33. Jonathan Engel, *Poor People's Medicine: Medicaid and American Charity Care since 1965* (Durham, NC: Duke University Press, 2006); Beatrix Hoffman, *Health Care for Some: Rights and Rationing in the United States since 1930* (Chicago: University of Chicago Press, 2012), 143–66.

34. University of Cincinnati/Cincinnati General Hospital/College of Medicine, "Hospital Construction Program (Out-Patient) Phase III," August 14, 1968, box 15, folder 1, Office of the President—Walter C. Langsam, UA-87-9, ARB.

35. Gene Inch, "Cincinnati: A People's Health Movement," *Health/PAC Bulletin* (September 1971): 2–7; "Report of the Medical Center Committee," July 9, 1971, box 3, folder 15A, Office of the President—Warren Bennis, UA-78-2, ARB.

36. Peggy Chenault to Rodger Mendenhall, April 9, 1970, box 23, folder 9, Office of the President—Walter C. Langsam, UA-87-9, ARB.

37. Chenault to Mendenhall, April 9, 1970, box 23, folder 9, Office of the President—Walter C. Langsam, UA-87-9, ARB.

38. "Health Group Wants Changes at General," *Cincinnati Post*, June 23, 1972.

39. William R. Meyers to Warren Bennis, December 14, 1971, box 3, folder 15A, Office of the President—Warren Bennis, UA-78-2, ARB.

40. Minutes of the Medical Center Advisory Committee, October 25, 1971, box 1, folder 7B, Vice Pres. & Director of Med. Center, Office of the President—Warren Bennis, UA-78-2, ARB. At this meeting Dr. Gall asked Charles Barrett to take the lead on the radiation issue.

41. Eric R. Chabrow, "JFA Report Critical of UC Radiation Project," *News Record*, January 28, 1772. See also *Radiation Experiments Conducted by the University of Cincinnati Medical School with Department of Defense Funding*, Hearing before the Subcommittee on Administrative Law and Governmental Relations, 103rd Congress, 2nd session, April 11, 1994; and the documents gathered by Martha Stephens for her book *The Treatment: The Story of Those Who Died in the Cincinnati Radiation Tests* (Durham, NC: Duke University Press, 2002): Martha Stephens—The Cincinnati Radiation Experiments: 1960–1972, UA-05-05. Stephens was a member of the Junior Faculty Association Committee that wrote the 1972 report.

42. Minutes of Medical Center Advisory Committee, February 9, 1972, box 1, folder 7B, Office of the President—Warren Bennis, UA-78-2, ARB.

43. Medical School Faculty Forum, April 25, 1972, box 1, folder 7B, Office of the President—Warren Bennis, UA-78-2, ARB.

44. Ibid.

45. Bobbie Sterne to Jane Earley, May 16, 1972, box 10, folder 172, Office of the President—Warren Bennis, UA-78-2, ARB.

46. "Committee Claims Hospital Overcrowded," *Cincinnati Post*, June 20, 1972.

47. "Vote Asked to Get Change in Hospital Administration," *Cincinnati Post*, August 16, 1972.

48. "Who's Going to Take Care of the Poor People?" *Cincinnati Post*, October 19, 1974; "Protesters: Pickets Demand More Money for Patients," *News Record*, October 15, 1974.

49. "Grievances and Fears," *News Record*, March 3, 1972.

50. Larry Jost, Assistant Professor of Philosophy, Paul Kaplan, Assistant Professor of Sociology, Glen Whaley, Instructor of Sociology, to Warren Bennis, November 17, 1972; Richard Towner to William Nester, November 20, 1972, box 2, folder 8d, Office of the President—Warren Bennis, UA-78-2, ARB; Author's email correspondence with Larry Jost, November 23, 2015.

51. Richard Towner to William Nester, June 18, 1973, box 2, folder 8d, Office of the President—Warren Bennis, UA-78-2, ARB.

52. "McDonald's Faces Hair Challenge," *News Record*, October 23, 1973.

53. "McDonald's Compromises on Hair," *News Record*, October 26, 1973.

54. "Letter," *News Record*, October 9, 1973.

55. Photo caption, *News Record*, November 19, 1974.

56. "Activism Gone: Students Today Concerned with Careers," *News Record*, October 9, 1973.

57. "Faculty Statistical Count Including All Appointments and Actions, October 6, 1970," box 3, folder 7, Office of the President—Walter C. Langsam, UA-87-9, ARB. See similar statistics for previous years in folder 8.

58. US Department of Justice, Overview of Title IX of the Education Amendments of 1972, https://www.justice.gov/crt/overview-title-ix-education-amendments-1972-20-usc-1681-et-seq.

59. Classifieds, *News Record*, February 25, 1972; "The Strawberry Statement," *News Record*, May 9, 1972; "Women Meet Today, Plan Upcoming Year," *News Record*, May 16, 1972.

60. Women's Center Steering Committee, "Statement on General Hospital to City Council," April 18, 1972, box 3, folder 15A, Office of the President—Warren Bennis, UA-78-2, ARB.

61. "Day Care Gains Momentum," *News Record*, May 9, 1972; "Group Requests Higher Priority for Day Care," *News Record*, May 16, 1972.

62. "UC Dedicates New Nursery Building," *Cincinnati Enquirer*, November 25, 1969; Letter to the Editor, *News Record*, September 28, 1973; "Child Co-Op Plans Event," *News Record*, November

30, 1973; "Money and Space Problems Hold Up Day Care Center," *News Record*, November 6, 1973. See also "History of the Arlitt Center," http://cech.uc.edu/centers/arlitt/about_arlitt/history.html.

63. "Child Care," *News Record*, May 27, 1975.

64. "UC Women Are Organizing," *News Record*, January 25, 1974; Kelsey Kennedy, "Women Helping Women Raises Awareness, Resources for Sexual Assault Survivors," *City Beat*, March 12, 2014.

65. "New Head Sets Women's Studies Goals," *News Record*, July 17, 1974; *University of Cincinnati Catalog*, 1975–76 (vol. 71), 96–97.

66. "Requests Expand Judaic Studies to Degree Program," *News Record*, January 7, 1975; "Anti-Gay Position Will Embarrass University," *News Record*, April 16, 1974.

67. Adrian Edward Hall, "Towers and Factories: The University of Cincinnati and America's Higher Education, 1960–1980," (Master's paper, University of Cincinnati, 2006); Lyman A. Glenny et al., *Presidents Confront Reality: From Edifice Complex to University without Walls* (San Francisco: Jossey-Bass Publishers, 1976).

68. "The Changing Face of Campus," *News Record*, April 30, 1964.

69. *University–Community Tension and Urban Campus Form*, Vol. 1 (1972), 28.

70. The groundbreaking for the EPA building was on June 28, 1972. See Herb Pence Jr., "Safeguarding Life's Quality," *Cincinnati Magazine* (September 1972), 36.

71. Savage, Chappelear, Schulte and Associates, Inc., "Comprehensive Study and Master Plan for Burnet Woods" (December 1972), 20.

72. "Burnet Woods Lodge Urged," *Cincinnati Enquirer*, March 6, 1975; "Burnet Woods Restaurant Out," *Cincinnati Enquirer*, April 4, 1975.

73. "New Stadium, Arena Proposed," *News Record*, July 16, 1975.

74. "UC Trustees Back Plan to Build New Center," *Cincinnati Enquirer*, October 5, 1977; "UC, Coliseum Won't Vie, Say Trustees," *Cincinnati Post*, October 5, 1977; "The All-Wrong Arena," *Cincinnati Post*, September 7, 1977. The arena gained the support of Myrl H. Shoemaker, an Ohio representative, for whom the building, completed ten years later, was eventually named. Shoemaker died of cancer before the building opened.

75. James K. Robinson, ed., *A Rededication to Scholarship: Papers Presented at the Dedication to the New Central Library, University of Cincinnati, April 25–27, 1979* (University of Cincinnati, 1980), 45.

76. Ibid., 1, 2.

77. *Report of the President: A Summary of the Sixteen Years of the Presidency of Walter C. Langsam, 1955–1971* (University of Cincinnati, 1971); "Vote for UC's State Affiliation," *Cincinnati Enquirer*, October 24, 1967.

78. "Putting UC in State System Called Boost for All Ohioans," *Cincinnati Post*, April 13, 1967; "U.C.'s Financial Dilemma Outlined," *Candid Campus*, November 29, 1972, box 2, folder 7C, Office of the President—Warren Bennis, UA-78-2, ARB.

79. "UC Confronts Issue of Going State," *Cincinnati Enquirer*, May 6, 1975; "UC Fighting Off State Takeover," *Cincinnati Enquirer*, May 5, 1975; "UC Heads toward State Control," *Cincinnati Post*, May 6, 1975.

80. Howard A. Mueller Jr. and Charles A. Berry, "A University within a City: Toward an Economic Profile of the University of Cincinnati" (January 1974), 1, box 155, folder 14, Theodore M. Berry Papers, ARB; "UC Report on Demography of Student Body," University of Cincinnati News Release, July 15, 1975, box 79, folder 5, Charles P. Taft II Papers, MSS 562, CHLA; B. Kesterson Dietrich, "Will UC 'Go State'? It's Now Up to the Voters," *Cincinnati Post*, October 27, 1975.

81. Warren Bennis, Guest Editorial, WKRC, June 3, 1975, box 78, folder 6, Charles P. Taft II Papers, MSS 562, CHLA; "Vote 'Yes' Thrice," "Student Forum," *News Record*, June 4, 1976; "Voters Approve State Status for UC," *Cincinnati Enquirer*, June 9, 1976.

Chapter 9 Toward a Third Century

1. With the shift from municipal to state ownership the board members were now trustees rather than directors.

2. "Winkler Named Acting President," *News Record*, July 20, 1977; "While You Were Away . . . ," *News Record*, September 30, 1970; "The Passage at UC," *Cincinnati Post*, July 2, 1977.

3. Dawn Fuller, "UC Enrollment History," September 14, 2011, http://www.uc.edu/news/ NR.aspx?id=14195.

4. John Bryan to Joseph Steger (email), September 4, 1999, box 16, folder 21, University College (8), Steger Papers, ARB. For a discussion of the danger of the "suburbanization of the intellect," a consequence of the urban university's turn toward suburbia, see Thomas Bender, "Scholarship, Local Life, and the Necessity of Worldliness," in *The Urban University and Its Identity: Roots, Location, Roles*, edited by Herman van der Wusten (Dordrecht, The Netherlands: Kluwer Academic Publishers, 1998), 18.

5. See for example, "Despite Report after Report, Unrest Endures in Cincinnati," *New York Times*, April 16, 2001.

6. Barbara R. Bergmann, "Bloated Administration, Blighted Campuses," *Academe* 77, no. 6 (November–December 1991): 12–16; John W. Curtis and Saranna Thornton, "Losing Focus: The Annual Report on the Economic Status of the Profession, 2013–14," *Academe* (March–April 2014): 7. For a longer discussion of these trends, see Benjamin Ginsberg, *The Fall of the Faculty: The Rise of the All-Administrative University and Why It Matters* (New York: Oxford University Press, 2011).

7. "UC, City Clash on Hospital," *Cincinnati Enquirer*, March 12, 1998. See also Linda Vaccariello, "Hospital, Heal Thyself," *Cincinnati Magazine*, October 1996, 60–67.

8. Robert M. Hutchins, *Freedom, Education, and the Fund: Essays and Addresses, 1946–1956* (New York: Meridian Books, 1956), 76.

9. Clark Kerr, *The Uses of the University* (Cambridge, MA: Harvard University Press, 2001), ix; University of Cincinnati Basic Fact Sheet, 2000, box 7, folder University Role, Steger Papers, UA-08-10, ARB.

10. The department changed its name to Africana Studies in 2009 to reflect the shifting nature of the field.

11. Patricia Hill Collins to Joseph Steger (email), June 25, 2001, box 9, folder 11-A, Afro-American Studies (2), Steger Papers, UA-06-09, ARB.

12. The 1990s planning effort was the most comprehensive and consequential of the university's history, but was part of a string of efforts. For the precursor to the Hargreaves plan see Glaser & Myers and Associates, *Ancillary Report: Part Two of the Developmental Plan, University of Cincinnati, 1982–1992* (Cincinnati: Glaser & Myers & Associates, and Woolpert Consultants, n.d., circa 1982).

13. Hargreaves Associates, *University of Cincinnati Master Plan 2000*, 6.

14. Ibid., 6; Hargreaves Associates, *University of Cincinnati Master Plan, September 1991*, 1, 13.

15. Dale McGirr, Ronald Kull and K. Scott Enns, "Town and Gown: Making Institutional and Community Development Work Together," [n.d., circa 2003], 7, box 11, folder Uptown Consortium, 406, Office of the President Subject Files, ARB.

16. Called the Technical School when completed in 1902, Old Tech originally housed science labs and drawing rooms. By the time Hargreaves began planning only Tanners remained.

17. The university also replaced a leaky roof on Zimmer Hall with a green roof, complete with patches of grass and two rows of trees, creating a very successful small quad between the engineering buildings and Rieveschl Hall.

18. *University of Cincinnati Master Plan 2000*, 23; "MainStreet, University of Cincinnati" (Marketing brochure, n.d., circa 2001), box 48, folder 401 City of Cincinnati (5), Steger Papers, UA-02-12, ARB. Not all of the imagined gateways were constructed, since Jefferson Quad was never built.

19. For descriptions of most existing buildings see Paul Bennett, *The Campus Guide: University of Cincinnati* (New York: Princeton Architectural Press, 2001).

20. Herbert Muschamp, "Eisenman's Spatial Extravaganza in Cincinnati," *New York Times*, July 21, 1996.

21. "UC Planning $17 Million Renovation of 'Iconic' Building," *Cincinnati Business Courier*, January 13, 2017. The use of "village" to describe a campus derives from Thomas Jefferson, who described his University of Virginia design as an "academical village." The term amplifies the separateness of the campus. Paul Venable Turner, *Campus: An American Planning Tradition* (Cambridge, MA: MIT Press, 1984), 3.

22. Morphosis website, http://morphopedia.com/p/architecture.

23. "Forbes: UC Named among the World's Most Beautiful College Campuses," *UC News*, http://www.uc.edu/news/nr.aspx?id=11524.

24. Nikil Saval, "If You Build It," *New York Times Magazine*, September 13, 2015, 48–55.

25. The Will of Charles McMicken, https://www.libraries.uc.edu/content/dam/libraries/arb/docs/university-archives/mcmicken-will.pdf, 22.

26. For a useful summary of the university's history of building and planning, see the *Campus Heritage Plan* (August 1, 2008), https://www.uc.edu/content/dam/uc/af/pdc/campus_heritage_plan/Campus%20Heritage%20Plan%20(13mb).pdf.

27. Quoted in Julie Irwin Zimmerman, "The Trouble with Townies," *Cincinnati Magazine*, September 2005, 48.

28. CUF is an abbreviation of Clifton Heights, University Heights, and Fairview, three small, contiguous neighborhoods along the university's western and southern boundaries.

29. Scott Enns to Lillian O'Neill (email), October 29, 2003, box 11, folder Uptown Consortium, 406, Office of the President Subject Files, ARB.

30. For a more complete accounting of UC's intervention in Uptown see Michael Romanos, David Edelman, and Mahyar Arefi, *Community Interactions and Collaborations Peer Institutional Study* (School of Planning, DAAP, 2006).

31. The Uptown Consortium was also instrumental to the redevelopment of Burnet Avenue north of Children's Hospital and Vine Street near the zoo, but these were lower priorities for the university.

32. In addition, a Taco Bell faced McMillan.

33. McGirr, Kull, and Enns, "Town and Gown," 406.

34. Andy Morgan to Nancy Zimpher (email), June 26, 2004, box 11, folder 406(4), Office of the President Subject Files, ARB.

35. McGirr, Kull, and Enns, "Town and Gown," 13, 14.

36. On the role of the UC Architect's Office in spurring and shaping neighborhood development, see Ray Bromley and Robert B. Kent, "Integrating Beyond the Campus: Ohio's Urban Public Universities and Neighborhood Revitalization," *Planning, Practice & Research* (February 2006): 45–78.

37. "Another Eminent Domain Fight Gets Ugly," *Cincinnati Business Courier*, May 24, 2004.

38. "Designing Clifton Heights," *City Beat*, June 8, 2005.

39. "Eminent Domain Ruling Overturned," *News Record*, February 7, 2007; Jake Mecklenborg, "$80M Mixed-Use Development Nears Completion in Clifton Heights," *Urban Cincy*, April 6, 2013, http://www.urbancincy.com/2013/04/photos-80m-mixed-use-development-nears-completion-in-clifton-heights/.

40. "UHCURC Update," Fall 2002, Issue 1, Volume 1, box 11, folder Uptown Consortium, 406, Office of the President Subject Files, ARB; Julie Irwin Zimmerman, "The Trouble with Townies," *Cincinnati Magazine* (September 2005), 50.

41. Brent Donaldson, "Bleak Street: What Will It Take to Raise Short Vine from the Dead," *Cincinnati Magazine* (November 2006), 94.

42. Monica Rimai to Zimpher (email), April 18, 2006, box 12, folder Uptown Consortium (11), Office of the President Subject Files, ARB.

43. John Linser to Zimpher (email), February 23, 2004, box 11, folder 406 (3), Office of the President Subject Files, ARB.

44. Uptown Consortium, Inc., Executive Employment Agreement, August 5, 2004, box 11, folder 406 (4), Office of the President Subject Files, ARB.

45. "Uptown Rebuilding Seen," *Cincinnati Enquirer*, March 14, 2008; "New Development Pours into Short Vine," *Cincinnati Enquirer*, June 27, 2014.

46. Nancy Zimpher to Tamim Chowdhury, September 14, 2006, box 12, folder Uptown Consortium (11), Office of the President Subject Files, ARB.

47. LaDale C. Winling, *Building the Ivory Tower: Universities and Metropolitan Development in the Twentieth Century* (Philadelphia: University of Pennsylvania Press, 2017), 185; "UC Projects Record-Breaking Fall Class," *UC Magazine*, August 17, 2016, http://magazine.uc.edu/editors_picks/recent_features/backtoschool16.html. For a brief, insightful article on these issues at the national level see Davarian L. Baldwin, "When Universities Swallow Cities," *Chronicle of Higher Education* (July 30, 2017).

48. "Education is not the filling of a pail, but the lighting of a fire," President's Report, University of Cincinnati, 1998, box 7, folder University Role, Steger Papers, UA-08-10, ARB.

49. Dawn Fuller, "Committee Evaluates Collegiate Structures for Undergraduate Education," *Campus News*, October 16, 2001. http://www.uc.edu/news/struc.htm.

50. "Final Report, Collegiate Structures Committee, University of Cincinnati," March 4, 2002. (In author's possession, courtesy of Kristi Nelson.)

51. Greg Hand, "UC Announces University-Wide Reorganization," *UC News*, May 24, 2002, http://www.uc.edu/news/creorg.htm; "UC Restructuring—Less 'Shuffle,'" *Cincinnati Enquirer*, July 15, 2002.

52. Catherine Gradey Strathern to Joseph Steer, October 3, 1997; Richard R. Klene to Joseph Steger, October 13, 1997, box 12, folder 21 University College (5), Steger Papers, UA-02-12, ARB. Dollar-return-per-dollar-spent data suggest that University College was indeed underfunded, as was Evening College. Both returned more money per dollar spent than the average college. See "Strategic Plan 1996–2001: College of Evening and Continuing Education University of Cincinnati," 16, box 3, folder College of Evening and Continuing Education Appendices 1, North Central Associate 1998–1999 Self-Study CITS-Finance, Admin. Services, Appendices, UA-99-35, ARB.

53. Anthony Perzigian to Diane Mankin (email), November 13, 2002; Diane Mankin to Anthony Perzigian (email), November 13, 2002, box 16, folder 21 University College (9), Steger Papers, UA-06-09, ARB.

54. Anthony Perzigian to University College Faculty and Staff (email), September 4, 2002, box 16, folder 21, University College (9)—Emails, Steger Papers, UA-06-09. ARB.

55. Ibid.

56. "2-Year Steppingstone to College Lost in UC Shuffle," *Cincinnati Enquirer*, September 11, 2003.

57. Anthony Perzigian Presentation, *Board of Trustees Records*, January 27, 2005, 104–5. Perzigian pointed out to the board that poor retention and graduation rates were at least partly responsible for the university's remaining in the third tier of the *U.S. News & World Report* rankings.

58. "Super Conference," February 1995, box 19, folder 55-G Conference USA, Steger Papers, UA-02-12, ARB.

59. "Historic Day for Big-East Bearcats," *UC Magazine*, August 2005. http://magazine.uc.edu/issues/0805/bigeastday.html.

60. "Cincinnati President Shows Moxie in Ousting Huggins," ESPN, August 24, 2005, http://www.espn.com/espn/columns/story?id=2141456.

61. "75-Foot-High 'Bearcat Bubble' Is Now Up," *UC News*, November 23, 2010, https://www.uc.edu/News/NR.aspx?id=12800.

62. "University of Cincinnati Sports Complex Adds Practice Fields," *UC Magazine*, March 17, 2010, http://magazine.uc.edu/editors_picks/recent_features/practicefields.html.

63. Coverage of the NCAA realignment is extensive, of course. For a concise description of the losers see: "Conference Realignment Era: The Losers," *CBSSports.Com*, April 24, 2013, http://www.cbssports.com/college-football/news/conference-realignment-era-the-losers/.

64. "Major Burden: How Universities Force Working-Class Students to Pay Thousands of Dollars in Hidden Fees to Athletic Departments Awash in Red Ink," *City Beat*, May 6–12, 2015, 15.

65. "UC Approves Plans for $87M Fifth Third Arena Renovation," *Cincinnati Business Courier*, December 15, 2015, http://www.bizjournals.com/cincinnati/news/2015/12/15/uc-approves-plans-for-87m-fifth-third-arena.html.

66. "Major Burden," 13.

67. Knight Commission on Intercollegiate Athletics, http://spendingdatabase.knightcommission.org/fbs/aac/university-of-cincinnati.

68. "Here's Where UC Coach Tuberville's Pay Ranks," *Cincinnati Business Courier*, October 14, 2015, http://www.bizjournals.com/cincinnati/blog/2015/10/here-s-where-uc-coach-tuberville-s-pay-ranks.html.

69. For the national story see Murray Sperber, *Beer and Circus: How Big-Time College Sports Is Crippling Undergraduate Education* (New York: Henry Holt, 2000). Sperber argues, "In the 1990s, university administrators began to use the idea of 'mission-driven athletics'; in other words, no matter how much money the athletic department loses, no matter how much bad publicity the coaches and jocks generate with misconduct and scandals, a school should promote its big-time college sports program as an essential element of its 'mission.' Of course, this 'mission' has little to do with education and everything to do with keeping enrollment high and tuition dollars flowing" (62).

70. John W. Curtis and Saranna Thornton, "Losing Focus: The Annual Report on the Economic Status of the Profession, 2013–14," *Academe* (March–April 2014): 11. See also a *Slate* essay on the rise in athletic coach salaries in comparison to the compensation of professors: "A Chart About College Coach Salaries That Will Make Academics Weep," *Slate*, April 7, 2014, http://www.slate.com/blogs/moneybox/2014/04/07/college_coach_pay_a_chart_that_will_make_academics_weep.html.

71. "Project a 'Good Marriage,'" *Cincinnati Post*, November 12, 2002.

72. Interview with Frank Russell conducted by Katherine R. Ranum, May 23, 2017.

73. Ibid.

74. "Nuns Find New Spot to Serve Up Pizza," *Cincinnati Enquirer*, April 23, 2004; "Once Evicted from Pizza Parlor Ministry, Nuns Set Up at New Site Thanks to UC Students," *News Record*, May 23, 2006.

75. Niehoff projects are accessible via https://www.uc.edu/cdc/niehoff_studio/niehoff_studio.html.

76. Alissa Weaver, "Urban Agriculture," 2009, https://sites.ucfilespace.uc.edu/studentwork/content/urban-agriculture; Gabriel's Place, http://gabrielsplace.org/project/about-us/.

77. Dominic Wolf, Yan Dai, Katie Poppel, Paige Vaughn, Jayson Lindsay, Justin Straub, Matt Eagle, Rocco Lombardi, Travis Hunt, and Zach Weber, "Wasson Way: Light Rail Transit," 2014, https://sites.ucfilespace.uc.edu/studentwork/content/wasson-way-light-rail-transit; Chris Allen, William Garde, Kayla Quinter, Alex Shumakh, and Eric Siegrist, "Environmental Aspects of Wasson Way: Hydrology, Green Infrastructure, and Re-envisioning Cincinnati," 2014, https://sites.ucfilespace.uc.edu/studentwork/content/environmental-aspects-wasson-way-hydrology-green-infrastructure-re-envisioning-cincinnati.

78. See Niehoff Studio data at http://www.uc.edu/cdc/niehoff_studio/Nov_18_15_inforgraphic_2M.jpg.

79. "Zimpher Outlines Four Goals for University," *Cincinnati Post*, October 20, 2005. For more on Zimpher's leadership philosophy see "Institutionalizing Engagement: What Can Presidents Do?" in *Creating a New Kind of University: Institutionalizing Community–University Engagement*, edited by Stephen L. Percy, Nancy L. Zimpher, and Mary Jane Brukardt (Bolton, MA: Anker Publishing Company, 2006), 223–41.

Epilogue We Will Be *in* Cincinnati

1. Office of the Chief Financial Officer, "University Current Funds Budget Plan, 2005–2006" (June 28, 2005), 9–12; Michael Mitchell, Michael Leachman, and Kathleen Masterson, "Funding Down, Tuition Up," Center on Budget and Policy Priorities, August 5, 2016. http://www.cbpp.org/research/state-budget-and-tax/funding-down-tuition-up.

2. American Association for the Advancement of Science, "Historical Trends in Federal R&D," https://www.aaas.org/page/historical-trends-federal-rd.

3. Reliance on adjunct instructors has clearly increased, but this is a trend that reflects administration efforts to control costs more than research faculty lack of interest in teaching undergraduates.

4. Clark Kerr, *The Uses of the University* (1963; rpt. Cambridge, MA: Harvard University Press, 2001), 212. The literature about higher education in crisis includes *The Embattled University*, edited by Stephen R. Graubard and Geno A. Ballotti (New York: George Braziller, 1970), a collection of essays that appeared in *Daedalus* over the previous year. The theme of crisis at that point entailed a lack of autonomy among universities, which had become beholden to government and corporations in the era of growth. See also *The Crisis in Higher Education*, edited by Joseph Froomkin (New York: Academy of Political Science, 1983), a collection of essays that describes the new crisis resulting from declining enrollments, rising tuition, and decreased state support. Each generation has its own crisis—at least one. See *The University in Ruins* (Cambridge, MA: Harvard University Press, 1996), in which Bill Readings describes the collapse of universities, bested by the postmodern challenge.

5. Anthony P. Carnevale, Stephen J. Rose, and Ban Cheah, *The College Payoff: Education, Occupations, and Lifetime Earnings* (Washington, DC: Georgetown Center for Education and the Workforce, n.d. [circa 2011]), https://cew.georgetown.edu/cew-reports/the-college-payoff/.

6. "Trending: President's Report on the University of Cincinnati," November 5, 2015, http://issuu.com/uofcincy/docs/trending6?e=12227993/31151518.

7. "What the Area Wants of UC," *Cincinnati Enquirer*, May 31, 2009.

8. Martha C. Nussbaum, *Not for Profit: Why Democracy Needs the Humanities* (Princeton: Princeton University Press, 2010), 10, 124.

9. Kevin Carey, *The End of College: Creating the Future of Learning and the University of Everywhere* (New York: Riverhead Books, 2015), 241.

10. Abraham Flexner, *Universities: American, English, German* (New York: Oxford University Press, 1930), 144. On the high hopes for the educational role of radio in the 1930s see Robert W. McChesney, *Telecommunications, Mass Media, and Democracy: The Battle for the Control of U.S. Broadcasting, 1928–1935* (New York: Oxford University Press, 1933), esp. 38–62.

11. The officer was also charged with manslaughter and murder, although after two hung juries those charges were dismissed. See "Charges against Ray Tensing Dismissed," *Cincinnati Enquirer*, July 24, 2017.

12. Exiger, "Final Report for the Comprehensive Review of the University of Cincinnati Police Department," June 1, 2016, https://www.uc.edu/content/dam/uc/publicsafety/docs/Reform/documents/FINAL%20REPORT.pdf; Robin S. Engel and Murat Ozer, "University of Cincinnati Police Department Traffic Stop Summary," University of Cincinnati Institute of Crime Science, July 31, 2015, https://www.uc.edu/content/dam/uc/ucomm/docs/ucpd-arrests-and-citations.pdf; Michele Ralston, "In Unprecedented Move, UC Board Approves Policy on Policing Standards; Hires Independent Monitor to Oversee Police Reforms," *UC News*, September 21, 2016.

13. Author's notes from All-Faculty Meeting, Great Hall, April 5, 2017.

14. J. Martin Klotsche, *The Urban University: And the Future of Our Cities* (New York: Harper & Row, 1966), 30; Thomas Bender, "Scholarship, Local Life, and the Necessity of Worldliness," in *The Urban University and Its Identity: Roots, Locations, Roles*, edited by Herman van der Wusten (Dordrecht, The Netherlands: Kluwer Academic Publishers, 1998), 27. As Bender phrased it, "By reorienting academic culture from the nation to the metropolis, and from national cultures to the metropolitan cultures in which universities are deeply implicated, one might thereby acquire important new resources for the making of the pluralized public culture that must be constructed in the coming generation—not only in the United States, but in every open, democratic society."

Bibliographical Essay

This essay describes the most important sources I consulted in writing this book. It is in no way exhaustive. I have organized the essay following my professional practice—describing archival materials first, then other primary sources, followed by secondary sources. This last section I have divided into works of general interest, those spanning places and times, categorized by topic. This I have followed with (nearly) chapter-by-chapter descriptions of works that pertain to narrower parts of this story.

❧ Archival Material

Most of the archival material I consulted can be found among the extensive collections of the University of Cincinnati Archives & Rare Books Library (ARB). Anyone interested in a systematic review of university history will find remarkable detail in the Board of Directors Meeting Minutes (after 1977, Board of Trustees), which are especially thorough in the late nineteenth century, a period about which they provide the best source on the institution.

Although they encourage a top-down perspective on the institution, the most important manuscript collections come from the desks of the university's presidents. The following collections were especially useful for the range and depth of documents included: Warren Bennis Papers (Office of the President), UA-77-10, UA-78-2; Walter C. Langsam Papers (Office of the President), UA-87-9; Joseph Steger Papers (Office of the President), UA-02-12, UA-06-09; Office of the President—Subject Files, UA-13-11, relating to Nancy Zimpher's presidency; and Raymond Walters Papers (Office of the President), UA-73-20.

I also consulted several special collections related to units within the university and particular events. The two most important are the Cincinnati College Records,

UA-82-1, which contains the bulk of the extant material related to the 1820s and 1830s, and the Cincinnati Observatory Collection, UA-79-43, which also contains early Cincinnati College materials. Of the others, among the most remarkable are the Campus Unrest Files, UA-04-012, which contain a wealth of material gathered to make sense of the unrest of the late 1960s. I also made good use of the Kettering Laboratory Publications, UA-02-22, which gather together the most important publications generated by Robert Kehoe and his colleagues; the Tangeman University Center Records, UA-15-03; and the WGUC Files, UA-87-4. UC archives also hold the papers of some individual faculty members. I accessed a select few: Ada Hart Arlitt Papers, UA-90-78; Carl Blegen Papers, UA-83-15; and Martha Stephens—The Cincinnati Radiation Experiments: 1960–1972, UA-05-05. I also visited the Zane L. Miller Papers, UA-05-10.

ARB contains a number of important manuscripts of local interest, identified as the Urban Studies collection. Many of these manuscripts come from Cincinnati politicians who dealt with university issues. I found most helpful: Bobbie Sterne Papers, US-04-11; Theodore M. Berry Papers, US-93-03; Myron Bush Papers, US-84-1; and Eugene P. Ruehlmann Papers, US-74-02. I also consulted some collections generated by other government institutions, including Cincinnati Park Board Records, ON-95-03; Clifton Town Meeting Records, US-77-7; and the Municipal Reference Library Files, US-04-09, which contain materials related to a wide variety of issues.

The Henry R. Winkler Center for the History of the Health Professions (WCA), also part of the UC Libraries system, holds an extraordinary wealth of information, only a tiny fraction of which I could examine. I used the Daniel Drake Materials, the Christian R. Holmes Collection, the Robert Kehoe Papers, and the Clarence Mills Papers.

Other archives in Cincinnati hold collections of use. Cincinnati History Library and Archives (CHLA) holds the Annette and E. Lucy Braun Papers, MSS 1064, and the Charles William Dabney Papers, 1905–1918, MSS 949, both of direct interest to university history. I also found useful materials in collections more focused on city issues, including the Cincinnatus Association Papers, MSS 617, and the Charles P. Taft II Papers, 1922–1977, MSS 562. The Lloyd Library, which specializes in the history of medicine and pharmacy, holds the Otto Juettner Papers, 1865–1922, and the George Rieveschl Jr. Papers, 1916–2007.

Three other local collections were especially valuable: materials related to Mercantile Library history, held at the Mercantile Library (ML) itself; the Burnet

Woods Collection held by Cincinnati Parks' Bettman Center (BCA) in Hyde Park; and the Art Academy of Cincinnati Collection held by the Cincinnati Art Museum Archives. Beyond Cincinnati, I visited several regional archives, including the Filson Historical Society (FHS) in Louisville, which holds the Samuel Brown Papers, 1817–1825. I visited Miami University Special Collections (MUSC), where I read the relevant parts of the John Hough James Collection, Diaries and Family Correspondence. Miami has also digitized and posted the William Holmes McGuffey Papers, which contain some letters of interest. Finally, I visited the archives at University of North Carolina–Chapel Hill (UNC), which holds the terribly useful Charles W. Dabney Papers, MSS 1412.

Beyond manuscript collections, the many student newspapers have been especially helpful. *Academica*, *Burnet Woods Echo*, the *Bearcat*, and early issues of the *News Record* can be found in ARB. Helpfully, the *News Record* is being systematically digitized and is word searchable at http://digital.libraries.uc.edu/collections/newsrecord/. I have also consulted city newspapers, most notably the *Cincinnati Enquirer*, *Cincinnati Times-Star*, and *Cincinnati Post*. Some decades of the *Enquirer* are available in digitized form, but I have also made use of the Newsdex service at Cincinnati Public Library.

In addition to these periodical sources, the university has over the years—in exponentially increasing frequency—produced hundreds of reports, authored by faculty, administrators, and consultants. Some of these reports were printed by the university and bound separately. They appear in the collections of the various libraries, especially Archives & Rare Books. I can claim to have read only a fraction of them.

❦ Secondary Sources
Higher Education

Not surprisingly, the literature on higher education in the United States is extensive. For the development of the university see James Axtell, *Wisdom's Workshop: The Rise of the Modern University* (Princeton: Princeton University Press, 2016), which describes the medieval roots of higher education, explores the contributions of Oxbridge and German universities, and finishes with a thorough exploration of elite universities in the twentieth-century United States. (It also has a valuable selected readings list, a wonderful starting point for anyone interested in exploring the literature on the longer history of higher education.) See also

Julie A. Reuben, *The Making of the Modern University: Intellectual Transformation and the Marginalization of Morality* (Chicago: University of Chicago Press, 1996), an intellectual history focused on elite institutions, mostly very dissimilar to UC. She describes the changing ideas of science as a driving force in the secularization of these elite universities. Also for the period from 1870 to 1910 see Laurence R. Veysey, *The Emergence of the American University* (Chicago: University of Chicago Press, 1965). Veysey provides a wonderful analysis of the creation of a distinctly American institution during the first revolution in higher education. He does this without mentioning the University of Cincinnati. I found Clark Kerr's *The Uses of the University* (1963; rpt. Cambridge, MA: Harvard University, 2001) to be especially helpful, not just in describing the postwar transition into the "multiversity," but for sparking thought about the role of higher education in the United States generally. Similarly, readers interested in an earlier conception of the American university might explore Abraham Flexner's influential *Universities: American, English, German* (New York: Oxford University Press, 1930).

Roger L. Geiger's *To Advance Knowledge: The Growth of American Research Universities, 1900–1940* (New York: Oxford University Press, 1986) is a remarkably thorough study of the nation's largest research universities. The likes of Johns Hopkins, Chicago, and Harvard occupy most of his attention, but Geiger well describes broader trends in university development. See also Dorothy Ross, *The Origins of American Social Science* (New York: Cambridge University Press, 1991), which traces the development of sociology, economics, and political science in the late 1800s and early 1900s. Those seeking a survey will find useful John S. Brubacker and Willis Rudy, *Higher Education in Transition: A History of American Colleges and Universities* (New Brunswick, NJ: Transaction Publishers, 1997), or John R. Thelin's *A History of American Higher Education* (Baltimore: Johns Hopkins University Press, 2004).

On land-grant colleges see the comprehensive but somewhat dated *Colleges for Our Land and Time: The Land-Grant Idea in American Education* by Edward Danforth Eddy Jr. (Westport, CT: Greenwood Press, 1956), and Allan Nevins's brief and lively *The Origins of the Land-Grant Colleges and State Universities* (Washington, DC: Civil War Centennial Commission, 1962). The collection edited by Alan I. Marcus, *Science as Service: Establishing and Reforming Land-Grant Universities, 1865–1930* (Tuscaloosa: University of Alabama Press, 2015), contains some useful essays, including Robert B. Fairbanks, "The Morrill Land-Grant Act and American Cities: The Neglected Story."

I also sampled other bicentennial books, including Curtis W. Ellison, ed., *Miami University, 1809–2009: Bicentennial Perspectives* (Athens: Ohio University Press, 2009), and Betty Hollow, *Ohio University: The Spirit of a Singular Place, 1804–2004* (Athens: Ohio University Press, 2003). Both are thorough institutional histories, well-illustrated and extraordinarily informative, though neither takes a critical scholarly stance. The number of college and university institutional histories is staggering, of course. Among the best, and most complete, is the multivolume *The University of Wisconsin: A History* (Madison: University of Wisconsin Press, 1949–), written by several of Madison's great historians: Merle Curti and Vernon Carstensen, the first two volumes, and E. David Cronon and John W. Jenkins the last two. See also Martin L. Friedland's remarkably complete *The University of Toronto: A History* (Toronto: University of Toronto Press, 2013).

✱ Urban Universities

After a long hiatus in attention to higher education in American urban history, two useful books appeared in 2017. Begin with Steven J. Diner, *Universities and Their Cities: Urban Higher Education in America* (Baltimore: Johns Hopkins University Press, 2017), which provides a national context for higher education in American cities, and which might be profitably read as a supplement to this book. See also LaDale C. Winling, *Building the Ivory Tower: Universities and Metropolitan Development in the Twentieth Century* (Philadelphia: University of Pennsylvania Press, 2017), a series of case studies around university engagement in urban planning. Unfortunately, none of the cases is very similar to UC.

I began my exploration of the relationship between city and university by reading the wonderful collection of essays edited by Thomas Bender: *The University and the City: From Medieval Origins to the Present* (Oxford: Oxford University Press, 1988). It contains essays on Florence, Paris, Leiden, Edinburgh, London, and New York City that raise a variety of questions concerning how urban universities have interacted with their cities—from curriculum to politics. In the long essay *The Urban University and the Future of Our Cities* (New York: Harper & Row, 1966), J. Martin Klotsche provides a positive assessment of the urban university's great potential to serve as a democratic engine and problem solver for an increasingly urban nation. See also Sharon Haar's very interesting exploration of planning and design of universities in Chicago, with a particular focus on the consequences of modernism for the University of Illinois–Chicago: *The City as Campus: Urbanism and Higher Education in Chicago* (Minneapolis: University of Minnesota Press, 2011). Readers interested in architecture should look at Andrew S. Dolkart's *Morningside Heights: A History of Its Architecture and Development* (New York: Columbia University Press, 1998).

Eager students of the history of higher education will enjoy the University of Akron's Parke R. Kolbe's straightforward description of the relationship between cities and universities in *Urban Influences on Higher Education in England and the United States* (New York: Macmillan, 1928), which is especially useful for understanding the 1920s. William S. Carlson, president of the University of Toledo, offered a thorough rumination on the mission and structure of the municipal university in the appropriately titled *The Municipal University* (Washington DC: Center for Applied Research in Education, 1962). In a brief book—just under 150 pages—Maurice Berube managed to describe the development of urban universities without mentioning UC once. See *The Urban University in America* (Westport, CT: Greenwood Press, 1978). Clearly influenced by the 1960s, Berube discusses open enrollment and the development of urban studies, but like many historians of higher education he seems to assume that his topic can be well covered by studying institutions in New York, Boston, Chicago, and Berkeley. Henry R. Winkler, "Higher Education in an Urban Context," in *Preparation for Life? The Paradox of Education in the Late Twentieth Century*, edited by Joan N. Burstyn (Philadelphia: Falmer Press, 1986) gives a more useful view from UC's historian-president. Very interested readers may enjoy some of the essays contained in *The Urban University and Its Identity: Roots, Locations, Roles*, edited by Herman van der Wusten (Dordrecht, The Netherlands: Kluwer Academic Publishers, 1998), including one by Thomas Bender on "The Necessity of Worldliness," which discusses cloistered universities, those that turn away from the city. On town-and-gown relationships see Mark Souther, "Acropolis of the Middle-West: Decay, Renewal, and Boosterism in Cleveland's University Circle" (*Journal of Planning History*, [February 2011]: 31–58). Souther, like many contemporary historians, is interested in the role of the university in urban renewal.

❀ UC Histories

The indispensable history of UC is Reginald McGrane, *The University of Cincinnati: A Success Story in Urban Higher Education* (New York: Harper & Row, 1963). Although its coverage ends more than fifty years ago (obviously), it is much more comprehensive than this book. It is also unencumbered by footnotes or bibliography. Ray-

mond Walters, *Historical Sketch of the University of Cincinnati* (Cincinnati, 1940), provides a good, brief introduction of the university's history. Walter Consuelo Langsam, *At the University of Cincinnati, 1955–1971* (University of Cincinnati Foundation,
1972), provides a quick sketch of his long career and the evolution of UC under
his administration, an era of rapid expansion punctuated by student unrest. For
an excellent illustrated history of the university, including hundreds of useful captions and short essays, see Kevin Grace and Greg Hand, *The University of Cincinnati*
(Montgomery, AL: Community Communications, 1995). Lena Beatrice Morton's
My First Sixty Years: Passion for Wisdom (New York: Philosophical Library, 1965) is the
autobiography of a prominent African American educator, who earned her BA
and MA at UC. She grew up in Kentucky and her parents moved to Cincinnati
specifically so Lena could get an education, first at Woodward and then at UC,
which she entered in 1918. I found Paul Bennett's *The University of Cincinnati: An
Architectural Tour* (New York: Princeton Architectural Press, 2001) very helpful, as it
contains the basic facts about all of the university's buildings. Eslie Asbury's *Reflections: An Anecdotal Account of the University of Cincinnati during the Last Sixty Years* (University of Cincinnati, 1976) is quirky and problematic, but not without value. Asbury,
a retired surgeon with long connections to the university, wrote the book at the
request of Warren Bennis. Those interested in the history of medical education in
Cincinnati should seek out Ellen Cangi's 1983 UC dissertation, "Principles before
Practice: The Reform of Medical Education in Cincinnati Before and After the
Flexner Report." Those interested in Blue Ash should seek out Robert Gioielli's *50
Years of UC Blue Ash College: Inspiring Student Success—Then, Now, Always* (Cincinnati:
University of Cincinnati Press, 2017).

❀ Cincinnati History

Most of the contextual Cincinnati historiography appears by chapter below, but
two books deserve mention here. Zane L. Miller, *Visions of Place: The City, Neighborhoods, Suburbs, and Cincinnati's Clifton* (Columbus: Ohio State University Press, 2001)
provides the long history of Clifton, although the university plays little role in his
narrative. Roger Fortin's *To See Great Wonders: A History of Xavier University, 1831–
2006* (Scranton: University of Scranton Press, 2006) provides a thorough history
of UC's in-city rival, written for the occasion of the university's 175th anniversary.
UC plays little role in Fortin's narrative, which is justifiably more concerned with
Xavier's Jesuit mission.

🌿 Chapter 1 A Frontier Institution

For local and regional context Richard Wade's classic *The Urban Frontier: The Rise of Western Cities* (Cambridge, MA: Harvard University Press, 1959) is still a valuable read. See also Daniel Aaron, *Cincinnati: Queen City of the West, 1819–1838* (Columbus: Ohio State University Press, 1992), the publication of a 1942 cultural history that was well before its time. Aaron provides excellent context for the foundation of the college and other cultural institutions, but he included just one brief section on education. For a valuable, more recent work, see Nikki M. Taylor, *Frontiers of Freedom: Cincinnati's Black Community, 1802–1868* (Athens: Ohio University Press, 2005). Taylor's focus is community formation—largely in response to rampant racism— and it includes significant discussion of the African American educational system.

See also Walter Stix Glazer, *Cincinnati in 1840: The Social and Functional Organization of an Urban Community during the Pre–Civil War Period* (Columbus: Ohio State University Press, 1999), which provides some very useful context at a critical period in the development of higher education. Wendy Jean Katz's *Regionalism and Reform: Art and Class Formation in Antebellum Cincinnati* (Columbus: Ohio State University Press, 2002) focuses primarily on three local artists, but it provides good cultural context in the 1840s and 1850s. See also Alan I. Marcus, *Plague of Strangers: Social Groups and the Origins of City Services in Cincinnati* (Columbus: Ohio State University Press, 1991), which describes the growth of municipal authority in the areas of health and safety in the 1840s and 1850s, connecting the empowerment of city governments with growing concern about immigrants. On the Western Museum see Louis Leonard Tucker, "'Ohio Show-Shop': The Western Museum of Cincinnati, 1820–1867," in *A Cabinet of Curiosities* (Charlottesville: University Press of Virginia, 1967).

For a fine secondary source on the Long expedition see Howard Ensign Evans, *The Natural History of the Long Expedition to the Rocky Mountains, 1819–1820* (Oxford University Press, 1997). Although he says little about Cincinnati and nothing of the college, Richard Rhodes wrote a terribly interesting biography of Audubon, which offers valuable impressions of Ohio River Valley in this period. See *John James Audubon: The Making of an American* (New York: Alfred Knopf, 2004). For his journals see John James Audubon, *Writings and Drawings* (Library of America, 1999).

Some very old secondary sources provide good information. John Parsons Foote, *Schools of Cincinnati and Its Vicinity* (Cincinnati: C. F. Bradley & Company, 1855), provides some useful information, albeit expressed in a great deal of flowery language. More useful is John Brough Shotwell, *A History of the Schools of Cincinnati* (Cincinnati: School Life Company, 1902). William H. Venable, *Beginnings of Literary Culture in the Ohio Valley: Historical and Biographical Sketches* (Cincinnati: Robert Clarke & Co., 1891), includes some errors and is little more than lists of institutions and publications, but is not without value, especially in its biography of E. D. Mansfield.

Readers interested in the early history of Cincinnati would do well to find several accessible primary sources, including Oliver Farnsworth, *The Cincinnati Directory* (Cincinnati: Morgan, Lodge and Co. Printers, 1819); and, Benjamin Drake and E. D. Mansfield, *Cincinnati in 1826* (Cincinnati: Morgan, Lodge, and Fisher, 1827). Two other Mansfield works are also of special interest: *Personal Memories, Social, Political, and Literary* (Cincinnati: Robert Clarke & Co., 1879) and *Memoirs of the Life and Services of Daniel Drake, M.D., Physician, Professor, and Author* (Cincinnati: Applegate & Co., 1855). For valuable descriptions of the young city and the Ohio River, which he traveled up and down, see Timothy Flint, *Recollections of the Last Ten Years in the Valley of the Mississippi* (1826; rpt. Carbondale: Southern Illinois University Press, 1968). Also of value: W. N. Blane, *An Excursion Through the United States and Canada during the Years 1822–1823* (London, 1824) and Charles Fenno Hoffman, *A Winter in the Far West* (London: Richard Bentley, 1835), which includes Hoffman's very generous description of Cincinnati's beauty in the mid-1830s.

The literature on Daniel Drake is quite extensive. Interested readers should seek out Drake's own writings, many of which are collected in *Physician to the West: Selected Writings of Daniel Drake on Science and Society*, edited by Henry D. Shapiro and Zane L. Miller (Lexington: University Press of Kentucky, 1970). This collection also includes excellent essays by Shapiro and Miller on Drake, Cincinnati, and the state of medicine during Drake's career. The many Drake biographies are short and flawed. Most complete is Emmet Field Horine, *Daniel Drake (1785–1852): Pioneer Physician of the Midwest* (Philadelphia: University of Pennsylvania Press, 1961). Horine's work is very detail-oriented and a bit of a slog. Those interested in this period, and Drake's role in it, will also find value in Stephen Szaraz's Harvard dissertation, "History, Character, and Prospects: Daniel Drake and the Life of the Mind in the Ohio Valley, 1785–1852" (1993). I also learned from Frank A. Barrett, "Daniel Drake's Medical Geography," *Social Science Medicine* (1996): 791–800.

❧ **Chapter 2** Shall It All Be in One Place? and **Chapter 3** To the Woods

To learn more about Cincinnati at the time of UC's founding see Zane L. Miller's *Boss Cox's Cincinnati: Urban Politics in the Progressive Era* (Chicago: University of

317

Chicago Press, 1968), and Steven J. Ross's *Workers on the Edge: Work, Leisure, and Politics in Industrializing Cincinnati, 1788–1890* (New York: Columbia University Press, 1985). On the city's strong economic foundation see Philip Scranton, "Diversified Industrialization and Economic Success: Understanding Cincinnati's Manufacturing Development, 1850–1925," *Ohio Valley History* (Spring 2005): 5–22. Steven K. Green provides an excellent explication of the Cincinnati Bible War in *The Bible, the School, and the Constitution: The Clash That Shaped Modern Church–State Doctrine* (New York: Oxford University Press, 2012). On Thomas Vickers and Alphonso Taft see George Augustine Thayer, *The First Congregationalist Church of Cincinnati (Unitarian): A History* (Cincinnati, 1917).

For a very readable long essay on the role of the university in the late nineteenth century, see Charles Franklin Thwing, *The American College in American Life* (New York: G. P. Putnam's Sons, 1897). On the development of German universities see Charles E. McClelland, *State, Society, and University in Germany, 1700–1914* (Cambridge: Cambridge University Press, 1980). For a study of Americans studying in Germany see Anja Werner, *The Transatlantic World of Higher Education: Americans at German Universities, 1776–1914* (New York: Berghahn Books, 2013), which focuses on student life and especially academic networking among Americans abroad. To learn more about the development of sports on American campuses, see Ronald A. Smith, *Sports and Freedom: The Rise of Big-Time College Athletics* (New York: Oxford University Press, 1988), which emphasizes English roots and student leadership.

🌿 Chapter 4 A Progressive Institution

For the national context during the Progressive Era start with Daniel T. Rodgers, *Atlantic Crossings: Social Politics in a Progressive Age* (Cambridge, MA: Belknap Press of Harvard University Press, 1998), which sets American politics in an international context, emphasizing European influences on governmental solutions to social problems. On higher education specifically, see *A City and Its Universities: Public Policy in Chicago, 1892–1919* (Chapel Hill: University of North Carolina Press, 1980), in which Steven J. Diner describes faculty and administrators engaging in urban reform as a means of asserting their own professional importance and linking university expertise to policy formation—a linkage that helped justify liberal reform through the 1960s.

Those interested in learning more about social settlements might go straight to the source: Jane Addams, *Twenty Years at Hull-House* (New York: Macmillan, 1910), published at the peak of the Progressive Era and reprinted many times since. For the longer view, and a scholarly perspective, see Judith Ann Trolander, *Professionalism and Social Change: From the Settlement House Movement to Neighborhood Centers, 1886 to the Present* (New York: Columbia University Press, 1987).

On cooperative education see Clyde W. Park, *The Co-Operative System of Education: A Reprint of Bulletin No. 37, Series of 1916, U.S. Bureau of Education with Additions* (University of Cincinnati, 1925), a brief and readable overview of the program written from a professor of English in the College of Engineering and Commerce. For a longer description see Park's biography of Herman Schneider: *Ambassador to Industry: The Idea and Life of Herman Schneider* (New York: Bobbs-Merrill, 1943). Schneider's own *Thirty Years of Educational Pioneering: The Philosophy of the Cooperative System and Its Practical Test* (University of Cincinnati, 1935) is mostly philosophical meanderings, useful only to those extremely interested in how he thought. For an accessible and nicely illustrated narrative of the entire history of the co-op system see M. B. Reilly, *The Ivory Tower and the Smokestack: 100 Years of Cooperative Education at the University of Cincinnati* (University of Cincinnati, 2006).

❦ Chapter 5 In the Service of the Nation

On World War I, start with Carol S. Gruber's wonderful *Mars and Minerva: World War I and the Uses of the Higher Learning in America* (Baton Rouge: Louisiana State University Press, 1975), which largely addresses faculty involvement in the war and their disappointingly quick and thorough adoption of the government's position. The book concerns mostly eastern schools (and the University of Wisconsin), but provides excellent context for the national story, including the creation of the Students' Army Training Corps. For a contemporary assessment see Parke Rexford Kolbe, *The Colleges in War Time and After* (New York: D. Appleton and Company, 1919). For a fine study of higher education with a focus on the international academic community during and immediately after World War I see Tomás Irish, *The University at War, 1914–25: Britain, France, and the United States* (London: Palgrave Macmillan, 2015). David M. Kennedy's *Over Here: The First World War and American Society* (New York: Oxford University Press, 2004) provides the broader context of the American home front. On Germans in Cincinnati during the war and after see Don Heinrich Tolzmann, *The Cincinnati Germans after the Great War* (New York: Peter Lang, 1987). For a quick but useful overview of higher education in the major western belligerent nations during both world wars see Willis Rudy's *Total War and the*

Twentieth-Century Higher Learning: Universities of the Western World in the First and Second World Wars (Madison, NJ: Fairleigh Dickinson University Press, 1991).

Contemporary sources provide details on the mobilization effort on campuses around the nation. See Frank Aydelotte, *Final Report of the War Issues Course of the Students' Army Training Corps* (Washington, DC: War Department, 1919); Committee on Education and Special Training, *A Review of Its Work during1918* (Washington, DC: War Department, 1919); C. R. Doley, *Final Report of the National Army Training Detachments* (Washington, DC: War Department, 1919). For a summary of the war's impact on higher education see Kolbe, *The Colleges in War Time and After.* For a comprehensive but uncritical study written in the afterglow of victory see Charles F. Thwing, *The American Colleges and Universities in the Great War, 1914–1919: A History* (New York: Macmillan, 1920).

Ronald L. Stuckey gathered together many of the Lucy Braun's publications and authored some brief biographical pieces. See *E. Lucy Braun (1889–1971): Ohio's Foremost Woman Botanist* (Columbus: RLS Creations, 2001). Those interested in learning more about Braun's work should turn to *Deciduous Forests of Eastern North America* (Philadelphia: Blakiston, 1950). She also published a number of interesting short articles and essays in *Wild Flower*, the quarterly publication of the Wild Flower Preservation Society of America. For the continued relevance of Braun's work see James M. Dyer, "Revisiting the *Deciduous Forests of Eastern North America*," *BioScience* 56, no. 4 (2006): 341–52. Margaret Rossiter has written two excellent surveys of women in scientific fields, much of it focused on academia. See *Women Scientists in America: Struggles and Strategies to 1940* (Baltimore: Johns Hopkins University Press, 1984), and *Women Scientists in America: Before Affirmative Action, 1940–1972* (Baltimore: Johns Hopkins University Press, 1998). For a very detailed description of early contributions of women to botany see Mary R. S. Creese, *Ladies in the Laboratory? American and British Women in Science, 1800–1900* (Lanham, MD: Scarecrow Press, 1998).

In 1936, the College of Medicine gathered together the Kettering Lab's published lead studies from the previous decade and bound them together under the title, *Experimental Studies on Lead Absorption and Excretion with Certain Practical Applications.* On lead research and the broader context of lead poisoning see Christian Warren, *Brush with Death: A Social History of Lead Poisoning* (Baltimore: Johns Hopkins University Press, 2000).

On the career of Carl Blegen see the fine collection of essays on his personal and professional life edited by Natalia Vogelkoff-Brogan, Jack L. Davis, and Vasiliki Florou: *Carl W. Blegen: Personal and Archaeological Narratives* (Atlanta: Lockwood Press, 2015). Blegen's own published corpus is extensive. I found of use: Carl W. Blegen and Marion Rawson, *The Palace of Nestor at Pylos in Western Messenia*, vol. 1, *The Buildings and Their Contents* (Princeton: Princeton University Press, 1966), and K. Kourouniotis and Carl W. Blegen, "Excavations at Pylos, 1939," *American Journal of Archaeology* (1939): 557–76. Very interested readers may enjoy Blegen's letters, gathered and edited by Robert D. Blegen, *Carl W. Blegen: His Letters Home, Book I—Life in Athens* (1994); *Carl W. Blegen: His Letters Home, Book II—From Distant Fields* (1995).

On the Great Depression and college campuses find Kevin P. Bower, "'A Favored Child of the State': Federal Student Aid at Ohio College and Universities, 1934–1943," *History of Education Quarterly* (September 2004): 364–87.

❧ Chapter 6 Growing Pains and Opportunities

The secondary material on postwar higher education is expansive. On the GI Bill see Keith W. Olson, *The G.I. Bill, the Veterans, and the Colleges* (Lexington: University Press of Kentucky, 1974). For a broader account of the GI Bill see Suzanne Mettler's *Soldiers to Citizens: The G.I. Bill and the Making of the Greatest Generation* (New York: Oxford University Press, 2005). Although it isn't easy to read, Stefan Muthesius's *The Postwar University: Utopianist Campus and College* (New Haven: Yale University Press, 2000) provides a useful analysis of the way Modernist architecture and planning ideas combined with university utopian ideals to re-create campuses around the United States, Britain, and Germany.

On UC's role in the race to develop a polio vaccine see David M. Oshinsky, *Polio: An American Story* (New York: Oxford University Press, 2005), the finest of many books on the topic. On Cold War threats and opportunities see Robert M. Hutchins, *Freedom, Education, and the Fund: Essays and Addresses, 1946–1956* (New York: Meridian Books, 1956). Hutchins, president and then chancellor of the University of Chicago, saw threats from above. On the national context of UC's growth see Clark Kerr, *The Great Transformation in Higher Education, 1960–1980* (Albany: State University of New York Press, 1991), which is not one of Kerr's best books, but it is useful and insightful nonetheless.

The literature on Kettering Lab and Robert Kehoe is extensive. I have been particularly influenced by Gerald Markowitz and David Rosner, *Lead Wars: The Politics of Science and the Fate of America's Children* (Berkeley: University of California

Press, 2013), part of a substantial literature in which Kehoe plays the bad guy. For a fuller articulation of the lead industry's long campaign to hide the dangers of lead from the general public, see Markowitz and Rosner, *Deceit and Denial: The Deadly Politics of Industrial Pollution* (Berkeley: University of California Press, 2002). Christopher Bryson offers a scathing indictment of Kehoe and the lab in *The Fluoride Deception* (New York: Seven Stories Press, 2004), which is well written, thoroughly researched, and largely convincing. For a more benign interpretation of Kehoe's work see Christopher Sellers, *Hazards of the Job: From Industrial Disease to Environmental Health Science* (Chapel Hill: University of North Carolina Press, 1997). Sellers places Kehoe at the center of the "environmental turn" among industrial health researchers, arguing that his work laid the groundwork for the environmentalist revolt against industrial pollution. William Graebner's "Private Power, Private Knowledge, and Public Health: Science, Engineering, and Lead Poisoning, 1900–1970," in *The Health and Safety of Workers: Case Studies in the Politics of Professional Responsibility*, edited by Ronald Bayer (New York: Oxford University Press, 1988) partly attributes the long delay in the regulation of lead to the Kettering Lab's hegemony in lead research. Benjamin Ross and Steven Amter's *The Polluters: The Making of Our Chemically Altered Environment* (New York: Oxford University Press, 2010) sets Kehoe's work in the context of the larger story of the industrial pollution of the environment and human bodies.

Clarence A. Mills's thoughts are most accessible in *Air Pollution and Community Health* (Boston: Christopher Publishing House, 1954). To learn more about the Donora disaster find Lynne Page Snyder's "'The Death-Dealing Smog Over Donora, Pennsylvania': Industrial Air Pollution, Public Health, and Federal Policy, 1915–1963" (PhD diss., University of Pennsylvania, 1994). Snyder made good use of the Mills and Kehoe papers at the Winkler Center. See also Devra Davis, *When Smoke Ran Like Water: Tales of Environmental Deception and the Battle against Pollution* (New York: Basic Books, 2003), which includes a shorter but useful discussion of Donora.

On UC basketball see *Bearcats! The Story of Basketball at the University of Cincinnati* (Louisville: Harmony House Publishers, 1998), by Kevin Grace, Greg Hand, Tom Hathaway, and Carey Hoffman, which includes a narrative of the long history of UC basketball and a trove of photographs. Oscar Robertson's autobiography, *The Big O: My Life, My Times, My Game* (New York: Rodale, 2003) sticks pretty close to basketball, but it also includes some interesting detail about his life at UC and in Cincinnati generally.

🌿 Chapter 7 A University at War with Itself

For more on the urban crisis with a special focus on the East Campus's neighborhood, see Charles F. Casey-Leininger, "Making the Second Ghetto in Cincinnati: Avondale, 1925–70," in *Race and the City: Work, Community, and Protest in Cincinnati, 1820–1970*, edited by Henry Louis Taylor Jr. (Urbana: University of Illinois Press, 1993), 232–57. In the 1970s the Carnegie Commission on Higher Education conducted a series of studies. The most directly relevant one appeared as *The University and the City: Eight Cases of Involvement* (New York: McGraw-Hill, 1973), by George Nash. On the overlooked size and impact of the black student movement, see Martha Biondi, *The Black Revolution on Campus* (Berkeley: University of California Press, 2012), which takes a national approach but focuses on New York, Chicago, and San Francisco. Cincinnati garners no mention.

For broader context of the civil rights movement in Cincinnati, see Thomas J. Sugrue, *Sweet Land of Liberty: The Forgotten Struggle for Civil Rights in the North* (New York: Random House, 2008). For valuable case studies, see Brian Purnell, *Fighting Jim Crow in the County of Kings: The Congress of Racial Equality in Brooklyn* (Lexington: University of Kentucky Press, 2013), and Clarence Lang, *Grassroots at the Gateway: Class Politics and Black Freedom Struggle in St. Louis, 1936–75* (Ann Arbor: University of Michigan Press, 2009). On Students for a Democratic Society see David Barber, *A Hard Rain Fell: SDS and Why It Failed* (Jackson: University Press of Mississippi, 2008), which sets the white New Left in the context of other movements, especially the civil rights movement, although he is not especially interested in the role of college campuses. For great detail on the New Left see Kirkpatrick Sale's monumental *SDS: The Rise and Development of the Students for a Democratic Society* (New York: Random House, 1973). On the influence of feminism on campus see Judith Glazer-Raymo, *Shattering the Myths: Women in Academe* (Baltimore: Johns Hopkins University Press, 1999).

🌿 Chapter 8 A University Without Walls

President Warren Bennis was a prolific writer, although the vast majority of his work does not concern the University of Cincinnati. Of particular value, however, is a collection of essays published as *The Unconscious Conspiracy: Why Leaders Can't Lead* (New York: Amacom, 1976), and *Today, Tomorrow…and the Day After: Four Writings by Warren Bennis, President, University of Cincinnati* (University of Cincinnati, 1972). To contextualize the People's Health Movement see Jonathan Engel, *Poor People's*

Medicine: Medicaid and American Charity Care since 1965 (Durham, NC: Duke University Press, 2006) and Beatrix Hoffman, *Health Care for Some: Rights and Rationing in the United States since 1930* (Chicago: University of Chicago Press, 2012). For a more expansive discussion of the radiation experiments see Martha Stephens, *The Treatment: The Story of Those Who Died in the Cincinnati Radiation Tests* (Durham, NC: Duke University Press, 2002). Stephens, a long-time member of the Department of English at UC, did extensive research and is at least partly responsible for the discovery (or uncovering) of many documents related to the cases. Eileen Welsome, *The Plutonium Files: America's Secret Medical Experiments in the Cold War* (New York: Dial Press, 1999), tells the Cincinnati story briefly as part of a broader exploration of radiation experiments in the United States. For the national context of affirmative action see Terry Anderson, *The Pursuit of Fairness: A History of Affirmative Action* (New York: Oxford University Press, 2004).

❦ Chapter 9 Toward a Third Century

In recent decades hand-wringing about the fate of the university has led to a blizzard of important works. Anyone interested in higher education in the late twentieth century must become familiar with the work of Derek Bok. He has written several books, but one might start with his first significant piece: *Beyond the Ivory Tower: Social Responsibilities of the Modern University* (Cambridge, MA: Harvard University Press, 1982). Those wanting to learn more about pressures on higher education at the end of the twentieth century would do well to start with David L. Kirp's *Shakespeare, Einstein, and the Bottom Line: The Marketing of Higher Education* (Cambridge, MA: Harvard University Press, 2003), which uses a series of case studies to explore the pitfalls of administration efforts to treat universities like corporations. See also *The University in Ruins* (Cambridge, MA: Harvard University Press, 1996), in which Bill Readings argues that postmodernism has demolished the university's mission—the reproduction of culture. I learned a great deal from Louis Menand's brief but insightful *The Marketplace of Ideas: Reform and Resistance in the American University* (New York: W. W. Norton, 2010).

See also Benjamin Ginsberg, *The Fall of the Faculty: The Rise of the All-Administrative University and Why It Matters* (New York: Oxford University Press, 2011), an assessment of the "administrative blight" that has crept across higher education, based largely on a career's worth of frustration with administration at Johns Hopkins and anecdotes about administrative malfeasance around the nation. Stanley Aronowitz's *The Knowl-*

edge Factory: Dismantling the Corporate University and Creating True Higher Learning (Boston: Beacon Press, 2000) has informed the discourse on higher education, but has not precipitated much "dismantling," although that might be too much to ask. Martha C. Nussbaum's *Not for Profit: Why Democracy Needs the Humanities* (Princeton: Princeton University Press, 2010) offers a strong defense of the liberal arts degree in arguing against the neoliberal model of higher education. James E. Cote and Anton L. Allahar, *Lowering Higher Education: The Rise of Corporate Universities and the Fall of Liberal Education* (Toronto: University of Toronto Press, 2011), maintains the position that the sky is not falling, but nonetheless decries the vocationalization of higher education in Canada. Another set of Canadian authors, Maggie Berg and Barbara K. Seeber, wrote the widely read *Slow Professor: Challenging the Culture of Speed in the Academy* (Toronto: University of Toronto Press, 2017), which makes the argument that the pressure for efficiency in academia is counterproductive given the amount of time needed to produce work or high quality, especially in the humanities.

Kevin Carey, *The End of College: Creating the Future of Learning and the University of Everywhere* (New York: Riverhead Books, 2015), is a thoughtful and readable rumination on just how disruptive the Internet will be to research universities. Carey learned a great deal from Richard Arum and Josipa Roksa, *Academically Adrift: Limited Learning on College Campuses* (Chicago: University of Chicago Press, 2011), which uses aggregated scores from standardized tests to argue that students don't learn as much as they should in their first two years of college.

Those interested in UC's planning should access the plans themselves: Hargreaves Associates, *The Master Plan: University of Cincinnati, September 1991* (San Francisco: Hargreaves, 1991); *The Master Plan, University of Cincinnati, Update I, September, 1995* (San Francisco: Hargreaves, 1995); *University of Cincinnati Master Plan 2000: Master Plan Update II* (San Francisco: Hargreaves, 2001). See also the earlier plans, including Glaser & Myers and Associates, *Ancillary Report: Part Two of the Developmental Plan, University of Cincinnati, 1982–1992* (Cincinnati: Glaser & Myers & Associates, and Woolpert Consultants, n.d., circa 1982), the precursor to the Hargreaves plan. For an excellent history of campus planning see Paul Venable Turner, *Campus: An American Planning Tradition* (Cambridge, MA: MIT Press, 1984).

For a more complete accounting of UC's intervention in Uptown see Michael Romanos, David Edelman, and Mahyar Arefi, *Community Interactions and Collaborations Peer Institutional Study* (School of Planning, DAAP, 2006), which also includes descriptions of similar interventions around twenty other universities, including

Akron and Ohio State. For a description of (and eulogy for) the University of Louisville's relatively short-lived Housing and Urban Development–funded intervention in the Russell neighborhood see John I. Gilderbloom and R. L. Mullins Jr., *Promise and Betrayal: Universities and the Battle for Sustainable Urban Neighborhoods* (Albany: State University of New York Press, 2005), which has a strong take-home message: universities inconsistently engage in urban problems because administrations have ever-shifting priorities. Perhaps even more useful is David J. Maurrasse's *Beyond the Campus: How Colleges and Universities Form Partnerships with Their Communities* (New York: Routledge, 2001), which includes insightful case studies of the University of Pennsylvania, Xavier University in New Orleans, San Francisco State, and Hostos Community College in the South Bronx. Maurrasse emphasizes the importance of an articulated mission related to community engagement. Nancy Zimpher provides a short autobiography and a description of her leadership philosophy in "Institutionalizing Engagement: What Can Presidents Do?," in *Creating a New Kind of University: Institutionalizing Community–University Engagement*, edited by Stephen L. Percy, Nancy L. Zimpher, and Mary Jane Brukardt (Bolton, MA: Anker Publishing Company, 2006), 223–41.

All types of scholars have taken up the topic of university athletics. See, in particular, Murray Sperber, *Beer and Circus: How Big-Time College Sports Is Crippling Undergraduate Education* (New York: Henry Holt, 2000), which argues that sports provide a distraction for undergraduates, allowing universities to serve them poorly while focusing on research and graduate students. For a philosopher's point of view see Peter A. French, *Ethics and College Sports: Ethics, Sports, and the University* (Lanham, MD: Rowman & Littlefield, 2004). For an exploration of the rise of big-time sports and the intractability of problems related to athletics (and administrators' reluctance to force reform) see John R. Thelin, *Games Colleges Play: Scandal and Reform in Intercollegiate Athletics* (Baltimore: Johns Hopkins University Press, 1994). For a thorough explication of why universities have pursued the commercialization of sports see Charles T. Clotfelter, *Big-Time Sports in American Universities* (New York: Columbia University Press, 2011).

INDEX

327

ABOUT THE AUTHOR

David Stradling is the Associate Dean for Humanities and Zane L. Miller Professor of Urban History at the University of Cincinnati. He is the author of several books, including *Where the River Burned: Carl Stokes and the Struggle to Save Cleveland* (2015), which he wrote with Richard Stradling, and *Making Mountains: New York City and the Catskills* (2007). He lives in Clifton, where he and Jodie Zultowsky raised two daughters.